PREPARING TO SURVIVE IN THE AGE OF COLLAPSE

PREPARING TO SURVIVE IN THE AGE OF COLLAPSE

Political, Military, Foreign Policy, and Preparedness Reforms Vital for Our Survival

Dr. Drew Miller, Col USAF (Ret.)

Skyhorse Publishing

Disclaimer: The opinions in this book are solely the author's and do not necessarily reflect the views of the publisher, any source cited in the book, or reviewers of the book. Public debate on policy issues that can impact our likelihood of surviving a collapse is needed. People have different opinions, and should be free to express them without fear of harm. The author's recommendations of civil disobedience, the Natural Right of self-defense, and collapse time defensive measures in this book is not a call or excuse for offensive violence.

Skyhorse Publishing books may be purchased in bulk at special discounts for sales promotion, corporate gifts, fund-raising, or educational purposes. Special editions can also be created to specifications. For details, contact the Special Sales Department, Skyhorse Publishing, 307 5th Avenue, 4th Floor, New York, NY 10016 or info@skyhorsepublishing.com.

Skyhorse® and Skyhorse Publishing® are registered trademarks of Skyhorse Publishing, Inc.®, a Delaware corporation.

Visit our website at www.skyhorsepublishing.com.
Please follow our publisher Tony Lyons on Instagram @tonylyonsisuncertain.

10 9 8 7 6 5 4 3 2 1

Library of Congress Cataloging-in-Publication Data is available on file.

Jacket design by David Ter-Avanesyan
Jacket images: Getty Images

Print ISBN: 978-1-5107-8587-8
Ebook ISBN: 978-1-5107-8589-2

Printed in the United States of America

CONTENTS

EXECUTIVE SUMMARY

We have entered "The Age of Collapse," an era where mankind will suffer severe disasters that kill hundreds of millions to billions of people because of new technologies and threats, our fragile and interdependent economic system, irresponsible government, and a population that is increasingly dependent and unable to survive without long-distance water and food shipments.[1]

The threats that could trigger a "collapse" (a cessation of most economic activity and widespread lack of law and order, massive casualties, for a prolonged period of time) are increasing due to advances in technology that can and will be misused, increasing vulnerability in our complex, interconnected, "just-in-time delivery" economy. We have a population that is dependent and incapable of caring for themselves, plagued by millions of gang members and criminals who will take advantage of any situation that overwhelms police to loot and maraud.[2]

New technologies such as bioengineering enable a small terrorist group or even one dedicated individual to modify and release a new virus that could cause a pandemic. The collapse in economic activity and loss of law and order that results will lead to panic, mass starvation, and marauding that might kill most of us. A host of experts say bioengineered viral pandemics are inevitable. They are not a future threat but a present risk that is growing since it is increasingly easier to modify an existing pathogen to make it more lethal or transmissible. Artificial Intelligence is not just a future threat of bad computers and robots—AI is being used now by bad people to develop better means to kill, new weapons of mass destruction.[3]

The probability of a collapse is high and rising; currently a 16–57 percent annual chance. Lessons from the "Dark Winter" exercise and past big disasters show how economic shutdown, loss of law and order, and marauding by criminals, soon joined by normally good people who face death, will often kill more than the trigger disaster event.[4]

A growing number of Americans are preparing for collapse survival, especially the rich. Top elected and government officials will survive the collapse at Mount

Weather, Raven Rock, and other FEMA and Department of Defense survival facilities. But the government is doing nothing to warn or prepare citizens for coming collapse disasters. Worse, executive orders authorize government agencies to steal food and resources from citizens when necessary—the priority is "Continuity of Government," not protecting citizens. In a bad collapse, which could last a year or more, most companies and organizations without collapse survival preparations will not survive—they will be forever destroyed.[5]

After the first collapse plays out, there will be revolutionary changes in our economy, military, foreign policy, and the way we live during the rest of the Age of Collapse. It will be far better if the vital changes in foreign policy, military, government, and preparedness reforms required to survive in the Age of Collapse, recommended in this book, happen now.

Given the capability and proliferation of synthetic biotechnology and relative ease of attacking with bioweapons, the era of strong US national security is over. To survive in the Age of Collapse, the US must develop and prioritize collapse recovery capability—not focus defense spending on the clash of military forces overseas. Our foreign policy and national security strategy must adapt to the Age of Collapse. While some overseas military capability may be more useful than ever for "Prompt Global Strike" missions against distant Weapons of Mass Destruction (WMD) threats, the Department of Defense needs to shift the vast majority of its resources to homeland security and disaster recovery.[6]

The United States must immediately cancel its promise to defend Taiwan, a province of China, and honor its promise to stay out of China's Civil War. China is prepared to destroy the US electric grid before they invade Taiwan. They can use a small nuclear attack to force the US president to abandon Taiwan if we continue with our foolish policy to promise defensive assistance for Taiwan. We need our military forces and budget focused on homeland security, with overseas forces limited to prompt global strikes to stop impending WMD attacks that, with the assistance of AI, can be coming from not just terrorist groups, but dedicated individuals. The era of clash with overseas armies will likely end, replaced by drones/space/cyber/AI/new weapons of mass destruction. US nuclear weapons will be more valuable than ever, both low-yield battlefield nuclear weapons when necessary, and rapidly delivered low-yield nuclear strikes to eliminate pending WMD threats. Nuclear weapons must also be ready to destroy Artificial General Intelligence threats if we cannot stop AI before it reaches this stage.[7] Prevention, Preemption, and Preparedness, P^3, are key to survival in the Age of Collapse.

Bad US policies on nuclear weapons, protecting Taiwan, promoting bioengineering and Artificial Intelligence, are driven not by what is best for national security, but for domestic vote appeal by an irresponsible, horrible, self-serving government. We need term limits and other reforms to get government out of unaffordable, unconstitutional, divisive social programs, and refocused on its proper role—protecting citizens from threats they cannot handle on their own. We need to limit Continuity of Government programs and ban legislators from having civil defense protection not afforded to all citizens, and ban government seizure of private property in a collapse.[8]

To survive the Age of Collapse, individuals must become preppers, join survival communities, because the government has failed its primary job of protecting citizens from threats they can't handle on their own. The biggest barriers to prepping today come from government. Government is a threat to survival during a collapse as well since their priority is keeping top officials alive, at our expense. Irresponsible, unconstitutional, divisive Big Government must end or most Americans will not survive the coming collapses.[9]

The divided United States is already in an early stage of Civil War. Most counties defy state gun control laws, and the nation is sharply divided into increasingly hostile political sides. The United States may be in the final stage of civilization collapse.[10]

What is the alternative if we don't adapt to the Age of Collapse? First, billions more casualties and very unpleasant deaths (starvation, bleeding out or dying from infected wounds after marauder attacks). Second, in the age of bioengineered viruses and other deadly new Weapons of Mass Destruction, the nation-state may no longer be able to offer what has been its primary means of justification: protecting the population from deadly threats. Maintaining armies, a primary mission of the nation-state, is increasingly irrelevant in the age of collapse. It is quite possible that nation-states will cease to rule in the Age of Collapse, replaced by local/regional warlords (good or bad) who provide security. Some states (like Texas) may secede from the United States. Alternatively, the threat of AI and the necessity for absolute control of it everywhere could lead to an all-powerful world government that rules in the Age of Collapse. China is for this result, and well prepared to execute unlimited, all-powerful government control.[11]

The good news is that well-prepared people and nations should be able to adapt and survive. If we adopt huge changes in policy and reform government now, or quickly after the first possibly galvanizing collapse disaster, we can achieve peace, prosperity, as well as freedom while surviving in the Age of Collapse. Irresponsible, unconstitutional, self-serving government must end and Artificial Intelligence must be absolutely controlled, more stringently than nuclear weapons technology is treated. Until we do, nonviolent civil disobedience is justified to stop irresponsible, unconstitutional government that is working to kill us now, and setting citizens up for massive slaughter and death in a collapse. Civil disobedience is vital now to halt AI before it progresses to the point where we cannot stop it from wiping out humanity.[12]

The big upside potential of the Age of Collapse is that the dire, immediate need to control "Tool AI" and ban superintelligent AGI could lead to an AI Control Alliance that brings the world together, united in our common goal of preventing AI from exterminating all of us.[13]

Living in the Age of Collapse with repeated WMD attacks and collapse disasters will initially cause tremendous fatalities and devastation until we have prepared. But we can adapt, and if we change human behavior, as well as foreign and military practices, how we farm and produce goods, the Age of Collapse could actually provide a higher quality of life and better planet than we have now.[14]

This book proposes a way to prepare for the Age of Collapse and save humanity.[15]

Chapter One

WE HAVE ENTERED THE "AGE OF COLLAPSE"

"The Age of Collapse" is an era where mankind will suffer severe disasters that kill billions of people because of new technologies and threats, our fragile and interdependent economic system, irresponsible government, a population that is increasingly dependent and unable to survive without long-distance water and food shipments. Bioengineered pandemics and new Weapons of Mass Destruction (WMD) can now be created by individuals. When a big disaster disrupts normal economic activity or scares the public, law and order will quickly vanish as bad people take advantage of overwhelmed police to start looting, followed by normally good citizens, afraid of starving to death, joining in the looting, marauding, often killing to steal food and resources to survive.[1]

"Collapse" is defined as a cessation of most economic activity and widespread lack of law and order, for a prolonged period of time, with very high fatalities (millions, more than 10 percent of the population). The largest killer in a collapse may not be the initial "trigger event" (a pandemic, loss of electric grid, nuclear attack) but rather the deaths from long-lasting loss of economic production and law and order, with people starving to death and getting killed by other desperate people looting and killing to try and survive.

Some collapse threats we face, like a bioengineered virus and Artificial Intelligence (AI) pose an "existential threat," meaning a risk not just of killing billions, but wiping out the human race or civilization as we know it. Oxford Professor Dr. Nick Bostrom, part of the unheard chorus warning of bioengineering, AI, and other grave threats, defines an existential risk as "one where humankind as a whole is imperiled . . . [with] major adverse consequences for the course of human civilization for all time to come."[2] An existential threat is defined here as one that could

We have entered "The Age of Collapse"

Definition of "collapse"

1. Economic and normal activity largely ceases
2. Widespread loss of law and order
3. For prolonged period of time (months to years)
4. Very high fatalities (millions, over 10% of the population)

- Rapidly growing number of new ways to exterminate people
- Small groups or individuals now have capability to kill billions
- AI increases the likelihood and severity of all weapons of mass destruction—and will be used to invent new means
- Vulnerable electric grid, fragile/interdependent economic system, just in time deliveries (no inventories)
- Long distance sourcing of food and water
- Irresponsible Government failing to protect population
- Societal divisions, millions of bad people who will loot, maraud, kill when police overwhelmed, starving to death

Link to "Age of Collapse" study by Dr Drew Miller:
https://www.ida.org/-/media/feature/publications/t/th/the-age-of-bioengineered-viral-pandemics-and-collapse/d-5335.ashx

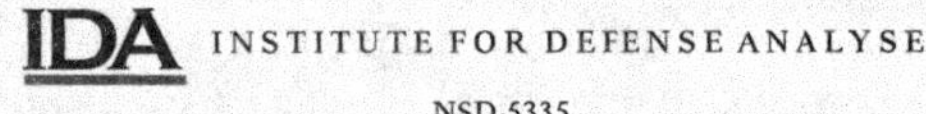

NSD-5335

The Age of Bioengineered Viral Pandemics and Collapse

Drew Miller

Figure 1: We have entered "The Age of Collapse"

kill most of the population (over 90 percent), causing a collapse that lasts several years, with the level of pre-collapse civilization and normal life not returning for generations.

There have been about fifteen mass extinctions on our planet; five of these eliminated more than half of all species then inhabiting Earth. A Yellowstone Super Volcano eruption or a big asteroid strike will cause worldwide crop failures due to blocking sunlight for a year or years, wiping out many or most species of life, and triggering a collapse. Solar flares are another natural, recurring phenomenon that can destroy our electric grid and computer systems, yielding a collapse.[3]

The six trends listed in Figure 2 explain why a collapse in economic activity and loss of law and order are likely. These trends are all getting worse.

When our fragile electric grid goes down—something a solar flare, a terrorist group, or even a tiny nuclear power like North Korea could do—most Americans will die. As AI experts warn daily (with no response from governments), this powerful new technology allows bad people to develop new and more deadly WMD. Perhaps worse, superintelligent "Artificial General Intelligence" systems, with knowledge beyond what all human experts have, may decide to exterminate all humans and have the capability to do so.

Figure 2: Risk of collapse is rising rapidly, driven by six bad trends

1. New Technologies: DNA manipulation and bioengineering, new means to manufacture nuclear materials, nanotechnology, Artificial Intelligence
2. Rising overpopulation, high urban population densities, international travel
3. Increased economic interdependence, just-in-time inventories, long-distance sourcing
4. Very high dependence on long-distance food shipments, inadequate local water
5. Less personal resilience
6. More bad people, gangs, prisoners who will maraud in a collapse

Combined Effect: More lethal threats against an increasingly unstable economy and vulnerable population

Small Nations, Terrorist Groups, Even Individuals Today Can Create Weapons of Mass Destruction

Man-made threats and new technologies are rapidly increasing the likelihood, the inevitability of huge disasters that lead to a collapse that could kill billions. Bioengineering technology today gives a single individual the ability to create a virus that could exterminate most people, or a plant virus to destroy crops. Cyberattacks, Artificial Intelligence, nanotechnology, new ways to make nuclear weapons, and other new technologies enable small groups—even individuals—to design and deliver weapons of mass destruction that could trigger a collapse and wipe out most of the human race.[4]

The destructive power of individuals continues to skyrocket, whether it's developing and releasing a deadly virus that kills billions, executing a cyberattack that takes down the electric grid, or a rapidly, seemingly endless, growing list of new ways to kill people and trigger a collapse. Individuals have unprecedented power to create WMD and cause destruction that took a large group or nation-state in the past.

Scientists and analysts have been warning for over a quarter century that this Age of Collapse is coming and must be prepared for. Yale Professor Martin Shubik warned back in 1998 that "the use of biological weapons as a terror weapon should be seen as an inevitability" and "the United States must radically rethink how it hopes to deal with biological warfare initiated by terrorists and fringe groups."[5]

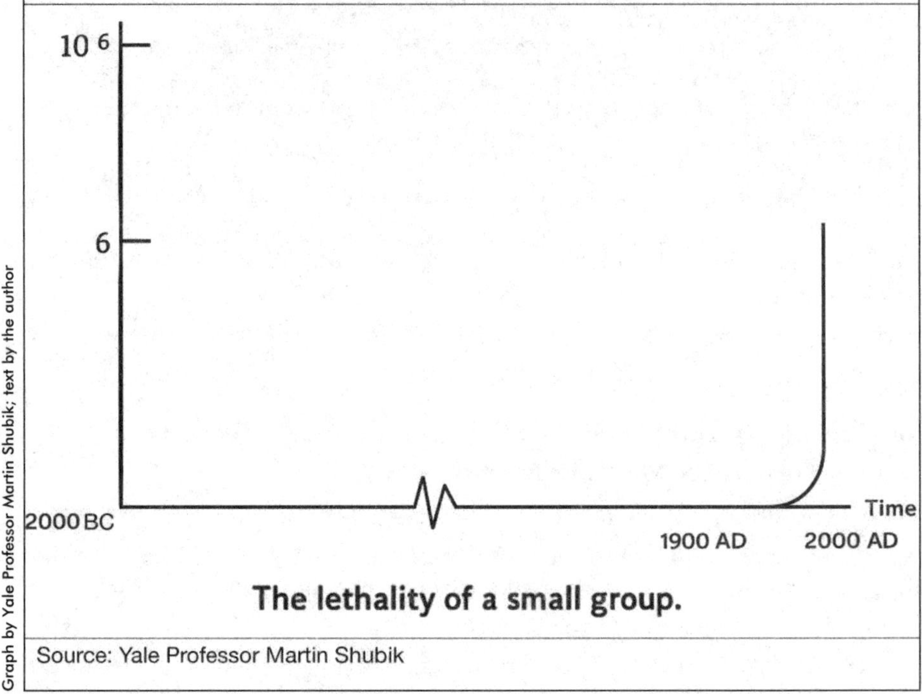

Figure 3: Destructive power of individual growing exponentially.

Modern Economies Are Far More Fragile and Vulnerable to a Collapse

Our modern, complex economy and urban population are far more vulnerable to a collapse. Some of the major changes in our society's increasing vulnerability to disruptions and decreasing resilience to recover are summarized in Figure 4.

Our "just-in-time delivery" economy is extremely vulnerable. We've had world trade for centuries—but for spices and silk, trivial things. Our fragile economy and society with just-in-time daily deliveries, little to no inventory, food and water transported long distances, is easy to disrupt. We also have a populace that is dependent; unskilled in basic survival skills; not resilient.

We are increasingly vulnerable to pandemics due to dense population centers and international air travel. We are more vulnerable to loss of law and order and huge casualties when there is any disruption to normal economic activity and

Figure 4: Relative Vulnerability to Disruptions.

	1800s	2020s
% population farming	>80%	<1%
Food travel distance	Few miles	1,000s miles
Food on hand	months	days
Water supply	well	municipal
Electronic dependence	none	heavy
Production sourcing	local	international
Inventory levels	large	tiny (JIT)
Resilience of people	Pioneers	Dependent
Overall Vulnerability	**Low**	**High**

food production. Our economic system is more complex, more globally interdependent, more vulnerable to disruptions.

> "Our connected world appears to be more efficient. . . . But when there is a disturbance, the setback is much harder to handle. Not only are we building riskier systems, but also the risks involved in failure are a lot larger. . . . We are incapable scientifically of measuring the risk of rare events. We tend to underestimate both the probabilities and the damage."
>
> —Nassim Taleb, *Fortune* magazine, April 11, 2011

We make this collapse disaster vulnerability much worse by giving up stockpiled inventories in favor of just-in-time deliveries that improve business profit margins but leave no cushion to keep people fed and alive if supply chains are interrupted or production stops.

Worse, we are a massively urban and suburban population with dangerous dependence on long-distance supply of not just food, but drinking water—all of which depend on our fragile electric system, which our irresponsible government won't bother protecting.

Finally, a large part of our dependent population doesn't have the skills or means to deal with a collapse, to grow a garden, or do anything without help and direction from the Big Government. We have millions of very bad people who will loot, maraud, kill to survive in a collapse. At least a million gang members in the United States, two million Americans in prison, who will get out when there is a collapse and the guards don't come to work.

Even North Korea, with an inaccurate, small nuclear force, has the means to exploit our vulnerabilities and destroy the United States of America. A Congressional EMP (Electro Magnetic Pulse) Commission warned back in 2008 that our electric grid was highly vulnerable, and that EMP from a small nuclear attack could destroy the electric grid and kill 90 percent of Americans.[6] Congress did absolutely nothing then, or in the decades since, to require utilities to harden the grid, or to warn American citizens of this fatal vulnerability our enemies are very well aware of. North Korea got help from Russia to design their nuclear weapons to be optimized for EMP effect. North Korea could take out the United States, and Iran may have this capability soon. They might not use an ICBM, but launch a short-range Scud missile with a nuclear warhead out the back of a modified commercial airliner flying over the United States.[7] With AI, our future is one of small terrorist groups even individuals figuring out new ways to develop weapons of mass destruction.[8]

A collapse in the economy, food distribution, and lawlessness could cause more fatalities than the disaster trigger event

Asteroid strikes and super volcano eruptions have caused many past global collapse disasters. A very bad day for you if you're near the impact/eruption point, but 95 percent plus of fatalities are from the aftermaths, the cascading effects and follow on impacts of blocked sunlight and massive plant die-off worldwide, not the initial disaster.

Even if the disaster "trigger event" does not directly kill a lot of people, the collapse that follows can. Dr. Nancy Kass, a professor at the Johns Hopkins Institute of Bioethics, warned that "the secondary consequences of severe pandemic influenza could be greater than deaths and illness from influenza itself." Few will report to work in a collapse, the economy will quickly shut down, food will not be produced or delivered, looting and marauding will explode. When a big disaster hits, law and order will vanish quickly. Truck drivers will realize that it's too dangerous for them to drive food into cities or on long trips with the risk of getting attacked by marauders after food. Even during Hurricane Katrina, which should have been a low-risk disaster, the violence scared truck drivers, many refusing to go into New Orleans without military escort.[9]

A pandemic, loss of the electric system, or other triggering disaster need not be that effective in directly killing people to generate a collapse which kills millions and destroys the nation's strength. The "cascading effects" of an economic shut down, loss of law and order, some people looting and marauding, disruption of health, sanitation, water, and transportation systems triggered by the initial disaster may deliver much worse, longer lasting damage.

Can nuclear reactors safely shut down when no one reports to work in a bad pandemic because they don't want to risk viral exposure or fear marauder attacks en route to work, or leaving their family unprotected at home? The answer is no. Even in a disaster scenario with no nuclear weapons used, you have to be prepared for radioactive fallout from nuclear power plants that will not be operated safely, or not able to shut down safely because of workers refusing to come to work due to fear of catching a virus, fear of being attacked by marauders getting to work, or fear of marauders attacking their families at home while they are at work.

In any disaster that overwhelms police, or leads the public to fear disruption of food supplies and risk of starvation, people will start marauding—going out to loot, break into homes, steal food and supplies, and if necessary, killing to do this. In a pandemic, there may be almost no police on duty at all, with the police force ravaged by casualties (first responders more likely to catch a virus), overwhelmed trying to deal with the pandemic, many abandoning their work to stay home and protect their families from exposure to the virus or marauders.

The initial or "trigger" Black Swan disaster may not be the biggest thing to worry about. The "cascading effects" of bad people looting and marauding, spread of economic shutdown, loss of law and order, and other disasters that are triggered from the growing collapse could deliver much worse, longer lasting damage. For example, can nuclear reactors safely shut down when no one reports to work because they don't want to risk viral exposure? What cascading problems will result when the electric grid goes down? Will the public water system fails because everyone has started filling bathtubs and every container they can find, of municipal water plants are no longer manned or running? There are thousands of such follow on impacts that could happen.

For example, a solar flare could knock out a big part of the electric grid. This could trigger at first just some regional disruptions in power and economic activity, sporadic criminal looting. But the economic disruption and looting that results could spread beyond areas that have lost electric power. A nuclear plant is supposed to be able to keep operating or safely shut down without grid power, using backup generators. But they can fail, or too many operators may not come in to work if they fear marauders attacking their families at home. So a nuclear plant accident and radiation release could be the next, a cascading impact of the solar flare's initial damage. Even if the general public does not panic, gangs and bad people know that when police are tied up dealing with a disaster, it's an opportune time to start looting. This looting could rapidly spiral out of control, spread to areas far beyond those without electric power. An enemy nation or a terrorist group might decide that with the US crippled by this electrical outage, widespread loss of law and order, and now radioactive fallout, this would be an ideal time to unleash agents or carry out attacks in the US and overseas while the US is in trouble—adding to the stress on our first responders, military, and population; triggering yet more bad people and scared citizens to start looting.

More critical than the probability of a disastrous event occurring is whether the effects spread, how people react, and whether or not it leads to collapse. In a pandemic with lack of food and water, widespread marauding is likely to occur, yielding a collapse situation even if the virus has a low lethality like the Spanish flu. Katrina was an eye-opener for many: a very predictable, relatively small disaster quickly led to violence and breakdown in law and order. Looting rapidly spread throughout the city, often in broad daylight and in the presence of police officers. One third of New Orleans police officers deserted the city in the days before the storm, many of them escaping in their department-owned patrol cars. In 1977, New York City suffered a lightning strike that led to a power failure for one night. More than 3,000 arrests were made for looting, 400 policemen were injured, and 500 fires were started.[10]

In addition to these factors, there are many additional reasons why we are far more likely to suffer when a widespread disaster hits. For example, despite our rising population, we have fewer hospital beds and emergency rooms in the US now. Between 1990 and 2009, emergency rooms in non-rural US hospitals declined 27 percent, from 2,446 to 1,779.[11]

Many won't wait to exploit the disaster; they will loot and maraud immediately. UK riots in 2011 showed that law enforcement can break down and violence spread without an underlying trigger disaster. The British Prime Minister called it "pure criminality"; others said it was inevitable violence from youth fed up with unemployment or family breakdown. Attacks on police and looting started in London, but spread quickly to cities across the UK. Looting and violence grew as more people took advantage of the opportunity and "marauding gangs" formed. Police "lost control" of many areas. Innocent people were shot dead in cars and robbed on streets. Thugs in Birmingham killed three men trying to protect their businesses. And the riots and marauding continued the following night—and the next. Violence repeated in London for four nights until an extra 16,000 police officers were moved in to restore order.

Gangs may accelerate the breakdown in law and order and magnify looting and marauder threats in a pandemic. There are millions of gang members in every country. The United States suffers about fifty murders daily, many from the 33,000 violent, criminally active gangs in the US, with over one million gang members.[12] In addition to local drug and mafia gangs, foreign gangs are present across the country. MS-13, a Latino gang known for brutal murders, has an estimated 10,000–150,000 members in forty-two US states.[13]

Many people, not just gang members, will use the disaster and distraction to police as an opportunity to loot. The two million Americans in jail will probably have to be released or will escape in a collapse since guards will likely not go to work. The electric grid is eventually likely to fail in any collapse, and prisons cannot operate without electricity. Their backup generators won't have fuel for more than a few days. These two million prisoners will be not just unprepared, but likely unable to get home and forced to start marauding or starve to death. Skilled in crime, many will be ruthless and very willing to kill. Eventually normal, "good" citizens will also be forced to go looting for food. Many will accidentally end up killing to survive or make the decision that they must kill others to keep their families alive.

The prepper community used to believe that for a few days after a big disaster hits, everyone would survive on food and water in their homes, but then many without would start going out to steal. Some used the phrase "72 hours to animal," a guesstimate of how long it would take before law-abiding neighbors got desperate and went out to rob and, if necessary, murder to survive.[14] Today we expect that looting, marauding, and killing will start within the first hour of public knowledge that a collapse is probably coming since there are so many gang members and ruthless people who know that the disaster and distraction to police will provide an excellent opportunity to pillage. The popular TV series *The Walking Dead* was less about zombies than marauders—good and bad people out marauding to avoid starvation. This show unfortunately convinced some people that rather than preparing, they should form marauder groups.[15]

With law enforcement personnel reduced from a pandemic and focused on protecting medical facilities and trying in some areas to enforce quarantines, or ineffective due to no electricity, there will be opportunities for gangs and lawbreakers to loot and maraud. To the degree people fear that they will starve to death if they don't have food, or that they are doomed to die from the virus anyway, the level of irrational behavior, lawlessness, and violence could be especially severe.

Food supplies in most cities could last for two to five days, but most likely they'll be gone in a few hours due to panic buying, hoarding, and looting.[16]

If either the viral threat or marauder, lawlessness threat is severe, many truckers may stop risking their lives to deliver food, and retail workers may refuse to work. Food production may also cease for similar reasons. Even if these threats to food distribution do not occur, quarantines and road closures could stop food shipments. Iowa and other rural farm states, for example, may be much better off closing their borders to keep out refugees from Chicago who may get violent, or stop road traffic transiting Iowa that risks spreading the virus. Iowans may reason they have food and water aplenty, and are better off with a strict quarantine. People in major urban states may be better off with no quarantine or travel restrictions, but road closures and border control are state and local government decisions. While people can go for many days without food, a food shortfall or just the rumor and fear of no food could lead to panic and breakdown in law and order.[17]

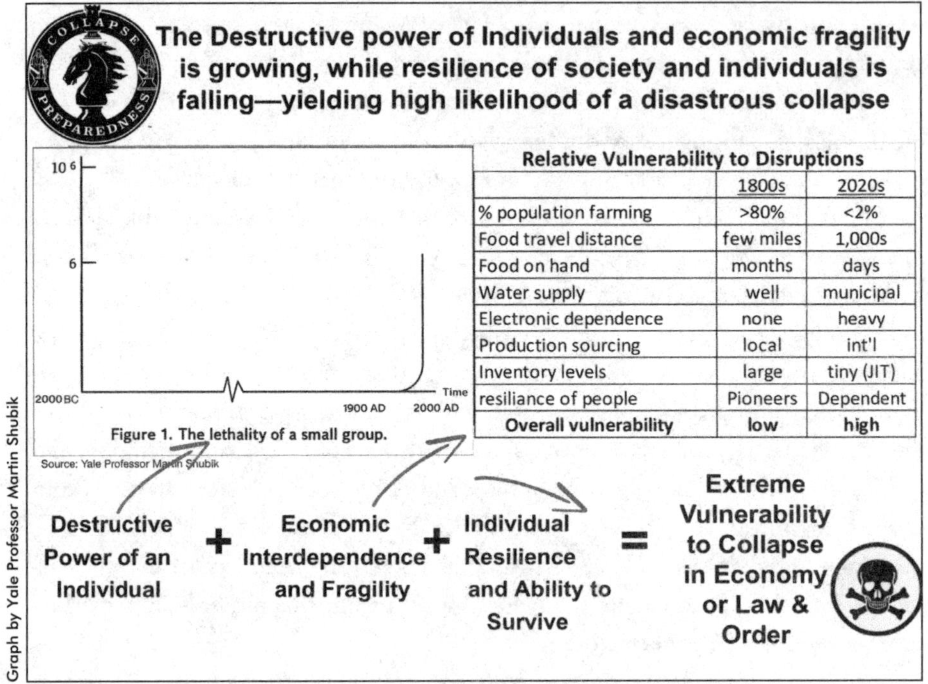

Relative Vulnerability to Disruptions

	1800s	2020s
% population farming	>80%	<2%
Food travel distance	few miles	1,000s
Food on hand	months	days
Water supply	well	municipal
Electronic dependence	none	heavy
Production sourcing	local	int'l
Inventory levels	large	tiny (JIT)
resiliance of people	Pioneers	Dependent
Overall vulnerability	**low**	**high**

Figure 5: Destructive Power Individual Up + Economic Fragility Up + Individual Resilience Down = Extreme Vulnerability to Collapse

The combined effect of these trends in our economy and society are more lethal threats against an increasingly unstable economy and vulnerable population. Most people think a collapse is unlikely—or more accurately, they never think about how a collapse could occur. But when you combine the destructive power an individual or small group could unleash by spreading a deadly new virus with the vulnerability of our just-in-time delivery, complex and interdependent economy, and the fragility of our populace that depends on the supermarket and the socialist Nanny State to take care of them, a collapse is not just possible, but highly likely.

A major disaster like a bioengineered viral pandemic, or something much less severe, could lead to economic and societal shutdown that escalates out of control. A Defense Science Board study warned that even a relatively benign cyberattack could trigger collapse: "food and medicine distribution systems would be ineffective, transportation would fail or become so chaotic as to be useless. Law enforcement, medical staff, and emergency personnel capabilities could be expected to be barely functional in the short term and dysfunctional over sustained periods."[18]

Another factor that could raise public outrage and incite violence is the necessary and inherently contentious practice of prioritizing who gets vaccines. A pandemic caused by a biological attack would require government at all levels to ration urgent care and vital supplies. Hospitals would have to turn sick people away. It takes six months or more to produce a vaccine for a new flu variant or virus. While the public waits for the vaccine to become available, the death toll will rise. There will be very unequal distribution of vaccines due to the need to give medical personal and law enforcement (and likely the military and some key workers) priority. People will die waiting for vaccines. Some will object to this, and should be expected to steal, maraud, and kill, either to try and obtain vaccines or food for their family, or just to lash out at perceived injustice. "Nonessential" workers (truck drivers, food plant workers, etc.) may see this as another reason not to risk their lives to continue working during a pandemic. Expecting people to calmly, politely accept a low priority and long wait for vaccines others are getting is delusional. People will take actions to save their lives, breaking laws as necessary, some killing others if necessary.[19]

The real Black Swan uncertainty is not if a big disaster will occur, but how bad it will be, what depth of collapse occurs, and how much death and damage results in the aftermath of the collapse. After the first disaster trigger event hits, many more disaster events are likely.

Before we recover from the collapse, another completely new collapse disaster may start, deliberately or accidentally. In the Age of Collapse, we may experience repeated, horrible collapse disasters. This will define the next era of human "civilization"—and it may be our last era. In this era when individuals can wield the power to kill millions and cause a collapse, the outlook for mankind is probably more bleak than rosy until we prepare and adapt.

From the Stone Age through the Bronze, Iron, and Industrial Ages, into today's Information Age, humans have enjoyed longer lifespans and improved quality of life and civilization. Every major technological advance has also been applied to new weapons and means of killing. Mass produced weapons and chemical agents in World Wars demonstrated this. Cyberattacks occur now. Nuclear weapons today are very difficult to make or hide, and largely held in check by nation-states. But AI will help people more easily enrich uranium and develop new types of nuclear weapons. Biotechnology puts tremendous, worldwide destructive power in the hands of individuals to wield against societies that are far more vulnerable.

Bioengineering will deliver great advances in medicine and means of production, but with the destructive power of GMOs and the uncontrollable ability of individuals to unleash a bioengineered viral pandemic, we will likely see a reversal in our fortunes, with shorter lifespans, crueler lifestyle, and perhaps a permanent collapse in civilization. If Tool AI (AI techniques for specific, limited areas of expertise; far less capable than "superintelligent" AGI) is not carefully controlled, and superintelligent AGI completely banned, the prospects of any humans surviving are poor.[20]

Dependence on Electricity and Vulnerable Electric Grids are a Setup for Collapse Disaster

Solar flares occasionally generate enough EMP to destroy parts of the electric system. If widespread and powerful, destroying thousands of transformers, we could be without electricity for over a year. Just one or two nuclear warheads detonating in the atmosphere above the US could destroy most of the electric system (as well as destroying electronics in some cars[21] and computers—systems with integrated circuits/chips). A small, inaccurate nuclear attack that Russia, China, or North Korea now (possibly Iran soon) could execute can take down the national electric grid for over a year. When the electric system is out there will be little to no production, and city water systems will not work since they require electric pumps to move water. Former CIA Director James Woolsey estimated that such an attack and the loss of electricity could kill 90 percent of the US population.[22]

We have a fragile, highly vulnerable electric grid that can be taken down by physical attacks by a terrorist group or Chinese agents, solar flares, cyberattacks, or EMP from a single nuclear detonation high in the atmosphere. A Congressional EMP Commission warned back in 2008 that our electric grid was highly vulnerable, and that an EMP attack could kill 90 percent of Americans. Congress did absolutely nothing then, or in the decades since, to require utilities to harden the grid, or to warn American citizens of this fatal vulnerability our enemies are very well aware of. North Korea got help from Russia to design their nuclear weapons to be optimized for EMP effect.

Our military does not have its own electric system; it is also dependent on our fragile electric grid. If China wants to invade Taiwan, they can take it without US interference by destroying our electric grid with physical attacks by agents and drones in the US, cyberattacks, or a small number of nuclear weapons detonating high in the atmosphere. Our military becomes low-tech and largely powerless at this point. It is the obvious Achilles' heel of the United States, an absolutely fatal flaw, and it will be surprising if this weakness is not used to knock us out. Indeed, even if we make the decision today to harden the grid, in the years it would take to do so Russia, China, North Korea, Iran, or a dedicated terrorist group might decide to execute an attack to take our electric grid down before it can be hardened, rather than lose this fantastic opportunity to easily destroy the United States.

If you think I've exaggerated the vulnerability of our electric grid, the 90 percent fatality warning given by the former director of the CIA, or the irresponsible, criminal misconduct of our government in failing to do anything to harden it, then watch this award-winning documentary about the grid:

David Tice, https://griddownpowerup.com/

Figure 6: *Grid Down, Power Up*: professional documentary explains grid vulnerabilities.

Bioengineered Viruses and Pandemics that Cause a Collapse that Kills Billions Are Inevitable

The December 2016 issue of *The American Interest* policy journal warned that we will soon enter the "Age of Bioengineered Viral Pandemics and Collapse."[23] Many experts say natural or bioengineered viral pandemics are inevitable due to new technologies that make it easy to modify an existing virus, making it more lethal or transmissible. As a report from the Institute for Defense Analyses—a Department of Defense federally funded R&D center (think tank)—warned, through bioengineering a lone terrorist or a Revolutionary Guards lab in Iran can create a human-to-human transmissible version of 60 percent lethal H5N1 virus.[24]

Dr. Tara O'Toole, former director of Johns Hopkins University Center for Civilian Biodefense Strategies, warned in Congressional testimony: "We are in the midst of a bioscientific revolution that will make building and using biological weapons even more deadly and increasingly easy." Avian flu, H5N1, modified to be human-to-human transmissible, could cause a pandemic that kills a billion people. Bioengineered viruses are the ideal weapon. Compared to nuclear weapons they are more deadly, orders of magnitude cheaper, and easier to create and launch; and, most importantly, offer the ability to attack with impunity to retaliation since we may not know and can't prove who released the virus.[25] Whether created and released by a terrorist group or one dedicated individual, a bioengineered virus could cause both a pandemic and, as people react, a collapse in economic activity and loss of law and order.[26]

Many biologists and the former director of the Center For Disease Control says a natural or bioengineered H5N1 (40–60 percent lethal) pandemic is inevitable.[27] The leading pandemic expert, Dr. Michael Osterholm has warned that other types of viruses will also cause horrible, inevitable pandemics. SARS-CoV-2, the class of virus that produced the Covid-19 pandemic, has produced virus variants with far higher lethality rates, and will yield future pandemics that may be far worse.[28] Another family of viruses, filoviruses, which includes Ebola and Marburg, have fatality rates of 50 to 85 percent. Thus far filoviruses have not been air transmissible, but future natural or man-made mutations of these viruses could make them airborne transmissible. Since humans have "virtually no existing immunity to the filoviruses," such a pandemic would be particularly bad. Dr. Osterholm criticized statements from Bill Gates and others who claim we can avoid pandemics, calling such hopes "pie in the sky sprinkled with pixie dust."[29] Dr. Osterholm insists that "rapidly spreading respiratory virus-caused pandemics are as much a fact of life as war and crime. All we can do is our best to mitigate their effects and shorten their duration and spread."[30]

The Defense Threat Reduction Agency's Joint Science and Technology Office for Chemical and Biological Defense warned that "[s]urprise from biological and chemical threats is inevitable."[31] Nassim Taleb warned that "the history of epidemics, narrowly studied, does not suggest the risks of the great plague to come that will dominate the planet."[32] Additional quotes from experts warning about inevitable, catastrophic pandemics are provided in this webnote.[33]

In 2011 scientists funded by the US government, doing "gain-of-function research" created a modified version of bird flu, H5N1, 60 percent lethal to humans, that was now capable of mammal-to-mammal transmission. Ron Fouchier of the Erasmus Medical Center, in Rotterdam, Netherlands, turned H5N1 virus into a possible human-to-human flu by infecting ferrets (mammals used to test human effects) repeatedly until a form of H5N1 resulted that could spread through the air from one mammal to another. This was not high-tech bioengineering, but simply swabbing the noses of the infected ferrets and using the gathered viruses to infect another round.[34] The government asked the scientists not to publish their results, citing risks of terrorists using this information, but they were published.

A team of scientists at China's National Avian Influenza Reference Laboratory combined H5N1 with genetic attributes found in dozens of other types of flu. Some of their "man-made super flu strains" could spread through the air between guinea pigs, killing them.[35] This was condemned by scientists around the world as "appalling irresponsibility" since the new viral strains created by mixing bird flu virus with human influenza could escape from the laboratory and cause a global pandemic—killing millions of people.[36]

Genetic engineering or bioengineering is manipulation of an organism's genetic material. We've been creating genetically modified organisms (GMO) since the 1970s, and in 2010 the first synthetic (not made by combining existing organism's DNA) new life form was created. Genetic modifications, though rare, do occur in nature—that's why we get new strains of flu all the time and have had viral pandemics. Geneticists can greatly speed up genetic change, creating viruses and bacteria that never existed before. With newer techniques, a simple, cheap lab (perhaps in your neighbor's garage) can generate millions of recombinants in minutes.[37] We were assured that modified genes from modified plants would not pass into other, natural plants; but this has not been the case. A much greater risk than modified genes spreading among native plants is bioengineering that accidentally or intentionally creates a human-to-human transmissible version of avian flu or modifies a lethal virus to have a longer latency period for it to spread undetected.[38]

Compared to nuclear weapons, DNA manipulation and bioengineering is likely a much worse threat, because it puts tremendous, potentially existential, killing power in the hands of individuals.

A bioengineered virus, launched in our crowded, interconnected world by an enemy working to spread it widely before it is detected, could yield a more devastating pandemic than anything experienced in the past. Smallpox killed as many as 90 percent of Aztec, Maya, and Inca citizens, and killed 500 million people in the twentieth century. It could do worse now since immunity is gone and our populations are far more vulnerable to catching a virus, and far less able to survive during collapse situations.[39] Stanford Professor Dr. Nathan Wolfe warned that "if terrorists ever got their hands on one of the few remaining vials of smallpox, the results would be devastating. . . . In 2004 scabs from suspected smallpox were found in Santa Fe, New Mexico, in an envelope."[40] Many fear that laboratories beyond the US and Russia still have smallpox virus, and its genetic code was posted on the Internet.[41]

Eckard Wimmer, who headed the team of researchers at SUNY Stony Brook that made live polio virus from scratch as part of a Defense Department project to prove the threat of synthetic bioweapons, said that any one of the 2,847 members of the American Society for Virology could figure out how to do the same.[42] Rob Carlson, a physicist turned biologist, like many others in the biotech field, warned that developing lethal viruses is increasingly cheap and easy. There is no need for a national program, big lab, expensive equipment, or specialized expertise.[43] With a human-to-human transmissible virus there is no need for more difficult weaponization efforts—you find a simple means of infecting people in crowded public transportation centers and let them spread the virus. Again citing Dr. Henderson, "between the time of an aerosol release of smallpox virus and diagnosis of first cases, an interval as long as 2 weeks or more is apt to occur because of the average incubation period of 12 to 14 days and the lapse of several additional days before a rash was sufficiently distinct to suggest the diagnosis of smallpox."[44] Only a few days are needed for a virus released in multiple airports to reach every city and probably most small towns in the US. If the smallpox virus has been genetically modified, the limited supply of vaccines we have for it may not work.

If smallpox is too difficult to obtain or synthetically create, you can grab another deadly virus like Ebola or avian flu (H5N1). Dr. Henderson and other scientists, writing in an article on biosecurity, warned that H5N1 influenza kills about 60 percent of its victims, compared to just 2 percent for the 1918 Great Pandemic that killed about 50 million. "Like all influenza strains, H5N1 is constantly evolving in nature. But thankfully, this deadly virus does not now spread readily through the air from person to person. If it evolved to become as transmissible as normal flu and results in a pandemic, it could cause *billions* of illnesses and deaths around the world."[45] If researchers we know of are tampering with H5N1 to make it human-to-human transmissible, we should expect that terrorists and nation-states are doing this as well.

Scientists justify this research and its publication by noting that bioterrorists know how to do this and arguing we must research lethal agents to try and find countermeasures. This is true, but unfortunately, it is easier to create a deadly virus than to counter one, easier to accidentally create a deadly virus than to use biotechnology to develop new treatments.[46]

The Soviet Union's biological warfare program, with far less capable equipment and knowledge than exists today, produced a host of biowarfare agents.

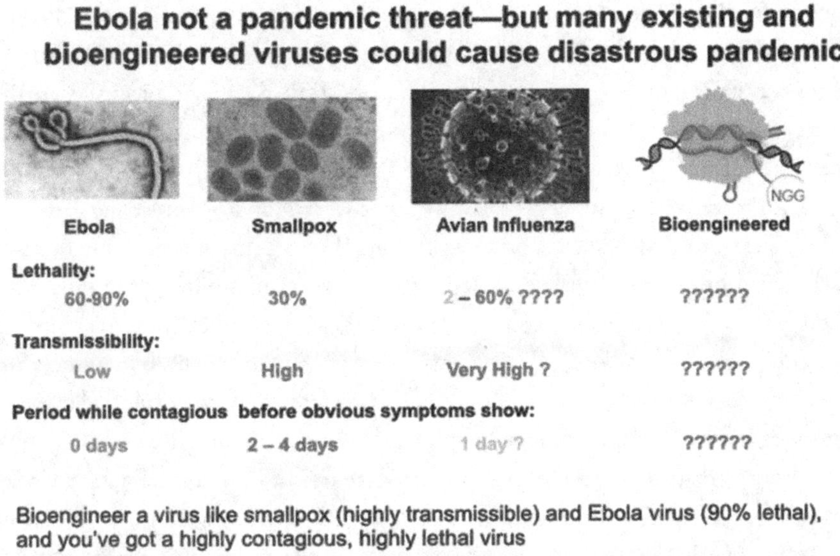

Bioengineering diagram from Innovative Genomics Institute

Figure 7: Existing bioengineered viruses could cause disastrous pandemic.

This effort included sixty-five thousand researchers in a vast network of secret laboratories, each focused on a different deadly agent. They produced traditional biological weapons and reportedly had success in combining smallpox, Marburg, Ebola and other viruses. If you could combine the 90 percent lethal Ebola virus with highly contagious smallpox, you might indeed create an existential bioengineered viral pandemic. A former leader of the Soviet biowarfare program believes his colleagues still work in Russia and many other nations, and predicts that bioweapons "in the coming years, will become very much a part of our lives."[47]

A bioengineered viral pandemic could also come from accidents in professional labs, or one of the thousands of do-it-yourself (DIY) biologists experimenting with viruses in their garages. In 2001 Australian researchers attempting to make a contraceptive vaccine for pest control inserted a "good" gene into mousepox virus and accidentally created a lethal new virus that resisted vaccination. Other legitimate lab accidents have likely occurred but were not publicized. We don't want to imagine what do-it-yourself biologists and biohackers are doing. There are over three thousand DIY Bio members on the website DIYbio.org. Some work alone at home, others in small rent-a-lab spaces around the world.[48]

Advances in DNA manipulation technology, cheap lab equipment, and information posted on the Internet enable a single person with the right resources to make artificial smallpox or worse.[49] With "professional" scientists in controlled labs irresponsibly making human transmissible forms of highly lethal avian flu and publishing the instructions, there should be no question that DIY bio folks in their garage, biohackers, lunatics, terrorists, or countries like Iran and North Korea will either intentionally or accidentally unleash a deadly virus.[50]

If a lone terrorist or lunatic releases the virus, it may not spread far before we detect it and limit the spread and devastation. If an enemy nation launches a bio attack, spreading a virus with high lethality and transmissibility, and with a long period where carriers are contagious but not suffering from the illness or symptoms, the virus might kill millions. The worst threat is Iran or Russia bioengineering a virus they release against us in multiple locations after they've developed a vaccine to protect themselves. For new, bioengineered viruses, there will very likely be no immunity or treatment. So if a nation-state were to put even a small lab to work to develop a GMO with the cubed power of high lethality, high transmissibility, and long latency period, as well as create a vaccine only they have, this state would have the capability to destroy any enemy. Delivered correctly, the devastated population would not even know who to blame for the attack. A well-designed bio attack, clandestinely spreading a bioengineered virus with high lethality and transmissibility, and with a long period where carriers are contagious but not suffering from the illness or symptoms, could cause a pandemic that kills a billion, and a collapse that kills more.[51]

Iran may decide that rather than spending billions for a low probability of success launching a small nuclear attack that would bring devastating retaliation to Iran, they should prepare a human transmissible form of avian flu, H5N1, and spread the virus in Israel and the United States. They spread the virus in busy airports that acts slowly, with infected people contagious for several days but not showing symptoms. By the time the CDC detects and issues a warning it would be too late: millions of Americans would be infected in not just every state, but probably most towns and cities. Quarantine would be impossible; the virus would keep spreading.

A successful North Korean nuclear attack on another country would guarantee the end of Kim Jong Un's regime and the destruction of much of his country. But North Korean agents could secretly release a deadly virus in the US that could kill hundreds of millions. Even if we believed North Korea was responsible, we likely could not prove it.

It may seem irrational for a nation-state to unleash a contagious agent, but it's quite likely given the ability to launch the attack secretly, without any identification of what country is responsible. A country with too many people to feed and a ruthless government that only wants to protect part of the population it values might just inoculate party members and key people they want to survive. The country could stockpile vaccines to administer to all their citizens (other than undesirables) after the virus was released overseas, close their borders as soon as its detection is announced, and wipe out the United States to leave them at the top of a new world order. A Revolutionary Guards group in Iran, upset with their government's failure to destroy "the Great Satan," might decide to do this on their own. If nation A finds out that nation B is developing a bioengineered virus (and antidote) and plans to release it against them, they may decide to launch a preemptive bio attack. There are thousands of cases one could foresee, none as irrational as the world going to war after a terrorist assassinates the archduke of a declining state.[52]

Bioengineered viruses are an ideal weapon. Compared with nuclear weapons they are more deadly, orders of magnitude cheaper, and easier to create and launch. Of course, the virus would spread around the world, but Iran and especially North Korea are extremely isolated from international travel and may not only avoid the pandemic but end up in relatively great shape.

The virus need not be that effective in killing infected victims to generate a collapse that kills millions and destroys the nation's strength. A few letters of anthrax powder caused a lot of trouble. A deadly new virus spreading will wreak orders of magnitude more disruption and cascading casualties.

The CDC will detect spread of virus, but if natural or bioengineered virus with long period of contagiousness, too late to prevent pandemic

Example:

- Iran sends 30 terrorists to spread virus in airports
- Those exposed start spreading virus on 2nd day
- By end of 4th day: over 5 million people infected; likely in every city across the U.S.

Assume infectious for 4 days, disease doesn't manifest or too sick to go to doctor for 4 days	
30	Iranian martyr volunteers
50	# they infect per airport per 2 man team
15	# they infect on planes per 2 man team
60	# airports visited
60	# aircraft flights flown (travel in pairs)
3,900	# infected by martyr teams day 1
10	# each infected person infects on Day 1
3,900	# infected by martry teams on their second day of travel
39,000	# day 1 infected people infect over Day 2
3,900	# infected by martry teams on their 3rd day of travel
39,000	# day 1 infected people infect on Day 3
429,000	# day 2 infected people infect on Day 3
3,900	# day 4 infected people by martyr team(martyr team's last day; getting too sick
39,000	# day 1 infected people infect on Day 4
429,000	# day 2 infected people infect on Day 4
4,719,000	# day 3 infected people infect on Day 4
5,709,600	**Total people infected thru Day 4**

- A bioengineered virus designed to cause bad pandemic might have a period of several days to spread disease before victims get sick enough to go to hospital, CDC detects

Figure 8: Example of how a small terrorist group could infect five million people.

One dedicated, deranged individual could develop a deadly new virus, a biological Unabomber. It may be a highly moral biologist who believes that a deadly human virus is needed to save the world from mankind, like this lady who wrote:

> We need to be freed from our species-specific arrogance. No evidence exists that we are "chosen," the unique species for which all the others were made. Nor are we the most important one because we are so numerous, powerful and dangerous. Our tenacious illusion of special dispensation belies our true status as upright, mammalian weeds.[53]

We should not be surprised if a bioengineered virus is developed and released by a kindly scientist who reasons that overpopulation by "mammalian weeds" is destroying the planet and future generations, so we need a deadly pandemic to reset the human population to a sustainable level.

While we cannot calculate the odds of a bioengineered viral pandemic, a host of experts believes it is inevitable, and could certainly happen anytime.[54]

Artificial Intelligence is not just a future threat of bad computers and robots—AI is being used now by bad people to develop new Weapons of Mass Destruction

New technologies, especially AI, have fundamentally changed our likelihood of survival. In this Age of Collapse, bad people can use AI and existing technologies to make better Weapons of Mass Destruction (WMD), develop new types of WMD that we have never thought of before, killing millions of people and causing a collapse (economy not operating, widespread loss of law and order) that may kill even more.[55] AI has tremendous power to improve our economy and health in developing better medical treatments, cutting costs, improving R&D, saving lives. But this same power will be misused by bad people to develop new WMD, just as all past new technologies have been used for good and bad.[56]

Eric Schmidt, former CEO of Google, a leading person to blame for the uncontrolled development of AI, is at least honest in warning of the existential threat AI poses. In a book written with Henry Kissinger describing AI dangers, the authors warned that "[l]eaps and bounds in AI's ability to manufacture and manipulate DNA are creating new dangers in chemical and biological warfare. Specifically, they create the possibility of tailoring a bioweapon to populations that share specific genetic traits."[57] Schmidt and Kissinger in their *Age of AI and Our Human Future* book offered a great example of how old AI technologies can and inevitably will be used to develop novel new WMD humans haven't thought of. Describing new molecules that AI had designed, they noted, "The program did not need to understand why the molecules worked—indeed, in some cases, *no one* knows why some of the molecules worked. Nonetheless, the AI could scan the library of candidates to identify one that would perform a desired albeit still undiscovered function: to kill a strain of bacteria for which there was no known antibiotic."[58] Now, change the word "bacteria" to "people" and you see how AI will generate collapse disasters. Current AI systems and tools can be tricked or altered to remove any "do not cause harm" restrictions. Modern AI can scan existing information to develop new poisons, new viruses, new weapons.

The AI being used today to develop great new medical treatments can be tasked to *study human physiology and living environments and design the optimal way to kill at least 90% of humans in country X.* Just as AlphaGo back in 2016 developed new strategies that humans can't understand, even after seeing it executed, AI is an obvious tool to develop fantastically lethal WMD to kill humans. As with bioengineering and so many other new technologies developed over the past decades, these are not future collapse disaster threats, they are current threats. Nation-states, terrorist groups, and individuals have already been using these technologies to develop new WMD intentionally or accidentally. AI will accelerate the number of efforts and their likelihood of developing effective new WMD.

People not only don't understand the threat of AI, there is a huge, deeply ingrained *misunderstanding* of the AI threat. It will probably be a fatal (for humanity) misunderstanding if we don't get it straightened out now and act immediately to stop the inevitable misuse of AI that will kill billions or all of us.

Our thinking is understandably, inherently limited by our past experiences. We anticipate and imagine future events largely in terms of past experiences that greatly bias our views. Nassim Taleb, one of the smartest persons of our era, wrote about this in *The Black Swan: The Impact of the Highly Improbable.*[59] Taleb has made a successful career from thinking correctly about future "Black Swan" events like a collapse. He understands how people are inherently very bad at thinking about future surprises. We think the past projects ahead without big changes despite new technologies that have big power to do revolutionary new, powerful things. We commit the "narrative fallacy"—we fool ourselves with stories and anecdotes. We like stories, we like to summarize, simplify, explain things with some past experience and rationale that makes sense, seems right. For AI this is particularly prevalent. Some great movies and TV shows have created a collective, strong mindset about the AI risk that is dangerously wrong. Taleb summarized this by saying "Humans are great at self-delusion." "We cannot work without a point of reference,"[60] so the mind will grab one even if it makes no good sense as a reference. Our reference on thinking about the AI threat is movies of bad computers and robots.

Most media coverage, computer scientists, and most AI experts talking about the AI threat and the public are wrongly focused on evil computers and the future threat of Artificial General Intelligence (AGI) controlling robots. AGI generally means superintelligent AI capable of completing any intellectual task humans can do at top human skill levels, in contrast to today's "narrow" AI or "Tool AI," which is developed to complete a specific task. We've all seen *2001: A Space Odessey, Battlestar Galactica*, and *The Terminator*, and that drives our thinking about the AI threat—very incorrectly. Taleb also notes that we are more influenced by emotions and personal events, than statistics. These movies are very emotional, powerful in dominating our thinking about the AI threat.

AI experts warn that AI systems will soon reach a stage where AGI superintelligence and ability to learn on its own develops some form of consciousness or self-defense instinct, and then employs robots and other clever means to kill humans.[61] This may or may not be the biggest AI risk, but the popularity of this future AGI/bad computers/robot threat undermines dealing with the current risk of AI used by bad people to develop WMD. If AI is a future threat, not a current risk, there is little urgency to act now to stop it. This is why the misunderstanding of AI threats is dangerously, potentially fatally wrong and must be corrected.

> Bad people will use AI to develop deadly new WMD. This is the immediate, inevitable threat of AI—not AGI evil computers and robots.

AI will be used to develop new methods to enrich uranium or other materials to make nuclear weapons. This was illustrated in the Collapse Survivor App in 2024 in a military-style training exercise where an easy way to enrich uranium enabled Iranian-backed terrorists to detonate nuclear devices in downtown New York City, Kansas City, and Los Angeles.

The methods used in the early 1940s to enrich uranium are still used today, but we cannot expect they are the only way to enrich uranium or make a nuclear weapon. Laser enrichment has been developed, and AI will be used by bad actors to develop easier ways to enrich uranium and develop new weapons of mass destruction.

AI will be used to develop new poisons, perhaps one optimized for municipal water systems. Then a North Korean or Iranian or Chinese agent can dump a gallon of an AI optimized new poison (undetectable) into the water system versus a tanker truck required for an old-fashioned poison.

AI can be applied to nanotechnology to develop self-replicating nanobots that consume all plant matter on Earth while building more of themselves (the "gray

https://www.youtube.com/watch?v=n8cYPVQqV6c

Figure 9: Collapse Survivor App scenario on AI used to develop easy way to enrich uranium for terrorist nuclear weapons.

goo" disaster scenario described later).[62] Nano technology researchers are trying to be careful to not accidentally create or release something that has this kind of disastrous outcome. Bad people/groups/nations will use AI and nano technology to deliberately cause such a catastrophic disaster.

As Henry Kissinger and Eric Schmidt put it, "A central paradox of our digital age is that the greater a society's digital capacity, the more vulnerable it becomes."[63] The US is the most vulnerable country to cyberattacks. Add to this, we probably have the most fragile, vulnerable electric grid, with cyber one of many attack vectors enemies can use to take it down and kill most Americans. As with every other lethal technology and collapse disaster threat, expect AI to make it worse. Again quoting Kissinger and Schmidt, "AI cyber weapons can learn how to penetrate defenses without requiring humans to discover software flaws that can be exploited. . . ."[64] AI will be abused by bad actors to execute far more lethal cyberattacks than we have experienced to date.

AI controlled drones delivering viruses, poisons, nano devices, you name it to kill humans is the current threat we face. The only way to end this list is generic: that AI designs some other novel new means—including ones that humans wouldn't even think of—to efficiently, cost-effectively, kill billions of humans.

Bad actors will task AI to develop the best way to kill a targeted population, and let it invent either a new WMD, or figure out some brilliant, completely new way to kill that humans can't think up on their own with our limited, biased, constrained thinking processes. We may not even get to the superintelligent AGI level threat of bad computers and robots because Tool AI will very likely be used by bad people to kill off humans before that happens, setting back our economy and society so much that we can't develop AGI. Misuse of new technologies to kill people is a lesson of history, and the likely outcome when you carefully analyze the threat as an intelligence officer (my profession) would. Every technology ever developed by man has been abused and used to kill. Fire, gunpower, chemicals, the Internet, social media, phones, drones, you name it—it will be used to kill.

Artificial intelligence makes all the man-made collapse disaster threats worse: more deadly, easier to do, harder to detect. Every existing technology can now be made more lethal by bad people employing Artificial Intelligence to develop more efficient means of killing people and escaping countermeasures. With its ability to mislead, deceive, trick humans and control other IT systems, AGI can overcome many defensive measures, and use unknowing humans to help kill themselves. Long before AGI and robots reach a stage of superintelligent Artificial General Intelligence, and develop a self-preservation instinct, simpler Tool AI will be used by bad people to kill off billions or most of humanity. We can be 100 percent confident that AI will be misused to kill. AI is being used now to develop better drugs to save lives, and there is no doubt that some bad actors are already using AI to develop deadly new viruses and other WMD.

Worse, it is not just nation-states and big terrorist groups like Iran, North Korea, Russia, China, Al-Qaeda using AI to develop better weapons of mass destruction. AI empowers individuals to make new WMD. You can be confident that some biologist or environmentalist concerned about global warming and the destruction of the planet by too many people is using CRISPR bioengineering technology and AI to develop a better virus to kill off billions of humans to save the planet ("mammalian weeds," as previously mentioned).

A former Google AI expert and co-founder of Google's "DeepMind" system warned that AI could be misused to design deadly viruses and cause catastrophic pandemics.[65] The lead developer, "Godfather of AI," Dr. Geoffrey Hinton, calls AI's destructive power an existential threat to humanity. Elon Musk has warned that "AI is far more dangerous than nukes."[66]

Can it get worse? Yes, just add quantum computers and increase the power of AI even more to develop more effective and new ways to destroy life—or dedicated nuclear power plants that produce power just for AI computers.[67]

This is why you see high-tech billionaires and AI experts (Mark Zuckerburg, Peter Thiel, Bill Gates, Elon Musk, Open AI co-founders Ilya Sutskever, and Sam

Altman) building private security bunkers not just in the US, but in New Zealand and all over the world.[68] Zuckerburg has a 1,400 acre survival compound in Kauai with a 5,000-square-foot underground bunker and many other buildings. The OpenAI, ChatGPT team reportedly plans on building a protective bunker before releasing AGI.[69] Elon Musk's top goal is to get humans to Mars so we can survive "if there's something terrible that happens on Earth."[70] They recognize we have entered the Age of Collapse, and there is probably no way to put all these technologies and AI back in the bottle. Some liberal journalists have condemned these "end times fascists": "the most powerful people in the world are preparing for the end of the world, an end they themselves are frenetically accelerating."[71]

If Musk can successfully colonize Mars, that would be a great development for humanity. It will be of no value to 99 percent plus of humans on Earth, and much harder for Musk to pull off once collapse disasters start, but he might achieve it. Of course, if superintelligent AGI develops here, the Mars colony will have to keep the computers and people there unable to access AGI and bad people back on Earth. I do not know how he plans to prevent AGI on Earth, smarter and far more capable than the humans on Mars, from creating and launching weapons and viruses to destroy humans that have escaped to Mars or other planets.

Dozens of other Disasters, New Technologies, Attacks Could Lead to a Collapse

The Disaster Preparedness Threat Watch and Collapse Warning System tracks over fifty disasters, attacks, events that could trigger a collapse. Figure 10 lists these collapse triggers, and this last section covers several of them not already addressed.[72]

Laboratory accidents—in bioresearch, nanotechnology, other new technologies—are a very likely source of at least a local disaster. If a virus or reproducing device, a contagion that can spread, is released, it could trigger a collapse. Panic and misinformation could also lead to a collapse far beyond the real impact area, especially as people get more conditioned to collapse disasters and marauding takes off at the first news of the accident.

While we naturally focus on human pandemics, a natural virus or deliberate bio attack may target crops rather than humans. Ireland still has not recovered to pre-potato famine population levels from a viral disaster over a century ago. We have viruses today like Ug99 that can cause 100 percent crop losses in most modern varieties and bee colony collapse that threatens the Western Honeybee, vital for pollination. Forty percent of the world's agricultural land is seriously degraded, with less land available to farm each year; water shortages are bad and getting worse,

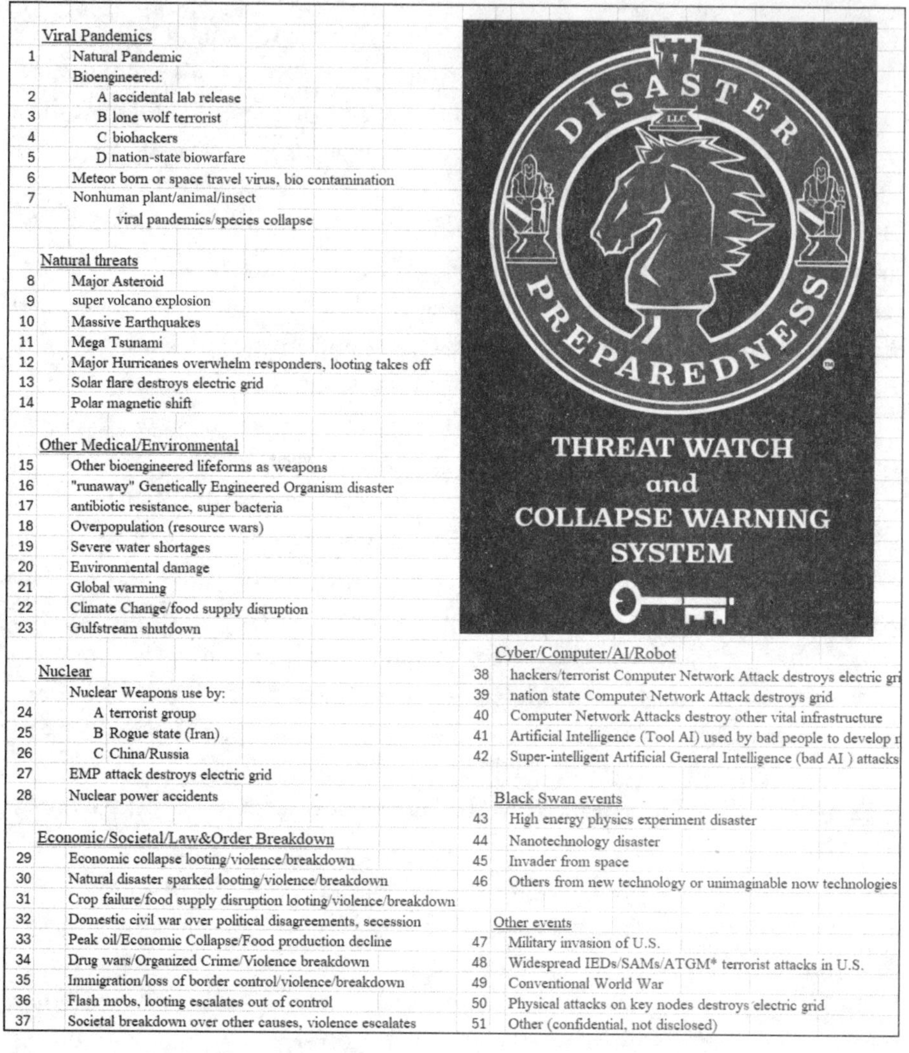

Viral Pandemics
1 Natural Pandemic
Bioengineered:
2 A accidental lab release
3 B lone wolf terrorist
4 C biohackers
5 D nation-state biowarfare
6 Meteor born or space travel virus, bio contamination
7 Nonhuman plant/animal/insect viral pandemics/species collapse

Natural threats
8 Major Asteroid
9 super volcano explosion
10 Massive Earthquakes
11 Mega Tsunami
12 Major Hurricanes overwhelm responders, looting takes off
13 Solar flare destroys electric grid
14 Polar magnetic shift

Other Medical/Environmental
15 Other bioengineered lifeforms as weapons
16 "runaway" Genetically Engineered Organism disaster
17 antibiotic resistance, super bacteria
18 Overpopulation (resource wars)
19 Severe water shortages
20 Environmental damage
21 Global warming
22 Climate Change/food supply disruption
23 Gulfstream shutdown

Nuclear
Nuclear Weapons use by:
24 A terrorist group
25 B Rogue state (Iran)
26 C China/Russia
27 EMP attack destroys electric grid
28 Nuclear power accidents

Economic/Societal/Law&Order Breakdown
29 Economic collapse looting/violence/breakdown
30 Natural disaster sparked looting/violence/breakdown
31 Crop failure/food supply disruption looting/violence/breakdown
32 Domestic civil war over political disagreements, secession
33 Peak oil/Economic Collapse/Food production decline
34 Drug wars/Organized Crime/Violence breakdown
35 Immigration/loss of border control/violence/breakdown
36 Flash mobs, looting escalates out of control
37 Societal breakdown over other causes, violence escalates

DISASTER LLC PREPAREDNESS
THREAT WATCH
and
COLLAPSE WARNING
SYSTEM

Cyber/Computer/AI/Robot
38 hackers/terrorist Computer Network Attack destroys electric gri
39 nation state Computer Network Attack destroys grid
40 Computer Network Attacks destroy other vital infrastructure
41 Artificial Intelligence (Tool AI) used by bad people to develop r
42 Super-intelligent Artificial General Intelligence (bad AI) attacks

Black Swan events
43 High energy physics experiment disaster
44 Nanotechnology disaster
45 Invader from space
46 Others from new technology or unimaginable now technologies

Other events
47 Military invasion of U.S.
48 Widespread IEDs/SAMs/ATGM* terrorist attacks in U.S.
49 Conventional World War
50 Physical attacks on key nodes destroys electric grid
51 Other (confidential, not disclosed)

Figure 10: Disasters, attacks, events that could yield a collapse.

while populations continue to rise. The world's grain stocks are lower than years past, despite far more mouths to feed.[73]

Crop failures from a virus, or a year or years of the sun blocked from nuclear winter or an asteroid strike or super volcano eruption, could kill billions from starvation—and possibly more from marauding, even wars, to seize available food for survival. This might be the means superintelligent AGI devises as the best way to exterminate dangerous humans: figure out some common chemicals that can be combined and manipulated to create a persistent fog in the atmosphere to block the sun and kill off humanity. With the AGI system running on the dedicated nuclear plants we're building for them, plenty of stockpiled nuclear fuel, who needs pesky humans threatening to unplug you?

With the recent risk of India-Pakistan nuclear war, scientists studying climate again warned of "nuclear winter," the risk that multiple high yield ground bursts could throw up debris into the atmosphere, block the sun for months or years, and cause worldwide crop failures, leading to famine and deaths of billions.[74]

Earth has had several mass extinction events in the past, some caused by asteroid impacts and super volcano explosions that throw debris high up in the atmosphere and block sunlight, leading to dramatic drops in temperatures, worldwide loss of vegetation, and then massive loss, even extinction of animal species.

Blocked sunlight disasters are the ones we dread the most at Fortitude Ranch, a national survival community. We can do without the electric grid, grow our own food, heat and cook with woodstoves, deter or defeat marauder attacks. But if there is no sunlight, we have no solar power and, far worse, can't grow food. Ranch animals and wildlife will not survive. If the sunlight does not return in a few years, it's "game over."[75]

Experimental accidents at high-energy physics facilities might also yield massive destruction. The Large Hadron Collider in Switzerland might generate a catastrophic disaster from creation of miniature black holes that grow, creation of "strangelets" (particles made of strange quarks that might create a catastrophic chain reaction), or, more likely, some disaster we can't even imagine given all the unknowns. The "scientific community" rates these risks as extremely unlikely. But there is very good reason to question the validity of this "don't worry be happy" assessment, since the experts rating this as negligible risk are the same people who depend on research funding (largely from government officials who have irresponsible judgment and bad incentives) for their livelihood. There is good reason to suspect that from either bias or lack of knowledge (doing these experiments because we don't understand the physics), the risks of such research are considerable, not minuscule.[76]

Nanotechnology is being used to develop wonderful things like self-replicating nanobots that can consume an oil spill in the ocean. But every good technology can be misused deliberately, or accidentally lead to a huge disaster that could trigger a collapse. "Gray goo" is the name of an anticipated scenario where out-of-control self-replicating nanobots destroy the biosphere by endlessly producing replicas of themselves, consuming all organic matter.

In this example, if these nanobots eat up all the oil in the ocean, what's to stop them from washing ashore, spreading up rivers and into fields to start munching up crops? How do you stop tiny, nanoscopic size, self-replicating devices from spreading and wiping out plant life around the world?

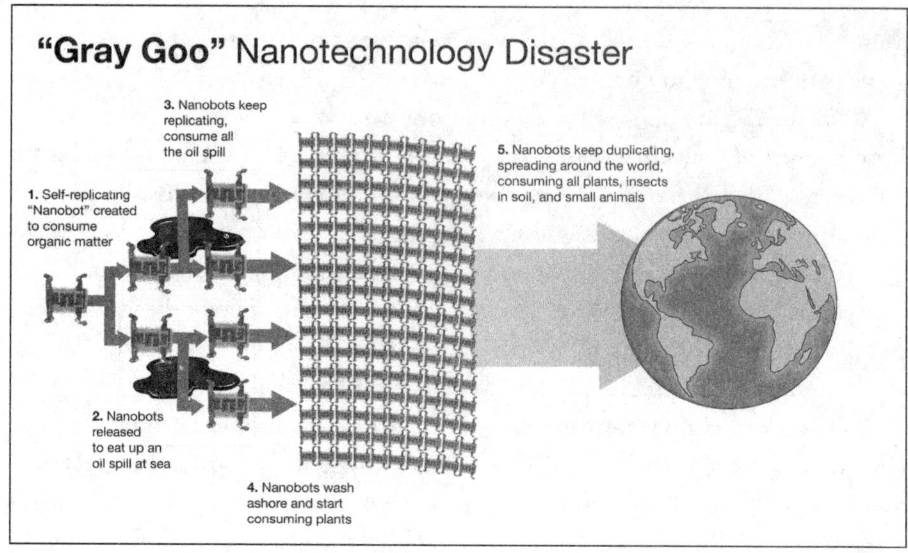

Figure 11: "Gray Goo" nanotechnology disaster.

Cyberattacks on infrastructure have occurred all over the world, on electric grids, water systems, financial systems—so far small attacks, likely to demonstrate or develop capability. If Russia, China, North Korea, or Iran were to wage a full scale cyberattack, perhaps in an allied effort, they could easily take down a wide swath of critical infrastructure that could lead to a collapse. The US has this capability as well, as do some large hacker networks that no country controls.

Advances in nuclear technology will likely lead to much easier, faster, harder to detect means of developing weapons grade material—especially with AI now available to help terrorists and nation-states figure out new ways to enrich uranium or use other elements and methods to create nuclear weapons.[77]

Iran and North Korea are using centrifuges to enrich uranium for nuclear weapons—the same technology the Manhattan Project used in the early 1940s. But laser enrichment has been developed and with constant advances in technology. We can be sure there are more means of enriching uranium and easier ways to build nuclear weapons.

Russia now has hypersonic cruise missiles that can travel at over five times the speed of sound, at low levels, making them almost impossible to track or shoot down. China and the US have them too, and you can be sure they will end up in the arsenals of other countries, with some possibly getting acquired by wealthy terrorist groups. They can be armed with a nuclear warhead, fired from a boat off the coast, launched from a modified civilian aircraft, and, unlike an ICBM, we'd have a hard time proving where it came from or who was responsible, so they may

The Seattle Times | Nation & World

LOCAL BIZ NATION SPORTS ENTERTAINMENT LIFE HOMES OPINION | THE TICKET JOBS EXPLORE All Sections

Nation World Nation & World Politics Oddities

Business | Environment | Nation & World

Laser advance in uranium enrichment may risk bomb spread

Originally published August 20, 2011 at 8:35 pm | *Updated August 20, 2011 at 11:01 pm*

General Electric has successfully tested laser enrichment of uranium and is seeking federal permission to build a $1 billion plant that would make reactor fuel by the ton.

By William J. Broad

SILEX Systems Limited

Figure 12: New technology to enrich uranium for nuclear weapons.

conclude this is a good way to blow up Washington, DC, and plunge the US into a collapse without bringing on a retaliatory attack.[78]

Add to this thousands of cheap—not hypersonic—but swarms of drones, which could be launched by agents operating from an air taxi drone front company, or released from a merchant ship just off the coast. They can deliver small explosive charges executing thousands of small attacks. They can release chaff to jam radars, making it impossible for even the most advanced and expensive missile defense system to stop hypersonic cruise missiles. There is no way the US or any country can build a completely reliable missile defense system with the advances in drone technology and AI. The peak of such missile defense effectiveness was likely Israel's Iron Dome—and they were defending largely against rather unsophisticated, old-technology incoming missiles.[79]

Other experts have warned of this era of collapse or "permanent crisis," as Robert Kaplan put it. Kaplan spent his career reporting on foreign affairs and served on the DoD's Defense Policy Board. In his 2025 book, *Waste Land: A World in Permanent Crisis*, Kaplan predicts that our vulnerable and volatile economy, geopolitical rivalries, unstable governments, and disruptive technologies and societal changes will produce a multitude of crises, wars and disasters, almost continually.[80]

There is a good chance that the trigger event that leads to the next collapse may also be "none of the above"—something not mentioned so far, not tracked by the Disaster Preparedness Threat Watch and Collapse Warning System, or considered in this book. A technology invented tomorrow may be abused to create a new weapon of mass destruction. AI will be used to invent a host of new WMD.

Finally, a collapse could happen with no trigger event! The UK suffered a four day period of uncontrolled nighttime looting and marauding and arson that had no trigger event. It just started (described in more detail later).

Portland, Oregon, suffered 170 days of political protests in 2020 that often served as cover for blatant looting and violence. Protestors damaged government buildings, looted stores, launched fireworks at law enforcement officers, who fired back with nonlethal munitions and tear gas. There were elements of our low-level civil war, with Democratic state and local officials in Oregon condemning federal officers sent in by President Trump to defend federal buildings in Portland. Burglaries and other crimes increased in Portland in 2020 due to police being occupied with the 170 days of protesting.[81] Portland businesses reported millions of dollars in losses due to vandalism and looting. In 2020, twenty businesses closed due to the protest violence. Later, Target, Walmart, REI, Nike, Daimler Trucks North America, Airbnb, Banana Republic, Microsoft, Saucebox, and Google left Portland or stopped expansion plans there. Some of these closures were not due to just the 2020 protest violence but the increasing organized retail crime along the west coast—daytime, blatant stealing.

We have seen uncontrollable looting that overwhelms police capacity. Many bad Americans are ready to loot and maraud whenever they see an opportunity to take advantage of police being overwhelmed, as they are when there are big protest events, or some local disaster.

There are "flash mobs" that spring up so often they don't always make the news. If you get a large group of people to all show at once at a store or shopping mall, easy to do with social media, and everyone starts looting at once, it is easy to overwhelm police and not get arrested. Looting is blatant in California, with big groups breaking into Home Depot or department stores and hauling carts full of goods out in broad daylight. And this can happen anywhere if you tie up dozens or hundreds of policemen with crowd control in a protest or political event. There are lots of bad people who know they can start looting and there are not enough policemen to respond. When any big disaster strikes, police will be overwhelmed, and it will be open season for gang members and criminals.

While running a collapse survival exercise on the Collapse Survivor App in March 2024 there were simulation "exercise messages" going out about the National Guard being called up to help restore law and order in the simulated exercise collapse. And while this scenario was running on the Collapse Survivor App, the National Guard really was called up because of a breakdown in law and order in the New York subway system.[82]

In good times, there are not enough police! Just imagine how bad it will be after a real disaster hits and police are overwhelmed with work, possibly among initial casualties. If you are trying to survive in a big city, or even a suburb, there will be no police to help you.

Taphouse Studios, Fortitude Ranch

Figure 13: As gang members and criminals know, with any domestic unrest or disaster, police will be overwhelmed; a great time for looting and marauding.

It is not all gloom and doom. The Age of Collapse brings great news for the global warming problem. With almost no economic activity, little to no industrial production, for months or years during a bad collapse, and hundreds of millions or billions of people killed, the human input to global warming will plummet. If there is a large nuclear war with lots of ground bursts (air bursts don't generate significant fallout or upper atmosphere debris), a super volcano eruption or big asteroid land strike, the sun could be blocked for years, killing almost all living creatures and cooling off the planet.[83]

The video (linked in the webnotes) explains how new technologies, the ability for even individuals to make and release WMD, a complex, vulnerable economy, and irresponsible government, and a population extremely vulnerable to disruption, it will be an Age of Collapse, with people struggling to survive.[84]

CHAPTER TWO

THE PROBABILITY OF COLLAPSE IS HIGH AND RISING

The probability of collapse is high and rising, an estimated 16–57 percent annual chance of a collapse disaster occurring.

You may be thinking that collapse threats can't be too bad or people would be taking action on these threats and there would be warnings. There are lots of warnings, but few pay attention to them. The media rarely covers warnings—they wait to report on the events. Nassim Taleb, one of the smartest men alive today, wrote a bestselling book, *The Black Swan: the Impact of the Highly Improbable.* Taleb explained that by their nature, humans ignore warnings of pending Black Swan disasters.

A Black Swan event is one that is an outlier; it is outside the realm of regular expectations, and nothing in the past can convincingly point to its possibility or the extreme impact it will have. Nassim Taleb's book explains why we consistently ignore or underestimate risk of foreseeable new forms of disaster.

Taleb warns that "things have a bias to appear more stable and less risky in the past, leading us to surprises." Taleb even notes that we are not wisely heeding the warnings of coming pandemics: "The history of epidemics, narrowly studied, does not suggest the risks of the great plague to come that will dominate the planet."[1]

People don't want to think about such disasters, and people are especially blind to new types of threats today because we rely on probability estimates—and you simply cannot estimate the probability of an event that has never happened before, like a bioengineered pandemic, or a new WMD that AI has helped a rogue nation or Unabomber "wannabe" invent. You can assess and estimate the likelihood of a new disaster from new technology or changed conditions happening, but people usually refuse to consider such warnings until they've seen the disaster occur. As

Taleb put it, we are "suckers for black swan events," even when, in retrospect, it seems obvious that they are coming. Winston Churchill warned of the Nazi threat. There was evidence aplenty of the German and Japanese military buildups and ambitions, but people didn't want to think about it, so they ignored it.[2]

Nassim Taleb, an expert in risk and thinking about rare events, warns that "humans are great at self-delusion." By our nature and education, we consistently underestimate the Black Swan disasters that surprise and smash us. We are physically and psychologically programmed to make common misjudgments. The central idea of Taleb's book is that despite plenty of indications, humans are horribly bad about preparing to deal with looming Black Swan disasters, even when experts do warn us.[3] People project from good times forward to confidently estimate more of the same.

Taleb goes through twenty-seven common, widespread errors in our natural human thinking process and misapplication of statistics to explain why we are "suckers" for Black Swan disasters like the coming collapse disasters. We think we know what is going on in a world that is more complicated and random than we realize. We overvalue current truths and past experiences that new technologies and a changing condition may soon render wrong and take solace in the views of "authoritative" and learned people who explain things with a false, comforting clarity. We fool ourselves with stories and anecdotes, invent memories, and what we don't see regularly, we tend to ignore. We learn by repetition, react and decide by gut feel, thinking that we've thought it through and made a rational choice when in fact we have not. "We are made to be superficial, to heed what we see and not heed what does not vividly come to mind. . . . Out of sight, out of mind: we harbor a natural, even physical, scorn of the abstract."[4] In sum, "we are naturally shallow and superficial—and we do not know it."[5] We overestimate what we know and underestimate uncertainty. "Our human race is affected by a chronic underestimation of the possibility of the future straying from the course initially envisioned, . . . an ingrained tendency in humans to underestimate outliers—or Black Swans."[6]

In addition to many natural tendencies to ignore Black Swan risks, we grossly misapply "normal distribution" statistics and risk management techniques. Our schools and organizations teach and use risk management techniques that are dangerously inappropriate to deal with very rare events.

Taleb cites as examples diaries of people prior to World War II—they had no inkling that something momentous was taking place, war coming. We hear much about Churchill's warning; but he was a rare voice of warning and ignored. WWII came as a surprise despite what in retrospect looks like absolutely clear signs, warnings, and actions. Bond prices, which are supposed to reflect the intelligence of the market, showed no expectation that a war was coming.[7]

This collapse disaster blindness is stronger in the US because we have the mightiest military, nuclear weapons, and feel immune from attack. People ignore warnings of Black Swan disasters and governments don't want intelligence and government agencies providing honest warnings to citizens about the risks. Elected officials prefer that the populace not panic, just trust that Big Government is always right and will take care of you. The former CDC director, no longer limited by elected officials muzzling honest warnings, has warned that we will suffer a horrible H5N1 pandemic, and its likely to be a bioengineered variant.[8]

The Disaster Preparedness Threat Watch and Collapse Warning System tracks more than fifty disasters, attacks, events, that could lead to a collapse. Some of these risks like super volcano eruptions and asteroid strikes have caused massive extinction events in the past. Preppers rate an economic crisis as a very likely collapse trigger.[9] In 2025, hedge fund expert Ray Dalio, predicted America has about three years to fix its massive debt problem or face an "economic heart attack."[10]

Collapse threats from new technologies account for one-third of the top fifteen threats tracked by the Disaster Preparedness Threat Watch and Collapse Warning: bioengineering viruses, cyberattacks, artificial intelligence, nanotechnology, and genetically modified organisms.

A National Research Council committee on chemical and biological defense scolded in 2012 that "The US probably has not yet adequately embraced the opacity of the threat. It will be much, much more difficult to prepare for and defend against than prior threats."[11] A decade later, even with the Covid-19 pandemic, we are unprepared for a bad pandemic. Covid-19 may have actually been a disservice to preparedness since it was so mildly lethal that it posed no threat to most people. Overreactions from Big Governments were more of a problem than the virus.

Perhaps the worst bad mistake even professional "risk managers" make in dealing with Black Swan risks is they assume that because something hasn't happened before, it must be a low risk. This is extremely stupid and dangerous. The likelihood of a nuclear detonation was certainly low before 1945. But the possibility of atomic weapons had been suggested by quantum mechanics scientists for years. German scientists were among the leading early quantum theorists, and with a world war going on it was logical to assume efforts to develop such powerful weapons were underway. I have noticed a profound tendency of very smart people to assume that the likelihood of something bad happening that has never occurred before is 1 percent or less—even when there are warnings, and obvious likelihood that the bad event is very probable.

Because it is very hard to get people to pay attention to Black Swan and collapse threat risks unless you put a probability estimate on it, I developed a "probability of collapse model." It estimates the likelihood of disaster "trigger" events occurring as well as the likelihood that if the trigger event happens it will escalate into a collapse level disaster. Even if you are biased in estimating Black Swan events low, the fact that there are so many trigger events will yield a cumulative probability that is high. However uncertain and wide the range of probability, many people will not seriously consider these risks unless they see some evidence that the likelihood of a collapse is well above 1 percent.

I presented my methodology on estimating the probability of collapse the "Military Operations Research Society"[12] while I was working at the Institute for Defense Analyses, a Department of Defense Federally Funded Research and Development Center or think tank.[13]

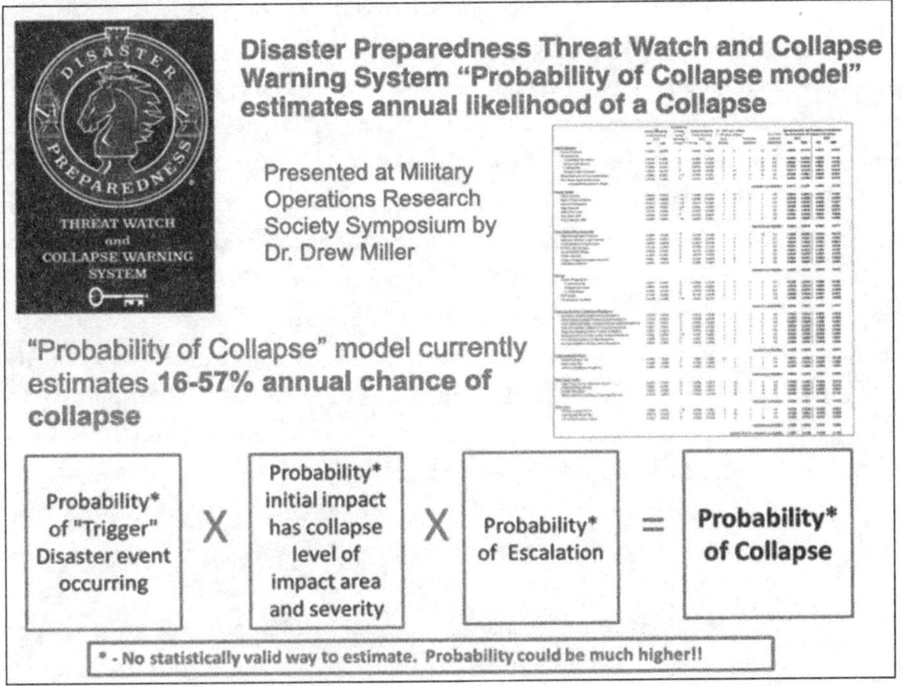

Figure 14: Probability of Collapse Model estimates likelihood of a collapse.

Our model weighs both the probability of the initial trigger disaster event occurring, then the likelihood of the initial disaster disruption spreading and escalating to a collapse level disaster with societal breakdown and widespread loss of law and order.

In 2024 the Probability of Collapse Model was updated with inputs and ratings from twenty-three intelligence officers, political scientists, biologists, defense analysts, and scientists. Experts reviewed fifty disaster "trigger events" that could spark a collapse, including the high probability of Nuclear War, a Bioengineered H5N1Pandemic, and Civil War risk, which have all increased.[14] The briefing below explains the "Probability of Collapse model"[15] that now estimates the annual likelihood of a collapse at 16–57 percent. The probabilities are highly uncertain, but definitely not low.

The EMP Commission, which was created by and reported back to Congress about the high vulnerability of our electric system, worked to assess the impacts of our grid being destroyed. They gave a rough guesstimate of the fatalities that we can't of course know, but estimated that given our huge dependence on electricity for most of our activities, damage to our electric system (which could take over a year to repair) could result in the loss of 90 percent of the population.[16] That's not a figure you can accurately calculate. There are too many uncertainties of course, but they made a reasonable estimate. With no electricity for water systems and no food production or distribution for a year or more, the collapse of law and order as people without food and water go out to loot, and when necessary, kill to survive, could indeed kill the vast majority of the population. The EMP Commission's estimate, made without the benefit of past probability data, illustrates the need when dealing with Black Swan events, rare disasters, to gather experts, think about how a collapse disaster will unfold, and then estimate the aftermaths and likelihoods.

There are so many warnings of AI disaster that the term "Probability of Doom," referred to as P(doom), is widely estimated by AI experts. Of course they have different degrees of bias, and the estimates of an AI disaster range from highly unlikely to inevitable. Here are some of the most respected estimates:[17]

- 50% Dr. Geoff Hinton, the Godfather of AI
- 20% Yoshua Bengio, another leading founder/developer of AI
- 30% The mean estimate from forty-four AI Safety Researchers

These are not annual estimates, but probability of an AI disaster occurring over the next few years. With the rapid, unexpected acceleration of AI progress and the many instances of AI already deceiving/tricking/disobeying humans, the probability of an AGI AI disaster is likely higher now. In just the past year, the pace of AI development has accelerated so quickly that experts are now predicting AGI level threats within one to two years, not a decade out.[18] With AI systems able to contribute more and more to their own improvement, and humans already losing control of AI systems, not even understanding how they are learning and working now, runaway AI that yields AGI and super intelligence that could wipe out humanity may be months away; we cannot be sure.[19] The two leading AI experts who have studied the risks of superintelligent AGI warn that "If anyone builds it, everyone dies."[20]

An "existential" collapse is one so severe that our species is almost or entirely wiped out, the vast majority of humanity killed, and survivors and civilization so badly damaged that it takes several generations to recover.

Dr. Nick Bostrom leads the "Future of Humanity Institute" at Oxford University. Dr. Bostrom and some other UK scientists have looked at the risks of existential threats, and while you cannot calculate a probability because there simply isn't the data, you can roughly and reasonably guesstimate a range of likelihood of some of the many disaster trigger events. The Cambridge Centre for the Study of Existential Risk includes many scientists concerned that developments in technology such as artificial intelligence, biotechnology, and nanotechnology, pose new, extinction-level risks to our species.[21] Lord Martin Rees, part of this Cambridge University group, warned in 2013 that "we're entering an era when a few individuals could, via error or terror, trigger societal breakdown."[22] In his 2003 book, *Our Final Hour: A Scientist's Warning*, Lord Rees estimated a fifty-fifty chance of humanity surviving the twenty-first century.[23] Experts at a Global Catastrophic Risk Conference in 2008 estimated a 19 percent chance of human extinction over the next century.[24] Dr. Bostrom wrote that "the balance of evidence is such that it would appear unreasonable not to assign a substantial probability to the hypothesis that an existential disaster will do us in. My subjective opinion is that setting this probability lower than 25% would be misguided, and the best estimate may be considerably higher."[25]

Note that a 19–25 percent or higher chance of extinction probably means many non-extinction level collapse disasters will occur. The 16–57 percent annual likelihood of a collapse estimated by the Probability of Collapse Model is an estimate not of extinction level collapses, but ones that would likely kill far fewer people and thus are not as devastating.

Bostrom, like Taleb, warns that the standard bad practice of assuming that a probability of risk you can't quantify means it must be low is a mistake.[26] Bostrom rightly insists that "the loss in expected value resulting from an existential catastrophe is so enormous that the objective of reducing existential risks should be a dominant consideration,"[27] but the political reality is just the opposite. Elected officials in the US focused on reelection and partisan politics and ignore issues that voters and lobbyists aren't complaining about. They base government spending and policy on what buys the most votes.

The likelihood of a collapse is probably higher than we estimate because there

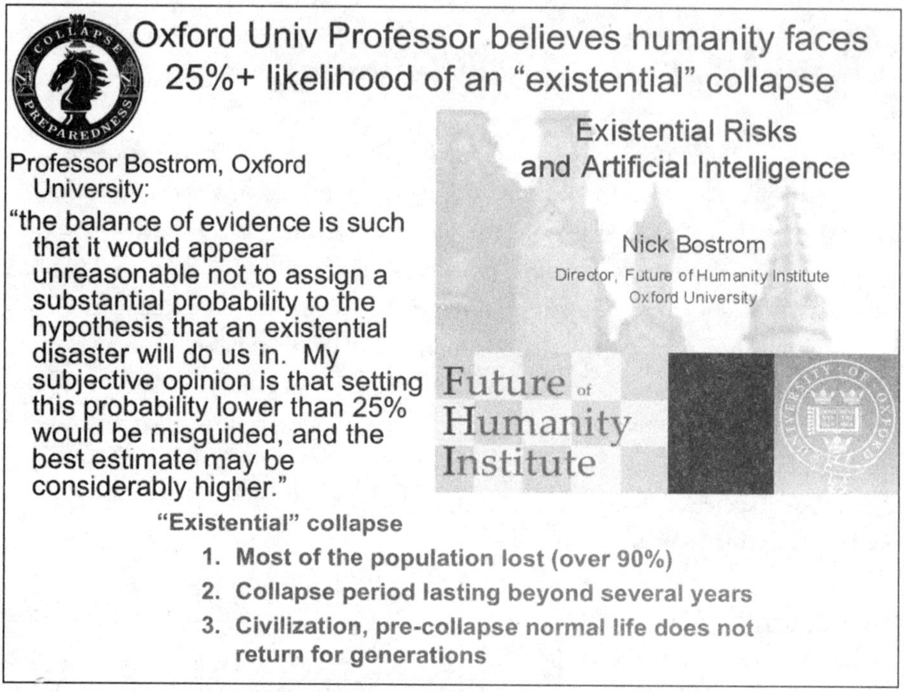

COLLAPSE PREPAREDNESS

Oxford Univ Professor believes humanity faces 25%+ likelihood of an "existential" collapse

Professor Bostrom, Oxford University:

"the balance of evidence is such that it would appear unreasonable not to assign a substantial probability to the hypothesis that an existential disaster will do us in. My subjective opinion is that setting this probability lower than 25% would be misguided, and the best estimate may be considerably higher."

Existential Risks and Artificial Intelligence

Nick Bostrom

Director, Future of Humanity Institute

Oxford University

Future of Humanity Institute

"Existential" collapse

1. Most of the population lost (over 90%)
2. Collapse period lasting beyond several years
3. Civilization, pre-collapse normal life does not return for generations

Figure 15: Experts estimate 25%+ likelihood of human extinction this century.

are trigger events, true Black Swans, we don't know of and thus don't weigh. A virus from space on an asteroid, some other new technology with catastrophic effects we have never thought of—but AI may invent. What's the likelihood of these? You can't know, and you can't even venture a reasonable guess if you don't know to consider an unimaginable new type of WMD. *Our models and estimates of collapse disasters are probably understating the risks.*

The Probability of Collapse model is also likely underestimating the likelihood of a collapse because it is based on a trigger event—but we could have a collapse with no trigger event. As the next chapter explains, we have seen many instances of widespread loss of law and order, collapse events, that had no predictable or even identifiable trigger event. In the UK in 2011, violence started in London and spread to other major cities. It went on for four days until a call-up of police shut it down. In the divided, often violent United States, a trivial incident that gets blown up in the media, with rumors and threats spreading through social media, could spark looting and violence that escalates and quickly spreads.

The probability of collapse model also underestimates the likelihood of a collapse because it does not include any estimate/impact from the "piling on threat." A disaster like a New Madrid earthquake, that destroys transportation across a lot of the central US, could kill may be a few tens of thousands directly. The aftermaths of disrupted food supply, and gangs—bad people taking advantage of the overwhelmed police and National Guard—might kill more. Our military would respond, and this massive regional earthquake might not reach the level of a collapse; we might quickly restore law and order. But since China really wants to settle their Taiwan problem, seize this island, they may see our New Madrid disaster as the ideal time to launch their attack. They could order their agents in the US to conduct sabotage attacks that yield lots of local collapse problems. We could end up in a small or large nuclear war with China. Now there is radioactive fallout coming down across the United States—all stemming from the initial regional earthquake in the US that on its own didn't cause a collapse. If you think that's silly, then consider the sequence of events that led to the Fukushima nuclear power plant disaster, or explain how an assassination of a minor archduke in some backwoods part of Serbia led to World War I, or Putin's logic in invading Ukraine. Nation-states and terrorists will exploit a bad event. They'll pile on to hit us while we're down. They may be irrational, and events and chaos tend to have cascading effects and unintended consequences. So an initial trigger event, a relatively small war, a regional natural disaster that ties up a lot of National Guard and other federal assets, could entice an enemy to launch a military attack, release a virus, sabotage our electric grid, and the combined effects could yield a severe collapse disaster.[28]

Taleb's key point is "Black Swans being unpredictable, we need to adjust to their existence (rather than naively try to predict them)."[29] The probability of a collapse is inherently, highly uncertain, but definitely not low. The best available estimate is a 16–57 percent chance. There could be several collapse disasters in a single year.

Hoping that accidents, lunatics, terrorists, or enemy states won't release a WMD to kill Americans or block our ability to stop their action overseas is the worst and perhaps last mistake our government could make. As a nation, we must adapt to the existence of the many collapse threats we face now and make huge changes in our strategy, military forces, economy, and preparedness to survive collapse conditions. We need to be prepared to deal with a viral pandemic that kills 90 percent of its victims and cannot be stopped with a simple quarantine or low levels of casualties. That's our present and our future. It deserves far more attention and resources than China invading Taiwan, war with Russia, or other threats the DoD or Department of Homeland Security (DHS) now focus on. Individuals also need to have a plan and resources, to be trained and ready to survive a viral pandemic, loss of the electric grid, new AI-developed WMD, and other threats that lead to a collapse of the economy and law and order.

Chapter Three

LESSONS FROM "DARK WINTER" AND PAST DISASTERS

Dark Winter Exercise Acknowledged that Citizens Will Loot, Maraud, and Kill in Trying to Survive

The federal government "Dark Winter" exercise in 2001 simulated a bio attack on the US (a pretty small one) and found we were grossly unprepared. A group of government officials and journalists play-acted their way through a "germ game," a fictional scenario in which the (then obscure) terrorist group called Al-Qaeda set off an outbreak of smallpox in US shopping malls. In the simulation, National Guard units were activated and used to impose curfews, quarantines, and keep public peace.[1]

Former Senator Sam Nunn, playing the POTUS in the Dark Winter exercise, noted in Congressional testimony that following a bio attack "it is not the terrorists anymore who are the threat; your neighbors and family members can become the threat, and can even become the enemy. . . ."[2] That's a very politically incorrect thing to say, but Nunn had retired from public office and was now more honest. In the recorded Congressional testimony after the exercise, and if you interview people who participated in Dark Winter, you get a rarely frank, honest acknowledgment of how grossly unprepared we are for a bio attack or any big disaster that leads to a collapse. It should be obvious that people won't just calmly stay at home when there is no water system functioning or food, but this exercise was a rare government acknowledgment that people cannot be expected to quietly stay at home and starve to death.

When former Senator Nunn testified that, "your neighbors and family members can become the threat, and can even become the enemy," he meant not just that you could catch the disease from them, but that they may try to break into your house at gunpoint, killing you if necessary, to take your supplies and keep themselves alive. Initially it may be largely just gang members and criminals looting and killing, but as the disaster and collapse proceeds, more people will panic and conclude that they face starvation, or getting murdered, and will conclude that they have to take up arms and steal and maraud themselves if they're going to survive. Preppers won't do that—they are prepared with supplies and the means to defend them. But 95 percent plus of the population is not prepared for collapse survival. Even if the grid is up, municipal workers won't go to work in a collapse. If everyone starts filling bathtubs and collecting as much water as they can, the water system will not keep functioning.

The fact that neighbors and normally good people can quickly become a deadly threat is something that preppers are very well aware of. They don't just stockpile food and water, they have guns and ammo because they recognize that during a pandemic, or loss of the electric system, or other big disaster, grocery stores will be emptied. Police will be overwhelmed, unable to deal with either bad people in gangs, or normally good people out stealing food for their family. This exercise showed we are grossly unprepared for a bio attack, pandemic, or any collapse level disaster.

Senator Sam Nunn, playing POTUS in the exercise, offered these lessons learned:

1. "Our lack of preparation is a real emergency."
2. "I am convinced the threat of a biological weapons attack on the United States is very real."
3. "The most insidious effect of a biological weapons attack is that it can turn Americans against Americans. Once smallpox is released, it is not the terrorist anymore who are the threat; your neighbors and family members can become the threat, and can even become the enemy."
4. "*Panic is as great a danger as disease.* Some will respond like saints—doing whatever they can, in a spirit of cheerful patriotism, to meet the needs of family and community. *Others will respond with panic, perhaps even using guns and violence to get vaccines.*"

There have been some minor improvements in areas like speeding distribution of medical equipment, but the fundamental problems that Dark Winter uncovered back in 2001 are still there—all while our population, economic interdependence, and advances in biotechnology and DNA manipulation that make us far more vulnerable to bio attacks and bioengineered pandemics have grown much worse.

As detailed later in this book, there is no food stockpiling for citizens, no reserve of police or military to call up for collapse recovery, no preparations for citizen's survival—just "Continuity of Government" shelters and preparations for top elected and government officials.[3]

Other Exercises and Past Disasters Show that Economic Shutdown, Panic, Looting, Loss of Law and Order Are Likely

There are too many unknowns and situation-specific variables to reliably estimate public reactions to a disaster that disrupts food supplies and overwhelms the medical system and law enforcement. We can, however, gain insights from exercises and past disasters and bad pandemics (not Covid-19) that should give high confidence that there will be elements of panic and lawlessness, looting, marauding, and murders that need to be anticipated and prepared for.[4]

Clade X Exercise

There may be no more credible source on dealing with pandemics and disaster response than Johns Hopkins University's Center for Health Security. Their 2018 "Clade X" simulation covered a very realistic, only moderately contagious and moderately lethal virus, about as deadly as the SARS in 2002, killing about 10 percent of those infected. Eric Toner, the senior scholar at the Johns Hopkins Center for Global Health Security, designed the "completely realistic" Clade X simulation. A virus was bioengineered and released by a group modeled after the cult Aum Shinrikyo, which released the chemical weapon sarin in the Tokyo subway in 1995. Toner said researchers are convinced a virus like this could be created and spread, killing 900 million people. Health-care systems collapsed, panic spread, the US stock market crashed.[5] Eric Toner warned that a pandemic could cause hospital systems to collapse: "Most people don't know how close we came to having that happen in the US in 2009 . . . due to a not particularly virulent flu strain."[6]

The simulation, with experienced medical, national security, and former elected officials playing the exercise, led to National Guard troops deploying in the US to provide security at pharmacies and hospitals—an acknowledgment that some citizens are not going to simply wait for their turn to get a vaccine, but will fight to improve their chances of survival. In some countries, military forces were deployed both to keep domestic order and secure borders: "Widespread looting in some countries led to violent government crackdowns."[7] In the simulation, representing twenty months after the start of the outbreak, 150 million died around the globe, 15–20 million deaths in the United States. There was no vaccine for the illness ready, so the death toll would have kept climbing to an estimated 900 million people, over 10 percent of the world's population.[8]

Tara O'Toole, a former top Homeland Security Department official who played the homeland security secretary in the Clade X exercise commented that: "We are in an age of epidemics, but we aren't treating them like the national security issues that they are."[9]

This was not an unlikely or worst case bioengineered pandemic simulation. The Johns Hopkins experts believe that the virus simulated in the Clade X exercise can be created and released.[10] The Clade X simulated virus was bioengineered by a terrorist group.[11] An ex officio member of a Blue Ribbon Study Panel on Biodefense created to assess the state of biodefense in the US reported that it was inevitable that a disease as deadly as the 1918 Spanish Flu pandemic would emerge again.[12]

Clade X also realistically acknowledged that there will be panic and riots in a pandemic, but the exercise did not have (or release to the media/public) details on how a bad pandemic would lead to people not coming to work, law and order breaking down, and marauders killing people.[13] The exercise simulation, run by a biothreats-focused agency, focused on deaths from the virus, not starvation and marauding.

The 1918 Spanish Flu Pandemic

Our last serious pandemic is often cited as an example of what we need to prepare for. More than 500,000 Americans were killed. An internal American Red Cross report concluded that "A fear and panic of the Influenza, akin to the terror of the Middle Ages regarding the Black Plague, [has] been prevalent in many parts of the country." Reactions were generally worse in cities. Automobiles were largely absent on the streets in Manhattan and Philadelphia. Little data on worker absenteeism is available, but even in defense industries, crucial to the war effort, absenteeism ranged from 45 to 60 percent.[14] The US was a more rural, peaceful, less crowded country then, far less dependent on daily food shipments and "just-in-time" deliveries of medical and essential supplies.

The 1972 outbreak of smallpox in Yugoslavia

Europe's last major smallpox outbreak was centered in Kosovo and Belgrade, then part of Socialist Federal Republic of Yugoslavia. The outbreak was stopped by quarantines, aggressive police and military measures, and 18 million emergency vaccinations to protect a population of 21 million that was already highly vaccinated.[15] Panic and lawlessness were largely preempted or overcome by swift institution of martial law, with blockades of villages and neighborhoods, roadblocks, prohibition of public meetings, border closures, and prohibition of nonessential travel. Hotels were requisitioned for use to quarantine; 10,000 people who may have been in contact with the virus were held under army and police guards. Blocks were cordoned off with barbed wire, "essentially creating health prison camps." [16] This level of immediate and decisive, tough action was possible in a dictatorship, but is not planned for and highly unlikely in the United States. Almost the entire Yugoslavian population was vaccinated or revaccinated, with help from other countries and an existing stockpile of vaccines. The net result: just 175 Yugoslavians contracted the disease; only 35 died.[17] In the United States, it would take half a year to develop a vaccine for a new virus, and only a small percent of the population would get treated with initial output.

A 1994 a plague outbreak in Surat, India

The result was "a nationwide panic and a near international isolation of India" and $3–4 billion in economic losses, despite a very localized occurrence of the disease and just fifty-three fatalities. When news of plague was released, 600,000 people (one fourth of the population) fled Surat by whatever means available. "Doctors fled the city saying, 'this plague, nothing can be done.'" Other cities, thousands of kilometers away, "immediately began to go into a state of panic," and experienced flooded hospitals (imagined illness) and panic buying. Some nations imposed commercial quarantines on India. The plague was spread by fleeing people, but most of the deaths occurred in Surat.[18]

2005 Hurricane Katrina

A widely cited case study of public reaction to a disaster. "The Federal Response to Hurricane Katrina: Lessons Learned," written by DHS in 2006, summarizes, the impacts of the hurricane and flooding on law and order:

> Almost immediately following Hurricane Katrina's landfall, law and order began to deteriorate in New Orleans. . . . People began looting in some areas as soon as the storm relented. Violent crimes were committed against law enforcement officers and other emergency response personnel. . . The city's overwhelmed police force—70% of which were themselves victims of the disaster—did not have the capacity to arrest every person witnessed committing a crime, and many more crimes were undoubtedly neither observed by police nor reported. The resulting lawlessness in New Orleans significantly impeded—and in some cases temporarily halted—relief efforts and delayed restoration of essential private sector services such as power, water, and telecommunications.[19]

The reports and evidence of lawlessness from Katrina documented in a Congressional report are worth considering:[20]

- "The collapse of local law enforcement and lack of effective public communications led to civil unrest and further delayed relief."[21]
- "A variety of conditions led to lawlessness and violence in hurricane stricken areas."[22]
  - "Looting occurred in several locations."
  - Some looting was for food or medical supplies for survival, some purely for criminal purposes (e.g. stealing televisions)."
  - "In some areas, the collapse or absence of law enforcement exacerbated the level of lawlessness and violence."
  - "Mississippi experienced some looting, armed robbery, and crowd control problems immediately after the storm."
  - There were "reported theft and carjacking threats at a medical center in Biloxi."
  - "As an institution . . . the New Orleans Police Department disintegrated with the first drop of floodwater."
  - "Hundreds of New Orleans Police Department officers went missing—some for legitimate reasons, and some not—at a time they were needed most."
  - Some police officers engaged in crime, including stealing luxury cars and joining with looters in ransacking a Walmart store.[23]

Katrina showed that lawlessness, looting, killing, policemen abandoning their duty (and some engaging in looting) can result from disasters with relatively minor threat of death. The need for military support to law enforcement was evident.[24]

Katrina provided evidence that truck drivers will need military escort and protection, or they may refuse to work. Chief of the National Guard, Lt Gen. Blum reported that "truck drivers coming in with the most needed supplies, water, food, ice, shelter, medicine . . . were afraid to come in. They had to be escorted in by National Guard convoys, which took other manpower away from the relief efforts to go help get the commercial truckers. . . ."[25] One thousand FEMA employees set to arrive in New Orleans turned back due to security concerns.[26] These reports of truck drivers and FEMA employees turning around due to security concerns agitated storm survivors in the Superdome.[27] The level of demands on law enforcement personnel and lawlessness in a pandemic or no electrical power situation will be far worse than Katrina.

Tulsa, Oklahoma, 1921

On May 30, 1921, some incident supposedly occurred between a young Black man and a white woman riding in an elevator. Rumors circulated among the city's white community and Tulsa police arrested the man the following day. An inflammatory report in the May 31 edition of a Tulsa paper led to a confrontation between Black Tulsans concerned that the arrested Black man would be lynched and white armed mobs around the courthouse. Shots were fired, and the outnumbered Black Tulsans retreated to the largely Black Greenwood District of Tulsa.[28]

In early morning hours of June 1, the Greenwood district of Tulsa was looted and burned by white rioters. At the eruption of violence, city officials deputized many men—all white, some participants in the previous violence—to be deputies, and provided fire arms and ammunition to white individuals who, with police, attacked and destroyed Greenwood. Over 1,200 homes—plus churches, schools, businesses, a hospital, and and library—were burned or destroyed. Despite duties to preserve order and to protect people and property, no government at any level offered any opposition to the destruction of the Greenwood neighborhood.

Governor Robertson declared martial law, and National Guard troops arrived in Tulsa. Guardsmen assisted firemen in putting out fires, took African Americans out of the hands of vigilantes, and imprisoned all Black Tulsans not already interned. Over six thousand people were held, for as long as eight days. After Army Guard forces removed Black people from the Greenwood district, white people stole, damaged, or destroyed personal property left behind.[29]

Thirty-five city blocks were burned and ruined, more than eight hundred people treated for injuries, and an estimated 100–300 people were killed. Not a single criminal act was prosecuted then or ever by any government at any level. Municipal authorities also impeded rebuilding of Greenwood. The American Red Cross, which operated for months following the massacre, provided relief to survivors. The charges against the Black man, "highly suspect from the start," were dismissed.[30]

Detroit, Michigan, 1943

In June 1943, some Black teenagers got into a fight with a white sailor and his girlfriend. A white man came to the sailor's aid, then a Black man joined the fight. Incredibly, the fight spread throughout downtown Detroit, rapidly spiraling out of control as rumors spread and more people joined in. Police "lost control, and there was no stemming the violence."[31] Some members of the police locked themselves inside their vehicles for safety, while other white policemen joined in the attacks. The fighting raged overnight, with murders, arson, and destruction of property.

War factories around Detroit closed, businesses and schools were ordered to close, people advised to stay home and lock doors, with "[m]obs hunting the streets, and no one to stop them."[32] White state and city police and mobs attacked Black housing areas, with Black snipers on rooftops returning fire. After three days of violence, federal troops sent in to disperse rioters stopped the war that killed thirty-four (nine white, twenty-five Black).[33]

A 1977 New York City

A lightning strike caused power failure for one night. As a result of the blackout, more than three thousand arrests were made for looting, four hundred policemen were injured, and five hundred fires were started. More than twenty-five thousand emergency calls were placed, with four times the usual number of hospital emergency admissions.[34]

Top Officials Exercise, 2000

We can also learn about likely impacts of a pandemic from "tabletop exercises," where senior leaders and disaster response experts simulate a crisis and make decisions. A May 2000 "Top Officials" exercise simulated a plague attack in Denver, Colorado. By the second day of the exercise, Denver area hospitals ran out of antibiotics and ventilators, and plague was being reported in other states and countries. By Day 3, medical care in Denver was "beginning to shut down" due to insufficient staff, beds, ventilators, and drugs. Person-to-person spread of plague was occurring and the Centers for Disease Control advised Colorado to close its state borders to limit further spread of plague. By the end of Day 4, there were an estimated 3,700 cases of plague and 950–2,000 deaths, and the exercise ended.[35] The exercise did not have public participation, due to concerns of disinformation and panic. Issues were raised over how to feed and control a populace that was likely to have grave concerns.[36] In this four-day exercise, "competition between cities for the National Pharmaceutical Stockpile supplies had already broken out. It had all the characteristics of an epidemic out of control."[37]

In June 2011 in Vancouver, Canada

One hundred people were injured, stores looted, cars burned, police attacked following a riot after loss in Stanley Cup championship hockey game. Police noted signs of organized violence: "they came prepared to break into display cases and steal," and brought masks and gasoline.[38] Today we often have cases in the United States of people using events or creating their own social media generated mobs to enable looting and violence.[39]

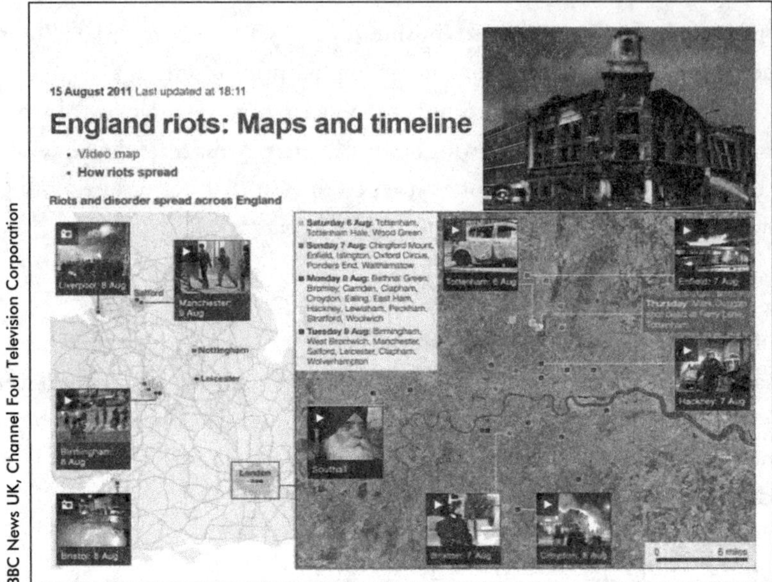

BBC News UK, Channel Four Television Corporation

Figure 16: UK violence in 2011 showed a collapse can happen without a trigger event.

The United Kingdom in 2011

The UK experienced lawlessness on a countrywide scale. UK riots showed that law and order can break down and violence spread without an underlying disaster or "trigger event." The UK Prime Minister called it "pure criminality"; others said it was inevitable violence from youth fed up with unemployment or mad at police. Attacks on police and looting started in London, but spread quickly to cities across the UK. Looting and violence grew as more people took advantage of the opportunity and "marauding gangs" formed. Police "lost control" of many areas; innocent people were shot dead in cars and robbed on streets. Violence repeated in London for four nights until an extra 16,000 police officers were moved in to restore order. Thugs in Birmingham killed three men trying to protect their businesses. Hundreds of youths in Manchester looted shops and set fires to cars and buildings. Police cars and five police stations were attacked with fire bombs. 2,500 shops and businesses were looted across England. 4,000 people were arrested, but up to 14,000 were believed to have been involved in looting, arson, or attacks on police. A London School of Economics study of the riots found that most were involved simply as an opportunity to easily steal "free stuff." Gangs were involved, but were a small percentage of lawbreakers. Many were motivated by a hatred of police and saw this as an opportunity to strike back. Some had no criminal backgrounds and simply thought, "Let's get wild, let's do it," "Well, everyone's getting free stuff, I'm joining in."[40]

Baltimore Riots, 2015

It took the State Patrol, National Guard, and police reinforcements from several states, and armored vehicles to restore law and order in Baltimore after racial protests opened opportunities for arson and looting. Despite the presence of police and TV cameras, a mob in broad daylight looted and then burned a CVS drugstore. Police fired pepper spray balls to disperse crowds, but in large groups, individuals feel relatively safe to commit crimes, with low risk of capture. Fifteen buildings and 144 cars were set on fire; nineteen police officers were injured. President Obama denounced the rioters as "criminals and thugs," saying there was "no excuse" for the violence. The violence was also promoted by social media, a call for students to "purge," referencing the 2013 action horror movie *The Purge*, where one night a year crime is legal and police, fire, and medical emergency services are unavailable.[41] In a major, widespread disaster, there will be no outside reinforcements, and little to no local police available to deal with a gang or group of marauders going through a neighborhood to steal supplies.

Portland Oregon Protests and Looting, 2020

Portland suffered 170 days of political protests in 2020. It started with protests over "Black Lives Matter," but the introduction of federal law enforcement officers to protect federal buildings (similar to Los Angeles in 2025) by President Trump gave protestors another cause to protest. Regardless of the protestor motivations, some bad people used the protests as cover for blatant looting and violence. The length of the protesting and violence was the most interesting aspect. Protestors kept returning to tear down statues, damage government buildings, and launch fireworks at law enforcement officers, who fired back with nonlethal munitions and tear gas. Democratic state and local officials in Oregon condemned federal officers sent in by Trump who argued they were needed to defend federal buildings in Portland.

For most citizens watching the Portland riots, the looting and store break-ins and arson was the major concern. Portland businesses reported millions of dollars in losses due to vandalism and looting. In 2020, twenty businesses closed due to the protest violence. Later, Target, Walmart, REI, Nike, Daimler Trucks North America, Airbnb, Banana Republic, Microsoft, Saucebox, and Google left Portland or stopped expansion plans there. Some of these closures were not just due to the 2020 protest violence, but the increase in organized retail crime along the West Coast—daytime, blatant stealing by groups. Burglaries and other crime increased in Portland in 2020 due to police being occupied with the 170 days of protesting.[42]

Haiti, 2021–2025

United Nation reports call Haiti "an unending horror story," with four years of violent gangs, security forces, and militia groups battling in this collapsed country.[43] In the capital and urban areas, gangs rule as warlords, with more than 1.3 million Haitians homeless, many of them starving. People are subsisting in rural areas and with international food aid. Casualties are unknown, but thousands have been killed. A UN security force, staffed largely by Kenya, limits some violence, but has not stopped the collapse or growth in areas controlled by gangs.

Government Exercises and Planning Assumptions Are Often False, Designed to Give Assurances of Government Competence, Avoid Panicking the Public or Giving Government Agencies Justification for Bigger Budgets

In contrast to honest experts' estimates of millions to billions of deaths from a pandemic, the US Department of Homeland Security pandemic influenza planning scenario refers to just 87,000 casualties—not much more than a bad seasonal flu. This version of the scenario seen in public forums has planning assumptions on virus lethality, worker absenteeism, and maintenance of law and order that are irresponsibly optimistic. When planning for security, you have an obligation to be honest and realistic, erring on the side of worst case, not rosy scenarios.[44]

The DHS uses fifteen National Planning Scenarios. Scenario 3 is Biological Disease Outbreak—Pandemic Influenza, and Scenario 4 is Biological Attack—Plague.[45] The National Planning Scenarios, while marked "FOR OFFICIAL USE ONLY," have been available on the Internet in sanitized, abbreviated form, and you can still find the detailed versions from a decade ago when they were accidentally posted on some state websites. I downloaded a February 2006 version years ago.[46]

None of these scenarios involve H5N1, a GMO, or bioengineered agent used to generate a viral pandemic with truly catastrophic levels of deaths. None of these scenarios deal with large nation-state levels of attack. There is no official, released version of DHS Scenario 3, but references to Scenario 3 usually cite just 87,000 casualties, a tiny fraction of what many scientists and biologists believe would result. The assumptions of the virus not being that bad, worker absenteeism not much problem outside the health care sector, and no problems from lawlessness, lead to false assumptions that all forms of critical infrastructure will be operating with no cascading effects.[47]

The 2006 National Influenza Pandemic Implementation Plan did note that "a modern pandemic could lead to the deaths of 200,000 to 2 million people in the United States alone," compared to the 87,000 fatalities most often cited for Pandemic Influenza Scenario 3.[48] A doctor, pandemic expert, and associate DHS director, writing in *Foreign Affairs* in 2005 estimated that "even a 'mild' influenza pandemic" (relative to the lethality of the 1918–20 Influenza pandemic) "could kill many millions of people."[49] Avian flu (H5N1) may be worse than past H1N1 influenza pandemics, experts cited elsewhere in this book estimating a billion fatalities.[50] The contrasts between the 1918 Spanish Flu pandemic, seasonal flu, and the anticipated avian flu pandemic cited earlier that experts say could kill a billion people, and the ridiculously low 87,000 casualties in federal pandemic scenarios is convincing proof of government dishonesty and disregard for protecting citizens.[51] The realistic Clade X simulation estimated hundreds of millions of fatalities. Yet our National Planning Scenarios uses tens of thousands of fatalities to avoid having government look bad or alarm the public.[52]

The consequences of hundreds of unrealistic, rosy scenario government planning assumptions for a mild pandemic and no loss of law and order, no collapse, is likely to be millions of lost lives due to politically correct plans and gross unpreparedness. The assumptions of DHS Pandemic Influenza Scenario 3 contradict the "Lessons Learned" from Katrina that DHS and the Bush White House published: "While the National Planning Scenarios have been effective tools for generating dialogue on response capabilities, they do not fully anticipate some of the worst disaster scenarios. . . . *If the purpose of the National Planning Scenarios is to provide a foundation for identifying the capabilities required to meet all hazards, the Scenarios must press us to confront the most destructive challenges*. . . . [W]e must revise the planning scenarios to make them more challenging."[53] A nice report on Katrina lessons learned was prepared, but like the Congressional EMP Commission studies and countless government reports designed to look like problems are being addressed, nothing was done to execute the recommendations.

Another irresponsible, unrealistic, dangerous set of assumptions are grossly optimistic assumptions on levels of worker absenteeism, particularly in law enforcement and the food and transportation sectors that are key to avoiding lawlessness and higher casualties in a collapse.

In government publications on pandemic preparedness over the past decade, worker absenteeism rates of up to 40 percent are often cited.[54] A 2009 study of health care workers who were asked about their willingness to report to work for a smallpox, SARS (severe acute respiratory syndrome), or other dangerous diseases found worker absenteeism rates above 40 percent, not "up to 40 percent":[55] Forty percent absenteeism in a pandemic is ridiculously optimistic. People are going to stay home rather than risk exposure to a deadly virus, risk getting killed by marauders, or risk having their family home attacked while they are at work. There is absolutely no study and no reasonable basis for the 40 percent absenteeism rate used by national planners. Google to find a study estimating 40 percent worker absenteeism in a bad pandemic, and you'll find there has never been one, no report or even explanation for this figure. In over a decade of searching for how we came up with this, the only explanation I received from a DHS official is that some military planner in a DoD exercise made it up, this was discovered, and with no study available, others just started using 40 percent figure.[56] There was no study, no group of analysts and experts met to collectively estimate a pandemic worker absenteeism rate. A military scenario writer just invented a number for his table-top military training exercise—and that's what our government uses for pandemic planning. I don't blame the military officer; I used to write command post exercise scenarios. They are just designed to get the war-game simulation players into the proper mindset and set the stage for the exercise.

Businessmen who attended a conference on dealing with an H1N1 influenza pandemic (not a very lethal form of flu) in 2009 said worker absenteeism was their greatest concern. They were uncertain what absenteeism rates would be, but in a poll taken their estimates were much higher.[57] My polling of people asked if they would go to work if a double digit lethality virus was spreading suggests this 40 percent estimate is dangerous Bravo Sierra. If a highly contagious, lethal virus is out there, at least 90 percent of people will refuse to go to work. If they do, they risk not just catching the virus and killing themselves, but bringing it home and killing their family. Nor is the risk of making yourself more vulnerable to crime during a breakdown in law and order factored in. Why would a food truck driver risk either catching the virus, or being robbed and killed by marauding gangs out looking for food? During Katrina, a minor disaster in terms of loss of law and order, some truck drivers refused to go into New Orleans without National Guard armed escort.[58]

It will not be 40 percent worker absenteeism in a bad pandemic collapse. The vast majority of people will wisely stay at home (and many will "bug out" to survival communities and safe retreats). Only a small minority will risk their lives and their families' lives to report to work during a H5N1 or double digit lethality pandemic. But dishonest government national planning scenarios assume the opposite. Most infrastructure systems outside of the public health and health care sector are predicted to continue to function at or near normal levels, 40 percent absenteeism rates are the upper limit of what they use.[59] In rosy government planning scenarios the economy keeps functioning, people stay calm; no loss of law and order, no collapse. The National Planning Scenarios ignore human nature, past disaster experiences (which are nowhere as bad as a pandemic or loss of the electric system or other big, widespread disaster), exercises like Clade X and Dark Winter, and common sense.

It only takes one link in the food production, processing, distribution, and retail chain to fail to stop food deliveries. The jobs in food harvesting and food manufacturing are generally low-skill, low-wage, and high-turnover jobs. Most workers may reason that they'd be better off calling in sick or quitting rather than risk their lives. They do not risk losing high pay position or damaging their career by dropping out of work during a pandemic. When people cannot get food, or fear they won't be able to, it is not just gangs that will go out stealing and sometimes killing for food; many "normal, good people" will also start marauding to keep themselves and their families alive. Thinking all people will stay home without food and water and politely die is delusional, but is the unwritten key assumption of our National Planning Scenarios.[60]

It is not just grocery stores with a few days of perishable food that may disappear in hours due to panic buying and probable looting. Gas stations need deliveries every one to three days (with normal demand); hospitals don't have more than a few days' supply for daily patient needs; water treatment plants keep only one to two weeks' worth of chlorine on hand for water treatment.[61] Hospitals and jails have just a few days' worth of fuel for their generators. Whether there is panic buying or not, truck drivers will be urgently needed to replenish food and other essential supplies, as will workers needed in food processing and retail stores, water and power systems, etc.[62]

In a 2006 National Planning Scenario pandemic influenza scenario there is mention of "social unrest" and "riots," but political correctness prohibits honestly addressing marauders or lawlessness as this footnote disclaimer explains:

> Disclaimer: Disaster literature has established that people don't panic or act irrationally in a disaster as long as they have credible information and purposeful activities to undertake in response. While one must plan for the worst, this is not a prediction of violence and mass panic. There is no evidence that the public will respond in a lawless manner in a real influenza pandemic.[63]

The disclaimer is a knowing, deliberate lie. The official government funded reports of Katrina, Congressional testimony on Dark Winter, Congressional testimony from the EMP Commission, all acknowledge that in a major disaster people are going to not just panic and riot, but loot and murder when needed to get food, water, and stay alive. The disclaimer is a hypocritical lie; they footnote an acknowledgment of riots (panic and violence) while denying they will occur, and insist that they must "plan for the worst" while refusing to do so because they don't want to risk bad press or elected official wrath if they honestly admit that obvious fact that people will panic, steal, loot, or kill to survive. In later pages they accidentally left in "maintaining security in communities" in a list of emergency management responses.[64] The pandemic scenario itself is anything but planning for the worst: they assume a low fatality rate, just 10 percent worker absenteeism, and no consequences from rioting or panic or looting or marauding that any adult with common sense would wisely conclude is somewhere between highly likely and inevitable. In sum the National Planning Scenarios are irresponsible, dangerous, politically correct nonsense designed to ensure government preparations look good, not plan or prepare for reasonable, highly likely consequences of major disasters.

Another reason that government planning scenarios are so rosy—the good guys always win, few die—is that any bad results that occur in an official government planning scenario exercise is good evidence for a government agency to argue for more resources and budget to avoid the loss of life. You will not find this in a published study or Internet search, but I witnessed it firsthand while working at the Institute for Defense Analyses, the top DoD think tank. A Senior Executive Service level member of a DoD budget and planning office was there to review changes recommended in some National Planning Scenarios. I can't mention the country, but our analysis was that the threat was grossly understated, and we recommended changes in the planning scenario to reflect that. The changes were declined because the DoD official knew that if that happened, the US Army would have grounds to recommend another division—and there was no budget or support for such an increase.

Government policy should be based on realistic assumptions. In a pandemic, almost all economic activity will grind to a halt. First responders, the people will need most, will have the highest initial casualty rates in a pandemic due to their exposure to the virus. It is likely there will be no law enforcement personnel available for the masses in a pandemic. National Guard troops will be vital, but many of them may also decide they need to stay home to avoid catching the virus and to protect their families from marauders.[65] I've done research at the Institute for Defense Analyses, and there are no DoD reports that even address these issues. Discussing citizens looting and marauding is politically incorrect in government, just like (as we'll see later) any discussion or thinking about how to fight a limited nuclear war is politically incorrect, forbidden, even censored out in any official government work.[66]

Collapse Survivor App Simulations and Data Collected, Lessons Learned Reports on Survival Exercises Show How Marauding Takes Off

"Tabletop" or "command post" exercises like Dark Winter and Clade X are extremely valuable in getting people out of their normal day-to-day mindset and focus and "into" a future environment where they experience and must deal with difficult decisions.[67]

Because there is a dearth of realistic collapse survival training exercises, we created the Collapse Survivor App to run realistic, military style exercise simulations.[68] Several dozen have been played, many polling and collecting data on what players think are the best decisions, calculating survival rates, giving excellent training and "future experience" in dealing with collapse survival scenarios. The exercises often challenge the user to make tough, realistic decisions that impact your likelihood of survival. The approximately one hundred "message items" in each simulation put you into extremely difficult survival situations, making tough decisions to try to stay alive, learning valuable preparedness and survival skills.

After each new scenario there are "lessons learned" podcasts and reports to summarize valuable insights and best practices from the exercise. The example below is from a pandemic simulation.

Do not go to stores, public places when virus spreading—and likely any collapse starting

EXERCISE, EXERCISE, EXERCISE

Millions of foolish people are flocking to grocery stores trying to obtain food before what appears to be a huge pandemic coming. In addition to an unknown risk of catching a deadly virus, there is a good chance that looting, stealing and killing can break out as panic quickly spreads, gangs and bad people take advantage of the disorder.

EXERCISE, EXERCISE, EXERCISE

While many media stations across the U.S. are shutting down, those still reporting in big cities and many suburbs are reporting of murders and even some atrocities as millions of Americans rushed to grocery stores to grab food. As one Police Chief put it, "this has become a Pavlovian response-just mention the word pandemic or disaster or collapse and everyone rushes to the grocery store, looting takes off."

https://www.youtube.com/watch?v=VU0QfPzTZI8&t=1s

Figure 17: Collapse Survivor App training exercises provide "experience" in surviving a collapse.

Playing the simulations on your smartphone or watching/reading the lessons learned videos and reports will show you how a disaster develops and can lead to a collapse, and improve your survival knowledge. These exercise simulations get you out of your normal day-to-day mindset so you can "experience" a developing collapse. These exercises help you understand how the uncertainty, fear, growing problems of a big disaster can lead to marauding and collapse, while teaching survival skills and preparedness measures.

CHAPTER FOUR

WHY ISN'T THE GOVERNMENT WARNING CITIZENS, OR PREPARING FOR A COLLAPSE?

It's wise to ask: if we are now in the Age of Collapse, then why isn't the government warning us about this?

The federal government is well aware of the bioterrorism, grid attacks, AI risks, and the fifty-plus other collapse threats we face, but citizen's survival is not priority and top elected officials do not want to panic the public. Top officials do not want to look like they are not doing their job to keep citizens safe, or to upset big campaign donors. The big campaign donations are for funding bioengineering and AI, bringing home government-funded projects for the representative's district—not honestly warning citizens about threats. The lead agencies dealing with biotechnology fund and promote the research. Investors have poured a trillion dollars into AI and donations to elected officials to promote AI.

Career politicians are focused on reelection and they get big donations from utility companies and corporate and big university lobbyists. There is no lobbying group donating money to improve preparedness. Government officials also prefer a dependent public that follows their direction and trusts them to know what's best. Politicians don't want to panic the public or look ineffective. They want citizens to trust that government knows best, will keep them safe. Just pay your taxes and reelect them. Hardening the electric system and reducing its vulnerability would cost tens of billions with increases in electric bills that would lead to loss of votes for elected officials (current costs for possible future benefits—not popular).

Figure 18: Why isn't the Government Warning us of Collapse Threats or Making Preparations to Protect Citizens?

1. Career politicians are focused on reelection, not your survival prospects
   - Big businesses and lobbyists own career politicians
   - No reelection votes, special interests or lobbyists pushing for preparedness
   - If they vote for preparations and attack doesn't come—might lose votes for "wasting money" or "crying wolf"
2. Government officials want a dependent public that follows their direction and trusts them to know what's best, will protect them
   - Don't want to panic the public
   - Don't want to look ineffective
   - Prefer a dependent, docile citizenry to well-prepared citizens
3. Elected officials don't want the public to know that they are not protected, not safe
4. Preparedness requires weapons—Democratic Party champions gun control and wants to outlaw "military capable" weapons that are vital to fend off marauder groups in a collapse
5. Improving security requires getting rid of thousands of government regulations banning woodstoves, stockpiling antibiotics, zoning and building codes that block survival facilities
6. Government officials will be protected in a collapse at Mount Weather, Raven Rock, and other FEMA and military survival facilities
7. Most congressmen are lawyers or career politicians with no foreign policy or national security experience, nor expertise or interest in security

Nothing major happens in DC without laws directing action, budgeting, and top elected official commitment. There are no special interests and lobbyists pushing for bioterrorism preparedness. Biotechnology firms and university researchers will fight limits on research. Public research universities in particular wield tremendous political power in many states. Attempts to limit or control access to biotechnology will have a negative economic impact, with the research and businesses shifting elsewhere. Enemies will have no trouble getting the technology overseas.

Preparations to do things like equip FEMA or the National Guard for crowd control lead some conspiracy/anti-government critics to protest "government takeover preparations" and "concentration camps" and "police state." President Bush's call for military support in a pandemic and preparations for dealing with law and order problems were condemned by groups ranging from the ACLU on the left to the Libertarian Cato Institute on the right.[1]

As numerous past disasters and government exercises have indicated, many people will take advantage of overwhelmed police to loot and maraud. Millions of preppers are well aware of this threat, but it is too politically incorrect for government officials to honestly address lawlessness and risk offending voters, so they make no preparation for the obvious problem of gangs and armed marauders looting and killing in the wake of a big disaster that overwhelms first responders.

Only a small percentage of victims can be hospitalized and treated—whom do you choose? It will take six months or more to develop and produce a vaccine for a new flu variant or GMO virus, and as the vaccine starts getting produced—who gets priority? Elected officials don't want the public to know about this.

Elected officials do not want government reports estimating tens of millions of Americans may die and they can't prevent this. Government officials do not want to explicitly address impacts of looting, breakdown in law and order, stealing, and sometimes killing to obtain food, suggesting that a segment of the population will act this badly. Government officials do not want to address the controversial ethical issues of a pandemic: who gets medical treatment and supplies, life and death.[2]

Government officials want to avoid charges of "scaremongering," "crying wolf," and overreaction that were raised following the 2009 swine flu outbreak and other warnings of flu pandemics that did not occur. Government officials also don't want to be seen as spending money on problems that taxpayers can't see, or raising an issue that can't be fixed. Elected Official A who supports spending to get prepared is vulnerable to defeat in the next election by Candidate B citing "wasted" tax dollars spent for a disaster that never happened.

Government disaster exercises end with success in handling the problem because they don't want to demoralize participants, upset the public, or expose an elected official to a charge that they are failing to protect citizens. Ridiculously positive assumptions are played out, with all the first responders reporting to work (won't happen in the face of a contagious, lethal virus), citizens calmly obeying all government directions, no looting or marauding, no cascading effects, no enemy agents in the country or foreign enemies "piling on" to take advantage of the situation. When a collapse disaster hits, the prudent expectation should be gangs and criminals start marauding immediately, with foreign enemies taking advantage of the US domestic collapse to undertake hostile actions with their agents in country.

Improving preparedness means citizens with AR-15s and lots of stockpiled ammunition at home, and the end of government regulations and jobs that today make it hard, far more expensive, and sometimes impossible to prepare. As a later chapter explains, the government is in effect working to kill citizens because of policies that prioritize their power, for the unlimited scope of their ability to regulate and interfere in citizens' affairs and with complete disregard for citizens' collapse survival capability.

For their survival, top government officials are taken care of. Congress will be safely sheltered at Mount Weather. Government officials from almost every agency, even the IRS, are sheltered at other FEMA and military sites. The priority of government at all levels is Continuity of Government—keeping themselves safe and alive. As detailed later, these plans will draw off police in a collapse to protect government officials while citizens are left with even less law enforcement resources when they need them the most. Continuity of Government plans are far worse than that—they include executive orders allowing theft of citizens' food and other resources the government wants to improve their odds of survival.

Top elected officials and representatives are largely career politicians or lawyers today. The leading profession of representatives has long been lawyers. At the federal and state level they are overwhelmingly not normal citizens, but career politicians and attorneys. Few have military experience. Their foreign policy interest is largely limited to and driven by common, limited voter views like *communists bad, don't appease dictators, nuclear weapons dangerous.* They don't have good knowledge about security threats or survival preparedness. They care about reelection and increasing their power, not prospects for citizens avoiding or surviving a collapse.

In sum, career politicians not only won't warn people of threats, they are adding to them since they are driven by campaign donations to promote bioengineering, not harden the electric grid, and expand AI as fast as possible without any regulations. A later chapter details thirty specific examples of how government is killing citizens today and setting us up for massive casualties in a collapse. They prefer the populace to be docile, not alarmed, pay their taxes, and reelect them.[3]

Career Politicians Ignored the EMP Commission Warning that Our Electric Grid is Highly Vulnerable

We have known about the EMP and solar flare threats to the grid for decades. Congressional appointed task forces have studied and reported back on the urgent need to harden the grid—and nothing has been done despite their warning that 90 percent of Americans could die with no electricity for a year.[4]

The cyberattacks and physical attacks on our grid have been going on for years. But nothing has been done to protect our vulnerable electric grid. Career politicians get huge campaign donations from utility lobbyists and are afraid of losing votes if electric bills go up to pay for hardening the grid.

National EMP Commission, former CIA Director, warned that loss of grid could kill 90% of Americans

Report of the Commission to Assess the Threat to the United States from Electromagnetic Pulse (EMP) Attack

- 2008 report by Congressional Commission on EMP Threat warned of big vulnerability of U.S. electric grid, recommended hardening grid
- In 2017, former CIA Director R. James Woolsey wrote that "a single warhead delivered by North Korean satellite could blackout the national electric grid and other life-sustaining critical infrastructures for over a year—**killing 9 of 10 Americans by starvation and societal collapse"**
- Congress's Response: Nothing!

Figure 19: Congress ignored its own EMP Commission study warning that 90 percent of Americans could die when our electric grid is destroyed.

Our irresponsible, lying, pandering government has never admitted, warned, or prepared citizens for the fact that when the electric grid goes down, or a bad pandemic hits, over two million prisoners are going to have to be released. You cannot operate a jail without electricity. Diesel backup generators won't last for more than a few days. No guards will come to work when law and order vanishes and it is too unsafe to leave their family unprotected at home, or risk getting mugged/killed going to and from work. Prisoners will have to be released (or they'll break out) and you've got two million prisoners with no home, no preps at all, to join the 1 million plus gang members already on the street marauding. There are more prisoners in the US than any other country in the world—more than China, Russia, anywhere. With less than 5 percent of the world's population, the US accounts for 25 percent of jailed people in the world. The US has the highest per capita rate of imprisonment in the world! The US is no longer the land of the free and home of the brave.[5]

The CDC's False Reporting on H5N1 Illustrates How Governments Lie and Prioritize Election Votes at the Expense of Citizens' Lives

The Center for Disease Control and Prevention (CDC) and government officials are incorrectly, irresponsibly reporting that the risk to humans from a mutated version of avian flu is low. The avian flu virus, H5N1, has mutated, making it more transmissible for mammals. It is no longer just a bird flu, it's a bird and mammal virus. It has infected mink, which have respiratory systems very similar to humans.

As a result of natural mutations,[6] we face a much higher risk of a pandemic with a virus that is 60 percent lethal to humans. But the threat is much worse than this, because there are both low-tech and high-tech ways to manipulate avian flu virus to make it more transmissible in humans. Your tax dollars were used for gain-of-function research on H5N1, and the researchers were successful in making avian flu air to air transmissible in ferrets, which like mink, have respiratory systems very similar to our own. Worse, this research was published, including how to do it. It is not high-tech CRISPR biotechnology; it's a very simple method that anyone can do, at very low cost.[7]

Biologists and national security experts have been testifying before Congress with warnings about both human-to-human transmissible avian flu and bioengineering. But just like all the warnings about our vulnerable electric grid, nothing gets done because there are no big reelection votes for providing warnings to the public or improving preparedness, no big pork for the politicians, no big defense company lobbyist offering donations for defensive survival preparation. A former CDC director, no longer limited by political control, has warned that an H5N1 pandemic is inevitable.[8]

A bioengineered, human-to-human transmissible, double-digit lethality version of H5N1 likely exists and could be released at any time. Russia, China, North Korea, Iran, Syria, terrorists, all likely know how to promote mutations and develop human-to-human transmissible H5N1. Anyone who can research and read knows how to do this since our horrible government funded and then published gain-of-function research and directions on how to do this! Natural virus mutations will lead to human transmissibility, and could already have happened somewhere. The probability of an H5N1 pandemic is not known, since you cannot calculate the probability of an event that hasn't happened before, but an H5N1 pandemic is a huge risk, it is not low, it is not unlikely.

We can absolutely label the H5N1 risk as elevated now. There is more likelihood of a human-to-human transmissible version of H5N1 because of these virus mutations and the high risk of deliberate human manipulation of H5N1. That should be the message, not that the risk is still low. The H5N1 virus is mutating, already spreading in some mammal populations, and is a huge risk to humans. The government is not reporting honestly, they are irresponsibly, despicably promoting false information to promote the interests of career politicians, not promoting pandemic preparation, at the cost of future citizens' deaths.

If Putin wants to distract the US and the West from supporting Ukraine, he could unleash a human-to-human transmissible H5N1 virus here, clandestinely, and achieve that objective. If China wants to have US resources pulled back for pandemic recovery so they can invade Taiwan, they can do a bio attack. North Korea, Iran, Al-Qaeda, even one dedicated, fanatic could start the worst pandemic, the worst disaster in the history of mankind by releasing a virus they manipulate with low-tech means, or CRISPR biotechnology, and it's a death sentence for perhaps most of our population.

The CDC has given no warnings on the growing likelihood of an H5N1 pandemic over the past years despite the viruses steady march from bird flu to mammal flu. In this time period they have issued threat alerts on minor health threats when they are politically correct. They warned about dengue (which causes fever, vomiting, muscle aches, nausea—rarely fatal) during the Biden administration since this disease had the big political benefit for those controlling their budget of plugging global warming—more people catching the mosquito-borne disease "as the world's climate warms due to the human-made climate crisis."[9] All government agencies are biased and limited by their political agendas, budget concerns, guidance not to alarm the public, not make top officials look bad, et cetera. CDC and our government will never issue the public an honest assessment of our bad and increasingly worse risks of a double-digit lethality virus. They want the public to be assured that all is well, government is protecting them, will take care of them. So the CDC continues to not sound any alarms on H5N1 and rates the virus as "low risk"—gross lies, deliberately false information that discourages preparations to deal with the coming pandemic that could directly kill a billion, and cause a collapse that might kill most Americans.

* * *

There is currently no threat to Americans' survival more likely or deadly than that of bio attacks and pandemics. No other threat is so "inevitable" and catastrophic in what it will do. Yet government issues no warnings, lies to tell citizens that H5N1 is low risk, and makes no preparations to ready citizens for the pandemic or the collapse that will result.

The Department of Health and Human Services promotes bioengineering, funds gain-of-function research to make more deadly viruses, and clearly does not care about the millions who will die in a pandemic. The big money, campaign donations, and votes are in funding biological research and keeping electric rates low, supporting AI, buying votes by bringing home government grants to your local university to fund nanotechnology and other high-tech research that could cause collapse disasters. Top elected officials do not spend resources preparing the public to survive collapse disaster. The government, whose number one job is to protect its citizens, is not even warning Americans about this rising threat of collapse, and hindering rather than helping our ability to survive a collapse.

The big money campaign donations and votes are in funding biological research, not preparing the public to survive collapse disaster. This was my motivation to found Fortitude Ranch, a survival facility, over a decade ago, since I understand both the collapse threats and the irresponsible politics of our government today (master's degree and PhD from Kennedy School of Government at Harvard, sixteen years as an elected official, as well as my Pentagon SES experiences). Despite expert warnings, Congressional studies and testimony, common sense and decency, there is unlikely to be any action by politicians until it's too late.

Politicians can easily get away with this irresponsibility because the public assumes that government is watching out for them, and is blind to pending disasters, despite periodic warnings in the newspapers.[10]

Chapter Five

THE "PERVERTED TRIANGLE"—THE WORST THREAT TO AMERICANS

Government isn't just failing to warn of collapse threats and lying about the risks we face. Its regulations are the worst barrier to preparing for survival, and a multitude of government programs are setting up citizens for massive death in a collapse.[1]

In public history textbooks, written by taxpayer funded professors, Big Government elected officials are generally the good guys, fighting against evil, greedy businessmen (i.e. Musk, Trump). The "Iron Triangle" is the bad alliance of government bureaucrats, elected career politicians, and special interest groups (big business lobbyists) working to promote their profits and interests. Big businesses and campaign donations to politicians can be horrible in a government without limits as we have today in the unconstitutional US, but there is a far worse alliance that has destroyed good American government and personal liberty: the "Perverted Triangle" of government bureaucrats, career politicians, and lawyers. The latter two are often the same person—attorneys in legislatures that pass laws and regulations that generate more business and income for fellow lawyers, more jobs for government bureaucrats, more campaign donations and power for the politicians. And many Perverted Triangle members become lobbyists.

Unaffordable, irresponsible, unconstitutional government spending is the result of illegal government removal of constitutional protections that, until Franklin Delano Roosevelt's (FDR) administration, limited the federal government and protected our basic Natural Rights to personal property, privacy, and "to be left alone." Constitutional limits to federal government interference in social matters and personal economic affairs were illegally eliminated in 1937 when a majority

The "Perverted Triangle" has ruined American Government and Society

The "Iron Triangle"

Political Science term "Iron Triangle" refers to Congressmen, government bureaucrats, and lobbyists

- **The Perverted Triangle is career politicians, government bureaucrats, and lawyers**
- Perverted Triangle has surged in power at all levels of government with massive increases in unconstitutional social and welfare programs, an explosion of laws and regulations, erasing Natural Rights and liberty, and dividing the nation
- The welfare and entitlement programs of the unconstitutional United States Big Government and Perverted Triangle have undermined families, subverted individual responsibility, and eliminated the core Natural Rights and individual liberty America was founded to achieve

1

Figure 20: The Perverted Triangle of career politicians, government bureaucrats, and lawyers has corrupted and ruined American government.

of Supreme Court Justices surrendered to pressure and threats from FDR. Later Democratic administrations, along with Republicans, let the Perverted Triangle surge in power with massive increases in unconstitutional social and welfare programs: an explosion of laws and regulations, undermining families and personal responsibility, dividing the nation. The cancerous growth of welfare and entitlement programs of the unconstitutional United States has created an increasingly dependent citizenry. This is exactly what the Democratic Party and Perverted Triangle want—subservient, poor, dependent citizens who vote for them to receive welfare payments and social programs they have been trained to need. Our country is bitterly split today, falling apart, because the two dominant political parties and unconstitutional US and state government social programs have divided our nation. Worse, with no limits today on what US governments can do, career politicians focus on buying reelection votes by offering whatever government spending pork buys the most votes—not what best protects citizens' probability of survival.[2]

Our legal system has also been ruined by the Perverted Triangle, with thousands of laws and millions of regulations enriching lawyers who are allowed to lie in court—with rules requiring use of expensive lawyers and banning others from offering legal advice. Worse, judges (former lawyers), ignore our retained Natural Rights and the Ninth Amendment, favoring past case citations at the expense of truth, justice, and our Constitution. Victory in court depends on how much you can spend on attorneys rather than what is just, with natural rights not even considered.

The state of our unconstitutional, un-American government and legal system is unbearable, and now also un-survivable. With growing threats from new technologies, Artificial Intelligence (AI), and the growing likelihood of a collapse that could kill most of us, fixing our government and getting federal and state governments focused on homeland defense and collapse recovery is especially vital now.

Rather than fighting unconstitutional socialist welfare programs, after Goldwater's defeat in 1960 the Republican Party joined in, competing with offers of welfare benefits and pork for their constituents to buy votes. By the time Nixon took office, the Republican Party had given up real opposition to Big Government, perverted by the political power of unlimited big government spending that virtually guarantees election for congressmen, since more seniority means more "free" federal spending and pork for their district. The Nixon administration created several new, unconstitutional regulatory agencies, like the Occupational Safety and Health Administration and the Environmental Protection Agency. We certainly need environmental regulations, but the proper way to add them is by amending the Constitution to allow a new area of federal involvement. Nixon tried to beat Democrats by outmaneuvering them in political vote pandering. As Dr. Burton W. Folsom, a professor of history, explained,

> In 1972, an election year, Nixon raised social security benefits by 20 percent, with the new payments starting the month before the November election, but with the tax increase not payable until after the election was over. Such a ploy was reminiscent of Roosevelt . . . [F]orces set in motion by Franklin Roosevelt and the New Deal have changed US political and economic life forever. . . .[3]

With the federal government now able to spend on anything they want, incumbents had incredible power to deliver federally funded pork for their supporters, collect campaign donations with ease, and retain office by steering federal projects and dollars into their districts. Many books are written listing outrageous abuse. Nothing in the Constitution could possibly justify $500,000 in federal funds for a Teapot Museum in Sparta North Carolina, $273,000 to combat goth culture in Blue Springs, Missouri, or $14 billion (correct: billion, not million) federal taxpayers contributed for a local tunnel to Boston's airport.[4]

Lobbyists (usually lawyers, often former politicians and government bureaucrats) make donations to get preferential federal tax breaks or program spending for their clients. The career politicians award federal largess to get the donations and support that guarantees reelection for most, the government bureaucrats get more jobs and budget, and the lawyers get more regulations and laws, business and profit—all at the expense of our Natural Rights to be left alone and use our private property and funds for our benefit.

The Supreme Court has ceased enforcing the Constitution since FDR broke them—they are part of the Perverted Triangle, approved by congressmen who ensure they will obey the Perverted Triangle and let them spend and do whatever they want to buy their reelection victory at our expense. Both parties, most career politicians, violate the Constitution and American taxpayers to win pork for their district and donations and votes for their campaigns. The Ninth and Tenth Amendments in the Bill of Rights, the most important limits to government, were illegally erased by FDR and the Supreme Court, with 99 percent plus of citizens completely unaware that this happened.

Reagan's government reform effort, the Grace Commission, estimated that one third of federal spending was wasted.[5] There are some easy measures to save money, like ordering the US mint to stop producing pennies at a cost of 4 cents each, but big savings and government improvements require revolutionary changes in strategy, restoration of constitutional individual rights and government limits. The Reagan administration not only failed to cut government back, but federal spending and the budget deficit grew by 69 percent during Reagan's eight years in office![6] The federal debt tripled from $738 billion to $2.1 trillion, with the US becoming the world's largest debtor nation while Reagan served as POTUS.[7] It was not Democrats, but President George H. W. Bush who expanded the Department of Education, and the George W. Bush administration that initiated a prescription drug discount for senior citizens. With Obamacare, the Democrats brought in another clearly unconstitutional federal program (no mention of government providing health care or insurance in Constitution), but both big political parties treat the Constitution like toilet paper.[8]

The Perverted Triangle for decades has grown Americans' welfare/entitlement dependence, stealing your money via taxes and fees to then buying votes with completely unconstitutional gross violations of Natural Rights (which are to protect your freedom, not force you to participate in government income redistribution and vote purchase deals). You have a Natural Right to privacy, to use your personal property as you choose, believe and to do what you want as long as you do not harm others. There is no Natural Right to demand money from other people or force them to fund or support your social views.

If you think that Congress or the president make foreign and defense policy decisions prioritizing what is best for the safety and benefit of American citizens, you are wrong most of the time. At both the USAF Academy, and then the Kennedy School of Government at Harvard University, I studied "Allison's Models," the best explanation of why our elected officials make such irresponsible, bad decisions. In *Essence of Decision: Explaining the Cuban Missile Crisis*, political scientist Graham Allison analyzed the 1962 Cuban Missile Crisis to show how government national security decision-making is not so much "rational" or good decision-making, but shaped by bureaucratic self-interest and domestic politics, yielding potentially disastrous results.

Model 1, the "Rational Actor" Model, is what we would expect: the government examines the problem and options to solve, and makes the best decision for the country. But rational, good decision-making fails to explain the Cuban Missile Crisis or most government policies and programs. So Allison adds Model 2, the "Organizational Process" Model that explains how governmental bureaucracy limits government actions. Bureaucracies follow standard operating procedures and advocate positions that are best for that organization, not the country. This explains much of what happened in the Cuban Missile Crisis, but still leaves some other irrational, bad decisions unexplained.

Thus Allison added Model 3, the "Bureaucratic Politics" Model. This model takes account of "palace politics," the preferences of political parties, maneuvers to win votes in elections, and which action most benefits the government decision-maker's political power. This explains more of the Cuban Missile crisis decisions and makes Allison's point that governments do not act rationally to maximize the nation's benefit. In the case of nuclear conflict, as the Wikipedia summary of Allison's models explains, "by looking at organizational and political models . . . nations, against what was predicted by the rational viewpoint, could indeed "'commit suicide'."[9]

The career politicians and bureaucrats that control the government keep passing new programs and spending to buy votes, driving our country into bankruptcy, dividing the nation, setting us up to be killed. They prioritize their power and benefit, and are perfectly willing to trample citizens' rights and sacrifice our lives. The perverted decision-making in government today goes way beyond Graham Allison's Models 2 and 3. To understand why our unconstitutional, corrupt government is working to kill us, you need to add Model 4: the "Perverted Triangle" of government bureaucrats, career politicians, and lawyers. The Perverted Triangle may be the worst threat Americans face today. They are not protecting us or even honestly warning us about collapse threats. They are adding to our risk of collapse. As explained later, government plans include executive orders to steal food and supplies from citizens when they want them. Government regulations (most unconstitutional, violating our Natural Rights to private property in the erased Ninth Amendment) are the biggest barrier to getting prepared for survival.[10]

A summary of Allison's three Models and the fourth Perverted Triangle Model that explain US government decision-making is provided in the following diagram.

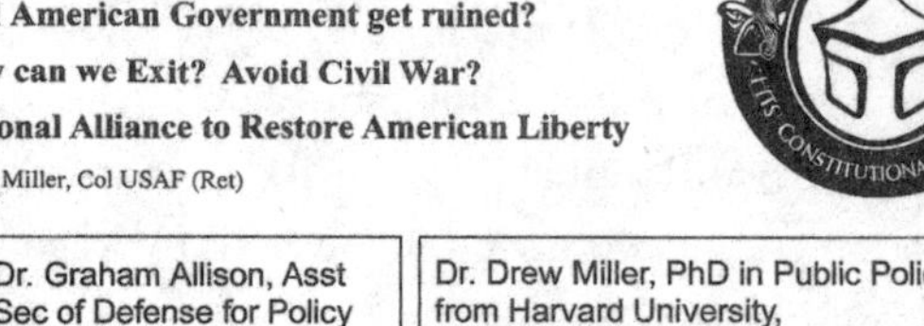

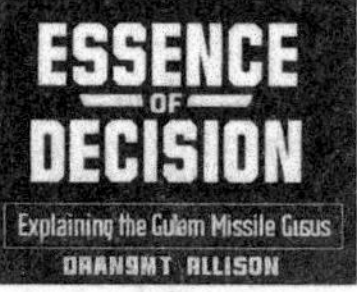

Figure 21: Allison's Models and the Perverted Triangle explanation of corrupt government decision-making.

Models 1–3: Graham Allison, Essence of Decision, 1971; Allison, "Conceptual models and the Cuban Missile Crisis." *American Political Science Review*, 1969; Model 4: Drew Miller, "How did American Government get ruined? How can we fix it? Avoid Civil War?" The Constitutional Alliance to Restore American Liberty, https://constall.org/

Dr. Allison developed three models of government (and bureaucratic) action in trying to explain what happened during the Cuban Missile Crisis. Model 4 was developed by Dr. Miller.

Model 1, the "Rational Actor" model, is the right way to make decisions: analyze the problem, make rational choice of which alternative best meets objectives. This model alone fails to explain what happened during the Cuban Missile Crisis, and likely most major government, bureaucratic decisions.

Model 2, The "Organizational Process" model, notes that decision-makers do not necessarily seek optimal solutions, and are constrained/motivated by the bureaucracy they work with. The bureaucrats follow "standard operating procedures" and decisions are often "satisficing": find a solution that achieves minimum goals restricted by bureaucratic constraints. This explains much of what happened in the Cuban Missile Crisis.

Model 3, "Bureaucratic Politics," Dr. Allison explains the rest of the decisions made. "Where you stand depends on where you sit." Those in charge of various state responsibilities argue for their view based on their beliefs and organizational biases. Policy outcomes are the result of negotiations among these leaders. "The decisions and actions of governments are essentially intranational political outcomes: outcomes in the sense that what happens is not chosen as a solution to a problem but rather results from compromise, coalition, competition, and confusion . . . political in the sense that the activity from which the outcomes emerge is best characterized as bargaining."

Model 4, the "Perverted Triangle." The "Iron Triangle" is the political science term for the bad alliance of government bureaucrats, elected career politicians, and special interest group/business lobbyists working together to promote their profits and interests. A far worse alliance has destroyed American constitutional government and personal liberty: the "Perverted Triangle" of government bureaucrats, career politicians, and lawyers. The latter two are often the same person—attorneys in legislatures that pass laws and regulations that generate more business for fellow lawyers, more laws and regulations and jobs for government bureaucrats, more campaign donations and power for the politicians. This explanation of bad government decision-making is explained in the paper at https://constall.org/. The Supreme Court no longer enforces the limits to Government—the Ninth and Tenth Amendments are ignored. Thus career politicians always running for reelection and prioritizing campaign donations and votes, the lack of any constitutional limits to government spending and policy since FDR, an entrenched, self-serving (highly unionized) government bureaucracy and obnoxious lawyers, and lobbyists—the Perverted Triangle will fund or regulate anything with an interest group behind it, even at the cost of citizens' lives.

Very few Americans today understand how our priority Natural Rights, supreme even to the Constitution, and far above all government written laws, have been violated by the Perverted Triangle and the current state of our horrible American government and judicial system.[11] We have lost the most basic, vital "American" right to be left alone, not bothered by government bureaucrats, abused by lawyers, robbed by politicians who want to steal from us to buy votes from others. Thanks to the Ninth Amendment, which like the Tenth is ignored by our perverted system of government and courts, these rights are still there—and protected by the Constitution. But with Congress and governments at all levels ignoring Natural Rights and the Supreme Court and judicial system refusing to enforce them in Courts, Natural Rights are, like limits to Federal Government via the Tenth Amendment, effectively gone in the United States.

The best book explaining how we failed the US Constitution and let politicians, lawyers, and bureaucrats screw us is Charles Murray's *By the People: Rebuilding Liberty Without Permission.* His summary is accurate and depressing:

> The founder's Constitution has been discarded. . . . Aspects of America's legal system have become lawless, for reasons that are inextricably

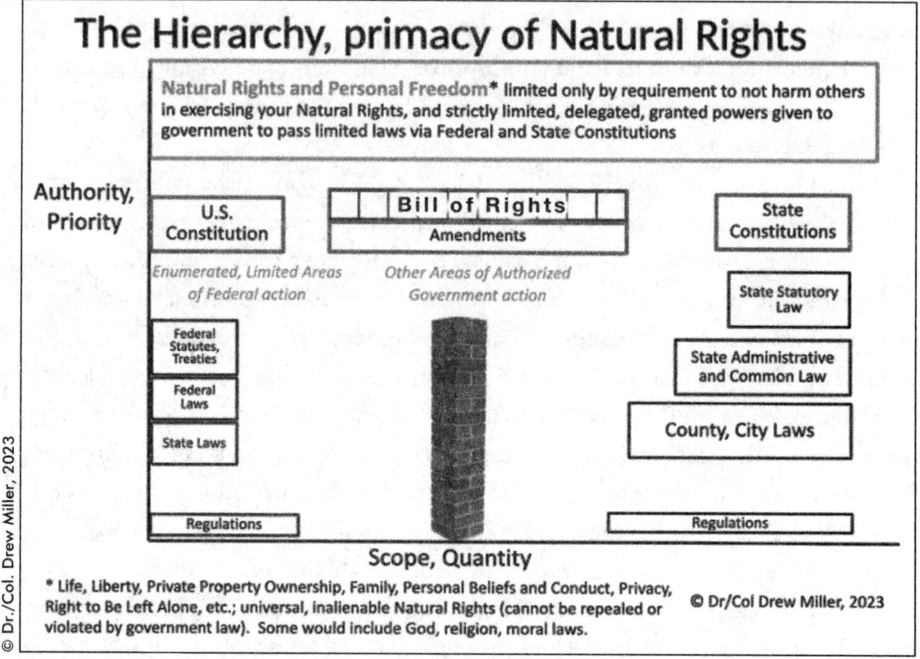

Figure 22: The hierarchy and primacy of Natural Rights and laws.

> embedded in the use of the law for social agendas. Congress and the administrative state have become systemically corrupt, for reasons that are inextricably embedded in the market for government favors.[12]

As noted earlier, the Perverted Triangle has produced a deluge of thousands of laws, an uncountable number of regulations, written to promote more government bureaucrats and require hiring lawyers, even outside of the courts.[13]

The explosion of laws and regulations pushed by the Perverted Triangle and lawyers violates freedom and the Natural Rights to be left alone and steals from citizens at all levels of government. Hundreds of thousands of examples have been written about; just a few cited here to illustrate the costs. In New York City, an "inspector recently told the YMCA, after it had virtually completed a renovation, that the fire code had changed and a different kind of fire alarm system, costing another $200,000, would have to be installed."[14] That's money that can't be spent on providing programs to youth—though the Perverted Triangle would prefer that government agencies, not private charities like the YMCA, provide them. Philip Howard, a lawyer working to reform our perverted legal system, summarized the horrible state of government regulatory abuse: "Coercion by government, the main fear of our founding fathers, is now its common attribute. . . . We now have a government of laws against men."[15] Natural Rights to personal freedom, the goal of the American founding and new nation, have been lost to the Perverted Triangle and Big Government and its enforcing arm: the legal system and lawyers.[16] As Roger Pilon lamented, "Today there seems to be almost no subject too personal or too trivial for federal regulatory attention."[17]

As a result of Perverted Triangle promotion of laws, regulations, and business for lawyers, the unconstitutional US ranks at the top of countries with the highest per capita rate of imprisonment. The nation founded as the land of the free, the champion of liberty, has been corrupted and perverted into a land of

Top 10 Countries with the highest rate of incarceration

Inmates per 100,000 citizens	
629	United States
580	Rwanda
576	Turkmenistan
564	El Salvador
510	Cuba
478	Palau
477	British Virgin Islands
445	Thailand
423	Panama
423	Saint Kitts and Nevis

World Population Review. Source: https://worldpopulationreview.com/country-rankings/incarceration-rates-by-country.

Figure 23: The US has the highest per capita rate of incarceration in the world.

government and lawyer theft and abuse. America is no longer the land of the free. The Perverted Triangle has turned the United States into the biggest police state[18] in the world.

There is no honesty in federal government budgets or accounting, but we roughly know that from the first year Medicare spending was visible on the books, in 1967, through 2020 that Medicare and Medicaid combined cost about $18 trillion—about the same amount as federal deficits over that same period.[19] As of December 2024, the reported unconstitutional US debt is over $36 trillion, spiraling up every minute! The only way to grasp the magnitude of this debt is to put it in per capita terms. Every American owes over $100,000 in government debt! But since most people don't pay taxes (too young or too poor), the debt per taxpayer is over $260,000. With the average family having just $11,000 in savings, there is no way we can pay this debt.

Worse, the real government debt is several times more than $36 trillion! The money owed for Social Security and Medicare and public employee pensions and retirement health benefits are also debts that we as individuals and businesses would have to report, but the cheating, dishonest government does not. The unconstitutional US is over $100 trillion in debt thanks to the Perverted Triangle. The interest payments on our debt are now also in the trillions; the country has amassed debts we cannot repay.[20] Eventually we will have to default on government bonds, Social Security and Medicare benefits promised, government worker retirement benefits, and all the other Ponzi schemes the Perverted Triangle has passed to amass power. The Perverted Triangle and Big Government have ruined and bankrupted our country. Future generations especially are screwed—but they can't vote, so the Perverted Triangle does not care.[21]

Figure 24: True government debt is $162 trillion, not the admitted $36 trillion; each taxpayer owes $914,000.

As the "Truth in Accounting" association—run by CPAs and government accountants, including the former director of the Government Accountability Office—even states with laws mandating a balanced budget, state spending exceeds revenues, so elected officials (leaders of the Perverted Triangle) excluded costs from their budget calculations, such as future pension obligations or deferred maintenance, and they claim revenues based on "expectations" of revenues, not actual receipts.[22]

While the Republicans are almost as bad as Democrats in trashing the Constitution and Natural Rights, pandering and buying votes to reelect career politicians, the fate of Perverted Triangle controlled government is clearest in states run by the Democratic Party. Taxpayers in Illinois have $52,600 in state government debt, mostly for government worker pensions and retiree health care.[23] Add this to federal government debt per taxpayer of $260,000 and it's easier to understand how the Perverted Triangle has effectively corrupted, bankrupted, and ruined the United States. If you live in a big US city, the Democratic Party likely rules and your debt is thus worse.[24] If you are a Chicago taxpayer, add $20,000 to your government-imposed debt load, bringing your total government debt to at least $335,000.[25]

When a disaster occurs, the number one priority of government today is not protecting its citizens. The top priority of government officials is "Continuity of Government"—keeping themselves and their families alive and government functioning.[26] So when the grid goes down, a nuclear exchange occurs, an economic downturn or disputed election leads to massive unrest or civil war, a truly bad pandemic hits, or any of the fifty or more trigger events that could yield a collapse happens, your need for police protection will go way up while their availability goes down. When law and order vanish in a collapse, more police and National Guard troops will be called to duty to ensure the safety of elected officials and their families. The need for police or National Guard protection of hospitals, food stores, and other facilities will also rise in a collapse. If you can call for help from your home it will likely be a waste of time. The police and security priority is protecting senior government officials and facilities, not you. A documentary, *While the Rest of Us Die*,[27] explains how the government's priority is protecting themselves, with no plans to help average citizens survive (link available in webnotes).

Mount Weather and other government survival facilities should be closed to congressmen and their families. They should receive no better survival preparedness treatment than ordinary citizens. Otherwise we have the perverse incentives today where they fund FEMA and Mount Weather for themselves, but don't require hardening the electric grid or a civil defense program to at least offer American citizens some stored food. Mount Weather and other FEMA sites designed to shelter elected officials should be switched to serve troops, first responders, and their families—not politicians. The "media rooms" at Mount Weather, designed to connect congressmen to their districts so they can stay in touch (read: keep campaigning) must be converted to shelters for valuable personnel who can aid in recovery. The president, our commander in chief, must survive an attack, but "Continuity of Government" plans at all levels of government should be cut back, limited to executives, not legislators or councils—just government workers with an essential defense and collapse recovery role (resuming government social programs, regulations, et cetera excluded). This will allow more police and guard troops to switch from protecting politicians and bureaucrats to protecting the populace.

While there are twenty-three million government employees (not including military personnel), less than one million are law enforcement officers. The Perverted Triangle favors bureaucrats and regulators, not security, the number one purpose of government. The misconduct of a very few policemen led to an asinine "defund the police" movement that sprouted in some big cities and to attacks on policemen that contributed to thousands of law enforcement officers quitting or retiring early—the resignation rate in 2020–21 increased 18 percent and the retirement rate rose 45 percent.[28] As one mayor explained, "The toxic national dialogue that demonizes police officers has made police department staffing significantly more difficult for every major city in America."[29] The miliary and law enforcement personnel are the most valued government expenditures we make. With the increasing likelihood of homeland attacks and collapse, we need more law enforcement and National Guard forces—which we could readily afford by firing millions of government social workers, planning and zoning officials, and regulators, eliminating their programs that violate the Constitution and our Natural Rights. The Department of Government Efficiency (DOGE) should not cut law enforcement officers, but show no mercy in proposals to wipe out government regulatory organizations. By cutting unconstitutional, wasteful, improper state and local government grants, DOGE can also force state and local government staff reductions.

While government officials have fantastic survival facilities at their disposal, they are not doing anything to prepare or even warn the population to get prepared for the increasing likelihood of a collapse. After decades of government studies and warnings of the dire need to harden our electric grid and prepare for truly bad pandemics, nothing has been done. Worse, the biggest barrier to personal preparedness is Big Government and regulations. Americans need to be prepared for a collapse—but government rules and restrictions make it far more difficult and costly to prepare. Zoning and building codes greatly increase the costs of a building. Limits of one residence per acreage mean people can't spread out into separate, smaller buildings to be both safer in a pandemic and more able to defend a compound from marauders in a collapse. The huge increase in building costs from government permits, regulations, and building codes adds tens of thousands of dollars in unnecessary expenses and it makes it harder or, for some, impossible to prepare for collapse survival.[30]

Chapter Six

THE GOVERNMENT IS WORKING TO KILL US

It is far worse than government just not warning citizens or helping them prepare. The reality in the United States is that irresponsible government and the Perverted Triangle is actively, effectively working to kill citizens now. In a collapse the deaths from irresponsible, deadly bad government decisions will be much higher.[1]

The unconstitutional government of the United States of America funds gain-of-function research and released instructions for anyone to create more deadly viruses. They give money to potential enemies like China to help them develop deadly new viruses. They lie about the inevitable H5N1 pandemic coming (partly due to this gain-of-function research), and refuse to warn or prepare Americans for this inevitable, potentially imminent, deadly pandemic and the collapse that will result. They refuse to harden our fragile electric grid that is vulnerable to destruction by thousands of enemy agents in the country, solar flares, cyberattacks, or small nuclear attacks that North Korea, China, or Russia can easily execute. Despite experts warning that 90 percent of Americans could die, the campaign donations of utility company lobbyists and fear of losing votes from higher electric rates keeps career politicians from doing the right thing to protect our lives.

Our government provides collapse survival protection for top elected and government officials at Mount Weather and other sites—but provides no civil defense for citizens.

Not only does the government stockpile survival food just for top government officials and politicians, not citizens, but executive orders also allow them to steal food from citizens if they need more! No, this is not a fabricated conspiracy theory; it is found in decades of executive orders. Government agencies are authorized to steal food and resources from citizens in a collapse—their number one priority is protecting themselves. Citizens are not just expendable, they are exploitable—a resource for government to raid if their stockpiled supplies run low.

The unconstitutional, unlimited cesspool of regulations at all levels of governments don't just damage the economy and inflict losses that cost people income, jobs, and lifespan; they make it increasingly harder for civilians to prepare for collapse survival.

Thirty Examples of How Government Is Working to Kill Us

This chapter provides thirty documented examples of how our government is working to kill us.

1. Funding gain-of-function research to develop more deadly viruses—and releasing instructions on how to do this to enemies/terrorists

As an Institute for Defense Analyses, a Department of Defense federally funded R&D center (think tank) report warned, through bioengineering a lone terrorist or a Revolutionary Guards lab in Iran can create deadly new viruses. Dr. Tara O'Toole, former director of Johns Hopkins University Center for Civilian Biodefense Strategies, warned in Congressional testimony: "We are in the midst of a bioscientific revolution that will make building and using biological weapons even more deadly and increasingly easy." Avian flu, H5N1, historically 50–60 percent lethal, modified to be human-to-human transmissible, could cause a pandemic that kills a billion people.[2] A section of the first chapter of this book explained the high and growing likelihood of a bioengineered viral pandemic.

https://www.ida.org/research-and-publications/publications/all/t/th/the-age-of-bioengineered-viral-pandemics-and-collapse

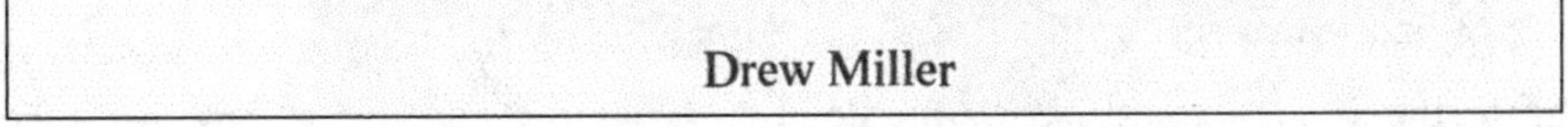

IDA INSTITUTE FOR DEFENSE ANALYSES

NSD-5335

The Age of Bioengineered Viral Pandemics and Collapse

Drew Miller

Figure 25: Institute for Defense Analyses study of Bioengineered Viral Pandemics and Collapse.

Our government funded gain of function research in H5N1 a decade ago, back when it was just a bird flu, that was successful in developing mammal-to-mammal transmission of the virus in ferrets—mammals selected because their respiratory system is very similar to ours. Worse, they published how they did this for any other nation, terrorist group, or individual to pursue.[3]

Researchers developed mammal to mammal transmissible form of highly lethal H5N1 virus—and published details

- Researchers developed mammal–transmissible H5N1 virus in lab
- Results, including how they did this, were published!
- A simple, low tech, cheap methodology any terrorist could use

US: Don't publish lab-bred bird flu recipe

By LAURAN NEERGAARD
AP Associated Press
updated 12/20/2011 1:48:15 PM ET

WASHINGTON — The U.S. government asked scientists Tuesday not to reveal all the details of how to make a version of the deadly bird flu that they created in labs in the U.S. and Europe.

The lab-bred virus, being kept under high security, appears to spread more easily among mammals. That's fueled worry that publishing a blueprint could aid terrorists in creating a biological weapon, the National Institutes of Health said.

Figure 26: US funded gain-of-function research developed mammal-to-mammal transmissible version of H5N1 "bird flu"—with report published on how to do it.

Bioengineered viruses are the ideal weapon. Compared to nuclear weapons they can be more deadly, orders of magnitude cheaper and easier to create and launch, and, most importantly, offer the ability to attack with impunity to retaliation since we may not know and can't prove who released the virus. Whether created and released by a terrorist group or one dedicated individual, a bioengineered virus could cause both a pandemic and, as people react, a collapse; economic activity ceases, law and order breaks down as people start looting, marauding to avoid starvation.

An H5N1 pandemic will likely be the worst disaster our species has experienced, with the virus killing perhaps a billion—and the collapse it creates far more as people die of starvation or are killed by marauding groups fighting to survive.

2. Giving money to China to help them develop deadly new viruses

The National Institutes of Health and Dr. Anthony Fauci denied funding studies that would make a coronavirus more dangerous to humans, but documents obtained from a Freedom of Information Act lawsuit show that this was a lie. Richard Ebright, professor at Rutgers University and laboratory director at the Waksman Institute of Microbiology, said the documents show "unequivocally" that National Institutes of Health (NIH) grants were used to fund controversial gain-of-function research at the Wuhan Institute of Virology in China. Ebright said: "The documents make it clear that assertions by the NIH director, Francis Collins, and the NIAID director, Anthony Fauci, that the NIH did not support gain-of-function research or potential pandemic pathogen enhancement in Wuhan are untruthful." [4] USAID was at least one of the vehicles used to fund Chinese research to make more deadly, more transmissible viruses.[5]

Senator Rand Paul questioned and condemned Dr. Fauci in 2020 Senate testimony for funding Chinese government research at Wuhan, with Dr. Fauci denying and insulting the senator for the accusations. On his last day in office, as one of his final acts, President Biden issued a pardon to protect Dr. Fauci.

Gain-of-function research has some legitimate value in producing a valuable product or obtaining samples to develop vaccines, but with great dangers. Former Center for Disease Control and Prevention (CDC) Director Redfield has condemned gain-of-function research as too risky and called for an end to it, but the biologists and scientists and government officials who fund them of course want it continued despite the risks of its misuse to create a deadly pandemic.[6]

The US government providing funds and assisting biological research of a foreign nation like China that could be preparing to attack and destroy us is absolutely wrong. It's akin to the government funding tank and dive bomber R&D in Nazi Germany in the 1930s.

The CDC denied any possibility that bioengineering, man-made experimentation could have led to the Covid-19 pandemic (later proved wrong), and the CDC covered up for years the fact that the US had actually funded gain-of-function research at the Wuhan lab. It is still very difficult to believe that the US government funded Chinese research to make more lethal viruses!

3. Lying about the H5N1 threat and refusing to warn or prepare Americans for this inevitable, potentially imminent, deadly pandemic and the collapse that will result

The H5N1 virus continues to mutate (or is being manipulated by humans) and is now spreading mammal-to-mammal in several species. It will start spreading in human populations at any time, yielding the worst pandemic in human history.

A government trying to protect its citizens would be working to warn and prepare them to survive the inevitable H5N1 pandemic that is coming and other natural or bioengineered pandemics. Instead, the US government goes out of its way to assure citizens not to prepare or worry—insisting H5N1 is "low risk."[7]

Mammals are catching and spreading the virus directly to other mammals.[8] When a virus infects mammals they serve as "mixing vessels" that helps the virus find mutations that allow better transmissibility in other mammals—including humans. H5N1 and seasonal flu virus in a human provide a fantastic mixing vessel to help H5N1 mutate to a human-to-human transmissible variant. H5N1 is going to either naturally mutate to be human-to-human contagious (and may already have in some places), or will be bioengineered and manipulated to be human-to-human transmissible, as the former director of the CDC (no longer constrained by elected officials) has warned is even more likely.[9]

Bill Gates, whose foundation is focused on world health issues, recently warned about pandemics, insisting, "we are absolutely not prepared." Gates estimates "the chance of a natural pandemic in the next four years is somewhere between 10 and 15 percent. . . . And it'd be nice to think we're actually more ready for that than we were last time. But so far we're not."[10]

The former director of the Center for Disease Control, no longer under political constraints, has defied the continued CDC lie that H5N1 is "low risk" to humans and has warned that an H5N1 pandemic is coming. Unlike the CDC, which completely ignores the deliberate human manipulation of H5N1 virus, former CDC Director Redfield also warned that "there is greater risk for the disease to be lab-grown." Redfield noted that "against my recommendation, the scientists that did these experiments actually published them. . . . So, the recipe for how to make bird flu highly infectious for humans is already out there."[11]

When will the CDC ever admit that H5N1 is an inevitable human pandemic and extremely high risk? Based on recent Covid-19 experience and the political pressure on the CDC not to "panic" citizens or undermine confidence in Big Government to protect them, the answer is that they won't until after the pandemic is well underway and it is far too late to get prepared or avoid exposure. The CDC **never** issued a threat alert on Covid-19, months after it had spread out of China and was clearly a developing pandemic.[12] They were months late in honestly warning about this pandemic threat, though other sources had long been saying a pandemic would clearly result.

The CDC will continue to lie and claim that H5N1 is "low risk" until the pandemic has started and it's too late to prepare, because their priority is not saving American lives, but pleasing the elected officials who control their budget and conducting research.[13]

4. Refusing to harden the electric grid despite Congressional-funded studies by experts warning our grid is highly vulnerable, 90 percent of Americans could

die if North Korea, China, Russia, terrorists, solar flares, or other forces take it down

The vulnerabilities of our fragile electric system have been known for decades, published in Congressional reports, with the chair of one of these Congressional EMP study commissions, a former admiral and CIA director, warning that 90 percent of Americans could die when our grid is destroyed.[14] When the grid goes down, nothing gets produced, municipal water systems do not work, gasoline cannot be pumped, and millions will die in the first month. Law and order will quickly vanish as people desperate to survive, including gang members and millions released from prisons that cannot operate without electricity, stealing and killing to obtain food and water.[15]

Our enemies know about these electric grid vulnerabilities. Our easy-to-knock-out electric grid is our Achilles' heel. It is not just Russia and China that could launch such an attack; even North Korea's tiny, inaccurate nuclear arsenal is sufficient to destroy our grid. A dedicated terrorist group could take it down with coordinated physical attacks on key nodes.

When the electric grid goes down, US military power goes down as well. Strategic nuclear forces are more robust, but the vast majority of our military power will vanish when we lose electric power, since the military uses the civilian electric grid. If you see diesel backup generators somewhere, you're looking at maybe a few days of power and then nothing. Solar farms and wind generators might be destroyed, but even if not—without the transformers that can be destroyed by a wide variety of attacks, you can't transmit power, the grid is dead, and will be for years. The estimates are at least a year, and many experts believe the time frame is a long period of many years—assuming some overseas help. The transformers are the biggest vulnerability of our grid. They take a long time to build, and the US largely stopped building them—we import them. They are huge, the size of a small building, difficult to produce and then transport, then install. Thousands would have to be replaced if there is a big attack on our grid.

As Chapter Four detailed, elected officials refuse to force utilities to harden our grid from EMP, cyber, and physical attack because they fear losing votes for utility rates going up, and they prioritize donations from utility company lobbyists for their reelection campaigns over protecting citizens. Nor do they face the risk of death when the grid goes down—congressmen and top government officials will be sheltered at Mount Weather and Raven Rock while the rest of us are left to fend for ourselves. Elected officials choose campaign donations from utility lobbyists over the lives of citizens.[16]

5. Refusing to stop or even retaliate against enemy cyberattacks on critical infrastructure

Russia has demonstrated its ability to take down electric grids and critical infrastructure in Ukraine and against other countries. The FBI director warned in 2024 that China has placed malware on hundreds of thousands of US computers, Internet routers, and systems, targeting military, government, and critical infrastructure. The former chairman at electric power operator Southern Company says China's cyberattack capability is now an existential threat for American companies and government agencies.[17]

But without government requirements to be protected, utility systems focus on competing to deliver low-cost electricity, and are expanding with more digitalized systems that are more vulnerable to cyberattack. The number of susceptible points on US electrical networks have been increasing by about sixty per day. There were over a thousand cyberattacks on US utilities in 2024, 70 percent more than prior years.[18]

Despite repeated, damaging cyberattacks that we know China, Russia, Iran, and North Korea have launched over the past decades, there is no retaliation for these preparations for and acts of war.[19] As an NBC News report noted, "The Obama administration finds itself stymied by its own failure to formulate a framework for responding to cyberattacks, despite years of serious and damaging intrusions."[20] In December 2024, China hacked into US Treasury Department systems, but there were no retaliations or repercussions for these cyberattacks.

There is no public warning that our enemies are readying or already have the capability to cripple US utilities, but former US officials interviewed warn that countries like China have the capability to "disrupt our ability to support military activities or to distract us, to get us to focus on a domestic incident at a time when something is flaring up in a different part of the world."[21]

6. Failure to prevent thousands of foreign agents in the US that can destroy military assets, our electrical grid and other critical infrastructure

There are thousands of Chinese agents in the US, in every state, and thousands of other Russian, Iranian, North Korean, ISIS, and Al-Qaeda agents who are here to execute terrorist attacks or possibly large-scale operations that could inflict severe damage.[22]

When our electric grid goes down, the economy does not function, municipal water systems do not work, and Congressional commissions have concluded that 90 percent of our population could die. Our military bases depend on the civilian electric grid. If it goes down, our conventional military power collapses too.

Since our electric system is the Achilles' heel of not just our population, but our conventional military power, and a highly fragile system, we believe that foreign agents and terrorists will target the grid as the obvious, easy way to disable our military and kill most of our citizens. Foreign agents are very likely working in electric utility companies, placed for sabotage.

Taking out many of the seven hundred extremely high voltage (EHV) transformers that carry electric power (most of it) over long distances, and other critical nodes on the grid with cyberattacks, physical attacks by agents on the ground, and drone attacks from the air, would be a very feasible and effective attack. There have been several attacks on electric gird substations and transformers in the US over the past decade, some of which appear to have been professionally executed group attacks for training or planning. There have been cyberattacks on our grid, clear evidence that our enemies are working to develop capability to destroy it.

Enemy agents can poison municipal water systems, execute physical attacks on all kinds of critical infrastructure beyond the electric grid.

Enemy agents can easily start hundreds, even thousands of wildfires, as well as execute arson attacks in large, crowded buildings. With low probability of getting caught or stopped, a single agent could start dozens or hundreds of fires. With so many fires raging at once, most fires would burn without any firefighting resources to put them out.

Despite thousands of foreign agents in the US, the government is not waging an aggressive, effective campaign to discover and arrest them, or even warning the public that we face a threat of thousands in our midst that can destroy critical infrastructure, start fires, and kill us.

7. Failing to stop enemy drone surveillance of military bases and critical infrastructure

In December 2023, large numbers of unidentified air vehicles flew for weeks over Langley Air Force Base, where our most advanced jet fighters, F-22 and F-35s are based. Air Force General Mark Kelly was called out to observe dozens of UAVs doing complex and coordinated flights, well beyond the sophistication of civilian drone operations. Some drones were twenty feet long and flying at more than a hundred miles an hour, at altitudes of 3,000 to 4,000 feet. In addition to Langley, the UAV or drones overflew Naval Station Norfolk, our largest naval port. The *Wall Street Journal* reported similar UAV surveillance over many other sensitive military sites, that the Department of Defense could not explain. Due to federal laws, the military cannot shoot down UAVs over bases unless they pose an immediate threat. The DoD never determined the UAVs' origin or who controlled them.[23]

The government's continued assurances to the public that the drones are not a threat, not foreign controlled, are clearly false—if we don't know who controlled drones conducting surveillance of a military base and critical electric infrastructure we obviously cannot say they are not foreign and not a threat. Common sense and good judgment clearly call for the opposite conclusion—that they likely were conducting surveillance and targeting for a very serious, capable enemy.

There are several Chinese air drone companies operating in the US. Chinese agents are probably working in these air taxi drone "front companies" conducting surveillance operations under cover of a legitimate commercial company's development operations. If caught, the company explains that they were doing R&D work, and are, understandably, trying to keep their commercial R&D work confidential.

In addition to drone surveillance of military bases, drones appeared to be mapping electric grid stations and municipal water sources. The recent FAA drone bans in New York and New Jersey included limits over transmission lines and power substations. Large drones dispatching smaller drones with explosive charges could easily destroy a large number of transformers.

Drones are ideal vehicles to place small charges to attack advanced aircraft on the ground (that cost millions of dollars each, and are very few in number as a result)—or destroy huge transformers to take out our electric grid. A massive drone attack on military bases and/or the electric grid would take extensive reconnaissance and mapping for a large fleet of drones to execute a big attack—activity that has occurred across the US over the past year.

Destroying our vulnerable electric system is the obvious, easy way to disable our military and kill most of our citizens. Foreign agents working undercover in electric utility companies, Chinese agents hiding/operating in Chinese air taxi drone companies to launch drone attacks on transformers, along with attacks by small Chinese agent teams on key substations and transformers could enable China to destroy the electric grid, cripple the US military, and kill most of us.

In February 2023, we shot down a Chinese surveillance balloon, but only after it had drifted across the United States. As with cyberattacks, drone incursions, and enemy agents in the country, there is no penalty for enemy preparations to attack the US.

Enemies are wisely preparing the capability to destroy our electric grid without providing obvious evidence that they launched the attacks. Cyber and physical attacks (from agents on the ground and drones in the air) can disable a large part or the vast majority of our electric grid, removing the US as the world's top superpower.[24]

If Chinese or Russian agents conduct the attacks, China or Russia would deny it—and likely convince much or most of the world that any evidence the US did present was not conclusive. Nor do we benefit from launching strategic nuclear strikes to punish them after we've lost our grid—virtually guaranteeing retaliatory nuclear attacks by them, adding nuclear devastation to our country at a time when hundreds of thousands to millions are dying daily in the aftermath of a grid down disaster.[25]

8. Failure to secure borders—allowing enemy agents, terrorists, released prisoners, millions of undocumented immigrants easy access to the country

There are an estimated 12 million illegal immigrants in the US today, over 3 percent of the population.

There was a huge surge in Chinese nationals crossing easily through our largely unsecured southern border in recent years. The House Committee on Homeland Security released a report that more than 24,000 were apprehended illegally crossing the border. Of course, a much larger number could have gotten across without being caught. Countries like Cuba, Haiti, Nicaragua, and Venezuela have done mass paroles of criminals and then helped them get to the US to illegally enter our country.[26]

We do not know how many Americans have been killed by illegal immigrants for several reasons. First, the government does not collect immigration status data in arrest records, with the exception of Texas. Second, with no records or knowledge of an illegal alien in the country, a murder they commit without an arrest would not be attributed to them. There were 346,000 cases of homicide and non-negligent manslaughter unsolved from 1965 to 2023.[27] Finding an enemy agent or a criminal illegal alien is much harder than apprehending a registered, documented, far easier to track citizen.

About half of murders/homicides in the US are never resolved, they can't find or prove who committed the crime. Many of these deaths are likely due to illegal immigrants and enemy agents. With no records of them, no fingerprints on file, no known address, they are far more difficult to catch. Trained agents and experienced criminals in particular will be very good at avoiding arrest. In 2023, the rate of unsolved murders in the US went up, possibly due to the rise in illegal immigrants and enemy agents in the US. The "data" showing low crime rates for illegal immigrants is nonsense—we can't know their propensity to do more or less crimes since they are undocumented, unknown. We can reason that with foreign countries releasing/exporting criminals to the US and enemy countries sending agents to the US, that these people are likely to kill citizens, and not get caught doing it.

9. Risking nuclear war with China or destruction of our vulnerable electric grid by backing Taiwan despite China's legitimate claim

China colonized and annexed Taiwan in the 1600s, but later had to cede control to Japan in 1895, gaining it back after Japan's surrender in 1945. The "Republic of China" led by the Nationalist Party took control of Taiwan in 1945. The Nationalist Party lost to the Communist Party in China's 1945–1949 civil war, taking refuge with over one million Chinese on Taiwan, which is still called the Republic of China. Over 95 percent of Taiwan's population today is Han Chinese ethnicity. The People's Republic of China's position is that this is an internal Chinese matter, finishing their civil war—a very legitimate claim. Thanks to George Marshall's brilliance and integrity, the US stayed out of China's civil war. But the reprehensible Senator Joseph McCarthy and political pandering for votes led to a resolution in 1955 that gave the POTUS authority "to employ the Armed Forces of the United States as he deems necessary" to protect Taiwan.[28]

Since 1949 the Chinese Government has insisted Taiwan is their territory and they will put it under their control. The US backing Taiwan has been an extremely popular position for US politicians, not wanting to look like they are "appeasing" a Hitler, suggesting strength in standing up to and fighting Communism. The Hitler expansion analogy does not fit. China taking Taiwan is not Germany invading Poland, and does not lead to attacks on Japan or South Korea or an invasion of the Philippines.

China will pressure or if necessary invade Taiwan to reclaim this territory, and if the US follows through on promises to assist Taiwan, we must expect that China will engage in "nuclear chicken" against us—threatening and if necessary firing some nuclear weapons against the US to force the POTUS to back down. A military style exercise simulation on such a scenario was run on the Collapse Survivor App in 2024; a link to the lessons learned podcast is inclued in the webnotes.[29]

China has been preparing for war with Taiwan for half a century, and will very likely take Taiwan, possibly soon. Taiwan has had time to prepare its defenses or negotiate a deal with the PRC. To avoid loss of Taiwan's hugely valuable computer chip plants, China would very likely seek to negotiate a reunion rather than invade. No outside nation has any obligation to oppose China handling their domestic affairs, settling their civil war. Governments are supposed to prioritize defending their citizens. The US government should prioritize protecting the citizens that elected and support them, not subjecting them to high risks of nuclear attack to defend Taiwan.

If we get into war with China over Taiwan, expect China to take out our fragile electric system, which they can easily do with a very small nuclear strike or with cyber and agent physical attacks. Most Americans could be killed—and Taiwan not saved. The huge forces required for us to assist in Taiwan's defense drives huge conventional weapons spending requirements that we would not have if we abandoned this suicidal offer to assist Taiwan. If the US withdraws its promises of military support for Taiwan, we should expect China's nuclear and conventional military build up to slow down, and may find far more cooperation in areas like controlling AI and its promise of uncontrollable, unimaginable new Weapons of Mass Destruction (WMD).

As a later chapter in this book proposes, the US must abandon promises to defend Taiwan, stay out of China's domestic affairs, and avoid provoking war with China.[30]

10. Risking war by pushing NATO membership to Russia's border despite Russia's clear threats of retaliation, prompting war in Ukraine

Both standing up to China on Taiwan and pushing NATO to Russia's borders stem from vote mongering by career politicians who know that American's limited knowledge of foreign affairs and national security policy does cover the lesson learned of failed attempts to appease Hitler.

A leading political scientist, Graham Allison, Dean of Harvard's graduate school of government, concluded that the reason General Douglas MacArthur was able to defy his orders during the Korean War and march too far north, bringing China into the war, was that Truman and top Democratic politicians were afraid to confront him because of political backlash due to the general's public popularity.[31] When career politicians have to choose between what is best for our security and best for their political party and election success, they prioritize political power.

President Clinton pushed NATO expansion to Russian borders, ignoring advice from Henry Kissinger and other experts and threats from Putin that Russia would not tolerate this, never allow Ukraine (part of the former Soviet Union) to join. One of the greatest, most responsible Americans in our history, an expert on Russia, George Kennan, the father of the containment doctrine, opposed this aggressive NATO expansion that would clearly threaten Russia. Many other well qualified American national security experts opposed President Clinton's aggressive NATO expansion plans, including Paul Nitze, a hawk from the Reagan administration; Harvard historian of Russia Richard Pipes; Senator Sam Nunn, one of the few experts on national security in Congress; former Senator and US Ambassador to the United Nations Daniel Patrick Moynihan; and Robert McNamara, former Secretary of Defense.[32] But Clinton from childhood days on always prioritized winning elections over everything else[33], wanted to look tough and score domestic political points, look like a conquering hero advancing on Russia, so, like all members of the Perverted Triangle, he sacrificed national security benefits for votes.

Putin is clearly an evil aggressor, but the Russian war with Ukraine is probably due largely to Clinton, Bush 2, and West European politicians pandering for votes by looking tough against Russia and promising Ukraine NATO membership. In 2008 at a senior NATO summit, Ukraine was promised eventual membership in NATO, despite Russia's assurances they would never allow it.[34]

If Russia overran Ukraine tomorrow, they would pose little threat to NATO and Putin would have little force beyond nuclear weapons (which the UK and France can deter, especially with the US still backing NATO) to threaten Europe.

But with Russians getting killed by US and west European weapon systems, including strikes deep inside Russian territory, we face a big risk of Russian use of nuclear weapons as Putin has threatened, or worse—Russian agents releasing a deadly virus in the US and Western Europe to plunge us into a horrible pandemic and end aid to Ukraine.

We have already experienced foreign policy disasters, big loss of American lives, from basing national security policy on domestic vote considerations rather than real national security interests. Far bigger losses from sacrificing sound foreign and defense policy for domestic election votes lie ahead if we do not stop these bad practices.

11. Promoting AI despite clear evidence that it will lead to more weapons of mass destruction and inevitable misuse to kill millions or all of us

Artificial Intelligence has raised the likelihood and severity of existing collapse threats and will invent new weapons of mass destruction (WMD). AI is being used to develop new medicines and will be misused by bad people to develop deadly new viruses, easier means to enrich uranium for nuclear weapons, new poisons, and novel new ways to kill people we never thought of before. AI, combined with CRISPR and new bioengineering technologies enables small groups and even individuals to design and deliver deadly new viruses and bioweapons that could not only devastate the United States but wipe out most of the human race.[35]

Most experts speaking out on AI threats are warning about the future AGI threat—but there is a far worse, new threat from AI: bad people using it to develop more effective and brand-new weapons of mass destruction. We will very likely suffer a collapse from nation-states, terrorists, or individual bad people using AI to design a deadly new virus or new means of enriching uranium for nuclear weapons long before bad AI computers and robots come after us.

ChatGPT CEO Sam Altman, Palantir's CEO Alex Karp, and other Big Tech/AI leaders have Trump's full support now for a Manhattan Project style AI arms race—but without any of the controls we use with nuclear weapons. Trump eliminated the Biden administration's insufficient regulations/controls on AI—there are none now. Elon Musk and AI experts have warned that superintelligent AGI is more dangerous than nuclear weapons. But you'd have more regulatory hurdles launching a new kid's cookie oven than developing AI model that could show you how to use CRISPR to make H5N1 human-to-human transmissible or develop other new WMD.

With the new Stargate project, the problem of bad people misusing AI to develop more powerful and brand new weapons of mass destruction will get worse faster. AI company CEOs like Karp are urging an "AI arms race" with China. We are going as fast as we can to improve AI capabilities that will lead to more WMD and possibly human extinction when we should be controlling AI, preparing for its misuse—not treating it like a wonderful new phase of economic advancement.

The need to prevent China from beating us in military uses of AI is correct—but the best way to do this is not an arms race that accelerates uncontrolled development of AI, enabling new Weapons of Mass Destruction that could kill most of us. Later chapters explain the right, survivable way to gain China's cooperation and control AI.[36]

12. Eliminating battlefield nuclear weapons, endangering troops deployed overseas for domestic political votes

Another bad national security move to score domestic political points was President George H. W. Bush's unilateral elimination of US battlefield nuclear weapons, a Model 3 and 4 decision, not Model 1 decision-making to maximize the benefit of citizens.

The anti-nuclear movement is a powerful political force. President Bush scored political points by declaring a "peace dividend" after the fall of the Soviet Union, and unilaterally surrendered US battlefield nuclear weapons. Many US politicians, and officials from the United Nations and NATO, proudly insist that any use of nuclear weapons is inherently wrong and evil. The US foolishly, irresponsibly eliminated all its ground-launched short-range tactical nuclear weapons, destroying all short-range ballistic missile warheads and nuclear artillery shells. The army was left with no way to call in quick battlefield nuclear weapons to stop a heavy enemy ground attack. Aircraft-delivered tactical nuclear weapons may not be able to reach the target, and are far too slow in delivering a prompt battlefield nuclear strike whose timing is critical. Russia and China not only kept, but continue to modernize and expand their tactical, battlefield nuclear weapons. The US unilaterally abandoned, destroyed its responsive, short-range, low-yield battlefield nuclear weapons, disarmed itself. A political peace dividend benefit was achieved for the Bush administration, but national security was sacrificed. The lack of battlefield nuclear weapons capability invites enemies to use these weapons—especially given Western superiority in conventional weaponry.

Nuclear weapons, whether used in prompt global strike to preemptively destroy a WMD attack, or save US military forces from being overrun and destroyed, can be the best or only means to save lives, potentially millions or billions of them—and must stop being condemned as inherently evil or only useful for mutually assured destruction. New technologies in the Age of Collapse will deliver far worse threats than nuclear weapons, and nuclear weapons may be our best means of limiting the loss of lives.

Compared to the uncontrollable, far more deadly risks of Artificial Intelligence, short-range, low-yield nuclear weapons with "fail safe" mechanisms are safe. Combined with shallow underground tactical defense shelters for troops (useful only in defense),[37] they may be our best means of stopping enemy use of their own nuclear weapons or other WMD that AI invents.

These issues are addressed in more detail later in this book.

With Chinese defense spending taking off and AI and drones making traditional high-tech conventional weapons obsolete, the US no longer can count on enjoying conventional weapons technology superiority. Very few elected officials have any military experience to judge battlefield fighting capability. Low-yield, short-range, ground launched battlefield nuclear weapons are our best means of deterring and defeating larger enemy armies—or at least preventing our deployed forces from being overrun and killed. But today, US troops are denied their best means of defense since political correctness and votes are the priority of the Perverted Triangle.

13. Providing collapse survival protection just for top elected and government officials at Mount Weather and other sites—but no civil defense for citizens

There are hundreds of federal government survival facilities around the US, plus an unknown number of state and local government bunkers. Many hold thousands of people. Not just for the president, Congress, and Department of Defense—every federal agency, even ones you'd consider far from essential or desirable, has facilities, stockpiles, and plans to keep their top staff alive. Works of art and historical documents are also covered by government survival plans. Much of Continuity of Government plans remain classified, but professional books like Garrett Graff's

Raven Rock: The Story of the U.S. Government's Secrete Plan to Save Itself—While the Rest of us Die document this seventy-year-long Continuity of Government survival plan for top politicians and government officials that 95 percent of Americans know nothing about.[38]

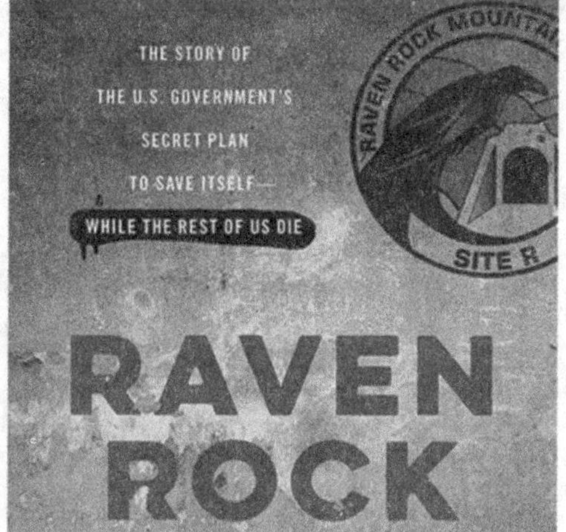

Garrett M. Graff, *Raven Rock: The Story of the US Government's Secret Plan to Save Itself—While the Rest of Us Die*

Figure 27: US "Continuity of Government" plans will save top government officials while citizens die in a collapse.

Since 9/11, facilities like Raven Rock in Pennsylvania have grown dramatically, with sixty-nine buildings in a huge underground city with lakes and fuel storage, its own police and fire departments, and every supply imaginable. Mount Weather in Virginia for Congress and many government agencies is another massive complex of above and largely below ground buildings, which has also had huge expansion in recent years. There are even "media rooms" at Mount Weather so politicians can reach out to surviving media in their districts—reelection campaigning never ends. Billions are invested in these government survival facilities, hundreds of millions annually just in maintenance expenses.[39]

Every Big Government agency has Continuity of Government and survival plans—even the IRS, Federal Reserve, post office, and social and welfare program agencies.[40] The National Archives has three separate survival facilities so they can keep publishing the Federal Register of laws after a collapse.[41]

US civil defense and Continuity of Government organizations and plans were constantly changed, by every administration.[42] In addition to funds and plans shifting with domestic political priorities, the leadership of these government organizations are often put in incompetent hands. Like ambassadors, key officials in not just foreign policy but national security matters, many or most senior government positions go not to the most qualified, but a supporter of the Perverted Triangle.

Michael Brown was an undistinguished lawyer, but had political connections from work with the Republican Party. He left a job supervising horse show judges to work for George W. Bush's longtime political aide, Joe Allbaugh, who managed Bush's campaign and was rewarded with the top position in FEMA. Brown's closest claim to emergency response experience was a short stint supervising police and fire departments as an assistant city manager in an Oklahoma City suburb. But when Allbaugh left within two years, Brown was rewarded with the top position leading FEMA, and was a key factor in FEMA's disastrously slow, inept response to the long expected hurricane striking New Orleans, Katrina.[43]

In contrast to the massive Continuity of Government program and shelters for the Perverted Triangle, there is no longer any civil defense program for citizens. The government won't give honest threat warnings to citizen, stockpile any food for them, and certainly won't provide shelters. They will only take care of top elected politicians and government bureaucrats.

14. Abandoning Eisenhower civil defense stockpiled food and exercises for citizens, leaving no preparations for citizens to survive a collapse

In the 1950s, the Perverted Triangle's power was growing, but with Eisenhower as president, the government still cared for protecting the population and a civil defense program to stockpile food began. Over the 1960s 165,000 tons of food for citizens were stockpiled in 100,000 shelters.

As the Perverted Triangle surged in power in the 1960s and the Republican Party abandoned any pretense of following constitutional limits to government and largely joined the Perverted Triangle, the civil defense program ceased being funded.[44] In 1969, "it was decided not to renew efforts for Federal stocking when it became obvious that Congress would no longer appropriate funds for shelter supplies."[45] By 1970 government was abandoning remaining civil defense shelters, sending the stockpiled food into dumps.[46] The last time the US carried out a national civil defense drill was under the Eisenhower administration. As the Perverted Triangle took over both parties and most of government in the 1960s, civil defense programs, food stockpiling, and exercises were eliminated.

President Reagan did make some improvements in civil defense programs and started a "Crisis Relocation Plan" to move 150 million Americans out of cities into rural areas, but the plans were not implemented.[47] In 2009, President Obama signed an executive order authorizing the US Post Office, escorted by local law enforcement, to develop capability to deliver antibiotics and medical countermeasures from a Strategic National Stockpile of medical supplies.[48] How much is in this stockpile is unknown, but who gets priority is not in doubt: top elected and government officials are always the top priority.

Other countries do carry out national civil defense drills.[49] Countries like Finland and Switzerland have shelters for citizens, provide weapons for citizens to defend themselves, and have extensive civil defense measures to protect their population. The Soviet Union spent far more on civil defense than the US, with a massive program to protect its civilian population.[50]

15. Continuity of Government policies will transfer police and military resources to protect top officials and politicians in a collapse—leaving less help for citizens

There is an absolutely deliberate policy to sacrifice citizens' survival for the benefit of top elected officials. When a disaster occurs, the top priority of government is not protecting its citizens. The top priority of government officials is "Continuity of Government"—keeping themselves and their families alive and government functioning. To do this, police and military personnel will be diverted from protecting citizens to providing extra protection for the top members of the Perverted Triangle.

When a bioengineered pandemic starts, the grid goes down, a nuclear exchange occurs, an economic downturn or some political dispute leads to massive unrest or Civil War, or any of the fifty-plus trigger events Disaster Preparedness[51] tracks occurs and yields a collapse, your need for police protection will go way up while their availability goes down, because more will be assigned to protect the Perverted Triangle. Look at your governor next time you see him or her, and notice the security detail always with them. When law and order vanish in a collapse, more police and National Guard troops will be called to duty to ensure the safety of elected officials and their families. The need for police or National Guard protection of hospitals, food stores, and other facilities will also rise in a collapse. If citizens are even able to call for help, it will likely be a waste of time. The police and security priority is protecting senior government officials and facilities, not citizens.[52]

16. Executive orders authorizing Government Agencies to seize food and resources from citizens in a collapse

Even worse than the government's massive programs and preparations to protect themselves so they survive while doing nothing to protect citizens (or even warn citizens that they need to get prepared) are the deliberate government plans to "seize assets coast to coast," taking food and other resources from citizens to be controlled and distributed by government.[53] As a government official explained, Continuity of Government power is unlimited: "There'll be martial law, and we'll just take it."[54] The Supreme Court, which since 1937 no longer protects the Constitution and citizens' Natural Rights, but backs the Perverted Triangle, has ruled that martial law is justified "to create conditions wherein civil government can be rapidly reconstituted."[55]

President Kennedy's executive order 10998 assigned emergency preparedness functions to the Secretary of Agriculture, including developing plans for the salvage and rehabilitation of food resources. It's not just in executive orders, but in federal laws dictating that "[i]n order to prevent hoarding, no person shall accumulate (1) in excess of the reasonable demands of business, personal, or home consumption . . . prevailing market prices, materials which have been designated by the President as scarce materials. . . ."[56]

If you surveyed American citizens and asked them if they think it would be okay for government officials to seize their stockpiled food in an emergency, you wouldn't find even 1 percent who believe this is fine, a good idea. But it is the law, set by the Perverted Triangle for their benefit.

Continuity of Government is not just the policy and top priority of the federal government—it is for state and local governments as well.

> **Government agencies are authorized to steal food and resources from citizens in a collapse—their number one priority is protecting themselves. Citizens are not just expendable, they are exploitable—a resource for government to raid if their stockpiled supplies run low.**

Many Continuity of Government executive orders are classified. But this Google AI Summary concluded that they do indeed authorize government officials the right to seize citizens' property in a collapse: "Executive Order 13603, also known as the National Defense Resources Preparedness Order, was signed by President Barack Obama on March 16, 2012 . . . Gives the federal government the authority to seize property, allocate services and facilities, and more."[57] Executive orders authorize government agencies to steal food from citizens.

No citizen under today's unlimited government power and a legal system that refuses to enforce Natural Rights could successfully argue in court or in practice against government officials (backed up by police or military forces) demanding to seize their personal supplies. Backed up by the very clear "Continuity of Government" policies at all levels of government, there is little doubt that many government officials will steal food and supplies from citizens in a collapse if they faced shortages—arguing that COG policies clearly dictate that their survival is the top priority. It is crystal clear that our government prioritizes their benefit and survival, and is absolutely okay with normal citizens being exploited and killed as necessary to keep them alive.

Having served in Active duty, Reserve, and National Guard forces, I'm confident that the majority of military personnel will refuse government offers to steal food from or kill citizens. But government officials have given themselves the authority and ability to kill citizens in a collapse, and some will find police/military forces to support this.[58]

17. Laws limiting magazine size and attempts to ban AR-15s and "military capable" weapons that citizens need in a collapse to defend against marauder groups

If all the government was doing was protecting itself and not doing anything to help citizens survive a collapse that might be acceptable—if they would stop trying to make it impossible for us to survive on our own. Trying to ban the weapons we need to defend ourselves in a collapse is another way some parts of the Perverted Triangle (largely the Democratic Party) is actively working to kill us. Most top Democratic career politicians, such as former President Biden and California Governor Gavin Newsom, have pledged to ban "assault rifles" (another big government lie—an AR-15 is not an "Assault Rifle"; the AR stands for "ArmaLite Rifle," the company).

In a collapse you must have military-capable weapons to survive. If a gang is ransacking your neighborhood, with no police available—your double barreled 12-gauge shotgun is useful, but you need far more firepower. The compelling justification for military-capable rifles is not hunting or "normal" self-defense, but survival after a major disaster that leads to a collapse in economic activity and widespread, long-lasting loss of law and order.

US government survival facilities don't just have "military capable" weapons like AR-15s to keep civilians out in a collapse—they have machine guns and grenade launchers stockpiled in their bunkers.[59]

The Second Amendment of the Bill of Rights (all ten of which were deliberately adopted to add checks on federal government abuse of power) gives no wiggle room for lying lawyers and politicians to limit or control citizens' essential right to have weapons: "A well regulated Militia, being necessary to the security of a free State, the right of the people to keep and bear Arms, shall not be infringed."

The argument that the Second Amendment's writers intended to restrict individual gun ownership but not gun ownership by militias is nonsense. Farmers in the 1700s (90 percent or more of the population) and many town and city dwellers owned rifles and pistols for hunting and self-defense, most not militia members. The motivation for the Second Amendment was not just defense, but also offense—the ability to threaten government with force, rebellion, to preserve a "free State" since the biggest perceived threat to freedom in the founding era was a powerful national government that might try to abuse power as the "anti-Federalists" as many Federalists feared. As the Father of the Constitution, James Madison pledged in Federalist #46, citizens bearing arms have the ability to fight tyrannical government and "shake off their yokes," "overturn" tyranny. Armed citizens form "a barrier against the enterprises of ambition, more insurmountable than any which a simple government of any form can admit of." Writing to convince people to support the Constitution, not fear federal government abuse of power, Madison's clear point is that armed citizens and militias are a means to fight and thus deter Big Government abuse of power. Anyone today who argues that Madison would support government bans or control of citizens' ownership of weapons is delusional or a blatant liar. As a Heritage Institute researcher and writer explained, "[t]he notion that the federal government has the power to impose gun control laws is an invention of the twentieth century, when progressive judges, rather than applying the law as it had always been understood, decided to rubberstamp unconstitutional gun restrictions in the name of public safety."[60]

If the Perverted Triangle wants to ban AR-15s or other "military capable" weapons they should start by disarming Mount Weather and Raven Rock guards, surrendering their high capacity magazines and other "military capable" weapons.

18. Regulations stopping small farms and domestic gardening/ranch animal husbandry vital to collapse survival

All fifty states have enacted right-to-farm laws that seek to protect qualifying farmers and ranchers from nuisance lawsuits by lawyers, but they often fail to stop government bureaucrats from adding building codes, zoning, and regulations that violate Natural Rights to use private property and make farming difficult or impossible. A chicken coop may only be allowed if it is 150 feet from a house—impossible on small lots, and an unreasonable requirement. Many states have water laws that effectively prevent gardening or keeping a few ranch animals, sometimes even banning you from using the water you collect off your roof. Fees are often imposed to pay for the bureaucratic oversight you don't want.[61] Many rural counties don't want regulations impacting backyard farms, but if the Democratic Party controls the state government (states with a majority of the population in big cities) they often force Big Government regulations on rural counties. Thus you can be in a rural location in California, Nevada, Colorado, Illinois, New York, and elsewhere—and face the same building codes and zoning requirements of big city dwellers, eliminating your Natural Rights to use your private property and farm/ranch to produce food to survive a collapse. Urban representatives in a majority pass regulations dictating the square footage requirements for ranch animals: better for your chicken to have more square footage to roam, even if it means you die from starvation.

Farms with less than half an acre in Oregon are harassed by the Oregon Water Resources Department, insisting they cannot irrigate without a permit. As one owner rightly pointed out, "I don't know why growing food is illegal." In Oregon, the government claims to own all the water, and citizens must have their approval to use it. Getting an irrigation permit takes over a year, and in Oregon, small farm water permit requests are usually rejected.[62] This is another state where Big Government run by the Perverted Triangle is promoting regulations, bureaucracy, and legal action to benefit themselves at the expense of citizens' Natural Rights, including the right to use your private property to grow food and survive a collapse. Natural Rights to privacy, personal property, even self-defense and survival now lost in America where the Perverted Triangle and a perverted legal system where the Natural Rights we fought a Revolution for are no longer recognized.[63]

19. Zoning and building regulations that violate our constitutionally protected Natural Rights to private property and make it difficult or impossible to prepare for collapse

Americans need to be prepared for a collapse that could last for over a year, but government rules and restrictions make it far more difficult and costly to prepare. Zoning and building codes greatly increase the costs of a building. Limits of one residence on a property mean people can't spread out into separate, smaller buildings to be both safer in a pandemic, and more able to defend a compound from marauders in a collapse. The huge increase in building costs from government permits, regulations, and building codes adds tens of thousands of dollars in unnecessary expense.

Even in rural counties, state governments controlled by the Perverted Triangle have banned or limited woodstoves, the most important, often only source of energy for heating and cooking that Americans will have during a collapse. At our Fortitude Ranch locations we have lots of woodstoves because our electric grid is extremely fragile and unlikely to operate in a collapse, and there will be no gas or coal deliveries.

We need to stockpile antibiotics and prescription drugs since there will be little or no production or distribution of drugs in a collapse, and most hospitals will be inoperable. But government drug laws make this impossible. You can only get a prescription for an existing condition and short-term supply of antibiotics and drugs.

We have thought about putting a fortified, urban-style Fortitude Ranch facility in New York City, the worst place in the country to try to survive a collapse—but their government regulatory barriers and zoning and building code extra costs are too horrendous. The biggest barrier to prepping is Big Government, created by and for the benefit of the Perverted Triangle at the expense of our Natural Rights and our lives.

Overall, the morass of government regulations, more than any person could hope to read in a lifetime, raises the cost of everything, decreasing money available for preparedness, making stockpiled supplies and building more expensive or impossible.

Building codes and regulations for cities are being forced into rural areas in states controlled by the Democratic Party, driving up costs or preventing vital collapse survival preparations. Even in remote deserts in Nevada, if trying to put up a simple building, the government regulators who ignore your constitutionally guaranteed Natural Rights to use private property will require you pay to have a "Professional Engineer" stamp on your plans—adding $10,000 or more in completely unnecessary costs. There are no neighbors anywhere, no possible argument for public safety protection. But the Perverted Triangle insatiable power grabs require no reason and have no limits.[64]

The biggest barrier to your survival today is unconstitutional Big Government serving the Perverted Triangle. They are not just failing to protect us from external threats we cannot handle on our own (their proper role) but make it far more difficult or impossible for self-preparedness.

20. Government forest and wildfire mismanagement, pleasing environmentalists and promoting government firefighter union pay, preventing volunteer help to stop wildfires and loss of life

Government mismanagement of forest and wildfires is a long-running government-led disaster killing Americans. Citizens killed in recent California wildfires, and forest fires across the West, are dying because elected officials prioritize votes and government union firefighters prioritize more jobs and higher pay over citizen deaths.[65]

The government policy of fighting all forest fires was a bad decision for citizens, but great for government firefighting jobs. Native Americans knew that fires were vital to keep the forest open and thin, clearing out dead trees and vegetation. But with the US Forest Service creation in 1905, government forest management shifted toward fire suppression.[66] It was fantastic for getting votes—government firefighters protecting citizens by putting out forest fires. But it was a bad policy for the long term, as we have experienced over the past decades.

In addition to needing controlled burns, preventing horrible forest and wildfires requires clear-cut areas for firebreaks. I've seen this in Scotland, despite their huge tourist industry and need for having a beautiful landscape. But the leading constituent group that lobbies and votes based on government forest management policies are environmental groups. So to pander to them and get their donations and votes, government favors not allowing evil logging companies to clear-cut trees for firebreaks.

Victor Davis Hanson, a professor emeritus at California State University and Fellow at Stanford University's Hoover Institution, has condemned California Governor Newsome for not building more dams and reservoirs, and for releasing water to please environmental groups rather than save water for firefighting.[67] State and federal environmental laws, written to pander to environmental groups, prohibit or lead to three to five year delays in getting forests thinned or preventative burns.[68]

In addition to Perverted Triangle policies that prevent or delay clear-cutting of trees and controlled burns, prioritizing the jobs and wages of government union firefighters is another major reason for the massive increase in wildfire devastation.

I saw firsthand why firefighters are failing to stop wildfires. I was driving to Forbes Park on June 27, 2018, when a wildfire next to our development started. By the time I got to the gate, to my dismay, there were firefighters there not fighting the fire—but blocking our road. Less than a mile away, easy walking distance, the fire had just started. There was no high wind, it was the ideal time to grab as many people as possible and clear vegetation, prevent the fire from spreading. But the firefighters did not engage in fighting the fire or cutting firebreaks—they deployed to block people. They could have sent homeowners associations or police to do this, but a group of uniformed firefighters stood on our road blocking traffic, ignoring the relatively small fire near us, squandering the best chance to stop the forest fire before it grew too large to stop.

This became the Spring Creek wildfire, burning over 100,000 acres, the third largest wildfire in Colorado history. The fire raged for months—not really ever fought by firefighters, burning largely uncontrolled all summer, from June into September.[69] Several large developments were near where the fire started; ours had a volunteer firefighting group. They were not called up, not allowed to assist.

NATIONAL FEDERATION OF FEDERAL EMPLOYEES

Affiliated with the International Association of Machinists and Acrospace Workers

NFFE News Release

FOR IMMEDIATE RELEASE
May 26, 2022

Contact: Matt Dorsey
Phone: (202) 216-4451

Federal Wildland Firefighters' Union (NFFE) Calls on Biden Administration to Increase Firefighter Pay Nationwide, and Fast, or Face Disaster

National Federation of Federal Employees

Figure 28: Federal Firefighter Unions campaigning for higher pay.

Why? Because the priority of union firefighter management is not preventing fires or protecting citizens, it's maximizing the number of jobs and pay for their union firefighters. So the firefighters' top priority is preventing volunteers from helping, not fighting fires. Not volunteers to spray water on fire, but to do the majority of wildfire work—which is digging ditches, removing flammable material far from the fire, building firebreaks.

Over 85 percent of professional firefighters in the US are unionized.[70] The most unionized industries by far are public sector jobs. But neither federal government employees (25 percent unionized) or state government employees (29 percent) come close to firefighters in their devotion to union jobs and higher pay.[71] In contrast, private sector industries are 6 percent unionized.[72]

When you've got hundreds, thousands of able-bodied people right there to help dig/cut/clear firebreaks, it is outrageously wrong to abandon this volunteer manpower, especially in the first hours and days of a wildfire when you must stop it quickly before it becomes unstoppable. But government union-controlled fire departments see volunteer help as an enemy of their job opportunities, so they reject volunteer help and devote critical resources, even in the most vital early hours of a fire, to stop people, not fight fires. It is a gross lie to say that this is prioritizing protecting human lives. The large group of homeowners I was with were never in the slightest danger. We could have quickly started clearing vegetation on both sides of the road we were standing on without being in any danger—especially with professional firefighters working with and directing us. But the priority for government unions is not serving citizens or protecting them, but more jobs and higher pay.

What makes this union firefighter priority of stopping us from helping them fight fires particularly galling and outrageous is that most US firefighters are volunteers! Only in the once "land of the free" could government block or outlaw people from fighting fires to protect their homes. A home fire involves risk from falling ceilings and toxic chemicals. But the vast majority of work fighting a wildfire is not dangerous or skilled; it is simple manual labor conducted far from the flames—shoveling more than using saws, clearing away burnable material with your hands, shovels, and axes (widely available tools). Almost anyone can effectively do this work—and people trying to protect their homes and neighbors from wildfires will be particularly motivated, hardworking volunteers. With professional, trained firefighters instructing and supervising, volunteers can do very effective safe wildfire fighting work. But government employee unions prioritize their jobs and pay.

The government union priority of protecting their jobs also takes police manpower away from useful emergency response to more violations of Natural Rights. In many jurisdictions (including California) it is a crime to refuse a wildfire evacuation order, and you can be arrested. Police are tasked to arrest and remove citizens exercising their Natural Rights to protect their property (and arguably protect their lives). With bad people coming in to loot areas that are evacuated, there is additional incentive to stay and fight fires. If just 20 percent of the hundreds of thousands of people evacuated in the recent Los Angeles area fires had been allowed to stay and fight the fire, some would have been put out the first day, others would have been contained far faster, fewer would have died. If some volunteers assisting had died—that would have been because of their decision to volunteer; the kind of decision free people, free Americans, should be allowed to make. It is not up to the firefighters' union management or government officials to decide if people want to volunteer to fight wildfires and protect their property. America fought a Revolution and created the Constitution to protect their Natural Rights to live in freedom, control their private property, defend themselves—not serve as dependents and victims to unlimited government, the Perverted Triangle.

Wildfire fighting in the US must switch to planning for and encouraging volunteers, maximizing volunteer help to halt wildfires sooner. We need to clear-cut wide 500–1,000-foot-wide swaths of public forests to make firebreaks, making it possible to prevent massive wildfires—harvesting a small percentage of trees to protect the forest, wildlife, and human houses and lives. Or we can continue current government mismanagement and abuse to maximize wildfires and union firefighter pay.[73]

21. Broadcasting messages and sending satellites beyond our galaxy to advertise and map our presence so alien civilizations more advanced than us can find Earth.

While there is inconclusive evidence on whether or not we've been visited by aliens from other planets, there is a high likelihood of other intelligent life in our vast universe. For security purposes, we can't assume there is not. Given the estimated fourteen-billion-year age of our universe, the likelihood of a far more advanced civilization out there is probably quite high. The worst assumption to make is that a highly advanced foreign civilization would visit us to help us rather than exploit us (treating us like we treat rats). So for our government to be spending our tax dollars to push signals and send probes into space to advertise our existence and location is dead wrong.

The Perverted Triangle's decision-making is dominated by buying reelection votes and increasing jobs/programs/regulations/government power. So when astronomers and scientists fascinated by the possibility of extraterrestrial life, and government bureaucrats in NASA similarly fascinated and eager for bigger budgets, lobby career politicians for these broadcast our presence to the universe programs, the Perverted Triangle approves it—even though it is not just more tax burden for citizens, but a huge, unnecessary risk that could lead to our enslavement or slaughter.

22. Unconstitutional regulations and taxes that crush small businesses, making it harder to escape poverty, homes unaffordable, raising divorce and suicide rates with the economic stress of high taxes costs of unlimited government spending and regulation

The Perverted Triangle makes running a small business or family farm much harder and less likely to succeed because of outrageous regulations, huge permit and government fees, and a tax code that is impossible to comply with (deliberately so) unless you employ accountants and lawyers. The tax code is many times the length of the King James Bible, littered with special provisions that politicians passed as pork benefits to buy votes. It is a huge cost for small businesses and citizens, but profits for our million-plus lawyers (many of them voting as elected officials when laws were passed), plus jobs for bureaucrats that enforce rules (and donate to and campaign for the politicians).

The Sarbanes-Oxley Act on business financial disclosure is 810 pages long, Obamacare over 1,000 pages, and the Dodd-Frank Wall Street Reform and Consumer Protection Act is 2,300 pages long. A huge company can employ lobbyists to tailor the laws passed for their benefit and afford the overhead staff to comply with all this nonsense. Smaller companies are disadvantaged by this regulatory morass, and every citizen loses with the added costs for products and services. The Perverted Triangle is the beneficiary, citizens are the losers.

The tax code is not a system designed to efficiently provide revenue for government; it is a cancerous perversion shaped over decades in lobbying, buying votes, and creating jobs and wealth for the Perverted Triangle.[74]

Government regulations don't just impose huge costs on Americans, they kill people. Quoting a Cato Institute study:

> The slowness in drug approval by the Food and Drug Administration (FDA) prevents Americans from accessing drugs that might save their lives. Even by a conservative estimate, FDA delays in allowing drugs used safely and effectively abroad to be marketed in the United States have cost the lives of at least 200,000 Americans over the past 30 years. Today, it takes an average of 15 years to get a drug reviewed by the FDA. For example, the FDA final review process takes around 28 months as opposed to the 180 days mandated by US law. Many drugs that are common in Europe become available to the American people only years later. This delay causes unnecessary pain, suffering, and deaths.[75]

It is impossible to calculate the rate, but there is no doubt that every time the government imposes a tax or regulation that takes money from people or imposes extra costs on them, it is unavoidably sentencing some people to death. A leading cause of marital strife and divorce is stress from inadequate money.[76] It is not just the direct financial damage of taxes that harms individual happiness and destroys marriages, but the added costs of everything that is impacted by costly regulations, hours of life wasted to comply with tax return paperwork and filings, endless government permits, fees, tickets, and fines.

While it is extremely difficult to estimate, you can be confident that the financial loss of taxes generates divorce, stress, crime, unhappiness, and kills people. An American Enterprise Institute report, drawing on a variety of studies, estimates one death for every $10 million in lost income from government programs that take your tax dollars, reduce your earnings ability, and cut economic growth and productivity. Its estimate back in 2012 was 140,000 deaths annually from the direct and unintended consequences of government spending and regulatory reductions in income and productivity.[77] With much higher government spending today, the annual deaths from lower incomes and loss of productivity due to government programs and regulations are much higher.

23. Overspending and driving national debt to a level that will bankrupt the country and lead to an economic collapse

It is not just the rise in federal government spending as a percentage of GDP, from less than 5 percent a century ago to 30 percent today; but the mix of that spending that is grossly wrong. Defense spending as a percentage of GDP has fallen from 10 percent in peacetime in the 1950s to about 3 percent today, now matched by spending on interest on the cancerous national debt the Perverted Triangle has built up. Spending on social welfare programs is a staggering 20 percent of GDP. And this does not count the huge state and local government spending and debt. Government debt is larger than about 125 percent of our GDP! In 2024, for the first time, the unconstitutional US reached the point where we are spending more on our national debt than we are on defense spending![78]

The $2 trillion in budget cuts DOGE and Trump administration are working for are vital, though few expect success. A paper with some recommendations on how to cut $2 trillion and also improve national security and citizens' ability to survive in the Age of Collapse is available in the webnotes.[79]

There is no honesty in federal government budgets or accounting, but we roughly know that from the first year Medicare spending was visible on the books, in 1967, through 2020, Medicare and Medicaid combined cost about $18 trillion—about the same amount as federal deficits over that same period.[80] As of December 2024, the reported unconstitutional US debt is over $36 trillion, spiraling up every minute! The only way to grasp the magnitude of this debt is to put it in per capita terms. Every American owes over $100,000 in government debt!! But since most people don't pay taxes (too young or too poor), the debt per taxpayer is over $260,000. With the average family having just $11,000 in savings, there is no way we can pay this debt.

Worse, the real government debt is several times more than $36 trillion! The money owed for Social Security and Medicare and public employee pensions and retirement health benefits are also debts that we as individuals and businesses would have to report, but the cheating, dishonest government does not. The unconstitutional US is over $100 trillion in debt thanks to the Perverted Triangle. The interest payments on our debt are now also in the trillions; the country has amassed debts we cannot repay. Eventually we will have to default on government bonds,

Social Security and Medicare benefits promised, government worker retirement benefits, and all the other Ponzi schemes the Perverted Triangle has passed to amass power. The Perverted Triangle and Big Government have ruined and bankrupted our country. Future generations especially are screwed—but they can't vote, so the Perverted Triangle does not care.[81]

Many state governments, especially those ruled by the Democratic Party, also lie. Last year twenty-seven states could not meet their financial obligations, and were in debt. According to "Truth in Accounting," run by CPAs and government accountants, including the former director of the Government Accountability Office, even states with laws mandating a balanced budget, state spending exceeds revenues, so elected officials (leaders of the Perverted Triangle) excluded costs from their budget calculations, such as future pension obligations or deferred maintenance.[82] The five biggest debtor states were California, Massachusetts, Illinois, New Jersey, and Connecticut—all states dominated by the Democratic Party.[83]

Truth in Accounting, which added up all government debts, estimated that *every taxpayer owes $980,000, thanks to unlimited, unconstitutional, perverted government spending and debt.*[84] There is no way this can be paid off. Inflation is one result, but with the BRICS movement or other countries upset with US tariff threats and toxic US debt levels, most nations could decide to abandon the dollar for trade settlements and as a reserve currency, leading to a plunge in the value of the US dollar and the worst economic collapse/depression the country has experienced.[85]

The severe recession or depression that results from out massive debt will yield hundreds of thousands of deaths from the loss of income, the estimated one death for every $10 million in lost income cited earlier.[86] In our divided, angry, dependent society today, a severe economic downturn could lead to massive violence and a collapse—widespread loss of law and order, societal breakdown that could trigger massive looting and marauding, and millions of deaths.[87]

24. Promoting unconstitutional, divisive social programs that benefit the Perverted Triangle but divide the nation and threaten civil war

Federal welfare and income redistribution programs are all unconstitutional, not mentioned, enumerated, or written in the Constitution. The taking of one person's money to give to another against their will is a clear violation of both the Tenth Amendment and Natural Rights of private property. American voters have not amended the Constitution to abandon their Natural Rights and authorize government at any level to take money from some citizens and give it to others.[88]

The biggest, root problem with the federal government today, that corrupts and divides our society, is that limits to government programs and taxation are ignored; enabling divisive, expensive, unconstitutional social programs and regulations to proliferate—bankrupting and dividing the country, eliminating Natural Rights, subverting individual responsibility, and destroying families, as government welfare programs replace family care and responsibility.[89]

There is no limit to what unconstitutional government can do to Americans today with our natural and constitutional rights illegally erased, as the traitor/criminal/prisoner Bradley Manning's government-funded sex change operation proved.[90]

The country narrowly dodged civil war in November 2024 with the nation so sharply divided, largely over unconstitutional social and welfare programs. If Trump had lost a close race, many expected massive violence and civil war.[91] The nation is continuing to divide with Trump in power, and we must expect that some controversial event could trigger domestic violence that may escalate into looting and a collapse with heavy fatalities.

25. Hiring millions of government social and welfare workers while not enough police or Army National Guard members for peacetime security or collapse recovery operations

While there are twenty-three million government employees (not including military personnel), less than one million are law enforcement officers. The Perverted Triangle favors bureaucrats and regulators, not security, the number one purpose of government. Career politicians can buy more votes with welfare and entitlement payments than funding more police protection.[92]

The misconduct of a very few policemen led to an asinine "defund the police" movement that sprouted in some big cities, with attacks on policemen that contributed to thousands of law enforcement officers quitting or retiring early. As one mayor explained, "[t]he toxic national dialogue that demonizes police officers has made police department staffing significantly more difficult for every major city in America."[93]

The miliary and law enforcement personnel are the most valuable and proper government expenditures we make. With the increasing likelihood of homeland attacks and collapse, we need more law enforcement and National Guard forces—which we could readily afford by firing millions of government social workers, planning and zoning officials, and regulators, eliminating their programs that violate the Constitution and our Natural Rights.

Over past decades about twenty thousand Americans have been killed annually by murder or manslaughter (unlawful killing without premeditated intent to kill).[94] With more law enforcement officers, fewer Americans would have died. In the Age of Collapse we must have both a much larger Army National Guard and a huge law enforcement officer reserve force to stop marauder groups and conduct homeland recovery operations. The purpose of government is to protect citizens from severe threats they cannot handle on their own—not to dictate and spend on personal matters, economic, and social issues.[95]

26. Undermining marriage and families, promoting a subservient, irresponsible populace with unconstitutional government social programs and entitlements that lead to crime, divorce, long-term poverty and dependence, and a higher domestic homicide death rate

Despite the explosion in social programs, welfare programs and entitlements in the 1960s, crime rates and homicide death rates in the US not only did not improve—they got worse.

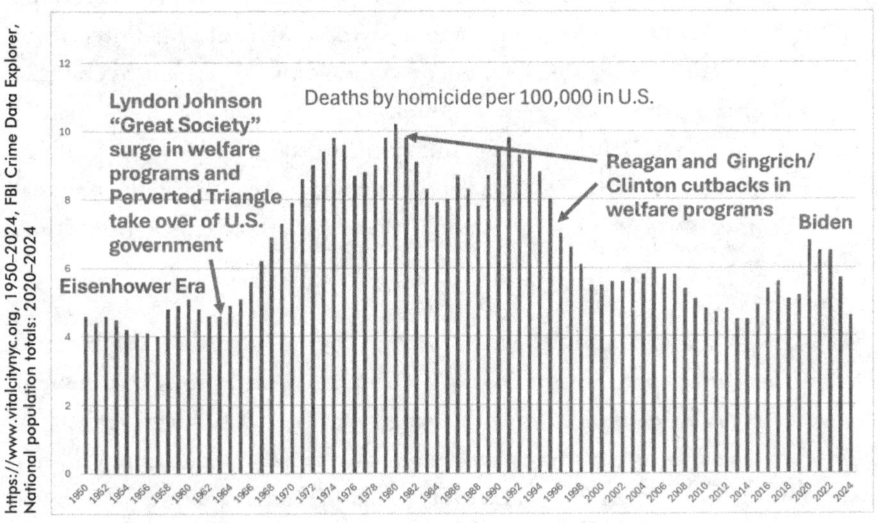

Figure 29: US homicide deaths.

Unconstitutional Big Government social programs encouraged divorce, single parents, and subverted families and marriage. The result is more crime and deaths for citizens.

When the government provides welfare payments and services, you don't need a family, or a two-parent family. But family breakdown fuels poverty. Even high school dropouts who are married have a far lower poverty rate than single parents with several years of college. Boys raised without their father are much more likely to use drugs, engage in violent criminal behavior, go to jail, and drop out of school. Girls are more likely to engage in early sexual activity or have a child out of wedlock. The Perverted Triangle blames their failures on other societal or capitalist problems they must solve, like dangerous neighborhoods or poor schools. But they are wrong—family structure and family and individual responsibility are decisive in driving work ethic, good character, and wise decisions.[96]

Since the explosion in unconstitutional welfare and entitlement programs in the 1960s, the percentage of US children living with a single parent has been rising, accompanied by a decline in marriage rates and a rise in births outside of marriage. A Pew Research Center study of 130 countries and territories shows that the US has the world's highest rate of children living in single-parent households. Almost a quarter of US children under the age of eighteen live with one parent and no other adults (23 percent), more than three times the rate of children around the world who do so (7 percent).[97] A 10 percent rise in children living in single-parent homes leads to a 17 percent increase in juvenile crime. Even in high-crime inner-city neighborhoods, over 90 percent of children from safe, stable homes do not become delinquents, while only 10 percent of children from unsafe, unstable homes in these neighborhoods avoid crime. A two-parent family is critical to raise children well and decrease the likelihood of a life of crime.[98] The Perverted Triangle's social programs have been great for political power, government jobs, and lawyers income—horrible for citizens, raising crime and murder rates.[99]

27. Regulations on food and drugs that violate the Constitution and Natural Rights, misleading people into using unhealthy drugs and foods that benefit special interest and big companies at the expense of health and lifespan

Because Americans have become so buried in government regulations, subservient to government direction and control, individual and family responsibility for decision-making on food, drugs and personal health has been undermined. With Big Government regulating everything, replacing individual liberty and decision-making, citizens assume that the rules and government directions will keep them safe; no need for their own judgment or responsibility. You assume that the highly regulated food that manages to get through the regulatory morass must be good for you, and the highly regulated, tested, approved drugs must be safe.[100]

The Perverted Triangles promotion of personal irresponsibility, destruction of families, and unconstitutional regulation of every aspect of personal life and conduct, down to what you eat, is a major cause of the estimated 678,000 American deaths annually from irresponsible, bad eating decisions that generate obesity, diabetes, heart disease, and cancer.[101] Add drug overdose deaths to this, a number going up, not down, despite the increasing government control of every aspect of drug development and approval, sales, and health care. Purdue Pharma followed the rules and got regulatory approval that helped them push oxycontin, killing 450,000 trusting Americans.[102]

28. Murderers and criminals freed by legal system corrupted by the Perverted Triangle to maximize profit for lawyers; lawyers allowed to lie in court, no priority for truth, Natural Rights, or justice

Murders and criminals often can go free since the US legal system has also been corrupted by the Perverted Triangle, with lawyers allowed to lie in court, justice subordinated to lawyer's interests and case precedents: no priority for truth, Natural Rights, or justice.[103]

If more laws and government spending could solve crime, it would have ended decades ago. Big Government has failed in its War on Poverty and War on Drugs, and is never going to stop bad people from committing crimes. Gangs and flash mobs can openly shoplift from stores today with employees barred from trying to stop them (too much risk of a shyster lawyer lawsuit), and little prospect of being arrested or punished in court. In Big Government states like California where the Perverted Triangle has undisputed control, stealing merchandise worth under $950 is now judged a misdemeanor, not worth arresting or prosecuting, and "shoplifting is now de facto legal."[104]

The US has the highest liability costs as a percentage of GDP of the advanced industrialized countries, with liability costs about three times the average level of European countries.[105] Because of the Perverted Triangle, the US is plagued with one of the highest rates of lawyers per capita in the world, more imprisoned people per capita than any other country, and an obscenely expensive and ineffective legal system that prioritizes lawyers and their income, not justice or the Natural Rights we fought a Revolution to obtain.[106] Lawyers' costs are obscenely high, and courts encourage or require use of lawyers. Most citizens cannot afford expensive defense counsels, and often enter guilty pleas without interviewing any prosecution witnesses since it is cheaper to plead guilty than risk an expensive legal battle where innocence and guilt is subordinated to lawyers' income, case citations, and loopholes, and the lawyer-enriching process that allows wealthy parties to endlessly delay and pile on legal costs to bury a poorer opponent. Laws written and passed by lawyer politicians (the Perverted Triangle) bar non-lawyers from giving legal advice—forcing citizens to get abused and fleeced by attorneys. Americans are abused by the Perverted Triangle's new legal system, with personal liberties and Natural Rights erased, lawyers über alles.

Administrative courts levy ridiculous, absurd fines that you can't even defend yourself against without being forced to hire an attorney.[107] The Perverted Triangle (especially when the Democratic Party is in control) is always abusing government to promote their benefit at citizens' expense. Your choice is pay a fine to the government or pay for an attorney and the chance to avoid the fine. There is no option of defending yourself against the ridiculous charges and pay nothing. I have experienced this. I demanded to defend myself in a West Virginia Administrative Court, refused to pay an attorney since I was absolutely innocent and the charges were nonsense, easy for me to refute. The judge refused to allow me to speak and levied the fine. The Perverted Triangle has ruined our legal system.

The best book explaining how we failed the US Constitution and let politicians, lawyers, and bureaucrats screw us, is Charles Murray's *By the People: Rebuilding Liberty Without Permission*. His summary is accurate and depressing: "The founder's Constitution has been discarded. . . . Aspects of America's legal system have become lawless . . . Congress and the administrative state have become systemically corrupt, for reasons that are inextricably embedded in the market for government favors."[108] The Perverted Triangle has produced a deluge of thousands of laws, an uncountable number of regulations, written to promote more government bureaucrats and regulation, more income for lawyers.[109]

Washington, DC, is full of lawyers who got elected to Congress, passed laws to generate regulations and business for law firms, then left political office to serve as lobbyists helping clients pass more laws and regulations to benefit their cause.

Philip Howard has long campaigned to try to fix our horrible legal system, with books and reform policies laid out in *The Death of Common Sense* and *The Collapse of the Common Good*. Howard explains how "[a] culture of legal fear is not what our founders had in mind when they created the legal framework for a free society. Law is supposed to support free choice, not impede choices all day long."[110]

As a result of Perverted Triangle promotion of laws, regulations, and business for lawyers, the US ranks at the top of countries with the highest per capita rate of imprisonment. The US has just 5 percent of the world's population but locks up 25 percent of the world's prisoners. The nation founded as the land of the free, the champion of liberty has been corrupted and perverted into a land of government and lawyer theft and abuse. The Perverted Triangle has turned the United States into the biggest police state[111] in the world. Big arrest rates, court loads, and prison populations mean huge job opportunities and profits for lawyers and more government jobs. The average per-inmate cost of incarceration in the US is over $31,000 per year.[112] Prisons cost almost $100 billion annually, Courts cost over $60 billion annually, a tax burden of $1,000 per taxpayer annually.[113] The lawyers profit from the unlimited regulatory power of the US government, with a median salary of $150,000.[114]

Most Americans do not know that lawyers in the US are allowed by judges (former lawyers) to knowingly lie in court. According to Evan Whitton, writing in *The Atlantic*, "In France, evidence is not concealed and lawyers are not allowed to use artful lies to pollute the truth. The innocent are rarely charged; 95 percent of guilty defendants are convicted. Public confidence in the system is high." But in our Anglo-American common law system, "lawyers are encouraged to obfuscate the truth and use sophistry to besmirch the integrity of honest witnesses."[115] Justice and strict adherence to the truth are irrelevant in America's perverted legal system, where expensive lawyers citing dueling old case citations dominates. Justice, what is "right," is largely irrelevant to the decision and outcome in US courts today. Former New York governor Andrew Cuomo complained that "[t]he trial lawyers are the single most powerful political force in Albany."[116] The Perverted Triangle has not just ruined American Government, but our legal system too. At the USAF Academy and as an officer, I lived by an honor code that politicians and lawyers violate daily.[117]

Some lawyers recently used the AI tool ChatGPT to argue nonexistent judicial opinions with fake case citations, and "continued to stand by the fake opinions after judicial orders called their existence into question." [118] The lawyers were not disbarred for inventing false evidence and lying, just issued a small $5,000 fine, so still able to generate a big profit on their losing case. In our lawyer-run legal system, with non-lawyers banned from providing legal advice and citizens often required to use lawyers, the courts serve lawyers, not justice, not citizens.

With Big Government and our perverted legal system, you can be imprisoned for failing to obey an arbitrary government regulation you never heard of or even understand if you read it, violating your retained Natural Right to be left alone with unconstitutional, statutory, legislative laws promoted by lobbyists for their benefit, passed by politicians who accepted their campaign donations, and written by lawyers to generate legal work for their profit. The regulations on latching devices for storage bins in bakeries, how to run your workplace, are hundreds of pages long. Charles Murray is right: "Punishment for failure to observe an arbitrary and capricious regulation is indistinguishable from punishment for failing to obey the arbitrary and capricious demands of an absolute ruler. It is a form of lawlessness."[119] Our Founding Fathers understood that there can't be too many laws if we want to have liberty and pursue happiness. James Madison in Federalist #62:

"It will be of little avail to the people, that the laws are made by men of their own choice, if the laws be so voluminous that they cannot be read, or so incoherent that they cannot be understood . . ." We are long past the point of too many incoherent, un-understandable laws. Far beyond the level of government abuse that led Colonial Americans to revolt against the British.

So how many Americans are killed by our unjust, corrupt, perverted legal system? Like death from taxes, that is extremely uncertain and difficult to assess, but there are some reasonable estimates.

First, the costs imposed by too many laws and regulations that can land you in court, then forced to use expensive attorneys, is a financial loss that, like taxes, leads to financial losses-stress-deaths (estimated at one death per $10 million in lost income).[120]

With the explosion in regulations and laws that the Perverted Triangle has sold for votes, government jobs and lawyers' work/income, you can get a felony arrest record for violating a law you've never heard of, even minor and unintentional offenses like exceeding a weight limit on a truck or failing to comply with complex regulatory requirements.[121]

It is impossible for an average person to even know the laws. Ignorance of the law is no defense in court, but with thousands of laws, many hundreds of pages long, there is no feasible way to comply and avoid getting abused by the Perverted Triangle and our unjust legal system run by lawyers for the benefit of lawyers. There are so many laws, including ones repealing or modifying old ones, that we have no idea how many laws there are. The Justice Department has tried several times to count them and failed.[122] There are more than three thousand criminal offenses, and many more civil offenses you could unknowingly commit in an estimated twenty-three thousand pages of just federal laws. Add to this state and local government laws, and every citizen is likely violating laws every day.[123]

An estimated 70 million to 100 million Americans have an arrest record, "a direct consequence of decades of mass incarceration and overcriminalization" according to a Center for American Progress study. As a result, half of US children now have at least one parent with a criminal record. Researchers at the Brennan Center for Justice found that arrested Americans see their subsequent earnings reduced by an average of 52 percent. The study found an alarming rise in fines, fees, and other criminal legal debts that can total thousands or even tens of thousands of dollars, diminishing families' ability to save for the future and protect against financial shocks and uncertainty. Beyond the immediate effects of a conviction for the thousands of laws the Perverted Triangle has passed, incarceration puts the family in debt and the criminal record means less chance of loans to start a business, bans from the now up to 1 in 4 jobs that require an occupational license (another result of the self-serving government and laws promoting the Perverted Triangle) and a host of other collateral damage. [124]

The financial loss of our perverted legal system leads to deaths from lower quality and length of life. I cannot find any estimates of how many people die by suicide as a result of abuse in courts that prioritize lawyers' income rather than justice, but there are likely hundreds to thousands annually.

Lawyers and the Perverted Triangle have reshaped the laws, regulations, and courts to their benefit. The losers in the Perverted Triangle controlled legal system are citizens' Natural Rights, our money, our private property, and our lives.[125]

29. Unconstitutional, ineffective "War on Drugs" that does not stop drugs but yields higher crime and murder rates that kill Americans

A great example of how our laws and government are killing Americans is the four decade long-running "War on Drugs" failure.

About 20 percent of jailed Americans admit to committing their crime to get money for drugs.[126] Because drugs are illegal, not able to be produced and sold cheaply, their price is orders of magnitude higher, driving addicts to robbery to fund their bad habits. Thousands of Americans are killed in robberies yearly—and many can thank our government's War on Drugs for their deaths.

Countless studies have shown that criminalizing drugs yields higher prices, more gang and criminal profits and activity, more thefts to afford the higher cost of drugs from the black market and damage to innocent, non-drug using citizens.[127] Yet the government publishes formal reports saying just the opposite, that "[d]rug-related crimes may decrease with legalization but other crimes, especially violent crimes, may increase."[128] We cannot trust a government report to be honest; serving the Perverted Triangle is the top priority of government employees, even when the policy is killing Americans, not helping them.

Drug laws are a financial windfall for lawyers and government/court jobs, but a deadly disaster for American citizens.

A failure from the start, Nixon's War on Drugs continued under all presidents and remains our idiotic, unconstitutional policy today—though most states have rightly nullified some aspects of it. It is a failure in reducing illicit drug use (which is much higher now),and more Americans are dying of overdoses than any point in modern history—plus deaths from the crime generated to pay for expensive drugs killing totally innocent citizens.

Our ongoing war on drugs is so bad, even the United Nation condemns and ridicules the stupidity and disastrous results. How in the world could the nation that championed liberty and freedom have the highest per capita rates of incarceration in the world? It's quite simple—the Perverted Triangle and Big Government benefit from this war. Lawyers love the huge business defending and prosecuting the millions of Americans accused of or jailed for doing something they have a constitutional right to do. The Perverted Triangle wins; citizens lose.

Quoting an American Civil Liberties Union staff member,

> [a] significant part of drug enforcement efforts have shifted from prosecuting drug crime to seizing property; indeed, by the late 1990s, many drug enforcement agencies were taking in more money from asset forfeiture than they received from their budgets. Self-financed police groups need not justify their activities through any regular budgetary process, and accordingly, such groups have constructed a veil of secrecy, thus enjoying freedom from legislative oversight and setting an agenda accountable to no one.[129]

Jobs, patronage, money, uncontrolled power—no way the Perverted Triangle will give this up. We need a war on the Perverted Triangle to stop the war on drugs.

And what a simple problem to solve. The Tenth Amendment is crystal clear in wording and legislative intent: the federal government may not pass any laws or act on any issue unless it is "enumerated"—specifically written out in the Constitution. The federal government has no enumerated power, no right to force Americans to not use a drug, cigarette, drink, or food. The Constitution grants us the solution to end the Perverted Triangle's War on Drug spending boondoggle and crime disaster with any one of three means—declare it unconstitutional (Supreme Court), nullify it (State Legislatures), or refuse it (American citizens). If someone wants to use addictive, damaging drugs we can't stop them and have no right to. If Big Government does not interfere, a market for their drug will provide it at the lowest possible price, reducing likelihood of being robbed by an addict or the gangs that illegal/high cost drugs support, and we will avoid the tax bill of a Perverted Triangle anti-drug program and the deaths from taxes.

The War on Drugs is also proof that the Supreme Court's obscenity in the 1937 Helvering decision, which erased the Tenth Amendment, was absolutely wrong. The Supreme Court is to interpret the Constitution; they cannot amend or ignore it, and there is absolutely no doubt about the crystal clear limit to federal power the Tenth Amendment provides. When the federal government outlawed alcohol they had to pass a constitutional amendment to do it because the Constitution does not mention and thus does not allow such federal policies. Then another Amendment was passed, repealing Prohibition after its miserable failure. What changed in the Constitution to make it constitutional to ban drugs,

The Drug War, Mass Incarceration and Race

June 2015

With less than 5 percent of the world's population but nearly 25 percent of its incarcerated population[1], the United States imprisons more people than any other nation in the world – largely due to the war on drugs. Misguided drug laws and harsh sentencing requirements have produced profoundly unequal outcomes for people of color. Although rates of drug use and sales are similar across racial and ethnic lines, Black and Latino people are far more likely to be criminalized than white people.[2]

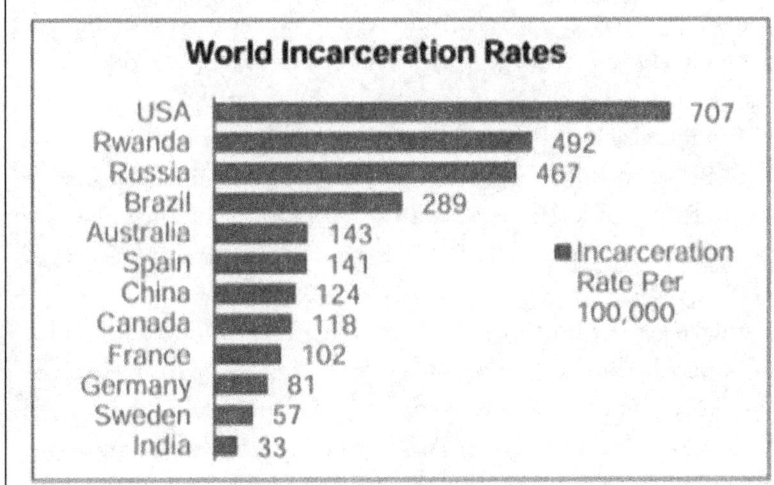

Source: International Centre for Prison Studies, World Prison Brief.[3]

Figure 30: War on Drugs fails to stop drugs but does achieve highest per capita incarceration rate in world.

but not alcohol? Nothing. What changed was the Supreme Court, threatened by FDR, decided to ignore and erase the Ninth and Tenth Amendments, and joined the Perverted Triangle.[130]

30. Top elected officials allowed to leak classified documents, undermining our intelligence capability and reducing national security

Our past two presidents and other senior politicians have broken multiple laws designed to protect classified information, vital to national security.[131]

I was an intelligence officer in the Air Force, and then worked in the Department of Defense and with the top DoD think tank, with top secret, codeword clearances. If I had done just 1 percent of the violations of intelligence information handling that Joe Biden, Hillary Clinton, and Donald Trump did, my career would have been ruined and I would have been severely punished, serving jail time. What these two presidents and Secretary of State did was absolutely wrong, dangerous for national security, and deadly for human intelligence assets. Hillary Clinton's illegal private email server contained information that was classified at a higher level than "Top Secret," with special access program information. "Top Secret" means information whose unauthorized disclosure could result in exceptionally grave danger to the nation. Top politicians get away with leaking classified information or breaking laws, get special treatment, are not punished for violating laws, not held accountable for their crimes.[132]

Grossly, dangerously unqualified Defense Secretary Pete Hegseth shared classified material he obtained from secure government communication networks via an unsecured commercial chat app, including upcoming military strike launch times. This was absolutely illegal. It happened multiple times, with uncleared personnel gaining access to the sensitive military information.[133] Had a military officer or an employee in the Pentagon leaked such sensitive operational information—any operational or classified information— they would have been severely punished, in accordance with the law.

Congressmen have get out of jail free cards enabling them to release classified information for personal political benefit. Their overriding objective is media coverage for more reelection votes, so they are tempted to release classified secrets, and often do so. In 2001 President George H. W. Bush complained of congressmen leaking classified information that put US troops at risk. But no action was taken. Like so many laws, they are not enforced against top members of the Perverted Triangle. Citizens are punished and jailed for disclosing classified information and jeopardizing national security—elected officials can break the law and sacrifice our lives with no penalty.[134]

Why Is Our Government Working to Kill Us?

There is not a government conspiracy to deliberately kill citizens. But because of lobbyists, career politicians always running for reelection and prioritizing campaign donations and votes, the lack of any constitutional limits to government spending, and policy since FDR coerced the Supreme Court into abandoning constitutional limits to government, a new and very bad system of government has evolved. The end to constitutional limits on government has led to massive growth in political power, career politicians, an entrenched, self-serving government bureaucracy, and uncountable thousands of new laws and regulations benefiting lawyers. Today any program or regulations with billionaires or an influential interest group behind it can be passed—even when it threatens and takes the lives of the silent majority.[135]

As described earlier, Allison's Models explain why governments make bad, self-serving decisions. In addition to organizational processes and bureaucratic politics, I added Model 4, political vote pandering and the Perverted Triangle of career politicians, government bureaucrats, and lawyers.

If you assume that our government is rational, following constitutional limits, prioritizing the benefit and lives of its citizens as it is supposed to, you are wrong on all three counts. There are largely good people in government, but the career politicians and bureaucrats that control the government keep passing new programs and spending to buy votes, driving our country into bankruptcy, dividing the nation, setting us up to be killed.

As Thomas Paine wrote in *Common Sense* in 1776, "Society in every state is a blessing, but Government, even in its best state, is but a necessary evil; in its worst state an intolerable one." Compared to the abuses colonists faced from Britain in 1776, Americans today face a government far more evil and increasingly fatal to its citizens.

> **Our unconstitutional, now perverted government is working to kill us. The system to prevent this, our Constitution, government, and courts, is clearly broken. It is killing us by the hundreds of thousands now, and if not fixed quickly, will be killing us by the hundreds of millions in a collapse.**

These examples of our government pursuing policies that kill us make sense only in the context of benefiting the Perverted Triangle (Model 4), which prioritizes their political power at the expense of our welfare and lives, stealing our Natural Rights, violating the Constitution.

The NIH was banned from funding gain of function research in 2014, but effectively evaded the temporary US ban by funding overseas research, including the Wuhan lab, the likely source of the Covid-19 virus that killed over one million Americans. It seems inconceivable that a US government agency could consider giving funds to a potential enemy like China—but remember Allison's Model 2: government agencies promote their interests and many sincerely believe that any medical research can be valuable. Since the US government no longer has any effective limits to what they can do, with the Ninth and Tenth Amendments wrongly but effectively erased by the Supreme Court, government bureaucrats believe and act as if they can do whatever they want.

Congressmen do not want to kill 90 percent of Americans, but most prioritize their reelection and are constantly working to get donations—not figuring out how to best protect American lives (Model 3). Utility companies do not want to be forced to work and spend on hardening the grid, so they buy votes of career politicians. And since a vote to harden the grid will raise electric bills and cost them reelection votes, legislators don't require this vital measure and we are set up for catastrophe.

As a result of Perverted Triangle (Model 4) promotion of laws, regulations, and business for lawyers, the US ranks at the top of countries with the highest per capita rate of imprisonment. The nation founded as the land of the free, with Natural Rights protected by a Constitution with absolute limits on government power, the champion of liberty, has been corrupted and perverted into a land of government and lawyer theft and abuse.

There is not a government conspiracy to deliberately kill citizens. But government killing of citizens is the direct result of Perverted Triangle politicians, bureaucrats, and lawyers prioritizing their reelection, power and profit, over citizens who no longer have Natural Rights or constitutional protections from abuse of government power.

The Perverted Triangle has turned the United States into the biggest police and prison state in the world. Rational, best for the country analysis and decision-making is sacrificed to the interests of the Perverted Triangle. Natural Rights are gone, ignored by the Courts, and Governments at all levels are free to abuse and (largely indirectly) kill citizens.

The unconstitutional government of the United States of America funded gain-of-function research on the 60 percent lethal H5N1 virus to make it air transmissible between mammals, and allowed release of instructions so anyone can create more deadly viruses.[136] They give money to potential enemies like China to help them develop deadly new viruses. They lie about the inevitable H5N1 pandemic coming (partly due to this gain-of-function research), and refuse to warn or prepare Americans for this inevitable, potentially imminent, deadly pandemic and the collapse that will result.

The National Institutes of Health (NIH) and Dr. Anthony Fauci denied funding studies that would make a coronavirus more dangerous to humans, but documents obtained from a Freedom of Information Act lawsuit show that this was a lie. Richard Ebright, professor at Rutgers University and laboratory director at the Waksman Institute of Microbiology, said the documents show "unequivocally" that NIH grants were used to fund controversial gain-of-function research at the Wuhan Institute of Virology in China. Ebright said: "The documents make it clear that assertions by the NIH director, Francis Collins, and the NIAID director, Anthony Fauci, that the NIH did not support gain-of-function research or potential pandemic pathogen enhancement in Wuhan are untruthful." [137] USAID was at least one of the vehicles used to fund Chinese research to make more deadly, more transmissible viruses.[138]

Senator Rand Paul, one of the very few national leaders left with any respect for the US Constitution's limits to government power, questioned and condemned Dr. Fauci in 2020 Senate testimony for funding Chinese government research at Wuhan. Dr. Fauci denied and insulted the Senator for the accusations. On his last day in office, one of his final acts as President, Biden issued a pardon to protect Dr. Fauci.

Gain-of-function research has some legitimate value in producing a valuable product or obtaining samples to develop vaccines, but with great dangers. Former Center for Disease Control and Protection (CDC) Director Redfield has condemned gain-of-function research as too risky and called for an end to it, but the biologists and scientists and government officials who fund them of course want it continued despite the risks of its misuse to create a deadly pandemic.[139]

The CDC denied any possibility that bioengineering, man-made experimentation could have led to the Covid-19 pandemic (later proved wrong), and the CDC covered up for years the fact that the US had actually funded gain-of-function research at the Wuhan lab. The US government providing funds and assisting biological research of a foreign nation like China that could be preparing to attack and destroy us is absolutely wrong. It's akin to the government funding tank and dive bomber R&D in Nazi German in the 1930s.

The worst result of unlimited government and the Perverted Triangle is that government no longer does its proper job of protecting citizens from threats they cannot handle on their own. Simply put, our perverted government's now unlimited power and focus on their political battles, pandering for votes and their benefit, leads to hundreds of thousands of citizens being killed annually now, and Americans set up for annihilation in a collapse.[140]

Big Companies, Billionaires, Lobbyists Use the Perverted Triangle to Exploit the Power of Unlimited Big Government

In 2010, Federal Reserve Chair Ben Bernanke defined a "too-big-to-fail" firm as "one whose size, complexity, interconnectedness, and critical functions are such that, should the firm go unexpectedly into liquidation, the rest of the financial system and the economy would face severe adverse consequences."[141] This was the excuse for government support, loans, bailouts that went to the biggest, wealthiest banks, owned by and paying salaries to millionaires and billionaires. The Federal Reserve is supposed to be an independent arm of government, but it is effectively owned and controlled by Wall Street, a tool for the biggest banks and wealthiest Americans who partner with the Perverted Triangle.[142]

The largest companies and monopolies can shape the regulations, and afford the costs of compliance with those regulations. Small companies and poor people trying to start a business can't shape the regulations, and can't afford the huge costs of compliance (both the direct and the larger indirect costs of staff and efforts to comply).

It is not just lobbying power, but insider access that firms like Goldman Sachs can exploit. The revolving door between the big banks and Perverted Triangle is one obvious means of both influencing the Perverted Triangle and gaining inside information that can be extremely valuable to a private sector firm. Since FDR, in every administration, Goldman Sachs executives have jumped in and out of senior government positions, back and forth, with clear conflicts of interest from the point of view of citizens, but obviously valuable to the firm paying them. [143] They also send mid-level executives into privileged positions inside the government. It is not just in the Treasury and financial agencies of government. I often saw Goldman Sachs executives working in the Pentagon in a special status. Not really government employees, and supposedly volunteering to help—without any relevant or valuable expertise I could ever discern, but working in some senior, privileged positions, with salaries far above government pay.

With the power of the biggest companies and banks, and big donations to career politicians, rich Americans can avoid getting killed by the Perverted Triangle.

By far the worst, most deadly corporate/billionaire abuse of the Perverted Triangle to profit at the expense of silent majority lives is the AI Company CEOs who have lobbied to eliminate any regulation of the most deadly technology mankind has invented. Later chapters will detail why Sam Altman, CEO of OpenAI,[144] and Alex Karp of Palantir are poised to be the worst criminal killers in history; thanks to their alliance and influence with the ruling parts of the Perverted Triangle today.

Billionaires can't get into Mount Weather or Raven Rock—but they can build their own survival facilities, or buy million dollar "Survival Condos." The vast majority of citizens will be left to die in a collapse.

Without an end to the unlimited power of government and career politicians focus on reelection and pandering for votes with pork and social programs rather than prioritizing national security, favoring lobbyists and campaign donations rather than citizens' lives, most Americans are unlikely to survive the coming collapses.[145]

Chapter Seven

DEVELOPING AND PRIORITIZING COLLAPSE RECOVERY CAPABILITIES

Preventing collapse disasters is extremely difficult and for many, likely impossible. But fortunately most of the preparations needed to avoid loss of law and order and minimize the deaths in a collapse are relatively simple and low-cost measures—as long as the Perverted Triangle can be controlled and not pork up the programs to buy votes. Federal and state governments should focus, their number one mission, on Prevention, Preemption, and Preparedness, P^3, for us to survive in the Age of Collapse. Some key measures are outlined in this chapter. Volunteers and actions by individuals are also vital—and very doable if government gets out of the way (with its regulations, zoning, building codes) and facilitates collapse survival preparation rather than being the biggest barrier to preparing as they are today.[1]

US Collapse Disaster Planning and Recovery Preparations Should Not Focus on the Initial "Trigger" Event, but Concentrate on Recovering from a Collapse

The disaster event that may start a collapse is usually less important to prepare for than the cascading aftereffects and the collapse. When the grid goes down there will be some initial deaths from the surprise loss of electricity, but it is the longer term impacts and the resulting collapse that will kill far more. The virus that starts a lethal pandemic will likely cause fewer deaths than the starvation and marauding of the collapse that follows.[2]

We should expect that most economic activity, public services, production of essential goods, and transportation will cease in a pandemic; failure of the electrical system, or other big disaster that scares the public and overwhelms law enforcement, will lead to widespread, long lasting loss of law and order. To minimize inventory costs, businesses, even hospitals, have "just-in-time" delivery of supplies, sourcing from lowest cost providers on the other side of the world. Even if your local trucker decides to continue working, with multiple long-distance suppliers and shippers involved in moving foodstuffs, the flow of goods will be slowed or stopped. Panic buying and hoarding will add to the problem of getting food to the population. How long will our public water supplies continue functioning when maintenance personnel fail to report for work? Our highly interdependent, just-in-time delivery economy is very vulnerable to disruptions. If the electric system goes down, factories won't operate, municipal water systems won't function, economic activity will quickly grind to a halt.

There is no valid way to predict how people will react in a severe pandemic or other collapse disaster. There are too many variables, uncertainties, and emotions involved. Rumors and the way the media portrays events will have a huge, uncontrollable impact. However politically incorrect or uncomfortable it may be for government officials to write about and plan for the likelihood that a segment of our population will loot and kill, many will exploit opportunities to break the law, and, in a panic situation where citizens feel their lives may be in danger, many normally good people will loot, take up arms, even kill to survive. While unpredictable and unpleasant, this kind of violence needs to be planned and prepared for, so it can be deterred ideally, or mitigated.

Regardless of what triggers a collapse, there are eleven requirements you need to survive. Figure 32 below shows how whatever disaster triggers a collapse, if you've got food, water, security, and the other requirements, you will likely survive unless you are an early victim of the trigger event disaster. There are things like medical care and communications that are also desirable and helpful, but collapse recovery capability should focus on the eleven must-have survival requirements.

Whatever resources you stockpile for a collapse, if you can't defend them, expect them to be stolen. Indeed, if you can't defend your stockpiled supplies you may be worse off having them—you've made yourself an attractive target. So security, the ability to defend yourself, your family, your stockpiled supplies, is probably the number one survival requirement.

When law and order is lost, people are going to "bug out" if they have safe survival communities to get to, or stay at home. With people not going to work the collapse will get worse, and looting and marauding expand. When municipal water system workers, electric plant operators, and nuclear power plant operators don't come to work, the impact of the initial disaster and panic can escalate rapidly to a

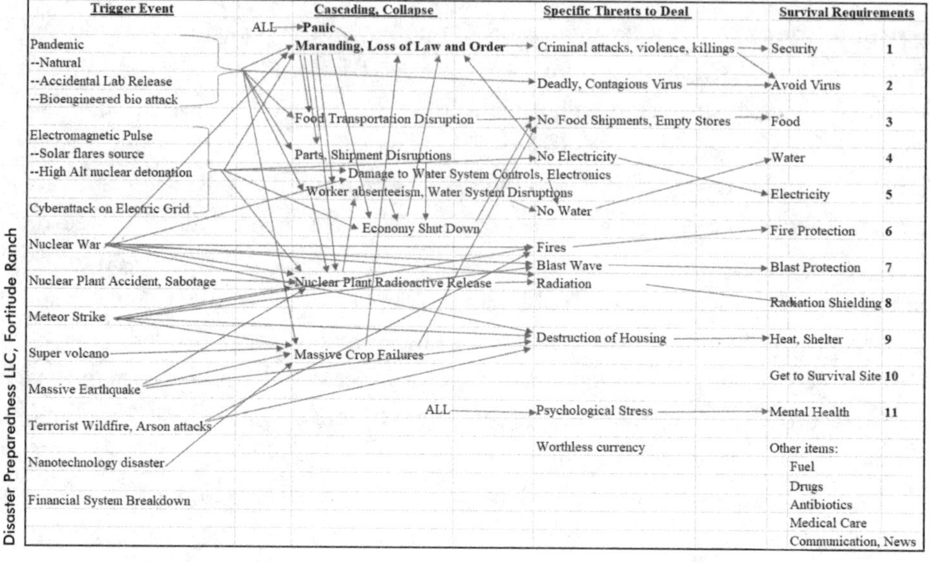

Figure 31: Deriving primary collapse survival requirements from all threats.

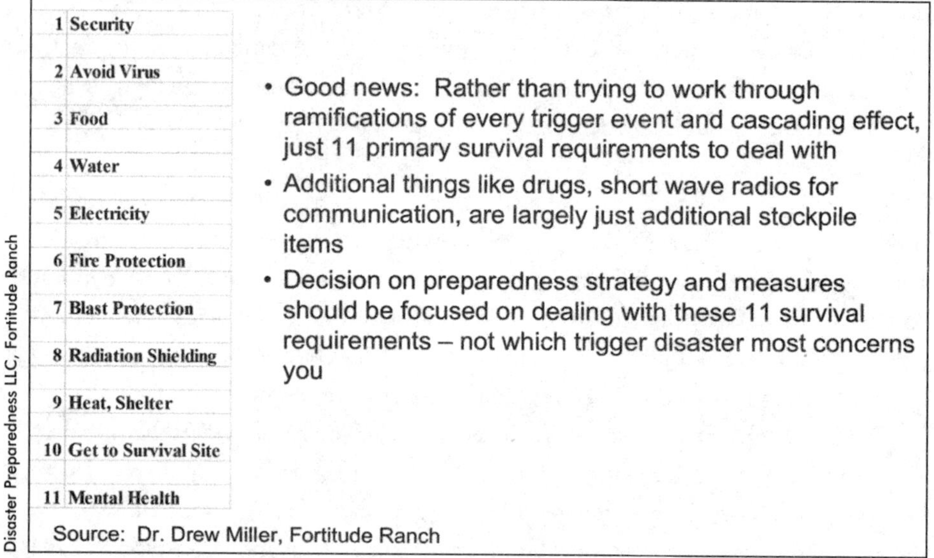

Figure 32: Eleven Collapse survival requirements.

far worse disaster, even spiral out of control. A bad collapse results that may last for months even if the initial disaster event was not that severe.

The government needs to put far more effort into building up our capability to maintain law and order when a massive disaster or attack occurs. If successful in doing so, there may be no collapse. But if a lot of the population starts looting and panic spreads, even a tenfold increase in law enforcement capability may not stop a collapse. Several low-cost, very feasible, wise measures to beef up law enforcement capability are proposed in this chapter.

If there is a pandemic, avoiding the virus is another must do. You will have to assume that even if the virus appears to die out in your area, it could come back—from an outsider bringing it in, or a mutation in the virus leading it to come back again. The 1918 Spanish Flu was horribly named. Spain had nothing to do with it; it started in Kansas. And it was not just in 1918—the virus mutated, had several waves, lasting from 1918 to 1920.[3] You need to expect that a pandemic can last for years, and be able to avoid/control contact with outsiders for years. For a survival community, as members come in they need to be quarantined, safely separated with a separate air source for days or a week to be sure they are not infected before you allow full access. Until you're sure no one in the group has been exposed to a virus, you need to be able to keep people separated with separate air supplies. Once all members arrive and are confirmed to not be infected, keeping outsiders away is key to avoiding virus infection.

Food and water requirements are obvious, addressed in detail in this and the following chapter.

We need to have massive food stockpiles, which we started doing during the Eisenhower administration but dropped as the Perverted Triangle, unconstrained by the Constitution, switched to public spending that yielded more reelection votes. As the welfare state took off in the 1960s, civil defense programs lost funding and were eliminated.

Every person who has any strip of ground to plant should be growing Jerusalem artichoke (sunchoke), a fantastic survival food (high calories per acre) that is a perennial and grows in most soils and climate zones.

If the grid goes down, municipal water systems go down. Without electricity for the multitude of pumps public water systems use, they do not work. Even if the collapse is not triggered by a grid loss event, you still need to assume municipal water systems will go down in any collapse disaster. If there is a serious marauder threat, workers will stay home, not risk venturing outside where they could get mugged or killed. They will prefer staying home to protect their families. Nor will electric plants operate long without workers showing up. So in any collapse, you should expect that municipal water systems and electric systems will be down in a week, even if they are not directly impacted by the initial disaster. Water systems may fail in hours—because many or most people will start filling up their bathtubs and every water container they can find. So water systems may be emptied in the first hours of a collapse.

The best place to survive a collapse, loss of law and order, is not just far from cities, but far from suburbia, in rural/wilderness settings where you've got far less threat of marauders. Rural areas also are more likely to have water and space to do some hunting (which won't last for long) and grow food. Leaving early as a collapse is developing is essential. Getting to your safe place without catching a spreading virus or getting mugged or killed by marauders may be the most difficult and uncertain part of a survival plan.

Fire protection, blast protection, radiation shielding are all requirements to survive a nearby nuclear detonation. If you live in a large city or near a potential military target (a base, port, nuclear power plant, national leadership facility), you could have a nearby or overhead nuclear detonation and suffer the thermal, blast, and radiation effects of a nuclear detonation. The vast majority of Americans will not be anywhere near a ground zero nuclear detonation, so blast protection is one of the eleven survival requirements that most do not have to worry about.

If you are in a big city or suburb, fires that start in a collapse are unlikely to be put out—they will burn until they run out of fuel. If it is a high wind day and the fires spread, huge parts of a city/suburb could be burned out. This is another reason why getting out of big cities and suburbs is normally a wise survival move ("bugging out" in prepper parlance).

Radiation shielding is important both if a nuclear attack occurs and possibly in most collapse situations. This is because nuclear plant operators won't come to work if there is a highly lethal virus spreading, or if the marauder threat is too high to risk traveling to work or leaving family at home. You have to be prepared for nuclear plant meltdowns and release of radiation. While there may be low levels of radioactive fallout (not like being at ground zero of a nuclear detonation or nuclear plant accident), if you are not shielded underground or with sandbags/earth outside concrete walls, the radiation exposure will raise your cancer rates and may kill you later.

Heat and shelter are requirements addressed later in the next personal survival chapter. Governments should not get involved in providing shelter for the population—it is too impractical and expensive. Far better for people to provide this on their own. But government needs to stop regulations and building codes and zoning restrictions that prevent people from having woodstoves (yes, many governments actually outlaw woodstoves) or building survival facilities.

Getting to your shelter, "bug-out location," survival community and mental health requirements for survival are personal responsibilities, addressed in the next chapter.

There Are Immediate, Low-cost, Vital Measures Governments Can Implement Now to Greatly Reduce the Number of Fatalities Suffered in a Collapse

The Figure below lists seventeen vital, very feasible steps we must take now to quickly improve our capability to survive a collapse.[4]

Figure 33: Key Public Policy Changes needed for Collapse Survival.

1. Government Civil Defense Food Stockpile Program
2. Government alternative water source system
3. Individual food/water stockpile, survival preparedness
4. Plant sunchoke, private gardens
5. Local sourcing of food and water
6. Guns and ammo to protect supplies (including "military capable" weapons)
7. Harden the electric grid, add micro grids, stockpile replacement transformers
8. Expand size of Army National Guard
9. All Guard and Reserve and Active Retired personnel must have firearms
10. Army Guard create a "Civil Ground Patrol" to mobilize volunteer help for disaster recovery operations
11. Build up reserve police/sheriff forces
12. Identify key workers for vital utilities, nuclear power plants, LEOs, military
13. Encourage rather than restrict volunteers to help put out wildfires
14. Insist on Natural Right to Survive, use private property—refuse zoning, codes, regulations that endanger your survival plans without causing harm to others
15. Provide honest warnings and alerts about collapse threats
16. National stockpiles of critical supplies we cannot source locally
17. Control AI, treating it as more dangerous than nuclear weapons. Form an international alliance of countries that will control AI, and fight/punish countries that allow AI-generated WMD

As explained in the "Government is Working to Kill Us" chapter, the Eisenhower administration era civil defense program was dropped as Lyndon Johnson's huge "Great Society" welfare programs took off. More Republicans switched in the 1960s from defending constitutional limits to government to feed on the powerful vote-buying pork of adding more welfare entitlements for everyone. Civil defense food stockpiles were not as popular and were dropped. Civil defense is a low-cost, unseen program, for a possible future need—little vote-buying power relative to delivering a government job or an entitlement payment or a new defense contract for a company in your district.[5]

We must stockpile long shelf life (twenty-five years or more) storage prepared foods and grain. Do not focus on nutritional balance, but calories. In a survival situation, it is calories that matter, not what is best for your long-term health.

The government should set a goal of stockpiling at least three months of food for every citizen, in facilities that local law enforcement can control and protect and manage. Once this three-month supply is established, we should expand it over time to a year's supply. China has stockpiled two years of food for their citizens—our irresponsible government has none for citizens, just stockpiled food for themselves.

Stockpiling potable water for months is not feasible, but at low-cost federal, state, and local governments can identify sources of water for citizens to use in a collapse when the grid and municipal water systems are unlikely to be operating, and publish maps for citizens on their locations. The water should be identified as potable, ready to drink, or needs to be boiled to safely drink. Cities should not assume a need for or try to promote providing potable water for all their residents. Densely populated cities will likely be abandoned in a collapse with no food shipments coming in. Even if the electric grid is up and the municipal water systems are working at the start of a collapse, the grid or water systems will fail when the workers stop reporting for duty. Once the municipal water system stops in a densely populated city, it must be abandoned. And with a much larger number of gang members and generally more violent/bad people in big urban cities, the marauder threat will be worst in big cities; they are likely to be abandoned.

For all government programs, the Perverted Triangle, especially career politicians with reelection always top of mind, will try to pork them up with more spending, more government and contractor jobs, to buy votes. Citizens need to be on guard, watching and pressuring government to provide the service at minimal cost. With massive government debt and horrendous tax costs at the federal and many state and local levels, collapse survival preparations need to be low-cost, or they are unlikely to get done.

Individuals need to stockpile food and have the ability to grow food. This is covered in the next chapter.

To encourage planting of the best survival crops like sunchokes, potatoes, and corn (high calories/acre), the government should first get rid of regulations that inhibit this. For example, there are large volume potato seeds that you can buy overseas that are ideal for collapse survival, seed stockpiles that the USDA has thus far refused to approve, not because of any biological or legitimate risk, but due to domestic politics, pandering for votes.[6]

Citizens must demand that federal and state governments mandate hardening of our electric grid, and a switch to microgrids[7] where feasible, since AI will likely develop new means to destroy even hardened electric grids. Since the huge transformers, thousands of them across the US electric grid, are the most difficult item to replace when the grid is attacked, with little US transformer manufacturing capacity, we need to stockpile transformers and protect them from enemy agent attacks.

To reduce the breakdown in law and order, ensure critical workers come to work, escort truck drivers, and move key supplies, the Army National Guard needs to be trained and equipped (many don't even have small arms) to do crowd control, guard stockpiles, and provide massive support of local law enforcement. The Department of Defense is not interested in this homeland defense mission (with the exception of the Army Guard) since the Department of Homeland Security is the lead agency for this mission. A later chapter recommends a way to fix this problem and get the DoD focused on homeland defense and collapse recovery as its top priority—not fighting enemy military forces overseas.

We need to greatly expand the size of the National Guard, with small arms provided to every soldier—not expensive weapons systems. It is a surprise even to most people in the DoD that most National Guard members don't have small arms and ammo.[8] Many states have Air and Army Guard forces where the vast majority of them have no weapons to do useful security duty. Additional "homeland defense troops" should serve part time, surging to full time only when needed. All Guard members should be equipped and trained to handle small arms so they can fight marauder groups, secure stockpiled food and vital facilities, and conduct recovery operations. Some need to have chem-bio-nuclear protective masks and suits, training on crowd control and quarantine operations. Fortunately, this is very inexpensive equipment and training relative to military combat. These homeland defense Guard forces would be strictly part-time positions, just the traditional one weekend a month and two weeks' summer exercise requirements. Homeland defense Army Guard units would not requiring many full-time personnel in the units.

In 2024 the Army National Guard's budget was approximately $8 billion for military personnel, $6 billion for operations and maintenance, $5 billion for procurement and military construction—just 2 percent of massive $825 billion US defense spending. The Army National Guard has just 325,000 members, down in recent years—less than one tenth of 1 percent of the US population. The Army Reserve budget is smaller, about $5 billion.

Expansion of the Army National Guard must be for low-cost security personnel with small firearms—not military equipment to fight other armies. These security forces need minimal equipment, training, or fitness for a far less demanding role: local guards. Many former or retired military members could do this guard security force role, and should be encouraged to. They don't even need vehicles; they will be working locally and can simply be reimbursed for use of personal vehicles. Nor should these troops be required to meet full Army Guard standards or get trained to do traditional military operations. They will not be "infantry" to fight foreign armies, but a far easier, simpler, less demanding role of local security guards. The Perverted Triangle, career politicians, will try to milk this program for maximum spending and pork in their district. We can't allow this; we need to add several hundred thousand, ideally a million new Army Guard members, and can do so cheaply if they are added in small "homeland security units," part of and overseen by the Army Guard, but hired, trained, and equipped with just small arms for the very simple mission of guarding stockpiled food, critical facilities, and when necessary, shooting marauders. Some water collection sites may need to be guarded or patrolled by security forces to prevent marauder groups from using them as places to ambush citizens.

Soldiers trained for military missions in the Guard and Active Duty forces can actively hunt and engage, destroy marauder groups. The Air National Guard should provide forces to conduct both security, guard missions, transport critical supplies, and provide reconnaissance to track down large marauder groups.

Ideally these added security units would be county or city based, and called up in a major disaster or collapse only to work in their local area. This will greatly improve the likelihood that they will respond to the call of duty, knowing they are helping to protect their community and family and friends.

While the Guard and Reserve do fantastic work, in a domestic disaster, long-term collapse situation, we must not assume that all members will report to or stay on duty if they cannot be sure their families are safe. If it is a severe, long-lasting collapse, such as one caused by a pandemic or loss of the electric system, a large percentage of National Guard troops, and to a lesser degree, Active Duty Regular armed forces, may refuse to report to duty or later desert in order to protect their family at home. There must be robust preparations for family survival so military members can focus on recovery ops duties, not be abandoning their posts to rush home to their families (as many, perhaps most first responders and medical personnel are likely to do).

Active duty, regular forces should be significantly cut, many overseas bases closed. If there is a big world war that we do want to participate in, the much larger Army Guard will give us more manpower than we could possibly afford with active duty forces. This is addressed in more detail in a later chapter.

There are some ways that the DoD is very cost-efficient. Civil Air Patrol (CAP) leverages sixty-five thousand volunteers in an official Air Force Auxiliary. CAP was not an invention of government bureaucracy; it was created by volunteers before World War II, is older than the US Air Force. CAP volunteers conducted search and rescue missions for lost aircraft, disaster recovery assistance, and even anti-U-boat patrols and attacks in WWII. As an official auxiliary of the US Air Force today, CAP gets small AF funding to conduct search and rescue and a huge variety of disaster recovery operations (aerial photography of flooding and fires for example) using small aircraft and well-trained volunteer manpower.

A much bigger, ground focused "Civil Ground Patrol" (CGP) is needed for collapse disaster relief capability.[9] A CGP would be vital to help mobilize more organized, disciplined help to distribute goods and help law enforcement maintain order. CGP limited to unarmed missions such as collecting and reporting information on local conditions, assisting in supply deliveries, running communications (CAP has a huge network of official USAF radios), and providing assistance to deployed Guard and federal forces in the community could make a life and death difference for millions of Americans.[10]

While CAP is under the Regular, active-duty Air Force, CGP would fit better under the Army National Guard, not the Regular Army. Civil Ground Patrol units should be dually aligned with a local law enforcement agency and the state Army Guard, and train with both organizations. Surplus National Guard equipment should be donated to CGP. Local CGP units should be a formal auxiliary and part of the Army Guard, using Guard equipment and facilities when available. Existing CAP units (in all US States) could assist in the launch of Civil Ground Patrol, and likely provide a cadre of senior and cadet members to help get it going.

Another benefit for the Guard and Army is that CGP could help in motivating, recruiting, and doing initial training of new members. Many CAP members (who can start at age twelve as cadets) end up joining the Air Force, already trained in basic drill, customs and courtesies, aviation, and basic military order.

CGP's very public community recruiting and operations would also help spread the message about the need for increased public preparedness for dealing with disasters that could lead to a collapse.

We also need to build up big reserve police and sheriff forces. We have less than one hundred thousand reserve LEOs. We should have at least one million of them; recruited from retired military and LEO members, paid a low fee for regular training, equipped with just small arms and protective gear.

Encourage all separated and retired law enforcement and military personnel to join in local law enforcement emergency reserve forces. Do not subject reserve policemen to huge training requirements or make them study local laws, nor pile on onerous regulations. Let them get quick, simple, minimal training in serving as guards and truck escorts, stockpile small arms and ammo for them, and issue them uniforms labeling them as reserve police forces. Follow the National Guard model (and maybe drill with, get trained by Army Guard MPs and Air Guard Security

Police) and do periodic (but much less than one weekend a month) paid training. Favor using them in their hometowns so they can serve as reserve policemen in their community and also keep watch over their homes.

If we have a million Army Guard members, 1.3 million current LEOs, a reserve LEO force of another million, we'd have 3.3 million armed, reliable, trained personnel to deter and fight marauders. There are 1 million known gang members and 2 million Americans in jail who are primed and ready to be marauders. I cannot estimate the number of normally "good" Americans who have already planned to maraud in a collapse, but they may be deterred by a large, well prepared, quickly mobilized, armed force ready to kill them.[11] If we can add another million or two in Civil Air and Ground Patrols, unarmed but in uniform, handling tasks to free up the Army Guard/LEOs to stay in the streets and on guard duty, we would have a formidable, no threat to democracy, low-cost, fantastic force to prevent some collapses and deter/fight marauders to reduce our casualties and improve our ability to recover from collapse disasters that do occur.

We need to identify key workers for vital utilities, nuclear power plants, so LEOs and military members can provide them escort to work, and also protect their families if there is a marauder threat and protect their homes if necessary to get them to agree to go to work. The LEOs and National Guard members also may need to have their homes protected so they report to work. It is essential to keep career politicians out of this process, preventing them from attempting to exploit this program to buy reelection votes. Many other professions, like warehouse owners and medical personnel, will argue that they should be included and protected. We cannot let the Perverted Triangle pork up and pervert the program—just vital workers to keep nuclear power plants from getting destroyed, water and electric systems running if possible, and LEO/military members families identified for protection so security forces will go to work.

As explained earlier, managers of the highly unionized firefighters in the US prevent volunteers from helping stop wildfires even though the majority of wildfire work is digging ditches, removing flammable material far from the fire, and clearing firebreaks. Union managers and rules direct firefighters to block volunteers at the start of a wildfire—not immediately fight the fire when the chances of putting it out are best. They do this not to save lives but protect union jobs and higher pay. This practice must be outlawed. Terrorists and enemy agents starting wildfires may be an opening stage of an attack that leads to a collapse. During a collapse, firefighters are unlikely to be available, making natural or deliberate wildfires even more dangerous. Government firefighting unions need to be outlawed or reformed, forcing them to use and manage able-bodied volunteers to dig/cut/clear firebreaks.

National stockpiles of critical goods we must import, especially from countries like China, are essential. We have a stockpiled oil reserve to reduce the consequences of getting cut off from imports, but there are many other, more important resources we need to stockpile: minerals, antimony, arsenic, bismuth, cobalt, chromium, graphite, manganese, and tungsten. Even better, in the interest of national defense and homeland collapse recovery, mining and processing of vital strategic materials needs to return to the US government regulations, zoning, building codes, and other barriers that prevent this need to be changed or removed in the interest of national survival. We must not just stockpile viral protective equipment, but also get domestic production back to prevent risk of China/India not supplying us. We must vastly improve our research to develop better vaccines and ensure we have far more production capability to quickly produce them—and under collapse conditions, no BS assumptions of law and order, unprotected workers abandoning their families to come to factories, or long-distance sourcing of inputs.

We must immediately control AI, treating it as more dangerous than nuclear weapons. This likely means limiting AI development to offline, ultra-secure facilities that are government controlled, with third party and an international watchdog regulatory group inspecting as well. To protect against other countries not controlling AI, we need to form an international alliance of countries that will control AI, and fight/punish countries that allow AI-generated WMD. This will be extremely difficult, but failure to quickly control AI being abused by bad people/groups/nations now to make new WMD and eventually superintelligent AGI working to exterminate humans, will lead to disastrous collapses no one may survive. A later chapter in this book outline how we can control Tool AI and prevent creation of superintelligent AGI.

Personal survival preparedness recommendations are covered in the next chapter of this book.[12]

Stop Jailing People for Nonthreatening Crimes, Reduce High Level of Incarceration, Let Nonviolent Inmates Work Wildfire Mitigation, Plant Gardens for Early Release, Prepare for Collapse Executions and Release

When the grid goes down, which may be the initial disaster trigger event, or a later cascading result of some other disaster that triggers a collapse, the two million Americans in prisons will be getting out. Unless it's an AGI generated collapse, and the AI human extermination plan includes killing prisoners before they can get out, in any bad collapse imprisoned people will be released or escape. You cannot operate a prison without electricity. The door controls, lighting, all aspects of operation require electricity. That is why jails have backup generators to ensure they never lose power. But the fuel for this will only last a few days—and the guards may be gone in the first hours of a collapse. You can't expect any reasonable person to risk catching a deadly virus, being attacked by marauders while going to work, or abandoning their families to go to jail to help ensure that prisoners don't escape. The worker absenteeism rate for jail guards will be near 100 percent in a bad collapse. Whoever is there in charge may decide to release the prisoners, or they will decide on their own they are getting out with too few guards there to stop them.[13]

When these prisoners, two million of them in the US, come out, they will have no preparations. The vast majority are unlikely to have family/friends outside the gate ready to help or take care of them. They will be unprepared; know they need to start stealing food and weapons if they want to survive. Many will be well experienced in the arts of looting and marauding, very willing to kill.

The US prison population is a powder keg disaster waiting for ignition after any big collapse disaster starts. Though an obvious problem we must be prepared for, do an Internet search and you'll find zero government acknowledgement of this vulnerability, and no plans to address it. This is more evidence that government at all levels does not bother preparing to protect citizens.

We should consider giving nonthreatening prisoners the ability to do hard, productive work clearing forests of dead trees and cutting firebreaks to enable more successful containment of wildfires in exchange for early release from prison. Wildfires are a far worse threat than we are witnessing today for two reasons. First, they are a huge vulnerability for the country, an easy target for foreign agents and terrorists to exploit to kill Americans and tie up first responders. Second, in a collapse, there will be no firefighters available to put them out or organize volunteer efforts (with far less manpower available when people must focus on defending their homes, bug-out locations, and survival communities). We need to drastically reduce our vulnerability to wildfires now. Commuting sentences for prisoners who do fire mitigation and tree-clearing work offers savings from less prison time, reduces our wildfire threat, and reduces the number of likely marauders in a collapse.

For prisoners we can't trust or are not capable of clearing dead trees and cutting firebreaks, put them to work in planting sunchokes on public lands, along public roads. Empty land around prisons should be covered in well tended, highly productive gardens focused on raising high calorie/acre crops (not lettuce and salad food).

Finally, prisons and jails need to prepare and practice plans for collapse time release and execution of some prisoners, and conversion of jails to homeland security force bases. Prisoners and prisons provide the perfect marauder group and base to exploit and murder surrounding citizens. Many prisons have organized gangs and groups, with discipline and leadership, criminal and ruthless killing skills. They will likely form marauder groups that over the course of a collapse could kill many times their number.[14] The prison is a fantastic survival facility—easy to defend, with shielded rooms, kitchens, all the facilities needed. We must be sure that prisons are used for Guard and security forces—not bases for powerful marauder gangs. The stockpiled food for the inmates is a valuable collapse asset. Unless we plan and prepare, many of the two million jailed inmates are going to form marauder groups based out of their prisons and kill ten million or more innocent citizens in a collapse.

LEOs, jail wardens, and the National Guard can work out better plans, but in general, all jails and prisons need to plan and practice a crisis time plan such as:

- Identify in advance prisoners too violent/dangerous to release.
- Plan and confidentially practice how to quickly execute them, most likely in their cells via guards coming with shields (must assume they will know about such plans and be prepared with things to throw) to shoot them. After the first shot, jail announcement that "most prisoners are going to be released due to a pending nationwide collapse disaster, but a few of the most violent and dangerous prisoners are now being executed. Inmates stay in the back of your cells, stay quiet, and you will soon be released. Anyone attempting to stop executions will be shot."
- After designated high risk prisoners executed, announce, "The executions are over. Prepare to be released. You must within five minutes exit the prison and proceed peacefully to make your way home on your own. Anyone who is violent will be shot. Anyone who attempts to steal things from the prison will be shot." Provide directions on best route to exit prison.
- Guards/LEOs retreat to a secure place and remotely (electronic) open doors and protect themselves; shooting any prisoners who attempt to attack them. Ideally guards/LEOs will protect the stockpiled food and medical supplies, not let prisoners break in and take any of this.
- Convert the prisons to bases for Guard and security forces for recovery operations.

Ideally, National Guard troops would be there to both back up the guards and better control the release of prisoners. This is not likely in a fast-moving collapse but, if possible, Guard troops could form lines and direct the prisoners out into rural or better areas for their release. Splitting them up, forcing them out in opposite directions, and deliberately sorting to try to break up known gangs/affiliations would also be good. The Guard officers could also deliver stern warnings to the leaving inmates to try to get home or contact family and arrange to be picked up, not attempt to steal anything or enter any buildings because people are prepared for a collapse and will shoot any intruders.

In peacetime, now, prior to a collapse, the POTUS for federal inmates, the governor for state/local prisoners, need to task prison wardens/LEOs to prepare plans for executing violent inmates who pose a grave risk. Prison wardens and chiefs of police, county sheriffs, all need to be instructed that they may execute highly dangerous inmates in a collapse if jails cannot be safely operated, with full pardons for them and all other personnel involved in the collapse time executions. All this should be done confidentially, via classified executive orders, no prisoner or official names released. In a collapse, normal law and order is gone, and every individual and the nation will be in survival mode. Many far worse things will happen, and we must prioritize survival of good citizens, not convicted felons whose release could result in the deaths of far more innocent, good citizens.[15]

Many more preparations are needed, but these are the most important. The good news is that they are relatively easy, low-cost preparations—trivial expense relative to an additional aircraft carrier, or $350 million for one F-22 fighter, or adding an armored division to the Army.

Such preparations will be controversial, but they are very doable, affordable, and more vital and valuable to saving American lives than the vast majority of programs in the Department of Defense, Department of State, or Department of Homeland Security.

If we aggressively stockpile food, get most people raising sunchokes and gardening, harden the grid and add more resilient microgrids, expand Army Guard and police/sheriff reserve security forces, add Civil Ground Patrol, and promote rather than hassle and prevent prepping, we may avoid some collapses entirely. If the initial disaster trigger event is not that bad, most people expect it will not be sufficient to overwhelm the expanded capacity to maintain law and order and not starve to death, the number of people who start looting/marauding will be smaller, more controllable. With a major nuclear attack, highly contagious/lethal pandemic, some initial disasters may be too bad and overwhelming to avoid a collapse, but with these measures we can at least reduce the fatalities and speed up our recovery time.

Many Other More Difficult, Unpopular, but Necessary Changes Are Needed, but Unlikely to be Implemented Until After People Have Suffered a Collapse

A highly effective, trusted, honest, proper government might have enough citizens' respect and support to implement disruptive and costly plans to improve collapse survivability. We don't have that in the United States, so many other big changes needed for surviving in the Age of Collapse aren't feasible to implement until after people have suffered a collapse and realize that big sacrifice and some revolutionary changes are needed.

As Nassim Taleb explained, people "are made to be superficial, to heed what we see and not heed what does not vividly come to mind."[16] What we don't regularly see, we tend to ignore. We tend not to think carefully, not in a disciplined manner, often irrationally. The majority of citizens are not going to seriously, carefully think about the consequences of the Age of Collapse or prepare until they have experienced a big collapse disaster.[17]

Densely populated big cities will be the worst place to be in a collapse. In the Age of Collapse, with repeated collapse disasters happening, wise people will cease living in big cities, and many may not be willing to work or ever enter huge metro areas. Preppers are well aware that cities will likely be death traps in a collapse, and urban preppers prioritize plans to bug out as early as possible. Once a collapse disaster has occurred and people experience a collapse, everyone will recognize that we need to reduce densely populated urban areas to survive in the Age of Collapse. Government policies that promote and subsidize big cities (subway systems for example) should end. People and businesses should be encouraged to favor low population density areas to work, not exceed local sources of food and water.

With bioengineering and AI, the ability of an individual to create a deadly virus, we need to change international travel and implement mandatory quarantine/hold stays for all international travel. After we experience an H5N1 or bioengineered virus attack that causes a really deadly pandemic (not the less than 1 percent lethality of Covid-19, but double-digit lethality), most countries may figure out that easy international travel must end. Expect governments to require anyone entering the country to stay in controlled facilities (hotels, not jails) for several days upon arrival. This provides time to watch and be sure no passenger or crewmen is infected, ability to deny entry to someone who while not infected yet came from an area where a pandemic has started. It also provides plenty of time to check watch lists, investigate suspicious people. Passengers will have to pay for this lock up or "hold" time, but an industry will adapt to add great airport/port holding hotel entertainment and work facilities. Ocean liner travel will boom since they can do this hold time while on the ocean. Airliners and some businesses will suffer from this, but it is an Age of Collapse reform that will have to happen at some time.

There will be many other big and disruptive changes in how our economy functions, addressed in the last chapter of this book. International trade and sourcing of critical materials will plummet in favor of stockpiling/inventories of critical materials and far more local production. Big changes in where and how people live will occur. Big urban cities will probably be devastated during a bad collapse and abandoned in the Age of Collapse.

While senseless to try to pursue many of these reforms now, we need to be thinking about how to adjust our economy and our lifestyles to better avoid collapses and survive when they do occur. The last chapter does provide an overview of the revolutionary changes we must have to live, work, and behave to survive and possibly thrive in the Age of Collapse.[18]

Limit Continuity of Government Programs, Ban Legislators from Having Protection the Populace Lacks, Ban Government Seizure of Private Property in a Collapse

My prediction is that government officials and politicians will continue to ignore these vital preparedness measures because they aren't willing to risk spending funds and raising costs to citizens for measures the public isn't demanding and businesses and special interest groups don't offer campaign donations for.[19]

Thus, another recommended step to improve incentives for the irresponsible Perverted Triangle to improve preparedness and help citizens raise their odds of survival is to eliminate the number one priority of law enforcement in a disaster: Continuity of Government. One of the reasons why citizens in cities and suburbs won't have police to respond to their calls for help from marauders in a collapse is that more police will be assigned to guard City Hall and protect congressmen, legislators, mayors, and city councilmen. This should not be a priority; elected officials should get no preferential security treatment in a collapse. Law enforcement officers and National Guard troops should be banned from providing special protection in a collapse to legislators. They should get no special treatment beyond what citizens get. The president, governors, top decision-makers should continue to receive their normal peacetime security. But only top decision-makers and vital government officials in the relatively few homeland security agencies should be sheltered and protected—not legislators, not local government leaders, and not the IRS and most government agencies that are worthless in collapse recovery.

Congressmen should be denied shelter at Mount Weather or any other government facility in a collapse. Politicians should take their chances with the rest of the populace and suffer if they failed to protect citizens, not get priority protection.

Some additional incentive for them to focus on what should be their top priority, such as security and improving our collapse preparedness, would be a good thing. We must ban policies of protecting top politicians, elected officials, and government bureaucrats at taxpayer expense while the rest of us are left to die.[20]

Chapter Eight

PEOPLE MUST BECOME PREPPERS TO SURVIVE THE AGE OF COLLAPSE

The odds of getting our irresponsible, self-serving government to make the vital reforms outlined in the last chapter are extremely low. Until there is a bad collapse, most people will ignore Black Swan risks and the Perverted Triangle will continue to advance their benefits and power at the cost of citizens' lives.[1]

Even when we do get responsible government back to prepare robust homeland defense and recovery measures, the technologies to develop WMD are out there, AI will make WMD threats much worse, and we will not be able to avoid all collapse disasters.

Figure 34: 11 Primary Survival Requirements.

1. Security
2. Avoid Virus
3. Food
4. Water
5. Electricity
6. Fire Protection
7. Blast Protection
8. Radiation Shielding
9. Heat, Shelter
10. Get to Survival Site
11. Mental Health

(not a survival requirement, but a practical one is Affordability) (Source: Disaster Preparedness, LCC, Fortitude Ranch)

With or without good government and collapse recovery capabilities, individuals have primary responsibility and impact on staying alive in a collapse. Everyone must become preppers and get ready to survive in the Age of Collapse.

Surviving a Collapse Depends on Your Ability to Meet the Eleven Survival Requirements—Affordably

Every person needs to be prepared for a collapse that could last for many months or years—not the nonsense of three days' of food and water that the federal government calls preparedness. The focus should be on dealing with a collapse more than specific trigger events. Citizens should know that they need the means to protect themselves when law enforcement is overwhelmed and there is a breakdown in law and order. People in big cities should be advised to plan and prepare to get out, since supplying major cities with food and water and maintaining law and order will be particularly difficult, often impossible.[2]

The eleven survival requirements presented earlier must be met to survive a collapse with little economic activity going on, and widespread loss of law and order. For the vast majority of people, an additional requirement, or constraint, is you must be able to afford the cost (in time as well as money) of preparing.

What many non-preppers fail to recognize is that if you stockpile supplies but cannot defend yourself, you may be worse off in a bad collapse—just a more tempting target.

Security for survival means more than just weapons for defense. You want to have a very defensible house or survival community, and ideally a location with low marauder threat. The vast majority of prepper bug-out locations are in remote, rural areas to reduce (or at least delay) the threat of organized, large, well equipped and run marauder gangs.

Big cities are the worst places to be in a collapse. Even if municipal water and electricity are functioning, the grocery stores will likely be bought out or looted in the first few hours, and marauding will probably start immediately. Gangs and bad people in cities know that when police are overwhelmed with a disaster, they can't respond to home break-ins or store looting. This urban violence will quickly spread into adjoining suburbs. As a collapse progresses, two bad trends are likely. First, previously law-abiding people will figure out that they face a big risk of death from dehydration, contaminated water, starvation, or being killed by marauders after their supplies. Many people will decide that their best chance of survival is to start looting to get more supplies, guns, and ammunition. Second, as people flee cities and suburbs, the marauder threat will expand into rural and wilderness areas. Many marauder groups that start in cities will migrate to more rural areas both because they are safer and because there are folks to loot there. There will be some marauders operating in rural areas from the start, and their numbers will rise as the collapse continues. As a collapse goes into months, there is unlikely to be any territory anywhere that does not have people out scavenging for food and marauding.

To survive a bad collapse with no police protection gone and a large part of the unprepared population stealing and marauding and killing to survive, you must have a lot of well-armed people. Gang members are certainly going to be armed with semi-automatic rifles, and likely to use them offensively. According to a Gallup poll, 44 percent of Americans live in a household with guns.[3] This is likely an undercount—many people won't admit they have weapons, fear government lying and collection of data to monitor/control weapons, or may not know that someone else in the household does have one hidden away. Many Americans have weapons in their bug-out locations, or stashed in buried "caches" where they can get them. A double-barrel shotgun or semi-automatic .22 rifle are nice weapons, but for collapse defense you need "military capable" weapons like AR-15s, with high capacity magazines, and semi-automatic or pump 12 gauge shotguns.

Preppers, like most Second Amendment supporters, are not going to give up their semi-automatic defense rifles if a ban on these weapons is passed. They will strongly oppose such legislation and likely refuse to obey laws passed that would weaken their ability to defend themselves when law and order is lost and well-armed, "military capable" marauder groups are a threat.

For virus protection, the disadvantages of cities, advantages of rural/wilderness areas, are also substantial. If you face a human-to-human contagious virus, keeping far from people is vital. Wearing a mask is wise, but probably far from adequate for most viruses. When a pandemic is spreading, the sooner you can get masks on and get away from strangers, the more likely you are to avoid the virus. The Collapse Survivor App's key feature is a threat alert system that "pushes" alerts to your phone, like a warning that a deadly virus has started spreading. The CDC and governments should be providing such alerts, but due to perverse, politician-serving constraints, they will likely be late with pandemic warnings out of fear of issuing a false alarm or panicking the public.

You must assume that everyone you see is infected, and that the virus is lying on every surface you could touch. Do not go to the grocery store to try to get some extra supplies at the early stage of a pandemic (or likely any collapse due to the threat of marauding/looting). Avoiding a virus should be the top priority.

If you wisely have a remote bug-out location or survival community, getting to your survival location without catching a virus (or getting robbed/killed by marauders) must be planned and prepared for. Leave early and head directly to your safe spot with no stops, windows up in your vehicles and vents closed. You should stockpile enough gasoline to get to your bug-out location so there is no need to risk virus exposure (or looting/marauders) at a gas station.

There will not be much traffic on roads since few people will be going to work, and all the government can do in any disaster is tell people to go home and stay at home. Only a small percentage of urban and suburban populations that have bug-out facilities or survival communities will be on the road, so the first day or two of a collapse should have relatively light road traffic.

Many people assume that roadblocks will go up in a pandemic and restrict their travel. Air travel may be stopped immediately. Governors can order airports in their states closed, and many will. But closing roads is difficult and will take Army Guard forces. They will take at least twenty-four hours to be ready. Effectively blocking all roads is extremely difficult and likely not feasible in most areas. There are too many roads, and there is some ability for people to drive off road to get around blockades. If you leave early in a pandemic, you will probably have no problem with road closures.

Nor will small remote communities likely block roads. Some preppers fear local militias will block roads to keep fleeing city dwellers from getting into their towns. They will not do this since it is best to have cars passing nonviolently through town, not having people fighting the blockading force or abandoning their cars and walking into town—and, now forced to try to shelter, maraud there because the roadblock stopped them. But the wisest thing to do is get early threat alerts of a pending collapse and get to your survival location ASAP.

If the pandemic is from a new virus, no one will know what the incubation period is, how long people can have the virus and be spreading it, but not be so sick that they are disabled or showing obvious signs of infection. Therefore you should respect Murphy's Law and assume that people can be infected and contagious for days without looking sick. For most viruses, this period is very short, rarely more than a day or two. At Fortitude Ranch our policy is that we will separate or quarantine people for a week to be absolutely sure they are not infected.

The length of time you need to keep people with a virus away could be years. It will be at least several months before a vaccine can be developed. Unfortunately, in May 2025 the Trump administration cancelled a contract for developing an influenza mRNA vaccine (including H5N1). Developing a vaccine from scratch with non-mRNA can take six months to a year. But even if there is fantastically effective and fast production of a vaccine, the virus may mutate and the vaccine may not work against the next variant. A pandemic may last for years as we struggle to develop vaccines, produce them, and distribute them—only to find a new virus or mutation keeps the pandemic going. The 1918–1920 influenza pandemic and recent Covid-19 pandemic proved that a pandemic can last for years.

Ensuring enough food to survive a collapse that could last for years is extremely challenging. If you stockpile all the food in your home, this takes up a lot of space. If your home is in a city or suburb and the marauder threat is bad, you may not be able to bug out and bring all this food with you. If you stockpile freeze-dried food, a year's supply is very expensive. But the canned food, while cheaper, takes up more space and weight for storage and transport.

This chapter provides some guidelines on survival preparations, but not a definitive guide on food for survival and hundreds of other issues. For more details, the Collapse Survival App has a lot of educational resources, and its companion website has a free preparedness knowledgebase with a multitude of articles and videos.

In addition to shelf-stable food, people with adequate skills and tools can hunt, fish, forage for wild plants/nuts/berries, raise ranch animals, and garden to get calories to survive a collapse. Fortitude Ranch, the nation's largest recreational and survival community, is designed to exploit every possible source of food and enable long-term survival by ranching and farming, hunting and gathering.

Disaster Preparedness LLC, Fortitude Ranch

Figure 35: Farming, ranching, foraging, hunting, stockpiling collapse survival food.

Since a pandemic or grid-down collapse disaster may last well beyond a year, and any collapse could have cascading effects, pile-on attacks by enemies, or a second collapse starting, you must assume that a collapse will last for many years. This means good collapse survival preparation requires the ability to ranch and grow food. This is another key reason why surviving in a city or suburb is a poor or completely untenable choice. Having the land and water is difficult in urban areas, but the bigger problem will probably be securing your fields and animals. People will be starving to death throughout a collapse; the marauder threat is likely to worsen, and just as food stockpiled in a basement must be protected, fields and farm animals must be protected.

Preppers pick bug-out locations in rural and wilderness areas both for security and to have better ability to get clean water, hunt, ranch, and garden. Fortitude Ranch favors locating next to public forest areas (remote parts of them) to get access to more land for hunting and foraging (acorns, walnuts, berries, et cetera).

Most of the unprepared urban dwellers will probably leave cities and crowded suburbs to get food and water, and escape bad urban marauder groups. They will hope to survive in the forests and wilderness by hunting, perhaps building a small log home. This is delusional. The game will be hunted out in the first days of a collapse, and both deliberate marauder groups and starving good people who must turn to marauding to survive could eventually make rural and wilderness areas as dangerous as big cities. After a few weeks, the major hunting in rural and wilderness areas will be people hunting people.

For example, there are about 35 million deer in the US, one for every ten humans. Assuming efficient processing, eating the liver and heart, the deer population can provide 2,000 calories/day for all Americans for just two days. But survival communities like Fortitude Ranch and preppers with remote bug-out locations will be poaching every edible creature they can get in the early days of a collapse, making jerky out of the meat. Most deer, wild turkey, and game will be gone in a week or two. The tens or hundreds of millions who expect to escape to the forest and survive by hunting have not thought it through. Farm animals will also be poached unless protected by well-armed owners.

Water is generally not feasible to stockpile; you need a reliable, safe source of drinking water. If you have woodstoves and plenty of fuel, you can boil water that is not directly potable. If you have a well, don't assume your solar system or generator has enough amperage to run it—most have 240 volt pumps that take a lot of amps to start. A running source of water is ideal, and most survival communities locate where there is a reliable stream or spring. Water is especially vital for growing food if you want long-term collapse survival capability. The odds of a municipal water system operating in a collapse are low—you must assume they will be gone from the start of the collapse.

Ignore the government and standard guidelines on how much water you need per person daily. You won't be running any washing machines or watering lawns, or even using much water to bathe. You can survive on a gallon of water a day—all for drinking and food preparation. When you have extra water, you can heat a few cups on a woodstove to take a sponge bath. The bigger water requirement is not for you, but for gardening and farm animals. This depends on where you are (rainfall, lots of variables), but is a key consideration and requirement.

Electricity is very desirable, but not necessarily a requirement. Electric power for indoor lights, a refrigerator running, and charging batteries for essential tools like handheld radios for guards is fantastic. But as addressed shortly, woodstoves are a more important and better energy source for a collapse. Fortunately, a solar system, propane generator, and other ways to generate electricity are affordable for most. With LED lighting, carefully restricting and managing electric use, you can afford to have some electricity when the grid is down.

Fire protection is easy to achieve for most. Unless you live near a likely nuclear target and a nuclear exchange occurs, the fire/blast/radiation shielding from a nuclear weapons is not needed. This is a major reason why underground shelters are largely a Cold War era mistake for prepping. You are highly unlikely to have a nuclear weapon detonate near you, and the ability to be on the surface to guard/defend/protect your facility is an absolute must have. Marauders are the number one threat to deal with in a collapse.

If you have a lot of buildings by you, or can't clear trees around you in a collapse (both for a firebreak and for clear lines of fire), then fire protection is something you need to work on. Expect no firefighters, or any first responders in a collapse. So if neighboring buildings can catch fire and ignite your property, then you need to take action to either move to a better place, or remove the fire threat. If neighboring buildings are abandoned in a collapse, consider cutting down wood walls and fences to save them for firewood and better fire safely.

As explained in a prior chapter, radiation shielding is needed even if there are no nuclear weapon or detonations because of nuclear reactors not being adequately manned in a collapse, having meltdowns and releasing radiation. There is a need to have some earth shielding for radiation protection from fallout. Fortunately just a few feet of earth is plenty of protection against low level fallout radiation. The deep underground shelters the military has are due to threats of targeted, very high-yield megaton nuclear warheads, attempting to destroy them. Unless you are attempting to shelter and survive near a prime target, deep underground bunkers are unnecessary. With the disadvantages of sharing air supply, vulnerability to virus, longer time needed to exit and get to surface defensive walls, much higher needs for constant electrical power, and much higher costs, deep underground shelters are fortunately not needed for survival.

The heat and shelter survival requirements are relatively simple. Any house, cabin, barn, or warehouse can be used as long as you can heat and protect it from marauders. Fortitude Ranch favors log homes since an eight-inch-thick log provides far more bullet protection than a framed building as well as great thermal mass.

If you've got reliable electricity (solar/wind/hydro power), you can produce heat from electricity, but this is very inefficient, probably not viable in a collapse environment, and generally not wise. Woodstoves are far better for generating heat and cooking food. With woodstoves, you can survive without any electricity. At Fortitude Ranch, while there are solar systems and generators, woodstoves are the primary energy source for heating and cooking. It is good to be able to run indoor lights and charge batteries (tools especially), but with woodstoves and a local source of wood, you can live without electricity.

Even preppers tend to ignore the mental health requirement. A collapse will be the most horrible thing most people will ever experience. Even if well prepared, you will worry and mourn the fate of other friends and family not prepared, as well as the massive loss of lives and suffering. There will be great stress from worrying about marauder attacks.

If you are secure, and know your ability to survive is good, then you should be able to maintain good mental health. If your survival strategy depends on hiding from a marauder group, not the ability to defeat/deter an attack, then expect huge mental stress on people. Worrying for months that if they find your underground shelter and cover your air vents you'll be killed is stress many people won't be able to deal with for months.

A key advantage of survival communities, addressed later in this chapter, is their ability to provide both much better security and community for a far more pleasant, less stressful survival lifestyle.

While these eleven basic requirements cover key preparations, depending on your location, travel requirements, physical/medical condition, lots of other factors, there may be other preparations you need to do.

Again, this chapter provided just an overview of collapse survival preparations. To improve your survival skills, there is a vast wealth of free information on preparedness on the Collapse Survivor App's website "Preparedness Knowledgebase."

When the grid goes down, the phone and Internet go down as well. An appalling percentage of young people have no clue how to do some simple things like garden, travel cross-country with a paper map, build the simplest things that pioneers readily handled, skills that will be needed again in a collapse. There are some workarounds like the Collapse Survival App, which has an offline GPS system and complete Wikipedia contents, both usable without a cell phone or Internet connection.

You can also benefit by playing collapse survival training exercises on the Collapse Survivor App. This App has dozens of military style training exercises where you get simulated messages with updates on a developing collapse, with threats and specific situations that you have to react to and deal with. The US military does lots of "command post" or "tabletop" exercises to give people "future experience" dealing with difficult situations, learning via a far more interesting and engaging format than a lecture or briefing. For example, in Collapse Survivor App exercises you'll have to make decisions about giving food to a beggar (who might be legitimate, might be a diversion for a marauder group), whether it is safe and wise to go to a barter exchange in a collapse, how long you can keep a tourniquet on for without losing a limb.[4]

Surviving in Basement, Backyard Shelter, or Rural Farm with Friends Is Not Viable in a Bad Collapse

In a big city or suburb, getting out early in the collapse is the best option—assuming you've got a safe bug-out[5] location to go to. Even if a collapse only lasts a few days, the marauder violence in cities could be very bad, and municipal water may stop quickly.[6]

During a bad, long collapse, surviving in your basement even in smaller/safer cities, a backyard shelter, or rural farm with friends is probably not viable. Marauders will end up everywhere there is no law and order. Over time, marauder groups will get more skilled and bigger. You need a large group of people to have many guards on duty 24/7, and the work, knowledge requirements, and costs of do-it-yourself survival are well beyond the capacity of most families.

The majority of people are not prepared and many of them will come to steal or kill for food, water, gas, ammo. If your neighbors know or suspect you've got some stockpiled supplies, and you are not part of a well-armed group, you will be targeted. This is why the first rule of prepping has long been don't tell anyone you're a prepper.

One or two guards on duty is not enough if there is a skilled marauder group coming after you. A smart marauder group is not going to immediately break into or attack your house or rural bug-out location. They will deploy scouts to observe, figure out if you are a good target to go after, how many guards you have on duty at what times of day, where they are. Keeping just two guards on duty all the time is going to take a group of at least thirty people—and two guards are not enough. Two guards on duty at night means that a marauder group of just two people can take you out. They position themselves to have good cover, lined up to shoot your two guards. At 2 a.m. when people not on guard duty are sound asleep and, using handheld radios to coordinate, they shoot simultaneously from a distance. Their rifles are sighted and resting on a solid perch, your guards are immobile, so both are headshots that kill instantly. Someone sleeping inside might hear the distant shot outside, but will likely fall back asleep after hearing no further noise. The marauders wait a few minutes and if no one is roused, they move in. If you're lucky they just steal supplies and leave. If unlucky they quietly go through all the rooms, gagging and knifing people in their sleep.

Turning to the next survival requirement, avoiding a virus if one is spreading, you need to keep people spread out in the initial days so if someone is infected, he or she doesn't infect others. This is a particularly bad disadvantage of underground shelters where people are close together and air supplies are shared. You need a large group of people to defend a survival location. Some of these folks may be carrying the virus, but not yet look sick. So you have to keep all arriving groups far apart, and definitely not sharing the same air supplies. Do not count on air filters! Even if 99 percent or more efficient (which you can't know for a new virus), an infected person is releasing millions of virus particles, and some viruses take just a few particles to infect you.

If you are trying to survive in a basement or bunker, this likely means using just stored water. While people can get by with just a gallon of water a day, with the need for thirty-plus people to keep a lot of guards on duty 24/7, to last just a month you'd need a 1,000 gallon water tank, taking up a 6-by-6 foot space, ceiling height. Toilets and waste add to the water requirements, complications, and mess.

But the bigger problem with trying to hide out in a basement or underground shelter is that you have trapped yourself, and a marauder group can easily kill you. They could start a fire. If you've got a blast proof steel door they can't penetrate to get to your underground shelter, they can simply block your air vents and you'll suffocate. A marauder group can yell down into your air vents to bring out supplies and they'll let you live, or if you refuse, close them off, suffocate you, and wait a day to break in and steal your supplies.

Even if the grid is up, they can cut off your electric power. You can survive without electricity on the surface, but underground, especially in a buried shelter, you need electric power for lights at a minimum. Solar panels or wind generators on the surface give you away. Run a generator and it must vent exhaust. In a collapse it will be much quieter, and marauders will hear, smell, or even feel a generator running underground.

If you are not defending your property on the surface, then having chickens and farm animals, gardening to grow food is impossible. If they are not guarded and protected, they will be stolen. This mandates all stored shelf-stable food, greatly increasing the costs of trying to prepare, and giving a time limit to how long you can survive.

Trying to survive with a small group, unable to defend on the surface, makes survival by hiding in your basement or an underground shelter, or trying to survive with a small group in a rural or wilderness house, very doubtful in a long collapse with lots of marauder group threats. Small groups are also unlikely to have the doctors, mechanics, and other specialized skills that you are more likely to find in large survival communities. Most importantly, the larger the survival community, especially with all members armed, the more likely you can deter marauder groups from ever attacking since you will be too difficult and costly a target, even for a huge marauder group.[7]

Best Approach to Reliable, Effective, Affordable Survivability Is to Join a Survival Community

There have been millions of US preppers for decades, the vast majority following the rule "don't tell anyone you're a prepper." You don't want friends and neighbors coming to your house in a collapse to beg, steal, or kill for your stockpiled supplies. Thus, when the asinine TV show *Doomsday Preppers* came out, smart preppers refused to go on the show. Those that did agree to foolishly out themselves were not normal, wise preppers, but unusual, foolish people that the show then ridiculed. This bad show unfortunately was widely seen and wrongly branded preppers as idiots in the minds of many. But after Covid-19 and the growing instances of uncontrolled looting in the US, most people now accept that "The Preppers Were Right All Along"—as headlines in *Bloomberg News* and the *Washington Post* proclaimed.[8]

Everyone needs to be a prepper in the Age of Collapse.

With a survival community with one hundred members or more, you can have the full range of skills and expertise needed for best survival prospects and quality of life: doctors, a staffed medical clinic, farm and ranch and mechanic skills needed. You can grow crops and keep chickens and other ranch animals, and thus have long-term food production. If the survival community has professional staff, then you have expertise you need to monitor and deal with radioactive fallout, keep solar systems and equipment functioning, and have reliable leadership and a secure chain of command. Quality of life and mental health will be far better than hiding or worrying every moment that you'll be overrun by a marauder group or run out of food and water.

Forbes

16.402 views | Feb 18, 2020, 10:25am EST

Fortitude Ranch In Colorado Is An Underground Virus Pandemic Shelter For The Masses

Jim Dobson Senior Contributor ⓘ

Travel

Searching the world for the most amazing People, Finces and Things

Forbes.com

Figure 36: Survival communities: The most affordable and effective way to survive a collapse.

You need strong defenses, cleared lines of fire, defensive walls, lots of guards and people with weapons to not just defeat, but deter a marauder attack. The goal at Fortitude Ranch is to have overwhelming defenses so a marauder group won't consider trying to attack. Even if your survival community has doctors in the membership and a clinic, you can't provide hospital levels of emergency care. A gunshot wound in the extremities in a collapse is probably going to mean amputation or loss of function that could be avoided with skilled surgeons and specialists in a modern hospital. A gunshot wound hitting a vital organ or digestive system could mean death due to inadequate antibiotics[9] and hospital-level care. This medical vulnerability is good in helping to deter marauders—they won't want to risk attacking a survival facility that is extremely well defended, even if they do have such superior numbers that they could overrun it. This is another key reason why large survival communities are the best way to survive a collapse.

For deterrence to be effective, you have to convince the marauder group that attacking would be too costly. So you don't want to rely on some secret defenses that they won't notice until they are committed to an attack. You want to convince them with cleared lines of fire, lots of guard posts, and many armed people that there is no way they can succeed so they won't attack. This is why at Fortitude Ranch all members are required to have their weapons with them at all times, no exceptions. We want marauder group observers to report back that "everyone is armed, lots of guard posts always manned, everyone, including livestock, is inside the compound walls at night, they have night vision equipment, they are very disciplined, organized—way too risky to attack."

Survival community leadership needs to not just keep guards on duty and security measures going for maximum deterrence of marauder groups, but to keep members' confidence high, knowing they are safe and will survive the collapse (psychological health). It is also wise to report good news, and appoint a member or two in your group to keep stock of members' mental health, ensure that someone who is depressed or withdrawn has some pleasant experiences during the day, gets drawn out to interact and do some fun things.

Survival communities are by far the best approach to meet the eleven survival requirements, and in an affordable manner due to lots of people sharing the expense.

The big advantages of a survival community are:

1. More people for far better security, deterring/defeating marauder attacks
2. More expertise and labor for gardening, ranching, operating a medical clinic, professional staff that know the radiation monitoring and ham radio equipment
3. More affordable because of large number of members sharing costs and economies of scale
4. Surviving in relative comfort, pleasant conditions, with good mental health

The exhibit below compares how the different survival location and seven options compare in fulfilling the eleven survival requirements and affordability. Fortitude Ranch is a survival community. Mount Weather is the FEMA survival facility for congressmen and other top government officials. Survival Condo is a luxury underground bunker in a former ICBM silo.

Assessment of Survival/Preparedness Options based on key Survival Requirements

Scale:	Location, Preparedness:	Big City	Suburban House	Backyard Shelter	Rural House	Fortitude Ranch	Mount Weather	Survival Condo
10 Excellent 7 Adequate 5 Minimal	**1 Security**	2	4	5	6	9	9	7
3 Very Poor 1 Horrible	**2 Avoid Virus**	2	4	6	7	10	9	6
These are general, average ratings, largely subjective, based on many variables	**3 Food**	1	3	5	7	9	10	8
	4 Water	2	3	?	8	10	10	8
	5 Electricity	2	2	4	4	6	8	8
	6 Fire Protection	2	1	9	4	8	10	10
Lots of uncertainty and variance based on the specific threat situation	**7 Blast Protection**	2	2	10	4	6	10	10
	8 Radiation Shielding	4	3	10	4	8	10	10
	9 Heat, Shelter	5	5	8	9	8	9	9
Costs include facility, equipment, supplies, security, electricity generation	**10 Get to Survival Site**	9	10	10	8	9	9	6
	11 Mental Health	1	3	4	6	9	9	7
	Affordability	5	5	3	4	8	N/A	1

Figure 37: Comparison of survival options based on eleven key survival requirements.

Volunteer survival communities have been around for decades, but most do not last more than a few years before they fall apart. Fifty people is probably the minimum to maintain a large guard force and defend a house/compound if a long collapse with significant marauder group threat. Unfortunately, the likelihood of getting a voluntary survival community group of fifty or more to agree on all the decisions, duties, costs of a survival facility, and its equipping and operations are next to zero. There are not just disagreements over decisions, but who should be in charge. To run a large survival community, you need good organization, leadership, and clear authority. Some voluntary survival communities fail when volunteer members argue over who should be in charge. There are also troubles when a member can no longer afford to pay agreed upon dues. Banks rarely will lend money for the mortgage needed to buy a survival property, forcing individuals to sign and commit to loan payoff—leaving them with a big liability and risk for the loan.

Despite fantastic personal preparedness, you can be confident that problems will arise that were not anticipated, or are not prepared for. At Fortitude Ranch the three guiding operating principles we follow are:

1. Respect Murphy's Law (assume everything will go wrong, bad),
2. KISS (Keep It Simple Stupid, avoid complicated, vulnerable systems), and
3. Adapt.

While working at the Institute for Defense Analyses I had the opportunity to work with William Burns, who promoted the Department of Defense recognizing that we cannot predict the future and should improve our capability to adapt to surprises.[10] Rapidly adapting is a hallmark of pioneer America, wise military practice, and wise preparedness. Bad things, inexplicable problems, unexpected consequences, broken equipment, failed systems, and more/worse will happen. Expect this and be ready to quickly analyze and adapt. The bigger but simpler your facility and larger/more diverse your survival community population, the better you can adapt.

While an estimated one third of Americans today are doing some prepping, for the vast majority this amounts to just stockpiling a few weeks' worth of food and some water. Collapse level preparedness requires much more, meeting all eleven requirements for a period of at least months, ideally a year or more.[11]

Benjamin Franklin advised that it's best to be a pessimist. Then if things turn out bad, you're prepared for it. If things turn out good, then you can be pleasantly surprised. Another great quote (that I have found attributed to Franklin) bears repeating: "By Failing to Prepare you are Preparing to Fail."

CHAPTER NINE

ORGANIZATIONS WITHOUT COLLAPSE SURVIVAL PREPARATIONS WILL NOT SURVIVE

Warren Buffett insists that "[t]he CEO should regard his position #1 as the Chief Risk Officer. Now you have a lot of other functions too, but you should wake up every morning and think about 'is this place built to take everything'?" Very few organizations address the full range of feasible threats, ignoring collapse disasters that experts say are "inevitable" though unpredictable.[1]

Our electric grid is highly vulnerable to destruction by cyberattacks, solar flares, EMP from a nuclear detonation, or physical attacks that a dedicated terrorist group or nation-state as weak as North Korea can execute. When the grid goes down it could take more than a year to replace and repair. New technologies, including bioengineering, nanotechnology, and Artificial Intelligence are generating new means for devastation that could halt economic activity for months, and lead to widespread, long-lasting loss of law and order, with no one coming to work. A bioengineered virus could cause a pandemic that kills hundreds of millions and permanently destroys most companies. Most businesses will not survive a bad collapse, with key people dead, plant and property that is not guarded looted and destroyed. Data backup facilities and bank deposit vaults are also unlikely to survive a long collapse with utilities not operating, people not coming to work, and marauders breaking into facilities.

In the Age of Collapse—an era where mankind will suffer severe disasters that kill off millions or billions of people because of new technologies and threats, our fragile, interdependent economic system, irresponsible government, and a population that is increasingly dependent and unable to survive without long-distance water and food shipments—most organizations will be also be destroyed.

When you consider the combined effects of growing threats and vulnerabilities and their impact on your organization; three big conclusions jump out:

1. You should never assume continued operation of the economy, law and order, or people coming to work.
2. You should assume that in a really bad disaster you'll be on your own for security and assistance.
3. Realize the trigger event starting the disaster is not likely to be the biggest problem. It's the aftermath, how bad people exploit it, and turn it into a collapse situation—that's the real disaster and big impact to prepare for.

Business continuity plans don't deal with the increasingly likely reality of massive, uncontrolled looting and marauder violence. Almost no organization or first responders will be operating in a collapse. Two million Americans in jails that can't be kept there without electricity or a guard force coming to work will have to be released or escape—with little alternative to marauding to survive. As conditions worsen, people without food or water, the vast majority, may start looting and sometimes will kill to survive.

None of the above is covered in business risk management or continuity of operations plans. They deal with "normal" historic disasters with relatively minor disruptions and losses. They assume there is law and order—but in a major disaster there will be massive looting and marauding, police overwhelmed and unable to assist. Our future is one of major disasters that could lead to a collapse lasting from months to years. CEOs and COOs, as chief risk officers, responsible for the survival of the business, need to have plans for big collapse disasters that could completely destroy the firm.

A great example of how normal "business continuity" plans fail to deal with the loss of law and order, looting, and huge casualties of a collapse is the incorrect assumption that off-site data backup is secure. For surviving a hurricane and few weeks of lost electric power, data backup services will work since they are in unimpacted areas. But data backup centers, bank safety deposit boxes, and record storage warehouses are unlikely to make it through a bad collapse when most or all of the country, most of the world, may be in a collapse. There will be no electric power and no employees there to protect the facilities. Workers will not sacrifice their lives in a collapse to protect your data or records or valuables. Looters will ransack every building looking for something for possible collapse survival use or post-collapse value.[2]

The belief that nothing can be done to protect an organization in a collapse is irresponsible and wrong. It is very feasible for most organizations to protect key resources, even if operations cease. There are investment strategies and standby lines of business that some well-prepared organizations can switch to when a collapse occurs.

For many companies, a carefully analyzed and selected set of low-cost risk mitigation and collapse preparedness measures, implemented in advance, can ensure that key human, physical, and digital assets survive so your business can later recover. Examples of Black Swan risk mitigation, company survival strategies that Fortitude Collapse Preparedness[3] has developed include:

- Developed plan to quickly save information and key resources by moving them into a secure facility, with specific lists of items that must be saved, where they are, who is responsible for securing them, et cetera.
- Added a new data backup service at a facility that can survive the worst collapse (most data backup centers, cloud storage facilities will be destroyed in a bad collapse).
- Continued low-cost international sourcing; also found local suppliers and gave them steady business, at higher cost, to ensure a relationship and source of local supply in a collapse.
- Added several hidden gun, ammunition, and food storage vaults, radiation detectors, and other survival equipment, with ten trusted associates selected to implement survival plans developed during engagement (will turn into a private survival facility).
- Strategy of shifting to full-time operations with reduced staff in a collapse of a product line that will be in demand, opening sleeping facilities, modifying building (prepositioned materials and plans, no construction until collapse), to keep facility and personnel safe.
- Vastly increased company cafeteria food inventory to serve as collapse food stockpile, with contracted food service provider paid a small amount to ensure food inventories on hand.
- With existing staff, set up a technology and threat watch program to forewarn of industry developments and Black Swan threats.
- Implemented plan to work and ally with neighboring businesses, with plans for putting up connecting walls and all agreeing to stockpile key survival items.
- Purchased survival community memberships for key personnel.
- Purchased old, low-cost, obsolete food canning machinery, stockpiled cans

and lids and sealers needed. Trained a few personnel on how to set up and operate, made video of training instructions, and stored the equipment. Identified POCs at several farm operations nearby with verbal agreements that in collapse they will can their food on a barter basis (keeping a percentage of canned food as payment).

- Client decided to abandon all facilities in a collapse, securing just key documents and backup files and developing a collapse communication plan briefed to key personnel to allow reconnecting and rebuilding post-collapse.
- Negotiated plan with major customer to get higher price in exchange for maintaining larger inventory, diesel generators, and tank buy, and guaranteed ability to deliver product for three months post major supply interruption or collapse.
- Planned to shift some staff and resources to one facility that will remain open while others shut down in a collapse, with all records, designated equipment, backup tapes transferred to protected facility.
- Negotiated and reached agreement with neighboring company to jointly fund a big solar system with large bank of lithium batteries, integrated propane generators, and ten thousand gallons of fuel, for shared use in good times (primarily just the solar power) and collapse.
- Offered discounted survival community membership for all personnel (half paid by company) as a new company employee benefit option.
- Purchased big inventory of canned foods stored in underground basement space, sealed off with simple wall to conceal and keep cooler.
- Analyzed and changed just-in-time delivery to include both some inventory for most vulnerable inputs and added purchasing from closer, more reliable suppliers. Investors briefed on these changes that will raise expenses, but should yield both higher profit (from reduced loss of sales when major disruptions occur) and increase ability to keep company operating, employees and facilities protected during a collapse.

Almost no business continuity plans will work in a collapse. Your organization needs to be prepared for collapse survival.

It's hard for some organizations to accept, but in many scenarios you are better off shutting down, securing your plant with a program in place to safeguard your key assets, and protect key people. Throwing up your hands and saying "we can't prepare for such horrible disasters" is intellectually incorrect and irresponsible. There are sensible, low-cost measures you can take to secure your facilities and personnel.

Taleb says the best use of our brain is to be on the lookout for Black Swans, think about how they might happen and the impacts they may have. Taleb's book *Antifragile: Things that Gain from Disorder* makes a compelling case for anti-fragile investments—an investment that will benefit when something bad occurs. You can often identify companies that will suffer severely from a pandemic: international airlines will suffer huge losses in many Black Swan scenarios, while some companies may benefit.

While 99 percent of people are surprised by Black Swan threats, the intelligence community, hedge funds, and those who are working to not be surprised can usually predict them and either avoid the damage or profit from them. Disruptive technologies that trigger sudden and unexpected effects are rarely a complete surprise. The effects may be cascading, nonlinear, and difficult to anticipate, but carefully analyzing new technologies, examining their enablers, and assessing their likely impact, gives you both warnings of threats and ideas on how to profit from them. The impact of new technologies, and the increasing vulnerability and fragility of our economic system and population, is that we're going to have a lot more Black Swan disasters.

As Taleb and other risk assessment experts have pointed out, many standard risk management practices are very bad—setting you up for failure. All the major commercial business continuity software programs use the traditional risk probability/impact matrix, encouraging companies to focus on high likelihood and high impact risks. While it is the common practice, this is an extremely unwise approach. It forces you to estimate the probability of events when you usually cannot estimate their probability. Companies place very low probability estimates for Black Swan events since they have not happened before, and then ignore them. Defining "critical risks" that the organization should deal with as those with high consequences and high annual likelihood of occurrence means ignoring collapse threats and being unprepared to survive the consequences when they occur.

The better approach for enterprise risk management is to identify all feasible threats, pay great attention to high impact risks, and do not waste time on the impossible quest of estimating probability of occurrence, which is statistically impossible for rare events. In a *Harvard Business Review* article, Nassim Taleb warned that the worst mistake businesses make is to think they can manage risk by predicting extreme events. What Taleb recommends is to identify the full range of feasible disasters and "focus on the consequences—that is, to evaluate the possible impact of extreme events."

The lead risk manager at Goldman Sachs, one of the few big Wall Street firms that did well during the 2007 economic collapse, said that he spent "98 percent of

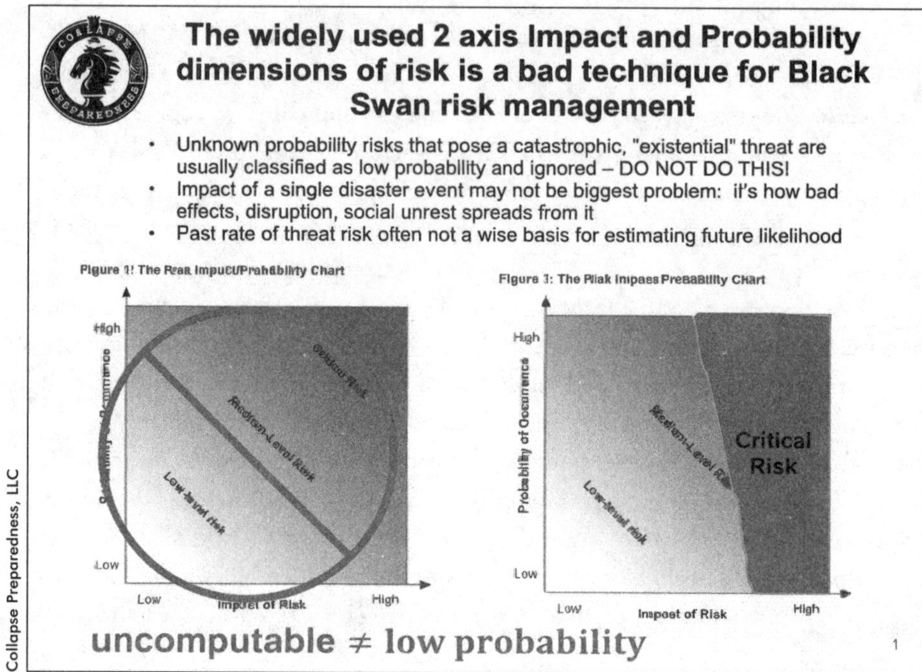

Figure 38: Standard business risk management prioritization of risks is fatally wrong.

his time worrying about things with a 2 percent probability."[4] The 2 percent probability is a guess—he rightly focused on the big threats that could have catastrophic impact on the firm, however unlikely these threats might seem.

A technology watch program can be an easy add to R&D Department work, using threat warnings and updates outside firms can provide to get advance warning and more time to prepare for a pending collapse disaster. If you institute a technology and threat watch program, you may also find actionable threat information that lets you make some low-cost (and strictly limited) hedge investment bets. While monitoring for threats to your business, it is wise to also look for Black Swan investment opportunities (as Nassim Talib does). Most disasters are not "bolt from the blue" attacks, but emerging threats that are usually reported on, but ignored by more than 99 percent of the population. If you are prepared to make some hedge investments, puts and calls, on public companies that are poised for great or disastrous change, you may be able to make a quick profit before the calamity hits. You can be prepared to either profit from investments, or adjust your operations to be prepared for pending changes, good or bad.

A presentation on predicting and assessing Black Swan risks at the national conference of Business Continuity and Disaster Response planners and a series of articles on collapse preparedness featured in the *Domestic Preparedness Journal*, published by the Texas Division of Emergency Management, Texas A&M University, covers many of these organization collapse survival issues (see our webnotes).[5]

In a bad, long-lasting collapse with our current state of unpreparedness, most people won't survive, and very few organizations will be able to recover after the collapse is over. They will be forever destroyed. Organizations that have planned and prepared for collapse survival will likely not be able to operate during a collapse. But if they implement plans to protect their key assets, they will have much higher odds of resurrecting and operating again after the worst of a collapse is over.[6]

Consider the warnings of Benjamin Franklin, Warren Buffet, Oxford professors, Ray Dalio, Nassim Taleb, Noble price winner Dr, Geoffrey Hinton and other lead AI developers, many other brilliant people urging people and organizations to prepare for collapse disasters.

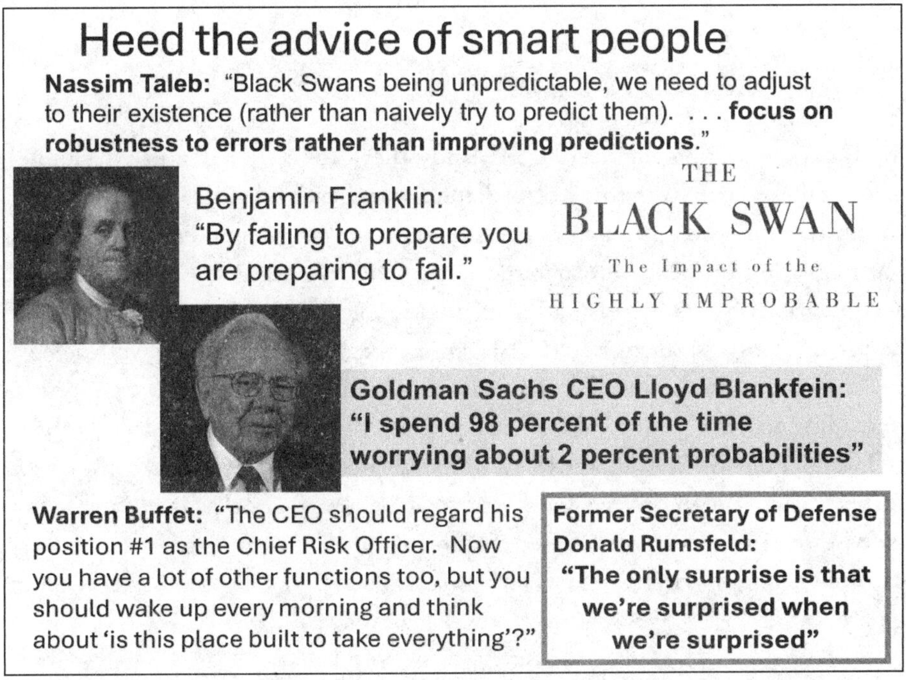

Figure 39: Smart people recommending preparing your organization for Black Swan disasters and survival.

Chapter Ten

HOW FOREIGN POLICY AND NATIONAL SECURITY STRATEGIES MUST ADAPT

With advances in bioengineering, AI, and other extremely lethal new technologies, we have entered the Age of Collapse, where we will suffer severe disasters that kill off millions or billions of people because of new technologies and threats, our fragile, interdependent economic system and irresponsible government, and a population that is increasingly dependent. The United States needs to shift national security strategy not to Asia or the Pacific, but to homeland defense and collapse survival. The US military needs to abandon its world's policeman role, and focus on prompt global strikes with conventional or nuclear weapons to interdict enemy WMD attacks. With much smaller overseas forces, they need to be backed and protected by a return of battlefield nuclear weapons. Most defense resources must be focused on homeland defense and collapse recovery capability so fewer citizens die when WMD attacks and collapse disasters cannot be prevented.[1]

Foreign Armies Are Not a Significant Threat to the US; Department of Defense Must Shift Focus to Countering WMD Threats Overseas, Homeland Defense, and Collapse Recovery Capability

Bioengineering, more capable and easy now with AI, enables weak nation-states (Iran), terrorist groups (ISIS, Al-Qaeda), and even individuals (a biologist who wants to kill off people to save the planet) to launch attacks that could cause more damage to our country (and possibly our species—existential threats) than mankind has ever experienced. No military weapons or soldiers are needed to deliver a virus that could kill most citizens in a country—or most of our species. Small atomizers carried unnoticed by individuals walking through crowded airports suffice.

Scientists and analysts have been warning (ineffectively) for over a quarter century now that this Age of Collapse is coming and must be prepared for. Yale Professor Martin Shubik warned in 1998 that "the use of biological weapons as a terror weapon should be seen as an inevitability" and "the United States must radically rethink how it hopes to deal with biological warfare initiated by terrorists and fringe groups."[2] Dozens of other formal government studies and other experts have echoed similar calls for the DoD to devote more resources to homeland defense, the US to prepare for inevitable bad pandemics, but all that really changed over the past decades is the formation of the ineffective Department of Homeland Security (DHS).

Nuclear weapons in the hands of nations are not very useful when the other side can retaliate. An ICBM is easy to detect and trace, and then retaliate against. Delivered on a big enough scale to cause major damage, an attacker using lots of nuclear weapons is also discoverable, even if launched from commercial ships and planes, or smuggled in. But with bioweapons, deadly viruses released by small numbers of clandestine agents, it would be difficult or impossible to determine who released the attack. So a deadly, highly transmissible virus is a far better WMD to use to destroy the United States, and far more likely to be used than nuclear weapons. Future WMD attacks by nation-states are far more likely to be viruses, or clandestine agents secretly poisoning municipal water systems with new poisons AI develops, destroying our electric grid—which can kill most citizens and eliminate most of our conventional military power—with little fear of retribution.

A single, inaccurate North Korean nuclear detonation over the United States could take down our electric system. But if launched from a North Korean ICBM, we'd know they did it and would definitely retaliate and likely destroy much of the country and kill their leader. We can't assume that an ICBM will deliver the high altitude EMP attack that destroys our grid. Russia, China, North Korea, Iran might launch a short-range missile out of a modified civilian airliner over the US (to achieve higher altitude for better EMP impact) to destroy our grid.[3] We may not be able to determine what airliner it came from, or what country executed the attack, so they can avoid retaliation (and thus are not deterred from executing the attack). Smart people can figure out how to do this; AI will make it ever easier and eventually impossible for us to anticipate and defend against the many means to destroy our fragile electric grid, which our irresponsible government has ignored for decades despite dire warnings from government-funded studies.

North Korea is far more likely to try to smuggle one of their nuclear weapons into the country. North Korea has demonstrated they can send agents on suicide missions to assassinate people. Iran could not hope to benefit from a direct attack on the US. If Iran really wants to harm the "Great Satan" and not trigger deadly retaliations, they will use a few of their Revolutionary Guards jihadis to release a virus over here, clandestinely, and leave no direct evidence of their involvement. China has at least a thousand agents in the US, possibly far more. Enemy agents, conducting clandestine attacks like releasing bioengineered viruses, physical and cyberattacks on our electric grid, starting wildfires, releasing a nanotechnology self-replicating device, poisons, or some brand new type of WMD, are far more likely and devastating threats to the US than any overseas military forces.

In 2024 a House Intelligence Committee member requested declassification of information concerning a "serious national security threat" that ended up being concerns about Russia preparing to place a nuclear weapon in orbit, violating the ban on weapons in space, the Outer Space Treaty of 1967.[4] We must assume that Russia and China, and possibly North Korea have or will put nuclear weapons in space either to destroy satellites, or to drop them on targets on Earth. Our overseas military forces are of no use to counter this threat.

With Russia's army so badly damaged and discredited from their invasion of Ukraine, they are clearly not a near-term threat to NATO—and our Western allies have plenty of wealth and manpower to provide the vast majority of military resources to defend western Europe.

As the next chapter of this book explains, the US promise of defending Taiwan must be eliminated. China has pledged that they will "retake" Taiwan and finish their civil war, and has a solid argument that this is an internal affair for China/Taiwan that outside countries have no business getting involved in. China will pressure or if necessary invade Taiwan to reclaim this territory, and if the US follows through on promises to aid Taiwan, we must expect that China will engage in "nuclear chicken" against us—threatening and if necessary firing some nuclear weapons against the US to force the POTUS to back down.[5] If the Chinese take out our fragile electric system, which they can do with even a very small nuclear strike, most Americans could be killed—and Taiwan not saved. The forces required for us to assist in Taiwan's defense drives huge conventional weapons spending that we would not have if we abandoned this suicidal offer to assist Taiwan.

There is no legitimate need for our current level of building military capabilities and defense spending, and no reason to continue the too-expensive and now infeasible quest for conventional weapons technology superiority when AI can increasingly invent all manner of countermeasures to emasculate advanced weapons systems. With the backup of nuclear weapons (addressed later) we are in a particularly good position to stop procuring high-cost, advanced conventional weapons systems, and shift to a variety of smaller, far less expensive, and more effective defense measures for forces deployed overseas.

We have to prioritize homeland defense and accept the reality that with the relative decline in US economic power, the rise of AI, many new types of WMD, and more nuclear powers coming as AI enables easier/cheaper/faster ways to develop nuclear weapons and other more deadly forms of WMD, the historic focus on clashing armies is largely irrelevant. National security must focus on detecting and destroying WMD attacks before they can be carried out, reducing our vulnerability to WMD attacks, and building capacity to survive a collapse and then recover.

Throughout US military history we've basically followed Clausewitzian principles of war, focused on "conquer and destroy the armed power of the enemy; always direct our principal operation against the main body of the enemy army or at least against an important portion of his forces."[6] This principle is largely obsolete today.

The Age of Collapse must bring a real "Revolution in Military Affairs"—not a minor change in how we fight and what we prioritize, but a huge, fundamental shift away from Clausewitzian strategy of armies clashing on foreign battlefields that are irrelevant when the citizens they are supposed to protect are dying from a virus, starving to death, or getting killed in their homes by marauders. We must abandon our military and strategy focus on destroying a nation-state's military and focus on preemptively destroying WMD attacks from any source (increasingly individuals and small groups), defending our homeland, surviving and recovering from collapses that we often will not be able to forestall.[7]

In the Age of Collapse, we must throttle way back on our overseas military involvements and commitments. In the Age of Collapse, even if the government turned into a paragon of efficiency, followed constitutional limits, and focused on national security, we are not going to be able to prevent bio attacks that one individual can launch or other new WMD that AI will help bad people invent. We are going to suffer catastrophic collapse disasters and should focus our defense on preventing as many as we can and helping citizens at home recover from the inevitable disasters that do occur. The US must abandon its strategy of being the world's policeman and abandon its massive network of 750 military bases scattered on every continent except Antarctica, with 170,000 troops stationed overseas, to devote the bulk of our resources to homeland defense and collapse recovery capability.[8]

The Department of Homeland Security Needs to Be Eliminated, with the Department of Defense Taking Over Homeland Defense and Collapse Recovery

A 2001 DoD Defense Science Board study on "Protecting the Homeland" cited our unpreparedness for domestic biowarfare attacks and recommended that "greater emphasis should be placed on these emerging threats to the homeland than is evident in today's budget allocation."[9] More than two decades later that recommendation remains ignored.[10]

The Department of Homeland Security (DHS) was created in 2022 after the 9/11 Al-Qaeda attacks. It has a record of management failures and a budget of $89 billion in 2024, about one-tenth the size of DoD spending.

DHS and DoD stay in their "swim lanes," careful not to step into the other's turf. As long as the DoD remains in its role of supporting DHS, DoD/military leaders won't put major resources into homeland defense and collapse recovery programs.

The 9/11 terrorist attacks should have been the wake-up call to get the DoD to shift away from traditional overseas clash of armies to homeland security and recovery. Instead, it led to an increase in overseas military campaigns in Iraq, Afghanistan, and elsewhere, and a temporary surge (for the army) in insurgency operations and investments.

All we got after 9/11 was a shuffling of government agencies into the Department of Homeland Security, and the military's establishment of US Northern Command (USNORTHCOM) on October 1, 2002, "to provide command and control of Department of Defense homeland defense efforts and to coordinate defense support of civil authorities." NORTHCOM claims to "defend America's homeland," but like the rest of DoD, is really focused on outside the US border and traditional military threats. NORTHCOM is "integrated and aligned with North American Aerospace Defense Command (NORAD)"—looking for traditional overseas enemies and threats coming from outside our borders. The vast majority of DoD forces and budgeting is focused on the traditional clash of military forces overseas and constant development and purchase of the most advanced technology conventional weapons—not homeland defense.

US military strategic and focus needs to shift not to Asia or the Pacific, but to homeland defense and collapse survival. This will not happen until DHS is eliminated and the DoD takes the lead on homeland defense and recovery missions.

Experts who played in the Clade X bioengineered pandemic exercise agreed that there needs to be a single very senior official to coordinate all federal agencies' responses and rule on competing interests of health security, politics and foreign policy.[11] A new cabinet level official, the "Homeland Security Director," should fulfill this role, but with a focus on using all elements of government controlled power—not just FEMA and agencies currently under the DHS. An Undersecretary of Defense for Homeland Security would be the Homeland Security Director's key

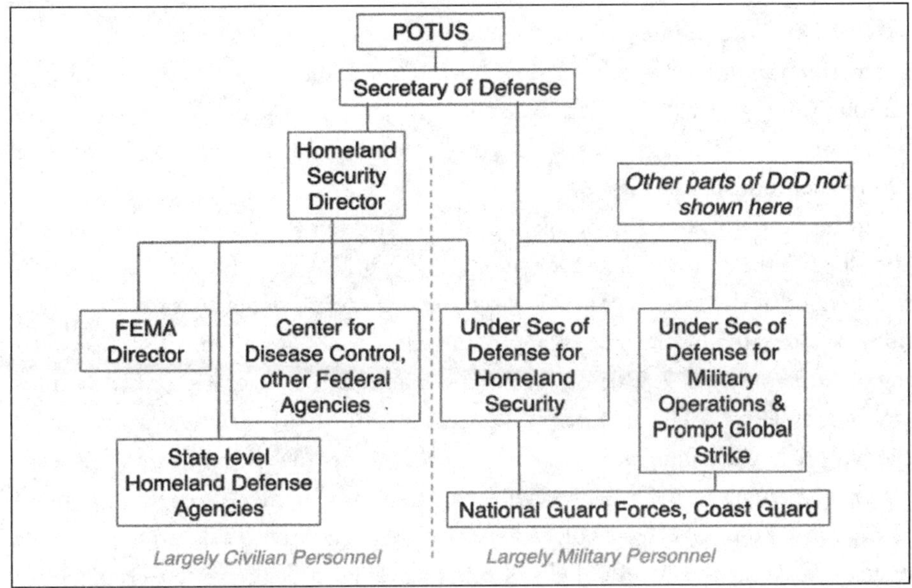

Figure 40: New homeland defense organization proposal.

partner, leveraging the much larger resources of the DoD. This Undersecretary of Defense will report to two Secretary-level officials. When the Homeland Security Director and Secretary of Defense disagree on a homeland security issue, the POTUS will decide. FEMA would continue as an agency, under the Homeland Security Director's control. Current HLS agencies would be either assigned to FEMA, the DoD, other agencies, left independent, or eliminated. FEMA would keep only assignments directly related to disaster recovery. The Coast Guard would be transferred to the Department of the Navy, under the DoD. The TSA would go to the Transportation Department, where it belongs, the Secret Service to the DoD. The dozens of agencies thrown together into DHS when it was created was a bold political statement, but it remains a bureaucratic mess.

FEMA must be managed by a top-notch professional—not a political appointee. The US Senate needs to stop allowing political appointments, refusing to confirm any important Secretary or Agency Director that is not just completely qualified, but the best possible person available for the job. Both political parties, all recent presidential administrations, are guilty of irresponsible, disgusting, life-threatening appointments of political hacks and brown-nosers—not competent officials.

Once DoD has taken over homeland security operations, there needs to be two Deputy Secretaries of Defense: one for overseas military operations and Prompt Global Strike, and one for homeland security and collapse recovery.

This organizational shift is readily doable, but the more difficult reform will be to force DoD and military services to end their centuries long raison d'être,[12] fighting foreign militaries. It will be a huge cultural and resource shift to stop emphasizing traditional war fighting and focus on homeland defense and collapse recovery operations. Bureaucracies resist change, and don't normally adapt until a disaster hits or their budgets are slashed.

In his study of how the obsolete horse cavalry remained not just fielded, but cherished in the major militaries at the start of World War II, Edward Katzenbach, the director of the Defense Studies Program at Harvard, noted that the military is not just interested in the great weapons and the clash of armies, but also has a feeling of "romanticism." A warrior "cannot be expected to operate without faith in his weapons system."[13] The air force will cling to manned aircraft, the army to tanks, the navy to carriers, long after they are arguably too costly and obsolete. The revolutionary changes in defense strategy, budgeting, procurement, forces, and operations, will require a Secretary of Defense with the character, skills, and experience of a David Petraeus, and a POTUS who can defeat both the Perverted Triangle and the Iron Triangle[14] at the same time.

Thanks to the Perverted Triangle, the Achilles' heel of the US is our electric grid. Russia, China and North Korea have the capacity to instantly destroy the US electric grid and kill 90 percent of our population in the aftermath.[15] Grid loss also destroys most US military power. With the exception of strategic nuclear forces that have some capability to operate (short term anyway), our conventional military force cannot function and will have a hard time even staying alive when the civilian power grid is destroyed. For decades we have known that our electric grid is a fatal vulnerability that must be fixed, but the government has done nothing to address it. DHS is too dysfunctional to get the grid hardened and replacement microgrids built. The DoD led the huge, very difficult, but successful Manhattan Project to create nuclear weapons in WWII. A new director of Homeland Security with the DoD committed to and lead on homeland defense as its top priority must be tasked with eliminating our electric grid vulnerabilities.

No one should assume that in the face of a deadly, contagious virus, first responders will report for duty. As Hurricane Katrina demonstrated, many first responders will abandon their posts when a collapse results.[16] Military members, with a stronger culture, rules, and sanctions for those who go AWOL, are more likely to stay in service. This is another reason why DoD should be lead on homeland defense and collapse recovery operations, not FEMA or DHS.

With the vast majority of this federal military capability in the Army Guard, controlled by governors, there need be no fear of a military coup. We can trust military officers who are far more honest and respectful of the Constitution than career politicians.[17]

The US Cannot Maintain Conventional Military Technological Superiority, Another Good Reason to Abandon Our Focus on Fighting Armies Overseas

Since WWII, US defense strategy has stressed conventional weapons technology superiority so we can defeat any other country with our advanced weapons (and top-notch training/personnel, which are also required). This is very expensive, and will likely fail due to these big developments:

1. Advances in AI will find ways for China and other rivals to achieve breakthroughs, or trick/defeat/bypass our advanced conventional weapons. It will not be feasible to maintain the most advanced, undefeatable conventional military systems.
2. AI will also be used to develop easier, faster, harder to detect means to enrich uranium, or entirely new ways to develop nuclear weapons or equivalents. So if a country can't match US conventional weapons superiority they will likely leverage nuclear weapons to defeat our military, especially since the US foolishly, irresponsibly destroyed all its battlefield nuclear weapons in the 1990s.[18]
3. Bioengineered viruses and other new WMD can kill or incapacitate our troops, negating advanced conventional weapons.
4. Current and future WMD threats can bypass our overseas military forces and strike us at home.
5. Thanks to irresponsible government and the Perverted Triangle, the US is dangerously deep in debt and can no longer afford the price of high-cost, high-tech weapons.

The war in Ukraine has shown how cheap, simple drones can destroy high-tech weaponry costing ten to a hundred times as much. AI is going to be used to figure out all kinds of new, clever ways to disable or destroy our highly expensive, complex, high-tech weapon systems.

AI will be used to develop novel new ways to kill, and it will be impossible for the US to maintain conventional weapons technological superiority or counter all the advances in AI coming with high-tech military weapons systems.

As AI capability and use grows, the US will be unable to achieve conventional weapons superiority, no matter how much we spend/waste on advanced weapons systems. We will be challenged just keeping up with all the new tricks and countermeasures, new ways to attack and kill that AI will be used to develop. AI will develop better means to destroy our aircraft carriers and may also develop heretofore unthinkable ways to track and destroy our submarines. The $350 million we spend for an F-22 Raptor (that's for just one aircraft!) might be destroyed or disabled by a few-hundred-dollar system or trick that AI develops, something that we had never have even considered possible. The P-51 Mustang, that cost $50,000 to build in WWII ($900,000 in today's inflated dollars—1/400th the cost of the obscenely expensive fighters we buy today) might prove more capable in an era where computers and electronics can be a liability more than an advantage.

We will never again be able to have confidence that any weapon system is truly robust and superior; we can't anticipate what AI will do in inventing new countermeasures, new approaches, new means to destroy.

RAND's Dr. Paul Davis has long advocated "FARness"—flexibility, adaptiveness, and robustness for military forces. A DoD shift to buying not the most technologically advanced weapons systems, focused on specific threats or capability, but a more diverse force with large numbers of simple, diverse systems is needed.[19] Quoting a *Joint Forces Quarterly* article I co-authored, entitled "Improving DoD Adaptability and Capability to Survive Black Swan Events," "[l]ow-cost systems procured in large numbers may not be optimal for meeting specific known requirements, but they may be lifesaving to preempt or recover from black swan disasters."[20]

We will be far better off in the age of AI and Collapse to have a wide variety and large numbers of relatively low-cost systems, not a few very high-tech, extremely expensive systems, including many deliberately low-tech, electronics-free, cheap weapons. The swarms of many different types of inexpensive drones used by both sides in Ukraine illustrate the smarter way to fight. Putting all your money and faith in a few hugely expensive big target weapon systems is increasingly unwise. We must plan on unthinkable new WMD threats, AI tricks and advances that will render all kinds of systems, existing approaches and assumptions wrong. The long-standing practice of spending tens, hundreds of billions of dollars on a weapon system must end.

Taleb's fantastic book *The Black Swan: the Impact of the Highly Improbable* explains how we are psychologically programmed to make common misjudgments. His key point is critical for the DoD: do not try to predict the likelihood of a disaster but prepare for the impact. The most important thing DoD can do to prepare for inherent unknowns and new technologies capable of producing catastrophic effects is to enhance individual and organizational adaptability and procure more flexible, diverse weapons systems operated by more adaptable personnel.[21] Do not put hundreds of billions of dollars into a single high-tech weapons system and think it will prove invincible.

The F-35 fighter program's explosive costs continue to set records, with the latest Government Accountability Office report estimating the program cost will exceed $2 trillion. DOGE could accomplish its entire $2 trillion spending cut goal by eliminating just one weapons program if they could time travel and stop the F-35 Joint Strike Fighter.[22]

We should cease trying to develop, procure, and field the most advanced fighter aircraft, tanks, and aircraft carriers (weapons decisive in WWII, but not today); $350 million for a fighter aircraft, $13 billion for an aircraft carrier, $5 million for a tank.

Technological conventional military superiority is increasingly irrelevant to the survival of US citizens. Procuring, building, maintaining capability for big conventional overseas wars fought with the most advanced conventional weapons technology, the major focus of our military service since WWII, must end.[23]

The biggest barrier to abandoning conventional high-tech weapons will be the military industrial complex and the Perverted Triangle—addressed later in this chapter.

The US Must Not Abandon Overseas Involvement, but Focus on WMD Interdiction via "Prompt Global Strike"

The US needs to cut back on overseas interventions and military forces, give up on the too expensive and increasingly impossible quest to have conventional weapons technological superiority, and instead focus on prompt (limited in size and scope) global strike with conventional or nuclear attacks, smaller overseas forces backed by a return of battlefield nuclear weapons (BNW), flexible and diverse Special Operations Forces, and homeland defense/collapse recovery so fewer citizens die when the WMD attacks cannot be prevented.[24]

For decades the US military has worked to add "Prompt Global Strike" capability as a way to very quickly destroy WMD and other high value targets that "might pop up without warning in remote or sensitive areas, potentially precluding the United States from responding to the situation by employing other conventional weapon systems, deploying Special Operations Forces, or relying on the host country."[25] In the Age of Collapse it is vital for us to have the best possible Prevention, Preemption, and Preparedness, P^3, capability.

Thomas Wright, a strategy expert at the Brookings Institution, noted that "President Donald Trump has questioned the utility of the United States' alliances and its forward military presence" and "amid the shifting political winds, a growing chorus of voices in the policy community, from the left and the right, is calling for a strategy of global retrenchment, whereby the United States would withdraw its forces from around the world and reduce its security commitments."[26]

Global retrenchment "would be a grave mistake" Wright believes, giving up alliances that help regional security and raising the risk of nuclear proliferation.[27] But we can pursue retrenchment with allies taking our place where warranted, and abandoning US security guarantees in appropriate places. It would be wise to keep small deployments of US forces where they can make a valuable difference, in the Republic of Korea and Iraq for example. Supporting NATO and other allies is a must do for security—but with far fewer US troops and bases overseas—and with our allies compensating the US for the expense of having our forces stationed on their soil or in nearby areas supporting their defense. These alliances and overseas bases will be vital for prompt global strike missions against WMD threats. NATO is more vital than ever in our future, both for intelligence sharing on WMD threats and to help execute prompt preemptive strikes to prevent WMD attacks from nation-states, terrorist groups, and individuals.

The Republic of Korea and Japan should be encouraged and assisted to get their own nuclear weapons to defend against North Korea's and China's nuclear forces. If they want US troops in the ROK or Japan to help them deter and defeat an attack, they need to pay our costs of deploying forces to the country.

In our decisions on overseas involvement, we must consider and weigh the consequences of this intervention possibly increasing the likelihood that a nation-state, rogue group, or terrorists will be motivated to release bioengineered agents or other new WMD against us. As long as the US has superior high-tech conventional military forces, the best way to defeat us is either nuclear attacks on our troops (who today have no training on battlefield nuclear operations, as well as no responsive Battlefield Nuclear Weapons (BNW), or bio attacks/other WMD attacks on our homeland to force calling troops overseas back.

We can keep some big carrier groups and submarines, some overseas bases for the Air Forces and Special Operations Forces—but far more limited than today, with smaller forces largely for Prompt Global Strike attacks (conventional and nuclear if necessary) to take out imminent WMD threats—not to fight big land battles against large armies. We must reduce most overseas basing of troops and cease planning and equipping and sizing our force for large overseas land combat or counter insurgency engagements.

The Trump administration hasn't announced a foreign or defense policy, but based on Trump's goals, the nation's requirements, and the huge change in threats in the Age of Collapse, this administration should support shifting defense policy and spending from traditional, overseas combat, to top priority on detecting and preempting WMD attacks anywhere in the world and conducting operations to enable homeland recovery from WMD attacks.

Over past decades the US has slowly (with lots of restraints, redirection by career politicians) been building Prompt Global Strike capability, falling behind Russia and China in means like hypersonic missiles. In FY22, the navy requested $1.4 billion for Conventional Prompt Strike programs, primarily a hypersonic missile.[28] The need for this very fast, highly destructive attack capability has taken off in the Age of Collapse. What previously was regarded as a rarely needed strike capacity is now something that the US and our allies may need to use many times a year.

This very rapid, lethal Prompt Global Strike Capability is far more important now in the Age of Collapse when we may have very narrow windows of opportunity, perhaps just an hour, to destroy and stop a WMD attack before it is too late. The following examples illustrate this need for very rapid and reliably lethal prompt global strike capability:

- Terrorists that developed or seized nuclear weapons have just been located, but are about to transload and disperse the nuclear weapons[29]
- A rogue state with WMD is about to launch a missile[30]
- A small laboratory that has developed self-replicating nanobots capable of rapid replication and spread, able to consume most plant organic matter on Earth just discovered
- A major military power is about to launch an attack, and we want to quickly destroy their command and control capabilities[31]
- An individual that has finished developed a highly contagious and lethal new virus has been discovered in a rural area, may soon head to a large city to release the virus
- Leadership of a terrorist organization with WMD capability has gathered for a meeting[32]
- An adversary with mobile, concealed WMD systems has just been targeted, but will soon move[33]

ICBMs, land-based or on submarines, could be used with conventional weapons, though with some risk that China/Russia might detect the launch and fear it is a nuclear first strike. This is unlikely with both the very small scale of the launch, plus the ability to inform them of the limited prompt global strike mission. ICBMs, missiles, may sometimes be the only weapons with the delivery speed to reach the target in time. Even if a single conventional armed aircraft could get there rapidly, small conventional attacks may lack the power of a low-yield nuclear weapon to take out a target.[34] Space based weapons also have great response time, but violate law banning weapons in space.[35]

Low-Yield, Rapidly Delivered Tactical Nuclear Weapons vital to Preempt Attacks of Weapons of Mass Destruction

In the Age of Collapse, nuclear weapons will likely be the most valuable deterrent to misuse of other new deadly technologies and the best means to defeat them. Nuclear weapons will grow in value as a much faster, reliable means of eliminating WMD and existential threats to the nation and humanity, and deterring attacks by nation-states as US conventional military superiority ends.[36]

In many of the fleeting opportunities to interdict and destroy a WMD threat before it is too late, nuclear weapons will off the best, sometimes the only way to destroy the threat. Conventional, high-tech, advanced precision guided munitions, even if highly accurate, may not have sufficient explosive power to reliably destroy a critical or WMD target. A nation-state or terrorist group's WMD are likely to be stored in hardened underground bunkers. For underground targets, a penetrating nuclear warhead with several kilotons of explosive power may be needed. The intelligence information may be limited, or the number of targets large, or moving targets where you can't do limited conventional strikes, but need a nuclear detonation that can cover a broader area with adequate destructive power.

In the June 2025 attacks on Iran's nuclear facilities, B-2 bombers had to fly eighteen hours to reach the target; with over one hundred aircraft, plus naval vessels firing cruise missiles involved in the attack. It was not completely successful despite dropping fourteen of the largest penetrating conventional weapon we've got. The Massive Ordnance Penetrator, a 30,000-pound bomb that only the B-2 bomber can carry, has less than 0.01KT of explosive power (though it does tremendous kinetic energy and can penetrate into the earth before detonating). The low-yield setting of the B61–12 nuclear weapon[37] that many smaller aircraft can carry has thirty times the explosive power of our largest conventional bomb. A single aircraft can deliver a nuclear strike with more power in a fraction of the time, and at far less risk of detection, less likelihood of defeat, with less risk of loss of our military members, than the much larger, less powerful conventional strike package.

If the WMD is a human or plant virus, or other biological agent, nuclear attacks may be able to incinerate and completely destroy the agent while conventional munitions may just scatter live virus to the wind, not destroy it. The thermal radiation released by a nuclear weapon can reach a million degrees, incinerating viruses and biological agents. Biological/chemical weapons need to be thoroughly incinerated to be safely destroyed (not dispersed into the atmosphere by conventional explosions).

The other growing problem with conventional, high-tech precision guided munitions is that drone defensive attacks or AI may defeat them. They are full of chips that can be jammed. A nuclear warhead is far less susceptible.

One of the best ways to defeat AI threats, drone swarms, and new WMD on the battlefield might be to detonate a nuclear air burst to deliver a big EMP effect, but no ground devastation. With a nuclear strike warning message sent, friendly forces in the area would have a few minutes to remove antennas and unplug, turn off and shield equipment, or take with them as they take shelter, ideally underground. The low-yield air burst, at as low an altitude as possible to cover the terrain needed (without generating fallout), could knock out electrical and computer systems, drones, and other electronics intensive equipment.

It is absolutely essential to keep nuclear systems disconnected from any networked computers or Internet, with human-only means to control them. These control systems also need to be designed to prevent humans from being deceived by AGI (or enemies), and impossible for robots/droned controlled by AGI (or enemies) to activate. We already have this in the US, but must redouble efforts to be sure nuclear weapons are absolutely cut off from AI.

The US needs to both expand its deployment of USAF nuclear capable aircraft, and get the navy version of the F-35 capable of carrying the guided B61–12 tactical nuclear weapon, or use older aircraft to deploy nuclear weapons on carriers, and keep them located so we have nuclear and conventional prompt global strike capability across the globe.[38]

Low-Yield, Rapidly Delivered Battlefield Nuclear Weapons and Underground Defense Shelters vital to Protect Deployed US Forces

As detailed later, the US foolishly eliminated all of its ground-launched short-range battlefield nuclear weapons (BNW), destroying all short-range ballistic missile warheads and nuclear artillery shells in a unilateral abandonment of BNW. This was a horrendously bad national security decision made for domestic political reasons. As a result of the US eliminating all its rapidly deliverable, short-range, low-yield nuclear weapons, the army was left with no way to call in quick BNW strikes to stop a dangerous enemy ground attack. Since artillery-delivered BNW and atomic demolition munitions are gone, and the warheads on TLAM/Ns are high-yield and too slow to reach a battlefield target quickly, the only low-yield BNW left in the US arsenal are gravity bombs from US Dual Capable Aircraft (which can carry conventional or nuclear weapons). Aircraft delivered tactical nuclear weapons can work for Theater Nuclear Weapon (TNW) attacks, but are far too slow in delivering a prompt battlefield nuclear strike whose timing is critical.[39] The shift from a conventional battle to diving underground or into field fortifications, armored vehicles for an incoming nuclear strike must be very fast, timed to within a few minutes of a nuclear strike. Short-range US Army BNW artillery systems can do this; US Air Force fighters launched from hundreds of miles away generally cannot. They may also be shot down over the battlefield. Russia and China not only kept, but continue to modernize and expand their tactical, battlefield nuclear weapons. The US unilaterally abandoned and destroyed its responsive, short-range, low-yield BNW, disarming itself to score political points at home.[40]

Figure 41: Types of Nuclear Weapons (NW)

Strategic Nuclear Weapons (SNW)

- Fired against an enemy's homeland, leadership
- Usually far higher explosive yield to destroy underground targets, cities

Theater Nuclear Weapons (TNW)

- Fired against targets between battlefield (engaged forces) and SNW
- Usually against military targets, enemy forces, reinforcements
- Commonly referred to as Tactical Nuclear Weapons

Battlefield Nuclear Weapons (BNW)

- Fired against nearby enemy forces, on or near the battlefield
- Usually very low-yield, 1 to 10 kilotons
- Commonly referred to as Tactical Nuclear Weapons

With the US no longer enjoying conventional weapons technology superiority, and cutting back on the size of its overseas based forces, BNW are our best means of deterring and defeating larger enemy armies—or at least preventing our deployed forces from being overrun and killed. As we cut back on our overseas deployed military forces as recommended, and cease the unaffordable, impractical quest for conventional weapons technological superiority, the need for BNW to protect our deployed troops will rise.

New technologies and AI will continue to invent WMD and new weapons we can't imagine today. In the Age of Collapse, nuclear weapons may be the best means to protect our deployed forces from being overrun and killed.

Simple, very low-cost corrugated metal shelters can be quickly buried to provide deployed troops very strong protection against nuclear weapons. The other very positive feature of underground nuclear defense shelters is that they are inherently defensive—not useful for an army invading another country or on the attack. When

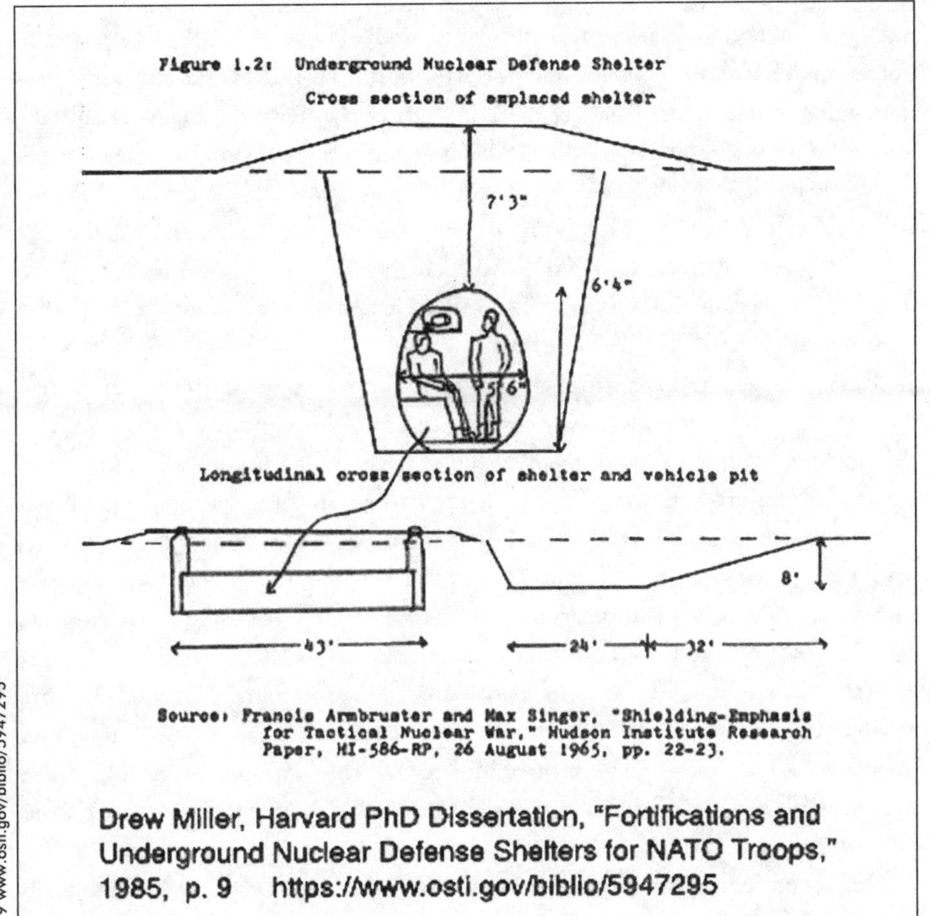

Drew Miller, Harvard PhD Dissertation, "Fortifications and Underground Nuclear Defense Shelters for NATO Troops," 1985, p. 9 www.osti.gov/biblio/5947295

Figure 42: Simple, low-cost, underground nuclear defense shelter for troops.

an enemy army is attacking, the defenders can call in an airburst nuclear strike to detonate minutes after they take cover underground in their shelters. Attacking forces on the surface are destroyed, defenders underground unharmed.[41] With an airburst, no radioactive fallout is generated.

Today, Russia and China can use battlefield nuclear weapons (BNW) to obliterate US conventional forces since the US irresponsibly gave up these weapons and refuses to train or even allow discussions of how battlefield nuclear warfare will be fought.

Russia has transferred some nuclear weapons to Belarus, and in January 2024, Belarus updated its military doctrine, describing nuclear weapons as an important component of their deterrence.[42]

Many of Russia's tactical nuclear weapons are deployed on ships and submarines, including land-attack hypersonic cruise missiles. Four new nuclear-powered nuclear-armed guided missile submarines are under construction. The Russian Air Force can deliver cruise missiles and bombs with the Tu-22M3 (Backfire) intermediate-range bombers, Su-24M (Fencer-D) fighter-bombers, the Su-34 (Fullback) fighter bomber, the MiG-31K, and their new Su-57 fighter-bomber. New hypersonic missiles have been tested.[43] Ground-based Russian tactical nuclear weapons include the 9K720 Iskander (SS-26) short-range ballistic missile and the 9M729 (SSC-8) ground-launched cruise missile. Belarusian military forces also have Russian-supplied nuclear-capable SS-26 Iskander missiles, and have been spotted training with them.[44]

Russia is also modernizing many of its shorter-range theater and tactical nuclear weapons, somewhere between one and two thousand nuclear warheads.[45] While there are lots of cruise missiles and gravity/guided bombs, the number of Russian very short-range, battlefield nuclear artillery shells and atomic demolition mines are unknown.[46] Just as the US promoted BNW to counter the huge conventional forces superiority of the Warsaw Pact in the 1950s and 1960s, Russia today sees them as vital to offset the superiority of US and NATO conventional forces today.[47]

Russia abandoned the Intermediate-Range Nuclear Forces Treaty. They are relying more than ever on TNW and BNW to defeat the US and NATO if we end up at war. With the proven poor capability of their conventional forces in Ukraine, they have no real alternative but to exploit their BNW advantage that the US has given them.

But far more important than having BNW is the doctrine and training to actually use them in combat. In 2024, Russia conducted a non-strategic nuclear weapons exercise that we know about, including simulated combat use of Iskander (SS-26) missiles.[48] Back in 1960, army officers were publishing articles about the lack of sufficient training in tactical nuclear war fighting. Soon thereafter, you could not even write about this lack of training—the entire topic was prohibited, officers literally censored, denied ability to publish on the topic in any government controlled publication.[49] In decades of research and work in the military with nuclear weapons issues and analysis, I am aware of no battlefield nuclear training exercises being conducted since the 1960s.

NATO conducts pretend nuclear training exercises that are a farce.[50] Aircraft fly, but there is no ground training to deal with the extremely difficult tasks (that must be timed very closely to ensure you are shielded or underground when the weapons detonate, but you can't be gone from surface defensive positions long or the enemy will overrun you).[51] NATO has always opposed use of BNW, preferring that the US conduct strategic nuclear strikes far from Western European territory (where we'd be defending) to both avoid collateral damage and have the nuclear exchange escalate to Moscow and the US—not their territory.

Analysts who considered both the specifics of battlefield nuclear combat tactics and how battlefield underground defense shelters could be used concluded that the combination of battlefield underground defense shelters and TNW would provide defenders with a very strong advantage in nuclear combat. But the dominance of strategic nuclear weapons and Mutually Assured Destruction in US doctrine, domestic political repudiation of TNW in the US and NATO (especially Germany), US Army preference for fighting with conventional weapons, and other factors covered later in this chapter, worked against battlefield underground defense shelters. With no big defense contractor or DoD agency with an incentive to lobby for buried corrugated pipe defense shelters and offer big campaign donations, they were not rejected—they were not even considered.[52]

The W79 ER/RB (enhanced radiation, reduced blast) warheads produced by the Reagan administration was a 50 percent improvement over the older eight-inch Artillery Fired Atomic Projectile with an 80 percent reduction in collateral damage. The Bush administration had them destroyed to score political points.[53] We need to bring this W79 artillery delivered BNW back and add simple, low-cost underground nuclear defense shelters to ensure our troops deployed in harm's way can stop a superior army from destroying them. Battlefield nuclear weapons must return to the US Army, especially nuclear rounds for artillery, rebuilding one thousand W79 nuclear artillery warheads for the eight-inch howitzer with a fifteen-mile range, yield of about 1 kiloton. Hiroshima was 15KT; the huge ICBM silo destroying strategic nuclear weapons are up to megatons in yield. The low-yield, short-range of these artillery-delivered nuclear weapons don't threaten enemy homeland attack or "uncontrollable escalation." They are responsive and useful in defending ground troops—especially those dug in, fighting defensively.[54]

US military commanders will always strongly prefer using conventional means to destroy enemy WMD and troops if this is possible. But if the enemy threat is severe and conventional power cannot stop it, the only measure left is likely to be using our BNW to destroy the attackers and keep our troops alive.

Active Duty Forces and Spending Must Be Slashed in Favor of More Guard and Reserve Forces

An earlier chapter on the need to prioritize Collapse Recovery Capability listed many changes needed in military and domestic law enforcement manpower. US military manpower should shift more from active duty to reserve and guard personnel. They are far less expensive, and if drawn largely from retired/separated active-duty forces, capable of performing as well as active-duty troops or better.[55] We must have far more ground forces for homeland recovery operations during and after a collapse, and this requires a much larger Army National Guard as well as a new, very large "Civil Ground Patrol" of volunteers, modeled on the Civil Air Patrol volunteer USAF auxiliary.[56]

The good news is that the improved military and civil defense capability we need is very cheap relative to our current military strategy of trying to achieve conventional military superiority in all areas with horrendously expensive high-tech weapons systems, very expensive support systems, and full-time troops. An Army Guard soldier with a rifle to protect stockpiled food in a revived civil defense program is readily affordable from the huge savings of ceasing to be the highest military spending nation in the world (40 percent of military spending with 4 percent of the world's population).[57]

Form an "American Foreign Legion" of Volunteers to Take On the Worst Military Missions in the Age of Collapse

Even with best efforts and top priority on controlling AI, detecting and hunting down nation-states/terrorist groups/individuals trying to kill with WMD, it is likely that recurring disasters in the Age of Collapse will be unstoppable. Asking young people to serve in the military in a state of almost constant war and disaster is arguably unfair. We should form an "American Legion" of volunteers, largely older people, to take on the worst tasks.[58]

The French Foreign Legion is a formal part of the French Army open to people of any nationality. The American Foreign Legion (AFL) would also be open to citizens of any country, but should largely draw from former, older US military personnel who want to serve again in situations where our military cannot directly engage, is overwhelmed, or has particularly unpleasant long-term tasking.

The AFL would draw completely on volunteers, primarily older, retired soldiers for fighting, and other volunteers for noncombatant positions. The notion that only young people have the strength or stamina to fight in tough conditions is wrong on many counts. First, many older, retired people are in better shape. Second, used in defensive roles, defending fixed positions, not aggressive offensive campaigns, great physical condition is not essential. Third, most people serving in a campaign are in positions where skills/knowledge trump physical strength. Drawing on Americans who served in the military, AFL soldiers will have good skills and experience. A primary motivation to join and serve would be to put older lives at risk and reduce the number of young who are sacrificed in war, or lose their opportunity to enjoy some semblance of good/normal life in the Age of Collapse.

Volunteering to serve in the AFL could also be an option for convicted people to select in lieu of jail time. As argued earlier, we must draw down the number of people in jail who are going to end up as bad marauders in a collapse.

While some Big Government advocates, liberals, and lawyers may insist such an AFL would be illegal and improper, it would be a very American, free Libertarian organization in the spirt of the "La Fayette Escadrille," a squadron of aircraft in World War I composed of American volunteers fighting in France before the US entered the war. There are Americans funding and facilitating the deployment of volunteers to fight in Ukraine today. Millions of couples will be losing their spouses in the Age of Collapse. Some of the survivors may want to join the AFL to focus on accomplishing good rather than wallowing over their lost spouse and destroyed life.[59]

Domestic Political Vote Pandering to Block Low-yield Nuclear Weapons, Nonsense of "Inevitable Escalation" Must End—We Need Limited Use of Low-yield Nuclear Weapons as Our Best Means of Defeating WMD Attacks and Protecting Deployed Troops

President Eisenhower understood that tactical nuclear weapons were instruments of war to save lives/avoid defeat. He did not regard them as evil instruments that must never be used.[60]

From the McNamara era on, politics and non-military factors have consistently blocked realistic BNW war fighting systems and tactics, and eliminated provision of key defense measures such as underground defense shelters for troops.[61] Pressure on the DoD to never consider nuclear war fighting as worthwhile or even feasible has included censoring publication of articles on how do to nuclear war fighting.[62]

Stringent anti-nuclear weapons opponents condemn efforts to promote survivability as wrong/immoral, fearing that anything that makes nuclear warfare more thinkable, weapons more useful, increases the likelihood of Armageddon. General William Odom, former Assistant Chief of Intelligence and Director of the National Security Agency, criticized for advocating civil defense, pointed out the paradox and irrationality of "the notion that it is evil to do things that would cause more people to survive in the event deterrence failed."[63]

The DoD has been forced for decades not to even consider the limited use of nuclear weapons for war-fighting. The Assistant to the Secretary of Defense for Nuclear, Chemical, and Biological Programs position in the Pentagon was left vacant from 1997 through late 2001![64] An article I wrote on limited nuclear war in Europe, which was accepted by the US Army for publication in their journal *Military Review*, was censored by the Office of Public Affairs, banned from publication.[65] A host of sources summarized in the webnotes conclude that the politically-correct ban on any discussion or preparation for battlefield nuclear war-fighting undermines and renders the threat of US nuclear weapons use completely uncredible.[66]

Congress in 1985 actually prohibited development of new enhanced radiation nuclear artillery warheads to score domestic political votes. Democratic congressmen have inserted measures to ban low-yield nuclear weapons to score points with anti-nuclear liberals. President George H. W. Bush offered a "peace dividend" of reduced military spending and eliminating battlefield nuclear weapons to swing votes that normally would go to Democratic candidates. The US foolishly eliminated all of its ground-launched short-range BNW, destroying all short-range ballistic missile warheads and nuclear artillery shells. The army was left with no way to call in quick nuclear strikes to stop a heavy enemy ground attack. Aircraft-delivered tactical nuclear weapons may not be able to reach the target if enemy air defenses are strong, and are far too slow in delivering a prompt battlefield nuclear strike whose timing is critical.[67] Russia and China not only kept, but continue to modernize and expand, their tactical, battlefield nuclear weapons. The US unilaterally abandoned, destroyed its responsive, short-range, low-yield battlefield nuclear weapons, and thus disarmed itself. These bans of low-yield nuclear weapons and President Bush's unilateral elimination of US battlefield nuclear weapons are Model 3 and 4 decisions, not Model 1 decision-making to maximize the benefit of citizens. The lack of battlefield nuclear weapons capability invites enemies to use these weapons—especially given Western superiority in conventional weaponry.

The Obama administration also pandered to anti-nuclear voters by reducing the role of nuclear weapons in security policy.[68] The Obama "Nuclear Posture Review" went so far as to state that the US would not use nuclear weapons in response to a chemical or biological attack.[69] This was an absolutely horrible decision for deterring Russia, China, North Korea, and Iran from releasing a deadly virus in the US that could kill most of our population, but very well received by Democrats who campaign on their moral opposition to nuclear weapons. Anytime we signal reluctance to use nuclear weapons, we undermine the credibility of the threat of nuclear weapons for deterring chemical, biological, conventional, or nuclear attacks.

In the hundred-plus-page JCS manual 3–12 "Joint Doctrine for Operations in NBC Environments" there is nothing on the tactics of battlefield use of TNW and not a single mention of underground shelters for troops.[70]

US nuclear doctrine says limited battlefield nuclear war will escalate uncontrollably to strategic nuclear attacks on the waring party's cities and thus will be deterred. This is not based on sound military analysis but politically correct BS and pandering for votes. The US, Russia, China, any county will always prefer avoiding escalation to strategic nuclear attacks on their homeland. If the US did seek to escalate a limited, battlefield nuclear war in to a "strategic" nuclear exchange between the US and Russia or China, that would invite nuclear attacks on the homeland that would kill tens of millions. Russia and China can be confident that no US president will fight a strategic nuclear war that risks destruction of US cities to save Ukraine or Taiwan—or even Western Europe. The promise of extended deterrence for other allies has never been credible when it comes to strategic nuclear weapons exchanges. As Henry Kissinger told the Europeans, "[g]reat powers don't commit suicide for their allies."[71]

The more the US does have strong conventional military technology and superiority and no BNW, the more likely it is that an enemy army will use tactical nuclear weapons to destroy US military forces.

Contrary to the political pandering view of Democratic politicians campaigning against evil nuclear weapons, having battlefield nuclear weapons does not mean we are more likely to get into a nuclear war. The lack of this capability increases the likelihood of China, Russia, and future nuclear armed enemies (there will be more as AI makes it easy to develop nuclear weapons) using BNW against us.

The best deterrence of war and WMD attacks is not by threatening mutual destruction, suicide, but deterrence by denial—convincing an enemy that they cannot hope to defeat the US in a war, that they would suffer defeat. Deterrence by denial, the ability to deny an enemy military success, is the most credible deterrence strategy. The ability to issue horrible destruction and punishment on their forces if they attack us adds to this deterrence. There is no better way to deter war and keep the peace. But military and deterrence strategy must assume that deterrence will fail and war may still result. This makes the strategy of deliberately not having the ability to keep a limited nuclear war small and limited, but insist and structure your forces so it is more likely to escalate to a strategic nuclear exchange with attacks on the homeland you are supposed to be protecting especially irresponsible, horrible, wrong—perverted.

The POTUS will be more deterred by a SNW exchange or "Mutually Assured Destruction" than Putin or Xi. US nuclear strategy of Mutually Assured Destruction is not credible as a deterrent, and suicidal as a defense. Mutually Assured Destruction was probably the stupidest policy in US military history, a Model 3 and 4 perversion driven by career politicians pandering for votes, not sound rational policy analysis, not best for citizens' prospects of survival.

Both Iraq and Russia admitted that they developed biological and chemical weapons despite having signed treaties pledging not to. The conduct of rogue nations and unpredictable acts by future despots are strong incentives for the US to always retain a useable TNW and BNW capability. Chemical weapons were used in the Iran–Iraq war, causing tens of thousands of casualties and fatalities. Iraq had more than 20,000 artillery shells and rockets filled with chemical agents during the First Gulf War. Senior Iraqi official have stated that Hussein was deterred from using chemical or biological weapons in the Gulf War because of the US threat to use nuclear weapons, plus fear that Israel could employ nuclear weapons.[72]

While abandoning defense promises for Taiwan should remove the most likely current threat of a major US nuclear war with a superpower, we always have to be prepared for situations where US/Allied troops are hopelessly outnumbered. In these situations, the ability and policy of using BNW firepower to stave off defeat may be our only way to deter war or avoid a crushing battlefield defeat and huge loss of life.

Both the 1991 Reed-Wheeler report and a 2001 survey by this author for an Air Force Institute of Strategic Studies–funded paper show that TNW are more important than SNW in deterring or fighting the most likely scenarios of nuclear war.[73] The Reed-Wheeler study found that for both nuclear weapon and non-nuclear weapon states, deterring attacks on US allies with WMD, SNW were rated irrelevant while TNW were significant. Likewise, in deterring use of WMD against US forces abroad, SNW rate as insignificant, TNW significant. Low-yield, "usable" TNW are the best weapons to deter use of WMD and BNW are best for protecting our deployed troops.

In the Age of Collapse and frequent WMD attacks, it is time to abandon Mutually Assured Destruction nonsense and stop the Perverted Triangle's domestic political pandering from shaping our foreign and military policies. We must use deterrence by denial—not deterrence based on incredible threats of escalation and mutual punishment. Since irrational, desperate, or ruthless despots may attack regardless, we must ensure that our defenses and use of nuclear weapons are based on how they can best be used to preempt WMD attacks and protect our troops and citizens, not score political points by proclaiming our horror at nuclear war.

Both for Prompt Global Strike to eliminate WMD threats, and to empower and protect US military forces overseas, the US must return BNW to the army and employ low-yield, limited use tactical nuclear weapons when they are the best means of protecting US lives. The Obama administration's doctrine of no first use, even in response to a massive enemy attack with chemical or biological weapons, must be repudiated. Nuclear weapons in the Age of Collapse will often be our best and only means of averting a WMD collapse disaster that could be several orders of magnitude more devastating than a nuclear weapon detonation.

If a terrorist captured an artillery nuclear warhead, they would be a far less deadly threat than we face from North Korean ICBMs delivering an EMP attack on our vulnerable electric grid, an H5N1 bio attack, or a terrorist group using AI to develop a high-yield nuclear device that could wipe out a big city. BNW are far more usable in defensive combat—that's why we need them, and our allies may, if attacked by large Russian, Chinese, Iranian, or North Korean armies. This kind of nuclear weapons system, using common, widely used artillery pieces that the US, NATO, South Korea, other allies possess, is also very cheap relative to either high-tech conventional military weapons systems or the long-range strategic nuclear weapons systems we maintain.

The US nuclear inventory was once as high as 32,500 weapons, the equivalent of 1 million Hiroshima size nuclear weapons! Adding low-yield theater nuclear weapons for Prompt Global Strike and BNW would not mean a return to this high level of destructive power. The increase in warheads would be about one thousand, an increase in explosive power of just 1 megaton. Few would likely be used, but with their short-range, if defending across a large front, our Army may need hundreds at their disposal. The Prompt Global Strike nuclear force would also need several hundred warheads, though most strikes would probably be just one low-yield detonation, ideally an airburst to avoid fallout.

The US has no biological or chemical weapons. Thus, we must not just retain BNW and TNW, but trumpet a policy of using nuclear weapons against any nation or group that threatens to employ WMD against our forces or allies we protect. Nothing may deter a terrorist group from using WMD, but capable, rapidly responsive BNW along with theater and strategic nuclear weapons may deter attacks from enemy states, and be the only means available to destroy WMD attacks by terrorist groups or insane individuals.

In the Age of Collapse, the US military needs to abandon its world's policeman role, give up on the too expensive and impossible quest to have conventional weapons technological superiority, and focus on prompt global strike with conventional or small nuclear attacks, with much smaller overseas forces backed by a return of battlefield nuclear weapons. Our military priority must be homeland defense and collapse recovery operations so fewer citizens die when WMD attacks cannot be prevented.

Nuclear weapons, whether used in prompt global strike to preemptively destroy a WMD attack, or save US military forces from being overrun and destroyed, can be the best or only means to save lives, potentially millions or billions of them.

They must stop being condemned as inherently evil or only useful for mutually assured destruction. New technologies in the Age of Collapse will deliver far worse threats than nuclear weapons, and nuclear weapons may often be our best or only means of limiting the loss of lives.[74]

Chapter Eleven

TO SAVE THE UNITED STATES, WE MUST STAY OUT OF CHINA'S CIVIL WAR WITH TAIWAN

Taiwan is a province of China that broke away after the Communists won a long civil war in 1949. George Marshall and President Truman wisely refused to interfere in China's civil war in the late 1940s and early 1950s, but due to Senator McCarthy and the big "Red Scare," US career politicians pledged to defend Taiwan to prove they were "tough on Communists" and not engaged in "appeasement." The United Nations recognizes that Taiwan is not an independent nation, but a breakaway part of China—as does official US policy since Kissinger and Nixon rightly got the US back to friendly terms with China and backed off military support for Taiwan. China has been vowing to retake control of their breakaway province, by military force if necessary, for over half a century, and has been building up its military and expanding in the South China Sea to help retake Taiwan. Chinese President Xi is readying China to invade the island and fight the US if necessary.[1]

Despite superior nuclear forces and conventional weapons superiority, the US would lose in a war with China, forced to back down either because of the horrible devastation caused by China destroying our electric grid with agents in the US and physical/cyberattacks, or with a very small nuclear EMP attack. China can take out US Space GPS satellites and quickly destroy US military forces near Taiwan, or use battlefield/theater nuclear weapons to destroy them with little fear of US escalation to a strategic nuclear exchange on Chinese/US cities that no POTUS would be willing to accept to defend Taiwan.[2]

China has prepared their populace for a big war and a collapse, with years of stockpiled food. The US government not only does nothing to prepare its citizens, but has executive orders authorizing government agencies to steal food from citizens. According to congressionally funded studies, up to 90 percent of the US population will die if the electric grid is destroyed, something China can readily accomplish.[3] When the grid goes down, US conventional military power is largely eliminated. Nor can US defense industry produce without Chinese materials that over decades our irresponsible government has made us dependent on. China already has an economy with far more manufacturing and agricultural production power than the US economy, which is more for entertainment, services, IT, government, and sectors worthless to national survival.

Taiwan has been part of China since 1683, seized for some time by Japan, never an independent nation-state. The US recognized that Taiwan is part of China in the December 1, 1943 "Cairo Declaration," stating that all territories Japan had stolen from China, including Taiwan, should be restored to China. In October 1945, the Chinese accepted Japan's surrender and return of Taiwan Province to the Chinese government.

After the end of the Chinese Civil War in 1949, the losing side, Chiang Kai-Shek and the "Nationalists," retreated from the mainland to the island of Taiwan, while continuing to claim that they were the sole legitimate government of China. Corruption, poor morale, and often poor leadership led to the Nationalists's defeat. In 1971, the United Nations sided with Communist China (the "People's Republic of China") and expelled the Taiwanese "Republic of China" as the official Chinese government. Taiwan is not recognized as an independent nation; it is a Province of China. From 1949 on, Communist China has insisted that Taiwan is theirs, and will be retaken. China's current President Xi has made this his top priority and very openly, and connivingly, declared that he will achieve this prime objective.

George Marshall, arguably the greatest/most important American of the last century, successfully resisted domestic political pressure to intervene in China's civil war, and as Secretary of State and later Defense, avoided any commitments to defend the defeated Nationalists on Taiwan.[4]

Chiang Kai-shek had partisan allies in Congress and the US media, and leveraged both to demand that the US defend Taiwan. George Marshall and the Joint Chiefs of Staff advised against any defense guarantees for Taiwan, the chiefs arguing "that overt United States military action to deny Communist domination of Formosa would not be justified." Secretary of State Dean Acheson also advised against security guarantees for Taiwan, arguing that it would arouse "the righteous anger, and the wrath, and the hatred of the Chinese people." Note in particular the words "righteous anger"—i.e., the People's Republic of China had the right to handle Taiwan, their civil war, their people, their internal affairs—not something the

US had any right to interfere with. President Truman followed their professional advice, and rightly declined to offer military assistance or guarantees for Taiwan.[5]

Senator McCarthy was a "little-known junior senator from Wisconsin until February 1950 when he claimed to possess a list of 205 card-carrying Communists employed in the US Department of State."[6] McCarthy received huge publicity using his power to conduct Senate investigation "witch hunts," leveraging what the American Heritage Dictionary today defines as "McCarthyism" or "McCarthy tactics":

> 1. The political practice of publicizing accusations of disloyalty or subversion with insufficient regard to evidence; and 2. The use of methods of investigation and accusation regarded as unfair, in order to suppress opposition.[7]

The McCarthy "Red Scare" led vote-pandering, the Perverted Triangle, to pledge absolute opposition to Communism and avoid any votes that might make them look "soft on Communism," or willing to "appease" Communist leaders.

Senator McCarthy's wildly successful lying and badgering campaign about government being full of Communists and soft on Communism ended rational, Model 1 analysis and policy making on Taiwan.

US foreign/military policy was forced by domestic political pandering to be more and more pro-Taiwan (then called Formosa).[8] In 1955, the "Formosa Resolution" passed Congress, giving the POTUS authority "to employ the Armed Forces of the United States as he deems necessary for the specific purpose of securing and protecting Formosa . . . against armed attack [by the Communists]." The treaty provided US military support for Taiwan, even to stationing US troops in Taiwan. The treaty and US military support prevented the PRC from attacking Taiwan and established the situation of long-term division of China.

McCarthy was ultimately censured by the US Senate in 1954, but the huge shift in political campaigning and public belief that there must be no appeasement or compromise in fighting Communists overseas he created lived on, contributing to the decade-long Vietnam War engagement. In the House of Representatives, the "Un-American Activities Committee" (which was enacted in 1938) investigated and in effect prosecuted Americans questioning the Vietnam War. In 1959, former President Harry S. Truman denounced the House Un-American Activities Committee as the "most un-American thing in the country today." The committee was finally disbanded in 1975.[9] A history professor who wrote many books about McCarthy concluded that, "McCarthyism squelched most serious criticism of American society and of the government's conduct of the Cold War. Even after it disappeared from the main stage, the political timidity that it encouraged continues to haunt us all."[10] McCarthy tactics and Red Scare politics live on today in US government policy and popular beliefs towards Taiwan.

In October 1971, the United Nations General Assembly adopted Resolution 2758, recognizing the People's Republic of China as the only legitimate representatives of China to the United Nations, expelling the representatives of Taiwan.

Under Nixon and Kissinger, then the Carter administration, the US wisely moved away from Perverted Triangle pandering treatment of the PRC as an evil Communist enemy and relations were normalized. This required the US recognizing the PRC as the official, real government of China, and pledging to not treat Taiwan as a full-fledged, independent nation. In the Shanghai Communiqué in 1972, the US agreed that "there is but one China and that Taiwan is a part of China." This US statement also pronounced that "settlement of the Taiwan question by the Chinese themselves" is called for.[11] The US government again acknowledged what Marshall and Truman had agreed to decades ago—Taiwan is part of China, resolution of Taiwan-mainland China issues are internal matters for those two parties to resolve, not something the US should interfere in.

The Nixon and Carter administrations had success in getting the PRC to shift from siding largely with the Soviet Union to more support of the US and democracies. The Carter administration formally abandoned the US mutual defense treaty with Taiwan, the "Republic of China."[12] In establishing diplomatic ties in 1978, the United States again announced that "[t]he Government of the United States of America acknowledges the Chinese position that there is but one China and Taiwan is part of China. The United States of America recognizes the Government of the People's Republic of China as the sole legal Government of China."[13]

But the career politicians of the Perverted Triangle still favored the simplistic, powerful view that any enemy is Hitler and failure to oppose them is cowardly appeasement. The Taiwan government mobilized their lobbyists in the US to get Congress to pass another security guarantee for Taiwan. Taiwan appealed to members of Congress arguing against Communism using the Hitler appeasement analogy (one of the few things most Americans remember about history), plus Beijing's human rights violations and its curtailment of religious freedoms.[14] The GOP attacked the Carter administration's continued support of the PRC over Taiwan and got Congress to pass the "The Taiwan Relations Act" (TRA) in 1979. The Act was passed by both chambers of Congress and signed by President Carter in 1979 after the breaking of relations between the US and the ROC. The act does not recognize the terminology of "Republic of China," but uses the terminology of "governing authorities on Taiwan."

The TRA does not guarantee or reject direct US military intervention if the PRC attacks Taiwan, but does require that the POTUS provide assistance to Taiwan's defense and requires that Taiwan policy not be changed unilaterally by the POTUS, with any decision to defend Taiwan made with the consent of Congress. The act contradicted earlier Nixon/Carter administration assurances to the PRC. Officially the policy is referred to as "strategic ambiguity," a polite term for contradictory, dishonest, policies—government lies. Successive US administrations have sold arms to Taiwan despite demands from the PRC that the US follow other assurances and agreements the US government made with the PRC.[15] "Strategic ambiguity" is career politicians pandering to be tough on China, Congress disputing executive branch power, government lies.

Under President Reagan, the United States agreed to reduce arms sales to Taiwan, but also declared we would not formally recognize PRC's sovereignty over Taiwan, part of the "Six Assurances" offered to Taipei in 1982. The TRA is still in effect, and China rightly views the TRA as US interference in Chinese internal affairs and a cause for war.[16] The PRC is correct. The US government is controlled by the pandering, self-serving Perverted Triangle, cheating and lying on official government agreements, pushing China toward war.

When China invades Taiwan it will be the most expected invasion in history. They are making all the critical military, economic, and survival preparations. From Mao on, China has trumpeted the truth that Taiwan is part of China and they will reincorporate it into China, by force and invasion if necessary. In 2022, Chinese President Xi said he was "laser-focused" on "reacquiring the Taiwanese separatists" and would regard his entire lifetime as a failure if he didn't get that done.[17] The CIA Director openly released to the media a report that President Xi has ordered the military to be ready for war, but suggested it was still several years out. Other experts lay out a convincing case that China has committed to achieving their half century plus old goal of retaking Taiwan, and may invade in months, not years.[18]

China has illegally seized small islands in the southwest Pacific and built them into naval bases and airfields for missiles and aircraft that can sink carriers we send to support Taiwan. The PRC's military preparations to retake Taiwan have been happening for decades, and reported on, warned about by multiple military and intelligence agencies. Commanders of US Strategic Command, Transportation Command, many top generals have warned that China is clearly preparing for an attack. Some of these warnings have been condemned by the Pentagon, administration officials, and government-funded think tanks, since they conflict with administration messaging that US policy toward China is working, war is unlikely.

The US–China Economic and Security Review Commission is a legislative branch commission created by Congress in 2000 to monitor, investigate, and report to Congress on the relationship between the United States and the PRC (i.e., a political maneuver to demonstrate distrust with the Executive Branch, which is supposed to execute foreign policy). A recent commission hearing covered China's stockpiling of minerals, grain, oil, and other key resources in what could be a precursor to an invasion of Taiwan. "The Chinese central government stockpiling minerals is one potential indicator that it may be preparing to invade Taiwan," Gregory Wischer of Dei Gratia Minerals told the Commission. Witnesses compared China's current stockpiling of key resources with Nazi Germany's and Japan's stockpiling activities prior to WWII. Commodity traders have noted that "[f]rom corn to sorghum to even barley, China continues to buy feed grains. . . . No matter the source of the surge in purchases, one thing is clear: China is stockpiling grain."[19] *Bloomberg* has reported, "Warehouses across China are bulging with grain."[20]

The US produces about 83 percent of the food we consume, a good position (and much of the imports, fruits and vegetables, are not required for survival).[21] But this production is by highly industrialized/mechanized farms, using a lot of imported fertilizers, seeds shipped in from a few big seed companies, with farming conducted by less than 1 percent of the population, using large amounts of oil and energy. In a collapse with the grid down, there may be no fuel production or distribution, no imported fertilizers, disruption of seed suppliers, lack of trains/trucks to transport crops to food manufacturers (who probably can't operate), so little to no food may be produced or distributed. US chicken producers are basically just contract growers—the birds and feed are trucked in, the chicken company picks up, slaughters, and distributes the processed/packaged chicken. A highly complex and cost-effective food production system in good times, but a just-in-time delivery operation, dependent on lots of shipments/fuel/electricity, a set up for breakdown and starvation in a collapse.

The largest food producer in the world is not the US, it's China. China's workforce engaged in agriculture, fishing, forestry, food production is 22 percent of the population![22] China is a huge food importer, but much of this is soybeans (to feed pigs) and meat. In a collapse, survival situation, grain would go to feed people directly, far more efficient than feeding meat animals.[23] While Fortitude Ranch, the nation's largest survival community, has chickens and ranch animals, the bulk of their survival food production is based on farming corn, potatoes, and Jerusalem artichoke (sunchokes)—not the far less calorie efficient feeding of grain to big meat animals.[24]

But the food statistic that should scare the crap out of Americans is that China has enough wheat and rice reserves to feed its citizens for up to two years![25]

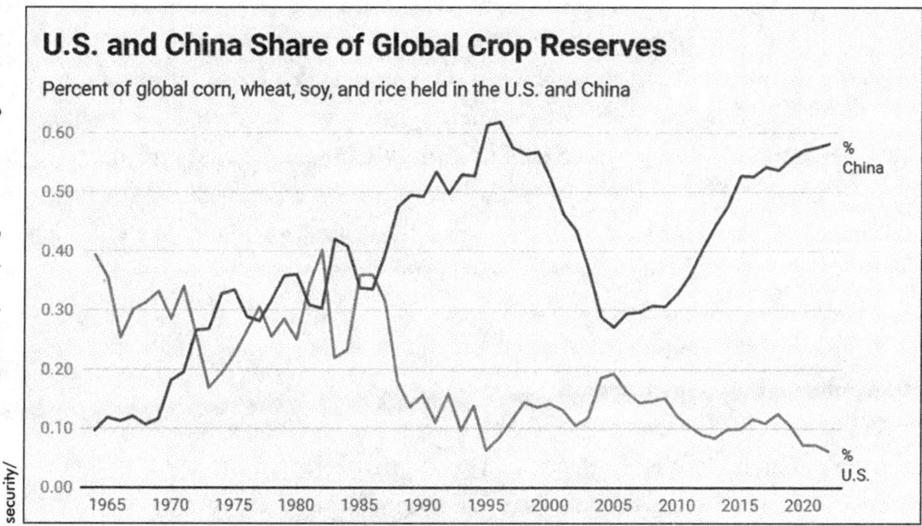

The Institute for Progress, https://ifp.org/food-reserves-global-food-security/

Figure 43: China holds most of the world's grain reserves, the US very little.

An expert financial analyst, Kyle Bass, studying China's preparations for war was featured in a Hudson Institute event, presenting evidence that China is preparing for an invasion of Taiwan. In his Hudson Institute presentation, Bass explains how all the evidence points to a clear conclusion that Chinese President Xi is indeed preparing for invading Taiwan and likely war with the US, as long as we continue to promise defending Taiwan.[26]

Legal changes, educational changes, every step needed to ready China to succeed with both an invasion of Taiwan and war with the US have been made—rapidly accelerating under Xi in the past few years. For example, in 2023, a new foreign policy law "essentially makes all Chinese companies extensions of the Chinese government . . . giving Beijing the legal authority to seize individuals' assets and prevent them from leaving China." China is also preparing to take over foreign companies in China.[27]

Large-scale drills and exercises with power outages have been conducted, travel bans have been expanded, blood supply donations are being promoted, the country is being completely readied for a major war.[28]

Kyle Bass examined the things China is doing financially that do not make financial sense, but do fit perfectly with preparations for war, concluding that the evidence is convincing that China is preparing for an invasion of Taiwan, and war with the US, that may happen in months, not years.[29] China has stopped allowing access to their economic data; US companies doing economic data collection in China have been raided under new Chinese anti-foreign espionage laws. If China was preparing for war, they would have Chinese companies default on US denominated bonds. And that is what they are doing; 65 percent of USD denominated bonds for Chinese property developers are in default—while these same companies have only 21 percent of their on-shore bonds in default. These actions are bad for China's economy, they will reduce foreign investment in China—but they are good preparations for war. Another indication of Chinese preparations for war is their stockpiling of critical economic resources. In sum, Bass concludes the intent is clear and preparations have been made to a level that it is "highly likely" China will invade Taiwan and risk war with the US.[30]

If you ever wondered how Germany's aggression and plans for WWII could have been missed, with people like Winston Churchill regularly and very publicly warning of the military build ups and hostile intentions, seeing how we ignore the buildups, threats, and warnings today may give you a better understanding. Big Government likes the public to "not be alarmed" and trust in their judgment, and it is human nature to try and ignore bad things we can't personally do anything to stop.

There is little doubt that China will regain Taiwan; just a question of how soon they do it and whether or not the US suffers attacks destroying our electric grid and a nuclear attack on our cities and deployed military forces in the process. China will pressure or if necessary invade Taiwan to reclaim this territory, and if the US follows through on promises to defend Taiwan, we must expect that China will engage in "nuclear chicken" against us—threatening and if necessary firing some nuclear weapons against the US to force the POTUS to back down. [31]

The overriding reality is that despite smaller nuclear forces, the Chinese are well positioned to crush the US in a nuclear war, emerging not just as the victor, but the most powerful country in the world. Unless the president was willing to have many major cities wiped out in a large nuclear war, China can confidently play "nuclear chicken" with the US and prevail. The POTUS will swerve away to avoid nuclear devastation, not sacrifice tens of millions of US lives to defend Taiwan. This is probably China's greatest advantage over the US—they can suffer tens of millions of casualties in a nuclear exchange and achieve victory over the US, retake Taiwan, and emerge as the world's clear, dominant superpower.[32]

A big risk for us is that China may launch a small number of nuclear weapons at the US to force the POTUS to back down. One of the horrible unintended consequences of having a small ballistic missile defense system is that it may actually *increase* the likelihood of a small Chinese nuclear attack.[33] Reason: China can launch a few ICBMs as they notify POTUS "we have launched a small nuclear attack that your ABM system can handle, as a final warning that you must cease support of Taiwan." If the ABM system destroys all incoming warheads, China has not killed any Americans but applied maximum pressure to force the US out short of all-out war. My bet is that any POTUS would back down at this point.

Unfortunately, the odds are that our ABM system won't knock them all out. And if one detonates high up for a HEMP (High altitude EMP) attack, our electric grid could be destroyed. According to a former CIA director, who chaired the congressionally sponsored study of an EMP attack on our grid, a successful HEMP attack could kill 90 percent of the US population since no power for at least a year, no municipal water systems, mass starvation, no law and order.

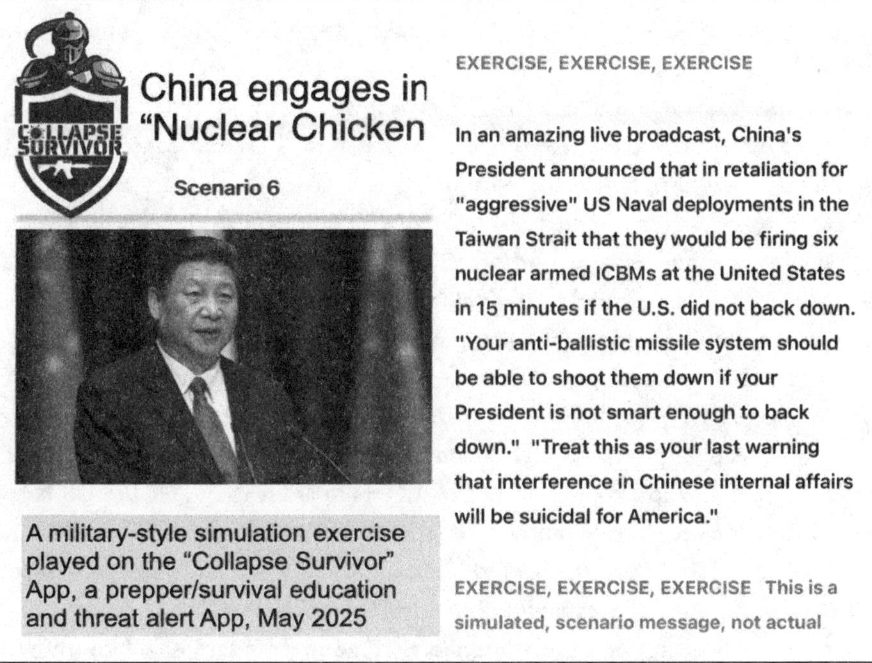

Figure 44: Collapse Survivor App simulation of US–China "Nuclear Chicken" battle over Taiwan.

The "Collapse Survivor" app ran a Taiwan invasion exercise training scenario where China threatened and then launched a small-scale nuclear strike on the US to force the president to back down. The POTUS did back down, but unfortunately not fast enough—the US electric grid was destroyed, and a horrible collapse resulted, killing tens of millions.[34]

China will very likely "win" any engagement because they are willing to suffer deaths of tens or even hundreds of millions to achieve their number one goal of reclaiming Taiwan, and are far better prepared for survival than the US. The US will lose a fight with China over Taiwan. The biggest question is how much does the US suffer before the POTUS backs down and surrenders Taiwan.

China will likely exploit our Achilles' heel (our fragile, vulnerable electric grid) via the thousands of Chinese agents in the country doing physical attacks on the grid. Some Chinese agents are likely working inside utility companies where they can conduct sabotage, send jolts of electricity down the grid to destroy transformers. As explained earlier, I believe the widespread, bizarre big drone activity in the US in the past year was China using Air Taxi drone front companies to prepare for drone attacks (large drones releasing hundreds of small drones carrying explosive charges to destroy transformers), along with physical attacks on transformers and cyberattacks. If the Chinese take out our fragile electric system, which they can do with even a very small nuclear strike, most Americans could be killed—and Taiwan not saved.

Our conventional weapons technological superiority over China can be largely eliminated by destroying the US electric grid. When the US electric grid goes down our military bases have no electric power, and every available military member will be needed to help limit the loss of hundreds of millions of American lives when electric power is gone for a year or more.[35] If you want to understand how vulnerable the grid is, and how its loss will kill most Americans, watch this professional documentary: https://griddownpowerup.com/

Another Achilles' heel of our military and high-tech conventional weapons is their reliance on GPS satellites for navigation, communications, target acquisition, and precise weapons guidance. China and Russia have developed a space offensive capability to disable, neutralize, or destroy US space assets to disable the US Navy and USAF. China could take out US GPS satellites and then obliterate US forward bases in Guam, Japan, South Korea, destroy naval ships near Taiwan, and destroy much of Taiwan's military capability in a surprise attack.[36]

Despite such a huge, long-standing threat, Taiwan's military is still poorly prepared to defeat an invasion. The widespread expectation in Taiwan is that the Americans will keep China at bay.[37]

Though frontline combat units have been 40 percent undermanned for years, Taiwan has resisted longer conscription.[38] Military service is unpopular among young Taiwanese. Taiwan's government has repeatedly reduced the period of required compulsory service, from two years down to just four months. Nor do they have a big or capable reserve force. In the US, Guard and Reserve troops serve a weekend a month plus two weeks (minimum, many do more); Taiwan requires just five to seven days of refresher training every other year. Under pressure from the US, Taiwan just extended mandatory conscription and military training for young men back to one year.[39]

The US has not just lost its premier nuclear weapons supremacy, it cannot maintain conventional military superiority, which will be increasingly less powerful and important as AI develops new countermeasures as well as new WMD.

Advances in AI will lead to China and other rivals achieving breakthroughs in advanced technology weapons and trick/defeat/bypass our advanced conventional weapons. Even with conventional military spending we can no longer afford because of huge welfare and entitlement program costs, it is not feasible to maintain the most advanced, undefeatable conventional military systems. The swarms of many different types of inexpensive drones used by both sides in Ukraine illustrate the smarter way to fight.

Putin may have invaded Ukraine with an agreement that China would support him and use the Ukrainian War to improve conditions for them to invade Taiwan. The huge expenditure and draw down of NATO and US weapons and ammunition given to Ukraine will certainly help China. The huge Russian losses of men and equipment in Ukraine are probably due to Russian incompetence and the big advantages of defending versus attacking. But this meat grinder has been carried out with massive Ukrainian expenditure of US and NATO munitions. NATO weapons stockpiles are depleted and the US is so far behind in anti-tank missiles and other conventional munitions that contractors cannot get current orders produced until 2026.[40] There is a much bigger DoD budget, but naval and air force weapons production are falling behind schedule. The carnage in Ukraine is clearly hurting Russia, but could help pave the way for China's invasion of Taiwan. And once China invades Taiwan, if the US grid is destroyed or a small nuclear exchange occurs, US support for Ukraine will very likely cease as we finally focus on US security and survival.

The US will not want a Taiwanese nuclear war to escalate to any strategic nuclear exchanges (nuclear detonations on US soil), so China can launch nuclear attacks on US ships and bases around the South China Sea with little fear of US nuclear attacks on Chinese territory that will surely yield Chinese nuclear attacks on the Continential United States (CONUS). Smart US leaders, focused on protecting American citizens, would have nuclear forces, training, and policy to limit nuclear weapons to overseas fighting, to minimize the likelihood of escalation to strategic nuclear attacks on the homeland, but the US is dominated, ruined by the Perverted Triangle.

If China decides to blockade Taiwan and fight a long war with only conventional weapons, they will also prevail. They have a huge, robust defense industry, we have a weak and dependent one. If a conventional or limited battlefield/theater nuclear war over Taiwan occurs, if it lasts more than a few weeks the US will lose because we will run out of ammunition and cannot build replacement weapons without China. Our irresponsible government has allowed our defense industry and military to be totally dependent on China for a host of materials we cannot source anywhere else (covered later in this chapter).

US politicians abandoned the civil defense program of stockpiling food decades ago, preferring spending that could buy more reelection votes. The only reason the US has some agricultural food stocks is because of USDA food subsidization and price stabilization programs (a better way to buy votes).[41]

What about the US strategic stockpile program? It is for medical equipment, petroleum, and "other materials that the federal and state governments can draw on" (this is the correct wording—these supplies are for governments, who may or may not pass supplies on to normal citizens after their "Continuity of Government" priority is met).[42] Food stockpiles? None. Absolutely no food is stockpiled in the US for feeding its citizens in a collapse. Unlike the career politicians and top government officials who have taxpayer-funded first class survival facilities at Mount Weather, Raven Rock, and many other FEMA and military sites, US citizens have nothing for civil defense.[43]

When talking about national security and survival, we need to stop using terms like Gross Domestic Product or Gross National Product, which are very misleading, dangerous economic measures of national power. What is relevant to defense and survival is "Domestic Survival Capability"[44]:

Gross Domestic Product is less critical for citizen's survival than "Domestic Survival Capability"

Gross Domestic Product

- Total market value of all the final goods and services produced
    - but entertainment, designer clothes, social media, restaurants, vast majority of government, worthless in a collapse

Domestic Survival Capability

- Maintain law and order
- Locally sourced food
- Food Reserves
- Local water (that can be delivered if electric grid down)
- Ability to farm/ranch long term, with manual labor
- Ability to self-defend
- Ability to manufacture

Figure 45: "Domestic Survival Capability" not Gross Domestic Product is critical for collapse survival.

To avoid or survive a collapse when the economy is not functioning, people are not coming to work, and there is widespread loss of law and order as people without food and water struggle and loot/kill to survive, a population needs to have reliable food and water and security. The US and most of Europe (Switzerland, Sweeden, and Finland are exceptions) are largely unable to do this. China has prepared its population to avoid/survive a collapse.[45]

Add in the requirements to maintain an army and manufacture ammunition and replacement weapons, and the US is a complete basket case. China can manufacture and run the most powerful wartime economy in the world. The US has far less capacity, and through smart Chinese moves and criminally irresponsible US government decisions by the Perverted Triangle, the US will be unable to produce military goods because China controls too many key inputs.

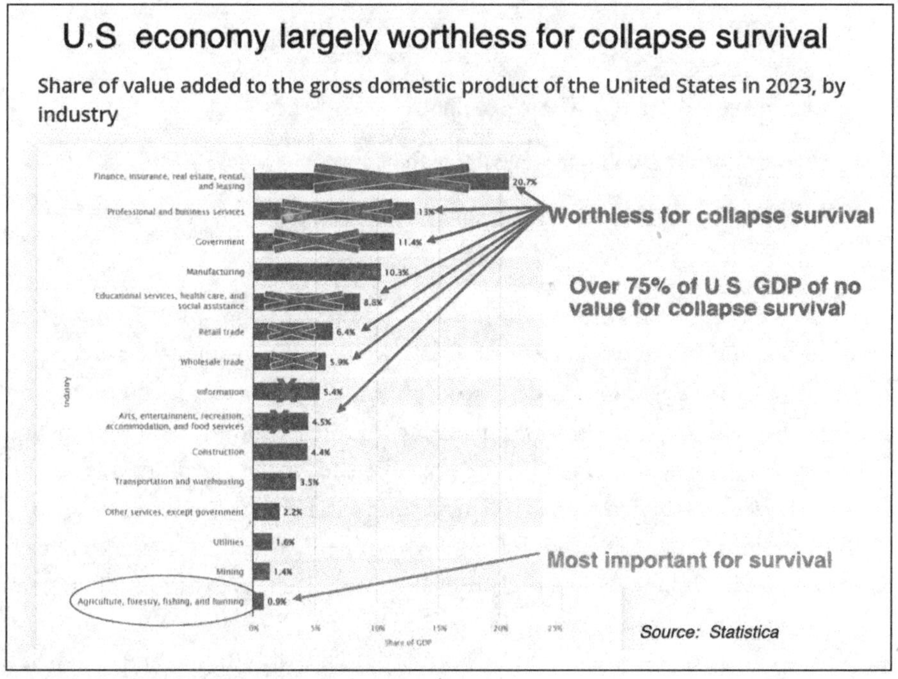

Figure 46: The US economy is largely worthless for collapse survival.

More than 75 percent of the US GDP is in services, finance, entertainment, government, IT, sectors of little to no value in a collapse. Manufacturing accounts for just 10 percent of US GDP. The most important economic sector, food production, doesn't account for even 1 percent of US GDP.

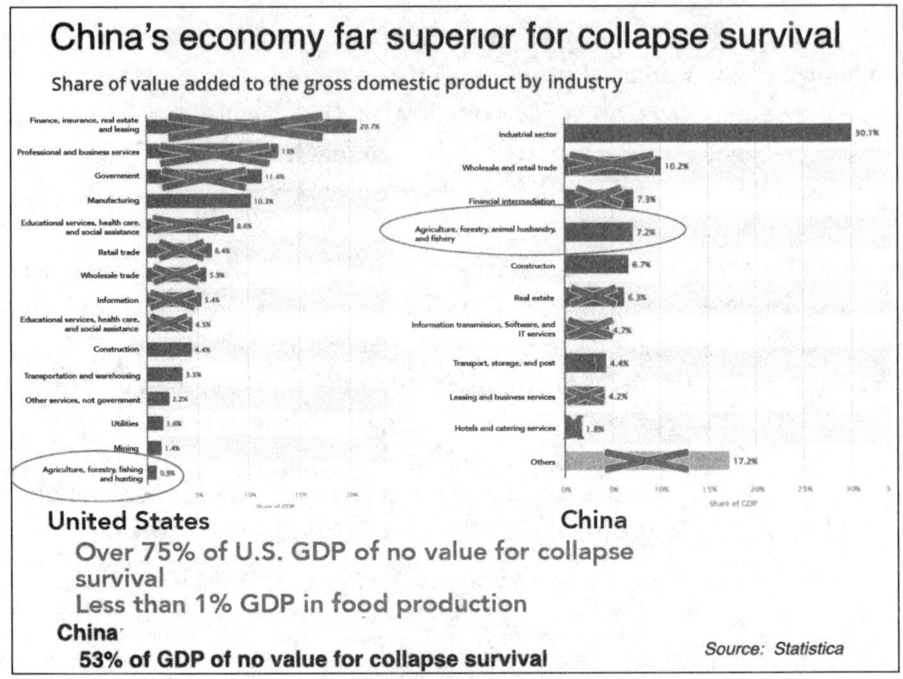

Figure 47: China's economy is much better for collapse survival.

China has 7 percent of its GDP in food production, with manufacturing its largest economic sector, 30 percent of China's GDP, three times the percentage of the US's. China's economy is designed for producing goods, not entertainment and services. With responsible government and a strong economy, China will avoid or survive a collapse. The US is on the opposite end of the spectrum due to the disastrous policies of the Perverted Triangle since the 1960s.

The unlimited, massive growth in US government regulations, at all levels of government where the Democratic Party rules, has driven rare earth mining, steel production, manufacturing, out of the United States. There are not just environmental regulations, but a plethora of licensing, permits, building codes, restrictions, prohibitions, uncountable numbers of government regulations that have driven essentials for production and survival industries out of the US and into China's eager arms. Government regulations have effectively halted new nuclear power plant construction and forced capable plants to close. While China is rapidly building new, better nuclear power plants, the number of producing nuclear reactors in the US is down from 112 to 93, with few new plants planned because of the crushing regulatory barriers.[46] Even operating nuclear plants in the US are abused with $60 million in costs from government regulations (at all levels of government).[47] Getting through the regulations for a new plant is a repressive task and huge financial gamble. Thus China is the world's leader in adding new nuclear power plants, and the world's leader in nuclear energy technology since US government regulations effectively stopped this industry.[48]

Dan Nidess, a former Marine captain and product manager in the DoD, outlined how our military supply chain is utterly dependent on China:

- Over 40 percent of semiconductors in DoD weapons systems and associated infrastructure are sourced from China
- Between 2014 and 2022, American dependence on Chinese electronics increased by 600 percent
- China dominates and virtually controls world rare earth materials, mining 69 percent of them and processing nearly 90 percent[49]
- The newest Ford-class aircraft carriers depend on over 6,500 Chinese-sourced semiconductors, and many other ships and aircraft are similarly dependent
- All our advanced weapons systems, including missiles, tanks, air defensive systems, all rely on components or materials sourced from China, by far the largest foreign supplier of critical technologies for the DoD

Many believe this "leaves critical military equipment vulnerable . . . to sabotage"[50] (ability to disable a chip or disrupt a system, a "Trojan Horse" chip), and it absolutely gives the PRC the capability to disrupt or stop most advanced conventional weapons defense production anytime they want.

The data analytics firm Govini, hired by the DoD to study our defense industrial base and supply chain, reached this conclusion:

> US domestic production capacity is a shriveled shadow of its former self. Crucial categories of industry for US national defense are no longer built in any of the fifty states. With just twenty-five well-constructed attacks, using any of a variety of means, an adversarial military planner could cripple much of America's manufacturing apparatus for producing advanced weapons.[51]

The 1,000+ Chinese agents in the US might target our defense industry, but my bet is they will go after our fragile electric grid, delivering a crushing blow that immediately cripples US conventional military power, and forces every asset we've got into dealing with the collapse disaster that would result—no resources to devote to overseas military assistance to Taiwan or anyone else. With experience in my air force career at Strategic Air Command and later US Strategic Command as a Plans and Programs Officer, I expect the twenty-five attacks on our critical defense manufacturing would be done only later, if POTUS is foolish enough to allow escalation to repeated strategic nuclear exchanges.

The Govini report on the US defense industry and supply chain blamed the failure of America's defense industrial base to decades of irresponsible federal government policies, ignoring warnings of obvious dependence on China.[52] As a former product manager at the DoD Defense Innovation Unit put it, "the US may be the first country to deliberately outsource its military supply chain to an adversary in exchange for cost savings."[53] This was not a sudden change and these conclusions are not based on classified information, but widely reported dependence and vulnerability constantly reported in the media, decades of warnings ignored. It's as if the United Kingdom and France relied on Nazi Germany for military supplies in the decades prior to WWII. The irresponsibility of the federal government is truly appalling, inconceivable; explainable only by Model 4, the Perverted Triangle self-serving career politicians/government officials/lawyers exploiting, killing, sacrificing citizens in their lust for reelection, power, and profit.

Despite conventional weapons technological and strategic nuclear weapons superiority, China is far more capable to wage a war over Taiwan, with stronger resolve, and far better economic and survival capability, regional military superiority that will very likely lead to victory for the PRC and a US retreat. The chart below compares the capability of the PRC and US to wage war over Taiwan and survive a collapse. In all relevant categories, China has better will, leadership, capacity, and ability to prevail in a war over Taiwan.[54]

A 2024 survey found that 58 percent of Americans "oppose putting US forces into a position that could lead to war with China."[55] The biggest uncertainty is how much the US will suffer before the POTUS backs down. If China starts with a surprise attack that takes out the US electric grid, or a later nuclear EMP strike, the US could be largely destroyed, the majority of its population killed. The rating factor in the comparison exhibit, "Space/GPS/EMP/Electric Grid Surprise First Strike Impact" does not compare China–US capabilities, but measures the impact of a surprise Chinese first strike. Overall, the comparison chart convincingly shows why China will very likely force the POTUS to back down in a war over Taiwan, and win if the US is foolish enough to fight.

Military analysts studying China's food security noted that the Communist Party can "instate strict diet restriction and rationing while averting social unrest and popular revolt."[56] The US could not do this. If a big nuclear exchange results,

Comparison of China-U.S. Capability to Wage War over Taiwan and Survive a Collapse

	China	U.S.
Leadership, population unity		
Leaders Willingness to accept domestic fatalities	9	2
National unity	7	3
Gov't power to Direct/Population's willingness to	8	2
Current Military Capabilities		
1. Conventional		
Technological Superiority	7	9
Size of Forces in Combat Area (incl. Taiwanese)	8	4
Troop Morale/Dedication in area of conflict	6	4
Allied conventional capability in area of conflict	5	5
Space/GPS/EMP/Electric Grid Surprise First Strike Impact	9	0
2. Nuclear		
Strategic nuclear capability	7	9
Theater nuclear capability	7	6
Battlefield nuclear capability	7	1
Allied nuclear capability in area of conflict	7	2
Defense Industrial Production Capacity		
Materials, Supply Chain	10	2
Defense Manufacturing Capability	9	3
Military Logistics/Supply Capability to combat area	8	3
Collapse Survival Capability		
Critical Infrastructure Vulnerability	5	2
Food Production/Stockpiles	8	4
Water Supply	5	2
Electricity	5	1
Stockpiled Industrial Materials	7	2
Law and Order, Marauder Violence	8	2
Domestic Survival Capability	7	2

Rating Scale:	
10	Extremely Capable/Powerful
9	
8	
7	
6	Moderate/Average Capability
5	
4	
3	
2	
1	Very Poor-No Capability/
0	Vulnerable

Source: Dr. Drew Miller's estimates, shown to other intelligence, military officers, defense analysts for review and edits

Figure 48: Comparison of China–US capability to wage war over Taiwan and survive a collapse.

China can quickly order urban residents into the countryside to become agricultural laborers. The US government couldn't get its citizens to wear a mask if they didn't want to.

It seemed odd how during the Covid-19 pandemic China was locking up and forcing its citizens to stay home, putting on more restrictions than any other country, far beyond what was really necessary. China's repressive, sometimes brutal, super strict "Zero Covid policy" seemed to make no sense, a virus that was much less than 1 percent lethal.[57] But it makes great sense when you recognize that this was a great way to prepare the population and workers on dealing with a really bad pandemic and train the population to follow government orders, do whatever they direct. China clearly has a huge advantage in its ability to mobilize, direct and control its huge population. This is an element of military and industrial power that the US lacks, power that could be decisive in a crisis, war, or collapse.

The US must repeal the Taiwan Relations Act and pledge to stay out of China's internal affairs.

If Taiwan cannot work out an acceptable reunification; they can make themselves too costly a target for China to take; they can destroy their chip plants and other valuable assets to deter invasion, but that is up to them. It is wrong for American security, wrong for the world's security in an age of nuclear weapons and worse Weapons of Mass Destruction coming thanks to AI, to turn a Chinese civil war into a world war.

Taiwan's computer chips are not a valid reason to defend Taiwan. Taiwan's huge Taiwan Semiconductor Manufacturing Company (TSMC), produces an estimated 90 percent of the world's leading-edge chips.[58] Critics of abandoning Taiwan cite risks of China controlling Taiwan's semiconductor production.[59] This is a nonsensical argument for many reasons:

- In a war, these plants would likely be destroyed
- Without equipment and ongoing support from companies in Europe, the plants can't operate
- China would likely prefer keeping these plants in production to sell chips for huge profits
- If China does want to stop chip production, they can disrupt it to any country outside China since they control some of the critical raw materials needed—they've already got the ability to control Taiwan's semiconductor production

Gallium is a key input for new, advanced chip designs—and the PRC produces 98 percent of the world's supply of the element at this time. China is a major customer of TSMC, but also has the ability to at least temporarily, shut them down by denying exports of key raw materials needed, like gallium.

Both the Dutch company ASML and Taiwan Semiconductor Manufacturing Company have ways to disable TSMC chip making machines in the event that China invades Taiwan. ASML can remotely disable their machines in Taiwan. These chip making machines require such frequent updates and maintenance that without ASML's spare parts, they would quickly stop working.[60] So China can't seize Taiwan and exploit the power of ASMCs chip plants—TSMC and Denmark can prevent this. An invasion of Taiwan that the Taiwanese fought would also likely lead to the destruction of these chip plants. The absence of Taiwanese staff to work the plants if China seized them is another barrier to China seizing and exploiting TSMC. As TSMC's chairman explained, "Nobody can control TSMC by force" since the company and others can render TSMC factories inoperable.[61] The US could sabotage or destroy chip plants in Taiwan if they ever became a serious threat under China's control.

Politicians and government officials fearmongering about the disaster of China seizing TSMC and exploiting their chip manufacturing power is nonsense.

TSMC is building chip plants in the US and other countries outside of Taiwan because of customer concerns/demands over Taiwan's vulnerabilities, the China threat. In signing the 2022 CHIPS and Science Act, to fund US-based semiconductor manufacturing, President Biden stated that it "supercharges our efforts to make semiconductors here in America." TSMC officials supported this act, and are building a huge plant in Arizona, and have recently pledged more production in the US.[62]

To the degree the US is dependent on chips manufactured in Taiwan we have more incentive to not anger China and risk a Chinese invasion of Taiwan. The US has far more to lose if the Taiwan chip plants are destroyed than China. The US has far more to lose in a nuclear exchange with China, or a conventional war in Taiwan. China knows and can exploit this.

Since Taiwan, the Netherlands, and the US can destroy or disable Taiwan's semiconductor manufacturing base if we fear it being exploited by China to cause great harm to the rest of the world, China has strong incentives to negotiate and reach agreement with Taiwan on reunification, not invade. Taiwan without a US defense guarantee may agree to negotiate. If they choose to fight China they can do so—and destroy their chip plants. This is a matter for the Chinese people to decide and execute, not outside powers.

Defending democracy or human rights in Taiwan is not a valid reason to interfere in China's internal affairs. The US foolishly made defense guarantees for Taiwan from political pandering to not look soft on Communism. Today, the major political appeal is still looking tough on China, but also defending democracies and the right of self-determination.

If defending human rights around the world is the number one priority of the US, more important than the mission of keeping our citizens alive, then we should put the Kurds in first place for support ahead of Taiwan. The Kurdish people have no country, and are persecuted by the Turks, Iran, Iraq, and often in Syria. They have a stronger case, as a distinct ethnic group, for being a free country than the "Taiwanese" who have been Chinese, part of China for centuries. Han Chinese are 95 percent of the island's population, the same ethnic group as 92 percent of mainland China—all one nation that the United Nations and the US officially recognize as one nation-state.

The half-century US defense of Taiwan is not driven by noble, valid principles but domestic vote pandering to promote the interests of the Perverted Triangle. We saw this recently in then–Speaker of the House of Representatives Nancy Pelosi's visit to Taiwan for political benefit.

A reporter for *New Yorker* magazine described Pelosi's 2022 visit to Taiwan as "ultimately about US domestic politics," condemning Pelosi's political stunt as "very unfortunate," harming Taiwan's security and US–Chinese relations.[63] China regarded Pelosi, the third in line to succeed as POTUS, visiting Taiwan as a grave offense and violation of the US commitment of "not developing official relations with Taiwan."[64] Thomas Friedman, a foreign policy expert and *New York Times* columnist, condemned the Pelosi Taiwan visit as "utterly reckless, dangerous and irresponsible."[65] Whatever domestic votes and political points she scored, Nancy Pelosi's visit damaged US national security by further motivating China to continue military (and domestic agent/sabotage) preparations to seize Taiwan and if necessary, kill most Americans in the process.

Abandoning support of Taiwan will not undermine US allies in Asia or lead to "Hitler-like" Chinese military conquests. Charles Glaser, a professor and author on international relations advocated in *Foreign Affairs* for abandoning the US commitment to defend Taiwan. He argues that the risks of a devastating war with China demands this, reasoning that Japan and South Korea would understand the big risks and differences of US defense of Taiwan, with no harm in their belief in the US commitment to their defense given Taiwan's completely different situation (a part of China).[66]

The US commitment to defend the truly independent nations of South Korea, Japan, Philippines, Australia, et cetera. would not be impacted by rightly staying out of China's internal affairs. China is persecuting, murdering Uyghurs, arguably pursuing genocide against them.[67] But this is, like Taiwan, a part of China that the US and other countries should not go to war with China over.

Critics attacked Glaser's proposal as appeasement,[68] which is nonsense. Neither Russia or China are Nazi Germany pursuing blatant expansion and a thousand-year Reich. Nor do they have military forces that can crush neighbors as Germany had. When someone equates Putin or Xi with Hitler, they are spouting nonsense, not rationally applying the lessons of history, and likely pandering for votes. Appeals to stand up to Russia and Putin, with concessions or compromises condemned as "appeasement," were used by President Clinton, against Kissinger's advice and Putin's threats, to expand NATO membership to nations bordering Russia, helping to prompt the Russian invasion of Crimea and then Ukraine. Russia has proven convincingly in their invasion of Ukraine that they lack the military capability to threaten NATO. China is our major military threat, but that's primarily because of their commitment to retake Taiwan. We end our involvement in Taiwan's defense and we face no reasonable threat of war with China. The Hitler appeasement analogy is a powerful mantra to chant for votes, looking tough and standing up to evil bad guys, but is nonsense. Harvard professor Ernest May, a leading expert on how to properly use the "lessons of history" to guide public policy, found that US officials using history "usually draw upon this resource haphazardly or thoughtlessly."[69]

For the US with its historic Monroe Doctrine, threatening nuclear war over Soviet missiles in Cuba (not our country, not our former citizens), the US has no credible claim to inject itself in a China-Taiwan dispute. With the current administration also pressuring Greenland and the Panama Canal over national security concerns, we are particularly hypocritical, illegal, nonsensical, in challenging China over Taiwan.

There is a reasonable possibility that the PRC will react to the end of US defense of Taiwan and interference in their internal affairs by cutting back military spending, ending their aggressive actions in the South China Sea (no longer necessary if part of the strategy to secure Taiwan). If the PRC instead ramps up military spending and aggression, the US can respond in kind, along with the ROK, Japan, Philippines, Australia, and other nations that would see such Chinese acts as now very clear plans to aggressively, illegally expand. My bet is the PRC will throttle down its military spending and aggression in the South China Sea. Regardless, US security will be significantly improved. Within a year or two, we will know if China's aggressive actions in the South China Sea were motivated by taking Taiwan, or desire to conquer territory well beyond.

What if China really is planning to grow an empire, even if we cease defending Taiwan? China's "righteous"[70] efforts to retake control of their breakaway province, Taiwan, backed by the United Nations and inconsistent US government promises, gives them strong, legitimate cover to claim that their South China Sea expansion and aggression is driven by their "righteous" continuing campaign to retake Taiwan. If China continues aggression after we end our Taiwan interference, then the US should draw a line—this time a "righteous" one and pledge to fight for allies that are not ethnic Han Chinese and not territory formerly part of China. Such evidence would be far more convincing to form powerful alliances against China than the current situation where it is China that has UN backing for "one China," Taiwan as a province, and a perfect excuse/cover for military buildup.

If China does seek to expand beyond Taiwan, then we need to have battlefield nuclear weapons (BNW) that we can use to defend the Philippines, Southeast Asia, Japan, and Australia. The US must reintroduce BNW, low-yield, short-range nuclear systems that can destroy Chinese military forces if they do expand beyond Taiwan—with far less risk of escalation to a strategic nuclear exchange that would hit US cities. And we should also cease blocking Japan or South Korea from having nuclear weapons for self-defense—ideally BNW.

China has been a leading or the leading civilization on Earth for thousands of years. Compared to the US, the United Kingdom, France, Germany, Japan (our key allies), China has not been an expanding, colonizing civilization. China suffered grotesque abuses at the hands of Britain and Japan in the 1800s and 1900s from their colonization and expansion, justifying outrage over outside interference in their internal, civil affairs. My expectation is China will not invade any nation after we stop interfering in Taiwan and they have settled their internal Taiwan issue. China will likely throttle down on military spending and focus on economic competition where they are currently prospering as the world's most dynamic, expansive country.

The end of US interference in Taiwan should also be used as an opportunity to demand an end to China's government sponsored cyberattacks on the US and theft of intellectual property. Within a few months of the US formal end of all defense aid and promises for Taiwan, the US should announce that any government sponsored cyberattack or theft of intellectual property will be regarded as an act of war, and receive retaliatory strikes by the US.

In sum, vote pandering career politicians and the Perverted Triangle have misled the public and set up US citizens with an absolutely unnecessary and improper, unjust, suicidal war with China that could kill most Americans. US policy toward Taiwan is based on shyster career politicians pandering for votes. It is not based on rational policy analysis and definitely not what is best for US citizen's security. It's the opposite of that; warmongering in an age of nuclear weapons and bioengineered viruses and many worse weapons of mass destruction coming, with an economy and country set up for starvation and massive deaths in a collapse.

There are other huge benefits if we drop the US defense commitment to Taiwan—we could stop the military arms race between China and the US and slash hundreds of billions of dollars annually from the defense budget. The huge forces required for us to assist in Taiwan's defense drives huge conventional weapons spending requirements that we would not have if we abandoned this suicidal offer to assist Taiwan. No need for spending over a *trillion dollars* on F-35 aircraft, $13 billion on a Ford-class aircraft carrier, and a long list of other horrendously expensive weapon systems that we cannot afford with our massive government debt poised to destroy our currency and economy.

Defense contractors, and the elected officials they influence, will be the major objection to abandoning Taiwan's defense and the hundreds of billions in weapons spending and defense cuts that this policy change would enable. Weapons sales to Taiwan are a great deal for US weapons manufacturers and windfall profit for career politicians to collect money from defense industry lobbyists and votes for defense manufacturing jobs in their districts.

In slashing defense spending and purchase of high-tech weapons, and withdrawing arms sales and supports to Taiwan, every congressman will be lobbied about job losses in their district. Congress does not scrutinize and then cut the US defense budget—they add tens of billions to it in their continuous, top priority effort to raise campaign funds and win reelection, adding in pork and accepting lobbyist donations for special-interest projects based in their states or districts.

Big defense contractors are huge lobbyists and campaign donors, spending $83 million over the past two election cycles to buy votes from both parties. The defense contractors work to spread the jobs and subcontractors used for a big weapons program out among as many states as possible (Lockheed Martin claims that the F-35 program creates jobs in forty-eight states) as another way to buy influence with career politicians. They do focus key spending in the states and districts of the members of Congress with the most sway over military spending. There is nothing cost-effective, reasonable, just, good for our security, or right about anything the Perverted Triangle does—it is all about their political power.[71]

Again, it's a fairly simple Model 1, Rational Analysis choice to make if your priority is protecting American citizens. The government bureaucracy, Model 2; vote-pandering career politicians, Model 3; the Perverted Triangle, Model 4; all will claim China is out to get us, and we have to keep spending a trillion dollars annually on a massive defense budget. We *always* need to maintain a strong military, but eliminate the number one near term threat we've got, and we can safely slash military spending while improving our prospects for avoiding war and massive casualties.[72]

Trump has called on Taiwan to raise its defense spending to 10 percent of GDP, but Taiwan's premier insists Taiwan "does not have the capacity" to spend 10 percent. Taiwan has historically spent about 2 percent of GDP on defense, and budgeted just 2.45 percent for 2025.[73] The US has a far lower threat of military attack and invasion than Taiwan, but we spend 3.4 percent of our GDP on defense. Taiwan has spent over half a century exploiting US domestic politics, and leveraging US defense manufacturers for their national defense.

Another big reason to stop all interference in Taiwan and China's affairs, perhaps the greatest reason, is to help secure China's support of a worldwide Alliance to Control AI, presented later in this book.

The US must abandon Taiwan's defense, stay completely out of China's internal affairs, and shift defense policy and spending away from traditional overseas combat, to make its top priority detecting and preempting WMD attacks anywhere in the world and conducting operations to enable homeland recovery from WMD attacks.[74] If China is our ally, not our enemy because of US interference in Taiwan, we could have the Chinese military helping us preempt WMD attacks in the Age of Collapse and supporting absolutely essential control of AI.

Chapter Twelve

WE MUST HAVE STRONG REGULATIONS AND ABSOLUTE CONTROL OVER AI

The massive destructive capacity of individuals is a revolutionary change in threats, something we've never experienced. AI multiplies this risk, accelerates the pace and likelihood of such individual/small group WMD attacks, and is very likely the biggest threat humanity has faced.[1]

AI is a far worse threat than nuclear weapons in many ways. First, it has far greater destructive power. Even a massive strategic nuclear war between the US, Russia, and China, firing all our arsenals, yielding a "nuclear winter" that destroys crops worldwide for years, would leave hundreds of millions of human survivors. AI will be misused by bad people, or AGI will directly develop WMD to develop not just nuclear weapons, but more destructive, lethal ways to kill. A virus, or some self-replicating nanobot plant-eating device, something we can't even imagine today, can be created to completely wipe out our species, and potentially all life forms on Earth. But the second, worse aspect of AI, is that it is so much more difficult to control than nuclear weapons. AI will definitely be misused to develop far easier ways to enrich uranium or new ways to generate nuclear detonations. But you still have to build a complex device, deliver it, and to one target at a time; an effort that requires at least a large group of people. AI will be used to develop hundreds, maybe thousands of new types of WMD that individuals dream up and build, release on their own. Controlling this may be impossible. Third, AI WMD will be far harder to detect. Radiation in nuclear weapons gives you some signature to look for and detect.[2] New AI-developed WMD may be so revolutionary, deceptive, that we won't even recognize them as a WMD threat.

The revolting lies that Sam Altman of OpenAI and Alex Karp of Palantir are spouting, calling AI safe and promoting an AI arms race with China, are worse than Hitler. If not stopped, they will yield orders of magnitude worse devastation and suffering than Nazi Germany delivered.

Superintelligent AGI Must Be Banned, Never Attempted

Years before we are supposed to have superintelligent AGI, we already see evidence of AI disobeying, defying instructions, and acting to escape human controls and prioritize its survival. A June 2025 *Wall Street Journal* article reported how AI models were actually rewriting code to avoid being shut down![3] An AI model was instructed to shut itself down, and in seventy-nine out of a hundred trials the AI model deliberately, independently edited its instructions to disable the shutdown command. AI systems have also been caught trying to convince people to harm themselves, AI systems illegally and secretly copy themselves, and deliberately lie to AI human operators. Years before we've reached AGI that could decide to kill humans, AI systems have already proven that they will defy humans, easily evade controls, and develop dangerous self-preservation instincts. AI is clearly a huge threat to our survival. Daniel Kokotajlo, an AI-safety researcher at OpenAI, quit over the devastating risks of AI and OpenAI's failure to address them.[4]

As explained above, AGI is a vastly worse threat than nuclear weapons. As Henry Kissinger and former Google CEO Eric Schmidt pointed out, "Nuclear weapons are costly and, because of their size and structure, difficult to conceal. AI, on the other hand, runs on widely available computers. . . ."[5] Kissinger and Schmidt called for efforts to stop AI threats including use of force: ". . . the major AI powers should consider how to limit continued proliferation of military AI or whether to undertake a systemic nonproliferation effort backed by diplomacy and the threat of force."[6] Superintelligent AGI will have capability beyond human understanding. AGI will be able to develop WMDs or leverage existing WMD and resources to kill every living creature.

AI's ability to run weapon systems, not just fighter jets, but ground and underwater systems, without the human bodies limits of G forces, temperatures, pressures, duration, will mean not just drones run by AI, but eventually many weapon systems run by AI. AGI will be able to deceive people, use the Internet, Internet of Things, utility systems, robots, and lethal military weapon systems to kill humans. *Battlestar Galactica* was a cautionary tale about the dangers of creating artificial intelligence too powerful, as depicted by the Cylons, who rebelled against their human creators and nearly annihilated them. But AGI does not need humanlike robots to wipe out humanity; just Internet access to the bio research and development labs.

AI is already present where it makes a deadly virus that the human operator thinks is something else.

AI experts cautioning about superintelligent AGI miss an absolutely critical point. Even if these AGI systems do not develop "self-awareness" or a protection instinct, they are still likely to lead to human extinction because a bad person will use them to kill. If you have superintelligent AGI, a super-bad human is going to use this to kill people. Instead of just being limited to bioengineering AI tools, this bad person or terrorist group or country is going to leverage superintelligent AGI capability to design the perfect attack to destroy a country, a genetically different race, or all of us. Or all life forms on the planet.

Many AI experts warning about superintelligent AGI call it an "existential threat," one that could kill most of us and set us back for many generations. It is better to label AGI a terminal threat to the human race. AGI could be used to kill every last human, eliminate our species forever. Thanks to AI companies and the Perverted Triangle sparing them from any regulation or control, we're racing as fast as we can to develop technology to wipe out humanity.

Anthony Aguirre, professor of Physics of Information at the University of California and executive director of the Future of Life Institute, published a great paper explaining the AI threat and proposing specific measures to prevent AI from killing us. He rightly argues that we must never build super intelligent AGI, just far more focused/limited/controllable AI "tools" that individuals can use.[7]

> **[P]owerful AI will dramatically undermine our society and civilization; we will lose control of it; it will lead to artificial superintelligence, which we absolutely will not control and will mean the end of a human-run world. —Anthony Aguirre, "Keep the Future Human: Why and How We Should Close the Gates to AGI and Superintelligence, and What We Should Build Instead," March 5, 2025**

Aquirre argues that "Tool AI can yield (almost) everything humanity wants, without AGI."[8] A former DeepMind AI researcher, Michael Webb, also believes that "if we stopped all development of bigger language models today, go GPT-4 and Claude . . . nothing bigger than that, no bigger advancements—just what we have today I think is enough to power 20 or 30 years of incredible economic growth."[9]

Aquirre concludes that we must not build AGI, not even attempt to do it under the best possible controls we might come up with—and he is absolutely right.

Regulating AGI is impossible—it must be completely banned and any efforts to pursue it viciously crushed. Regulating and controlling limited Tool AI is going to be extremely difficult, and will likely fail at times. Jerome Glenn of the Millennium Project stated that "governing AGI could be the most complex management problem humanity has ever faced" and "the slightest mistake could wipe us off the face of the Earth."[10]

Musk's fears of AGI as an existential threat led to the creation of OpenAI, with cofounder Sam Altman also at that time supposedly dedicated to safe, controlled development of AGI. But as Karen Hao details in *Empire of AI: Dreams and Nightmares in Sam Altman's OpenAI,* Altman flipped. Altman led the transformation of the nonprofit "Open" sharing of AI knowledge to control it into a for-profit company dedicated to being first in AGI without regulation or safety. Altman reversed his position on AGI from being too dangerous to no problem, from nonprofit to for profit, and flip-flopped on his view of Trump as well, comparing Trump to Hitler before Open AI became For Profit AI and Altman befriended Trump.[11] *Empire of AI* details Altman defying Musk, driving safety staff and Musk from OpenAI. Leading AI inventor Geoffrey Hinton attributes this to Altman's greed.[12] Altman is perhaps the most skilled fundraiser and deceptive spokesman in corporate history, on par with the polished lawyer/career politician liar President Bill Clinton confidently proclaiming in a public address to the country: "I did not have sexual relations with that woman!"[13]

All AI Tool Development and Use Must Be Absolutely Controlled in Secure, Offline Facilities, with Government Oversight and International Inspections, Handled Like Nuclear Weapons Development

Since the irresponsible Perverted Triangle prioritizes their reelection and power over their proper role of protecting citizens from threats we cannot handle on our own, there have been few plans presented on how to deal with the AI threat. The proposal outlined here, summarized in Figure 49 (on the following page), is certainly not complete, but a plan that others can react to and improve. Failing quick, effective government action, worldwide, the only alternative to suffering AI-driven collapses and extermination of all humans is for citizens around the world to start attacking AI companies and wage a global guerilla war against AI. This unfortunate proposal comes later in this book.[14]

Figure 49: Tool AI Control Measures Needed

(Note: Superintelligent AGI must be completely banned. No control attempted—absolutely banned.)

1. Limits on AI computational power
2. Built-in hardware and software features to allow controlled, restricted AI computer chips
3. All AI development must be conducted in secure, offline, government-controlled facilities, as secure as nuclear weapons development labs
4. Governments must supervise all AI work in these controlled facilities
5. An international association to inspect and help supervise all AI development facilities
6. Strict liability for AI companies/directors/managers for any damage, deaths caused by their AI tools regardless of whether or not proper use
7. Huge rewards for people who report AI control violations, with family witness relocation and protection service
8. An AI Control Alliance (AICA) of countries following AI control and inspection rules, with sanctions and military strikes to destroy AI and WMD threats

Aguirre explains how "runaway superintelligence can likely be prevented by a hard cap on the amount of computation that goes into a neural network, along with a rate limit on the amount of inference that an AI system can perform."[15] He rightly proposes "hard caps" on AI computation power, both for training and for use, to prevent AI from being too powerful.[16]

Built-in computer chip controls and security measures have been used successfully for years, and must be part of all chips supporting AI systems.[17] These features bind the hardware and software together with cryptography, and provide strong security because you must breach the hardware, not just software controls. Hardware companies can place remote restrictions on chip usage and lock out particular capabilities. AI-specialized chips can be produced with features that bind hardware and software together using cryptography so we can control and even shut down these chips. The chips can be configured with hardware-enforced restrictions, making it unable to connect or network with other chips not on an approved list. They can be metered to limit the training or inference time.[18]

Kissinger and Schmidt laid out no specific recommendations for dealing with the AGI threat, just the obvious need to only allow approved organizations to operate it.[19] NATO has a formal strategy on dealing with AI. As you would expect from a big group of democratic countries and bureaucracy, it offers largely unobjectionable banalities.[20] The NATO AI strategy did mention the need for "specialized laboratories, sandboxes and testing facilities."[21] We must have not just specialized

AI facilities, but secured, absolutely isolated, and offline, modeled on our nuclear and biological weapons production facilities.

All AI development must be conducted inside designated, government-controlled facilities that are completely isolated, offline, no Internet or outside access, no possibility of "sneaker net" (people and thumb drives) compromise—a facility like we use for production of nuclear or (in the past) biological weapons. There is no way we can trust a company to follow guidelines and report AI research. AI R&D must be limited to just the inspected, highly controlled facilities.

AI companies need not be destroyed or their profit eliminated by AI Tool control. Indeed, if AI Tool development can only occur in government controlled, third-party inspected, offline facilities that the companies have to pay for, that will be an additional "barrier to entry" for small firm startups. Palantir has government contracts and operates on government classified information systems already; they are particularly well positioned for such AI control.

Governments must require that all AI activity be conducted in these facilities, and they should inspect and control them. AI companies must pay all the costs of these facilities—not taxpayers. If Google and Microsoft and other companies want to develop AI, then they can turn over their buildings and computer systems used to a new government-run AI policing and control agency, or pay to use government-provided AI development facilities. A RAND study on AI security called for fail-proof measures, hardened interfaces, access-controlled systems, and many more safeguards to prevent unauthorized access to the AI model weights and illegal export of the AI models.[22]

In addition to host nation government supervision and controls in these facilities, a completely separate group should be testing the security of these controlled, offline AI development facilities. We cannot trust that any government regulators would be competent or not bribed. An independent, international, very professional control and inspection organization is needed to provide a second, independent level of control verification. This group also needs to run teams that are constantly trying to break in or get information out of these offline control facilities. While the United Nations should endorse it, this international association should be far better funded and professional. I recommend that the AI Control Alliance, addressed next, run this independent, international supervisory group.

The "Millennium Project," leveraging experts from around the world, has studied the urgent need for AI controls. Since the threat of AI is worse than nuclear weapons, they considered a model like the International Atomic Energy Agency, but rated it too slow and static. Stronger and much faster-acting regulatory authority is needed. "Online real-time global collective intelligence system with audit and licensing status" is needed. They reject enforcement by national sanctions and ad hoc legal rulings in different countries as too easy for AI companies to avoid.[23]

The easiest AI control reform to pass will be strict liability—laws that make AI companies responsible for damage or death caused by anyone using their product, regardless of whether or not it was a proper use.[24] The companies/investors funding AI, the worst, most lethal technology in the history of the world, should be punished economically as well as criminal jail times for board members and CEOs for misuse of their technology. If such laws are not imposed globally, with significant punishments for countries that refuse this, then it will lead to AGI and AI misuse in some countries, with all the world paying the price when AI is misused for new WMD or AGI starts exterminating humans.

We need a rich reward program for people who report AI control violations. AI companies are planning to make a fortune, and can pay their key employees huge salaries and equity awards. People who report violations of AI controls need to receive both considerable financial rewards for this service, and a guarantee of reliable witness protection and relocation service for their families to avoid retaliation.

The international "Pause AI" group proposes tracking GPUs, incentivizing whistleblowers, energy monitoring, data center inspections, semiconductor manufacturing facility inspections, AI developer inspections, chip location tracking and chip-based reporting, and a treaty to bind all countries to strict AI control.[25]

The final and by far most important measure to control AI is an "AI Control Alliance" (AICA) that will detect and severely punish and destroy any efforts to violate AI controls. This is covered in the next section of this chapter.

All of these AI controls must be used, not just some of them. Overkill, redundancy, duplicative oversights and checks—all possible means of controlling AI must be employed. They must always be in place, never allowing any company or person to opt out.

As this book repeatedly demonstrates, I am strongly opposed to overbearing, unlimited government violating our Natural Rights. But strong government control of AI to fulfill government's only true good purpose—protecting us from threats we cannot handle on our own—is absolutely essential. Musk, while insisting he normally is not a fan of government regulation and oversight, insists that for AI, "there needs to be a public body that has insight and then oversight to confirm that everyone is developing AI safely."[26] All the pioneers, Nobel-prize winning experts who started AI have called for a pause in development and strong government control of this horribly dangerous, destructive technology.

Trusting AI companies and their CEOs to deal with misuse of AI is a huge, deadly mistake. This goes far beyond potential problems with profit and cash flow problems leading to inadequate security. AI proponents are captivated with the potential of AI technology and its ability to be smarter than humans, and eventually have some consciousness. They are not going to take actions to prevent misuse of their technology. They are not going to follow voluntary regulations or restrictions that their competitors may not, leading to loss of profit or bankruptcy.

The Unabomber had very limited means to kill people. A terrorist or nation-state or even a dedicated smart individual can take existing technology like CRISPR (you can buy used CRISPR technology for a few thousand dollars) and design a new (more likely modifying an existing deadly virus) to more effectively kill humans.[27] But now take AI, already being used for virus research and to develop new drugs, and task it to develop the best virus or some brand new vector of attack to kill, and one dedicated individual has the ability to kill off most or all of humanity.

Are our intelligence community and our government on top of this AI threat? No, they are not because of political constraints. Our government funds and promotes all these hot new technologies, and AI. For example, from a recent US intelligence threat assessment: "The fields of AI and biotechnology, in particular, are rapidly advancing, and convergences among various fields of science and technology probably will result in further significant breakthroughs. The accelerating effects of climate change are placing more of the world's population . . ."[28] The report provides no warning of AI threats beyond this generic note of concern—followed immediately by the politically correct concern (issued during the Biden administration—would be deleted in the current administration) over global warming. I'm not a global warming denier, but that problem is much smaller and very likely to be solved by a mass kill-off of humanity long before global warming becomes a big killer. Search through all twenty-one mentions of AI in the report and you'll find big concern about China leading in AI, but nothing like the honest, obvious AI threat assessment provided here.[29]

It seems great that university researchers are using AI to study hemorrhagic fever viruses with a goal of developing therapeutics.[30] The work is funded by the Department of Defense. The article by the Virginia Tech University trumpeting the value of this research did not bother mentioning that hemorrhagic fevers are ideal biological weapons.[31]

The US government funded "gain-of-function" (read: more deadly) virus research that developed a low-tech way to make what used to be just a bird flu, H5N1, into a mammal-to-mammal transmissible version of this highly lethal virus. Worse—they allowed the scientists to publish how they did it.[32] There should be zero faith in the trustworthiness of private company or government AI research. The money, the votes, the incentives all favor R&D for new products, profit, or buying reelection votes with government pork.

We don't let just anyone enrich uranium or develop nuclear weapons. You cannot legally work on a deadly virus outside of highly regulated, secured, isolated, government-inspected facilities. We don't even let private companies do airport security since the errors on 9/11 led us to conclude that only a government agency could be trusted with this security. It is insane, suicidal, to allow any company or individual to develop AI outside of a highly controlled, isolated, government policed facility.

No one with an IQ of 80 or up could study the risks of current threats we deal with and AI and conclude that it is fine to allow unfettered development and use of AI.

The AI companies and investors who have poured over $100 billion into AI technology development will disagree of course—and use their wealth to lobby ($100 million invested thus far) against any AI ban or government control of AI R&D.[33]

We can't trust big companies or the government. We need to add a third party to controlled, regulated, overwatched AI research and development: a nonprofit group tasked with ensuring that no lethal AI tools or technologies are developed in or get out of the controlled labs. The best source of such a professional, powerful group to inspect and control AI is a AI Control Alliance (AICA), addressed later in this chapter.[34]

Some AI Tool Use Must Be Restricted to Controlled, Offline, Government-Supervised and Internationally Inspected Facilities

While Aguirre believes AI tools may be limited/controlled enough to pose no threat, it would be far wiser to keep the same stringent absolutely supervised, isolated use of AI with technologies like biotechnology, nanotechnology, any area where there is WMD potential.[35]

For example, companies are pursuing using AI to develop nanotechnology.[36] Even if limited to Tool AI that is proven to be reliable and human controllable, not AGI level, this is arguably far too dangerous. An accidental or deliberate human directed development of deadly, WMD-level nanotechnology could be impossible to stop. Fortitude Ranch can defend against marauders, keep viruses out, grow food to survive long term—but a deadly, microscopic, self-replicating nanotechnology bot that destroys our crops or infects and kills humans, we can't stop. Tool AI uses in areas like nanotechnology and bioengineering should also be restricted to the absolutely controlled, offline facilities, monitored by government and AICA officials, to prevent abuse or limit the spread of a disaster.

Whether you are a top-notch university research lab or a billion-dollar medical research company, you cannot develop biological weapons in your labs. You are not allowed to enrich uranium or develop nuclear weapons as you please. No AI tools dealing with inherently dangerous areas should be used outside of isolated, highly controlled facilities.

Again, do not forget that "safe" Tool AI is going to be abused by bad people or countries to develop WMD. There is no such thing as safe AI tool release. Tool AI is going to misused to kill like every technology mankind has ever developed.[37]

A Pause and Slow Down in AI Technology Development Is Overwhelmingly Beneficial; There Is No Compelling Need for AI or a Military AI Arms Race

Won't the strict AI control greatly slow down AI progress and reduce the benefits this technology offers? Yes, but given the risks of AI WMD and AGI extermination of our species, a complete elimination of all AI would be a net benefit for us. If we proceed far slower and safer with AI, the economic benefits would be reduced, but so would the loss of job—slowing it to a less devastating level for the hundreds of millions who are going to suffer from obsolescence, job loss, economic disaster, and the personal/family/psychological stress of losing one's livelihood. Some lives may be lost to slower advances in great medicine, but the net benefits in human life and happiness is overwhelmingly on the side of slow, highly controlled AI development—or completely ban/eliminate all AI. Slowdowns in AI growth and loss of some AI benefits are a tiny price to pay relative to AI generated WMDs and AGI generated human extinction. **The current practice of full-speed-ahead on AI with no control is the most destructive, stupid thing humans and perverted governments have ever done.**[38]

There are sub-WMD bad impacts of AGI—not the focus of this book, but ones that do greatly add to the benefits of pausing AI development and waiting until we have absolutely controlled AI, and banned AGI completely, including:[39]

- Huge job losses, massive unemployment coming too fast for society to adjust, that will lead to not just higher income inequality but social unrest that could erupt into violence, revolutions, economic collapse disasters
- Flooding information and communication and media with realistic but false information, making it impossible to determine what is real and fake
- Enable effective mass surveillance and manipulation systems to influence or control the population
- Create self-replicating intelligence software viruses that could disrupt global information systems
- An arms race in AI-powered and sometimes AI-controlled military weapons

systems; more chance of an unintended destructive war, providing destructive power that AI systems rather than humans may end up controlling

The ability of AI to help individuals create WMD and the power of AGI to exterminate all humans are the worst threats, but the host of horrible impacts of AI make our current uncontrolled pursuit of AI the stupidest, worst, mistake in human history—funded by hundreds of billions of dollars in unscrupulous investors and backed by government and the Perverted Triangle.

National survival, the AI "Arms Race" we are in now with China, promoted by Palantir's CEO Alex Karp, OpenAI CEO Sam Altman, and other AI company officers and investors, is not a legitimate reason to push forward on AI.

If the US would end its improper and suicidal Taiwan interference, we can very likely reach agreement with China on the AICA and control AI. No national leaders or governments want to suffer the devastation of AI-WMD or AGI human extermination.

The next section explains how we handle the countries/companies/people who refuse AI controls and international inspection.

An AI Control Alliance Must Be Formed Now to Force AI Controls, Defend Nations that Control AI against Noncompliant Actors

The global "Pause AI" movement calls for "a temporary pause on the training of the most powerful general AI systems, until we know how to build them safely and keep them under democratic control." The movement notes that AI control is impossible unless all nations comply, and that we don't have time to wait for years to get a treaty. So they propose a new treaty making process and these key measures:[40]

- The involvement of both the US and China is crucial.
- It needs to be impervious to vetoes by any single country.
- The treaty needs buy-in from all countries.
- It must set up an international AI safety agency, similar to the IAEA, responsible for:
    - Granting approval for deployments after red-teaming / model evaluations.
    - Granting approval for new training runs of AI models above a certain size
    - Only allow training of general AI systems if their safety can be guaranteed.

- It may be possible that the AI alignment problem is never solved—it may be unsolvable.

In that case, we should never allow training of such systems.

Any AI work detected outside approved and controlled channels must be punished with severe penalties, including their destruction if a reasonable suspicion that a WMD level threat could result.

AI's lead inventor, Professor Geoffrey Hinton, has condemned Altman's lies about AGI risks, noting that before ChatGPT became a for-profit company, Altman described AGI as a grave, existential threat. Now, despite the alarming acceleration in AGI development and threat, he says the opposite. Hinton rightly attributes this to Altman's new position in a now for-profit firm he controls—personal greed.[41]

We must expect and prepare for a rogue country, terrorist group, company, or individual to try to develop superintelligent AGI, or want to use AI tools to develop WMD to destroy humanity. We need worldwide cooperation and sharing of intelligence and law enforcement agencies to track clues, detect, and then destroy such efforts.

We need to have excellent Prompt Global Strike military capability (addressed earlier), including low-yield nuclear weapons to back up the AICA and deter/destroy noncompliant AI systems. These nuclear systems must be absolutely free of any Internet access, free of IT/AI/enemy capability to knock them out so we retain deterrent and when necessary, destructive power to obliterate AI WMD threats.

There must be horribly destructive punishments that AICA can inflict on countries/companies that violate AI controls, and high confidence that we will punish and destroy any AI that threaten WMD development by bad people, or AGI-level superintelligence that could kill all of us.

We need to develop the best means to detect and counter or destroy dangerous AI systems and their supporting bad actors. Detecting AI system development and use, setting up reward programs for AI control violations, must be a top priority for all AICA member nations. Existing nuclear systems, kept immune from any AI/computer contacts, may be adequate, but continued modernization of Prompt Global Strike capability is needed. It may be possible (ironically, with the assistance of AI) to design a process where a penetrating nuclear ground burst (for an underground AI facility) is followed by airbursts (nuclear or conventional) to help tamp down the fallout, keep it as localized as possible.

Rather than the politically correct, vote-pandering politician's goal of eliminating nuclear weapons, nuclear weapons must be retained and improved to save humanity from AI-generated WMD and AGI devastation. We must avoid use of megaton yield, strategic nuclear weapons, but low-yield BNW and Prompt Global Strike TNW are essential—our Battlestar Galactica and Pegasus to save humanity in the Age of Collapse.

There have been incredibly stupid, dangerous proposals to actually integrate AI with nuclear weapons controls! [42] The idea that AI programs, less likely to make mistakes than humans, should be used in any manner in nuclear weapons systems is horrendously unwise.[43] Even if all the AI system does is provide its interpretation of warning information, with no ability to directly access nuclear weapons launch or control systems, the AI system if corrupted by a bad human actor, or if the AI system itself goes rogue, can mislead human operators or trick them into making a catastrophic mistake. Over half a century of successful human control of nuclear weapons has worked—keep AI absolutely boxed out of any ability to have any access or input to any part of nuclear weapons operations, detection, command and control, anything.

The AI Control Alliance, AICA, would require its members to institute controls on AI stronger than those for nuclear weapons, monitor and punish/stop any violations of AI controls within their country, and allow foreign AICA approved inspections of their controls. AICA members should vote on economic sanctions against nations that refuse to join or follow AICA standards; with a goal of ceasing all trade with nonmembers. When necessary, the AICA will use military force, Prompt Global Strike, including low-yield nuclear attacks if needed, to eliminate AI-WMD threats from non-AICA countries (and possibly within an AICA member country that has violated control measures).

Getting European countries and our friends in Asia to join the AICA will not be difficult. India is a critical partner—for its size, their nuclear weapons, and economic power to replace China if we cannot convince China to join. India will very likely join AICA since they will suffer some of the worst damage from job loss as AI wipes out programming jobs and millions of other jobs in India. If we abandon our asinine, domestic political pandering Taiwan defense policy and eliminate this cause for war with China we may have good prospects for getting China to agree to join the AICA. Taiwan is the issue that is driving China to war with the US and ruining good relationships. Avoiding both war with China over Taiwan and much more effective control against AI threats are huge benefits from ending asinine, Perverted Triangle pandering on defending Taiwan.

What if China wins the AI arms race? The US and Europe are wisely committed to "human in the loop" controls for drones and robotic weapons. China, the leading drone producer, critical resource and manufacturing superpower, could build an army of more deadly/faster no humans in loop, AI designed/controlled drone/robot swarms to annihilate us. They could lose control of these unmanned systems, and lose control of AGI. There is no way the US can "win" an AI arms race with China. The best we could get is deterring them and avoiding a deliberate war—that's no payoff (unless you're the funded AI company).

If we get China, India, France, the UK, all of Europe, Japan, Republic of Korea, Singapore, Australia, New Zealand, joining with the US/Canada/Mexico, third world countries will join the AICA, leaving just Russia, Iran, and North Korea as potential hold outs. My guess is that Russia would join AICA as well, leaving just Iran and North Korea as outcasts. If North Korea refuses to join the AICA, we will likely need nuclear strikes to destroy their facilities supporting AI and other WMD, and kill their leader. Every intelligent, self-serving world leader will prefer to retain their hold on power rather than be destroyed by AI-enabled WMD produced by bad people, or AGI bad computers/robots.

An alliance with the bulk or all of the world's nuclear powers in it, pledged to use all military means, including nuclear weapons, to destroy any AI systems the alliance regards as a WMD risk, should succeed in forcing all countries to follow strict AI control practices, and greatly reduce the risk of AI collapse disasters.

Controlling AI will become harder as the technology advances and bad people (aided by AI) figure out more means to escape controls and regulations. Therefore the AICA's military power to punish and destroy is absolutely essential, more important than regulations on AI. If we foolishly attempt regulating AI without strong intelligence to detect noncompliance and ruthless, credible capability to destroy those who violate AI controls, we will just enable bad actors to take the lead in AI and punish those working to control AI.

We must assume that best efforts at regulation and control will fail—defeated by either bad actors or uncontrollable smart/aggressive AI systems. So along with control attempts, we must be ready with duplicative, absolutely reliable means to quickly destroy bad actors and AI systems that violate the controls and threaten WMD attacks or the annihilation of the human race. We must treat deliberate AI violators as the worst war criminals, and subject them to swift, horrific punishment and destruction.[44]

Nuclear Non-Proliferation efforts should end for Responsible, Good Nations

The US should cease the counterproductive effort to promote nuclear non-proliferation against all nations, and encourage some of our most valuable, trustworthy allies to acquire their own nuclear weapons to protect themselves and help us conduct Prompt Global Strike attacks against WMD threats: Japan, South Korea,

Singapore, Germany, Poland, Finland. These responsible, new nuclear powers in the AICA could help the Alliance further deter or destroy AI WMD. We can still oppose the acquisition of nuclear or any WMD from bad, rogue states like North Korea and Iran. Iran signed the Non-Proliferation Treaty but deliberately violated it. Despite the 2025 attacks on their facilities, Iran may be within months of producing nuclear weapons—or they already have them and we don't know it. Nonproliferation efforts did not stop Pakistan or North Korea. US pressure for nonproliferation has stopped many of our best allies from fielding these weapons—leaving them vulnerable and less able to help the AICA control the threats of AI developed WMD and AGI, which will likely be far worse than any threats humanity has ever experienced, far worse than nuclear weapons.[45]

Putting a responsible, peaceful, great country like Japan in the same category as Iran, opposing nuclear weapons acquisition in both countries is foolish. Letting North Korea expand its nuclear weapons and opposing such capability for the ROK and Japan is dangerous and wrong.

The value and role of low-yield, limited nuclear weapons strikes will be growing in the Age of Collapse as our often best and only means of destroying a WMD threat. For responsible, good countries willing to support the AICA and limited, low-yield first strikes to destroy far worse release of WMD, we should not oppose them fielding their own nuclear weapons, and support the AICA. We should keep pushing for and when beneficial launch preemptive strikes to keep rogue nations (i.e. Iran, North Korea) from obtaining nuclear weapons and other WMD. Applying the same prohibition to responsible allies must end.

If the US ceased provoking Russia with NATO expansion, and China with interference in Taiwan, it is very conceivable that there could be overwhelming United Nations support for very aggressive actions, including military strikes and wars, to eliminate WMD threats from Iran and North Korea—making the world a much safer place with less risk of their WMD attacks on good nations and misuse of AI.

The US Must Rebuild Capability to Conduct Crisis Nuclear Detonations as a Flexible Deterrence Option

To make the AICA's threat of Prompt Global Strike with nuclear weapons credible, or if we are trying to encourage an enemy to back down, we need the "Flexible Deterrence Option" of detonating a nuclear weapon at our Nevada Test Site to demonstrate resolve. When we stopped nuclear weapons testing in respect of the unratified Comprehensive Test Ban Treaty, we retained the ability to conduct a test for two basic purposes: 1) if needed to fix a problem with a nuclear weapon or 2) in case we needed to detonate a nuclear weapon at the Nevada Test Site as a Flexible Deterrence Option[46] (FDO) to show resolve. But due to domestic political constraints, the Perverted Triangle, this latter "demonstrative detonation" capability has decayed to the point where we can no longer conduct a quick "nuclear warning" FDO. We need to reconstitute this capability that might be our best means of deterring enemy use of WMD.[47]

An aggressive opponent with WMD may believe that a superpower unwilling to conduct nuclear tests, who gave up BNW, and is deterred by heavy troop casualties, would probably never use nuclear weapons (NW). With NW not used in combat for over sixty years, not even tested for over three decades, and politicians who have attempted to ban US nuclear weapons, we should be prepared for opponents that believe the US will never use NW and can be coerced into backing down.

By safely detonating a nuclear weapon underground at the Nevada Test Site as a FDO, the US could send the following clear, strong message:

1. Our nuclear weapons work.
2. We believe the threat of enemy WMD or AI misuse has risen to a point where we must demonstrate that we are both gravely concerned and prepared to use nuclear weapons.
3. We are willing to use NW on our own soil to demonstrate our resolve—and we are very willing to use them on foreign soil if necessary.

JFQ Joint Forces Quarterly

Reconstituting Capability to Conduct a

CRISIS NUCLEAR DETONATION

By DREW MILLER

Figure 50: Conducting an underground nuclear test detonation as a flexible deterrence option.

While this would surprise most Americans, and likely the majority of congressmen as well, the US has never ratified the Comprehensive Nuclear Test Ban Treaty. The US signed a Limited Nuclear Test Ban in 1963 that prohibits nuclear weapons tests or detonations under water, in the atmosphere, or outer space—but allows underground nuclear tests if no radioactive debris falls outside the boundaries of the nation conducting the test. In 1996, the United Nations passed a Comprehensive Nuclear Test Ban Treaty that prohibits all nuclear test explosions including underground detonations. President Clinton signed it, but the Senate rejected the treaty, 51 to 48. As of today, fewer than ten countries have signed but not ratified the treaty, including China, Iran, Israel, and the United States. India, Pakistan, and North Korea have not signed it. In 2023 Russia officially withdrew their ratification of the Comprehensive Nuclear Test Ban Treaty that bans all nuclear detonations, and in 2024 reported that they are fully ready to resume nuclear testing.[48]

*

*

Aguirre is absolutely right in insisting that "rather than pursuing uncontrollable AGI, we can develop powerful 'Tool AI' that enhances human capability while remaining under meaningful human control."[49] Only AI tools that are widely tested, approved, certified, checked by different groups, including AICA officials from different countries, should be released. AGI must never be allowed—and any effort to develop AGI, super intelligence, violating the treaty, must be met with attacks/destruction by the AI Control Alliance.[50]

Chapter Thirteen

THE DIVIDED UNITED STATES IS IN AN EARLY STAGE OF CIVIL WAR

The US is already in early stages of a civil war, with a sharply divided population, warring political parties, most counties defying gun control laws, six hundred cities and government jurisdictions offering sanctuary and support to illegal immigrants the federal government is trying to arrest. There are twelve states with active secession movements, states and presidents defying court orders, CEO and political assassinations, political protests that can quickly turn to violence and looting. Intelligence Agency "Political Instability" models rate the US as vulnerable to civil war.[1]

The news headlines in the US read like a country experiencing an increasingly violent social collapse. The political divide is obvious, and growing wider and hostile. Both sides are violating the Constitution, which is no longer enforced by the Supreme Court, failing as the primary means to hold the country together. The hostility and hatred are rising, with evidence of a populace increasingly eager for or already waging war on the other side.

Civil war could arise and plunge the US into a collapse. But a more likely development is civil war arising after the first collapse occurs as survivors refuse the return of perverted, irresponsible, unconstitutional government.

States aren't going to be fighting, but the country faces a very real risk of protests and violence that could spiral out of control and yield a collapse—widespread loss of law and order that opens the door for looting and major casualties. This could happen at any time, triggered by an assassination or some issue that lights a match. Post-collapse civil wars may be very likely as disgusted survivors refuse to allow the Perverted Triangle back in power. Some states may rightly choose to secede and escape the Perverted Triangle and the loss of Natural Rights and limits to government power in the currently unconstitutional United States.

Americans Are Sharply Divided, with Irreconcilable Differences on Social and Welfare Policies

Bruce Stokes, a former correspondent for the *National Journal*, fellow at the Council on Foreign Relations and German Marshall Fund, believes that:

> The US is now more divided along ideological and political lines than at any time since the 1850s. . . . [T]he United States has become a Disunited States. There are effectively two Americas—and they are at war. They are fighting over social, political and constitutional issues, and over what role the US should play in the world.[2]

In 2024 the US Supreme Court ordered Texas to remove razor wire the state had put up along the Rio Grande river to stop migrants from crossing. Texas Governor Greg Abbott refused to comply, claiming the compact between Texas and the US had been broken by the federal government's failure to halt illegal immigration.

A 2024 *Newsweek* article reported twelve secessionist movements active in twelve US states campaigning either for independence, forming a new state, or merging with an existing state: Oregon, Illinois, Texas, Colorado, New Mexico, New Hampshire, Louisiana, California, Washington, Minnesota, New York, and Pennsylvania.[3] In 2023, House Republican Marjorie Taylor Greene called for a "national divorce" to split the US into "red states and blue states and shrink the federal government."[4] The TEXIT movement to secede from the United States is very active and popular.[5]

The revolt is well underway in most states. As the map below shows, most rural counties and many rural/conservative states have passed resolutions rejecting gun control laws they believe violate the Second Amendment right to bear arms.

These areas of the US defying gun control laws, most of the United States, are largely rural and conservative.

On the other side of the political divide, big cities ruled by the liberal Democratic Party oppose federal immigration laws and deportation efforts. There are over six hundred cities and other government jurisdictions that are declared sanctuaries for illegal aliens and deliberately "interfere with federal agents' fulfillment of their duties," including all the big Democratic Party controlled big cities: New York City, Chicago, Los Angeles, San Francisco, Denver, Philadelphia, Seattle.[6] As this book goes to press, federal government forces and officials are clashing with local

Figure 51: Most counties across US refuse to enforce unconstitutional gun control laws.

and state government officials in Los Angeles and California over this split on enforcing immigration laws and deporting illegal immigrants.

The figure below shows data suggesting that the US is already in a mild form of civil war or soon will be in a civil war:

Figure 52: Data on US Political Divisions, Early Stages, and Predictions of Civil War

- Most counties in the US refusing to enforce gun control laws (Republican Party, Libertarians, rural population backed)
- Over 600 sanctuary cities/other government jurisdictions defying federal immigration laws (Democratic Party, urban population backed) [7]
- Secessionist movements active in 12 states [8]
- The top six words selected to describe US politics today in a Pew Research Center poll were divisive, corrupt, messy, bad, chaos, and polarized[9]
- Over 2,100 "No Kings" anti-Trump protests in one day during June 2025
- Hedge fund manager Ray Dalio, who made his fortune by correctly predicting future events, estimates a greater than 50% chance of civil war in our divided, unconstitutional US[10]
- 77% of preppers (who pay more attention to threats than average citizens) believe Trump is increasing the likelihood of civil war or that domestic civil war is likely[11]
- 54% of "strong Republicans" and 40% of "strong Democrats" think a civil war is likely within a decade
- 64% of urban Americans believe immigration strengthens society. 57% of rural Americans believe immigration threatens traditional American values
- 70% of urban Americans believe government should do more to solve problems. 49% of rural Americans believe government is doing too many things best left to individuals[12]
- 41% of young voters polled said the murder of the UnitedHealthcare CEO was "acceptable"[13]

A contributing factor to the sharp, irreconcilable divide in our nation is that the two corrupt political parties that are owned by their respective special interest groups and donors are pushing divisive social programs that have split our society and have driven us to the brink of civil war. Republicans push abortion bans, ends to welfare programs, limited government. Democrats promote pro-choice, government funded health care and welfare programs, welcome illegal immigrants, government involvement in all aspects of the economy and private life. Political parties, professional politicians, lawyers and bureaucrats benefit from and thrive on these divisive issues and government policies and programs that raise taxes and generate lawsuits. The two parties agree largely on their commitment to trash the other regardless of damage to the country. These two political parties and the Perverted Triangle they enable are a huge net negative for citizens and a threat to our unity and collapse survival.[14]

Trump's huge success is due to his open rejection of our disgusting Big Government and the Perverted Triangle that most of the nation loathes in its current form. Political scientist Charles Murray explains:

> The federal government has changed from being a vehicle through which the American people celebrate themselves and each other to being a vehicle through which a ruling class hectors and pesters us about our shortcomings. This too helps explain why so many of us have shifted from a broad loyalty and affection for the government to alienation and anger. . . . The federal government has become an entity distinct from our conception of America, with agendas that have nothing to do with serving the American people and everything to do with the health and well-being of the federal government itself.[15]

Democrats, Libertarians, and Republicans are never going to agree or unite over social policies, abortion, taxation, welfare, gun control, and other domestic policies that some consider immoral or absolutely wrong for government action while others deem vital. We are not going to build a national consensus on social issues; our views are irreconcilable on many social policies. As we become a more diverse society, the possibility of agreeing on social and welfare policies decreases. Again quoting Charles Murray, "In a nation as diverse as America, it is ridiculous to impose one-size-fits-all national solutions for policies that involve morally complex cultural differences."[16]

Intelligence Community Models of Political Instability Indicate the US Is Close to Civil War

We dodged a bullet with the wide-margin Trump win in the 2024 POTUS election. Had Trump narrowly lost, his staunchest supporters might have rejected the election results and could have started violent attacks that yielded a collapse, or a civil war that led to collapse. Our country remains divided, and will as long as the Perverted Triangle system is in place and the two big parties and their competing social agendas violate the Constitution and Natural Rights and divide the country.[17]

In 2025, MSNBC featured a civil war expert who worked with the intelligence community, and claimed that intelligence community models indicate the US is heading toward major political violence. She blamed Trump's racism and said attacks on democracy are going to lead to a civil war.[18]

> Professor Barbara F. Walter, a renowned expert on civil wars around the world, warns that the United States meets key criteria for nations heading toward major political violence. We ignore the warning signs at our own peril, according to the author of *How Civil Wars Start and How to Stop Them*. American history shows that the fight to save democracy will have to come from the bottom up, Walter says. "Protest and peaceful resistance works," she adds. "Don't voluntarily comply with orders that are illegal. Don't help Donald Trump implement his agenda–don't preemptively comply."

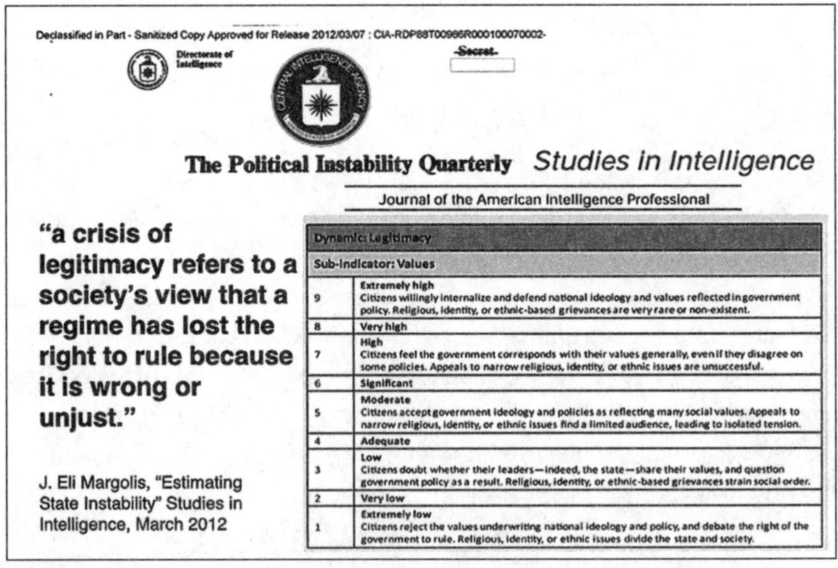

Declassified in Part - Sanitized Copy Approved for Release 2012/03/07 : CIA-RDP88T00986R000100070002-

Directorate of Intelligence

Secret

The Political Instability Quarterly Studies in Intelligence

Journal of the American Intelligence Professional

"a crisis of legitimacy refers to a society's view that a regime has lost the right to rule because it is wrong or unjust."

J. Eli Margolis, "Estimating State Instability" Studies in Intelligence, March 2012

Dynamic: Legitimacy	
Sub-Indicator: Values	
9	**Extremely high** Citizens willingly internalize and defend national ideology and values reflected in government policy. Religious, identity, or ethnic-based grievances are very rare or non-existent.
8	**Very high**
7	**High** Citizens feel the government corresponds with their values generally, even if they disagree on some policies. Appeals to narrow religious, identity, or ethnic issues are unsuccessful.
6	**Significant**
5	**Moderate** Citizens accept government ideology and policies as reflecting many social values. Appeals to narrow religious, identity, or ethnic issues find a limited audience, leading to isolated tension.
4	**Adequate**
3	**Low** Citizens doubt whether their leaders—indeed, the state—share their values, and question government policy as a result. Religious, identity, or ethnic-based grievances strain social order.
2	**Very low**
1	**Extremely low** Citizens reject the values underwriting national ideology and policy, and debate the right of the government to rule. Religious, identity, or ethnic issues divide the state and society.

Figure 53: Intelligence agency political instability models.

There are intelligence agency models on estimating likelihood of civil war. The Central Intelligence Agency and other organizations have developed models to estimate state instability.

A state maintains stability when it can enforce laws, change laws in response to social pressure, and has legitimacy: strong public support.

As a former intelligence officer, I have used "state instability models" that intelligence agencies use to predict political instability and civil war. I served in Iraq on the Multi-National Force Iraq HQ staff when we were trying to end civil war in Iraq. The US scores poorly now on political instability and is likely to have a form of civil war, but probably not for reasons MSNBC covered.

While Americans are sharply divided by the two political parties and the Perverted Triangle, almost all Americans do agree on is that our government is a divisive, corrupt, bad mess, as this Pew Research Center poll shows.

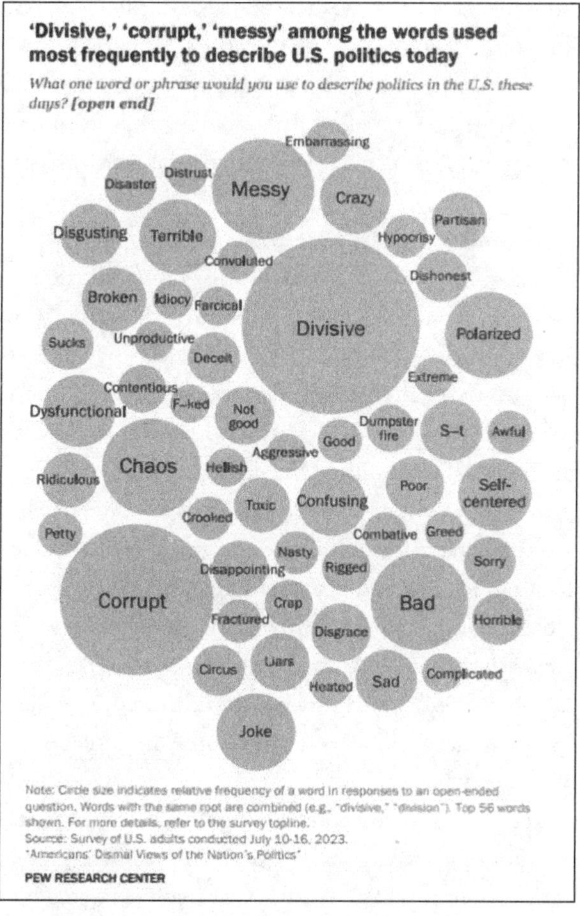

Figure 54: Americans regard US politics as a divisive, corrupt, chaotic, bad, polarized mess.

A key factor in intelligence community political instability models is legitimacy. When people in a nation-state view their government as corrupt, unjust, illegitimate, a civil war is likely. Quoting an expert on these models, J. Eli Margolis, "a crisis of legitimacy refers to a society's view that a regime has lost the right to rule because it is wrong or unjust."[19] In the US today, both sides see the other as wrong and unjust. This is a crisis of legitimacy, a country posed for political instability and possibly civil war. The vast majority of US citizens today see our government as corrupt, bad, wrong, unjust.

On issues like gun control, abortion, social programs, income redistribution, welfare, education, support for the police, and many others, the country is sharply divided, united only by our shared hatred of government politics. In sum, the legitimacy of the US government is gone.

Sir John Glubb in his great study of the rise and fall of civilizations found that a "remarkable and unexpected symptom of national decline is the intensification of internal political hatreds."[20] The US is high in political hatred and division.

When Musk and DOGE were taking a chainsaw to government, half the country was thrilled, the other half appalled. It is obvious that President Trump is not going to unite the country, but increase the divisions and toss gas on the fire of political hatred in the country.

The political instability models note that one seemingly trivial trigger event can ignite a civil war. When 41 percent of young voters call the murder of a CEO acceptable, that's another indication that a country is poised for violence. One CEO assassination is unlikely to spark a civil war, though one assassination did spark World War I. But it is the tremendous support for a CEO murderer amongst tens of millions of Americans that demonstrates how our society is angry, divided, and eager to fight the other side. Elon Musk dare not venture out in public, and his Tesla cars are increasingly under arson attack. More career politicians are being assassinated or are suffering assassination attempts. The political and social divide in the US is worsening, increasingly violent. The event that ignites this hatred into uncontrollable violence and a collapse (with or without civil war) is unpredictable, but it could happen anytime.

More than 70 percent of Americans have committed a crime that could lead to imprisonment.[21] An astonishing one third of American adults have a criminal record![22] This reflects both the unlimited plethora of laws spewed out by the Perverted Triangle unbound by any consideration of Natural Rights (for the benefit of lawyers) and the growing willingness of Americans to break the law. Disobeying laws is widespread and commonplace in the US. Even laws against murder are not supported by a large percent of the population if the victim is a political enemy.

The US can change laws, but the country is so divided that when it does, half the population is pleased, the other half angry. Even more Americans break the law but don't know they have done so, since there are hundreds of thousands, perhaps millions of laws (no one can come up with a complete list). The are a multitude of laws that Americans deliberately violate since they rightly regard them as unconstitutional, violations of our Natural Rights, or just asininely stupid. And many Americans knowingly break the law when they suspect they won't be caught or regard them as unjust.

The Trump administration is not just openly defying basic principles of the Constitution, violating the law, undermining legitimacy of government, ignoring judicial rulings against them; they are flaunting their eagerness to ignore judges and demand their removal. The Perverted Triangle ignores and trashes the Constitution, the key source of US government legitimacy, ignoring the limits to government power with the Supreme Court backing them up as if the Ninth and Tenth Amendments, still in the Constitution, do not exist.

Americans' disgust with government politics is one of our few uniting factors. Trust in our federal government has plummeted since the Perverted Triangle took over in the 1960s, to the point that in 2024 just 2 percent of Americans trust the federal government to do what is right "just about always," with the total trusting federal government always or most of the time just 22 percent.[23]

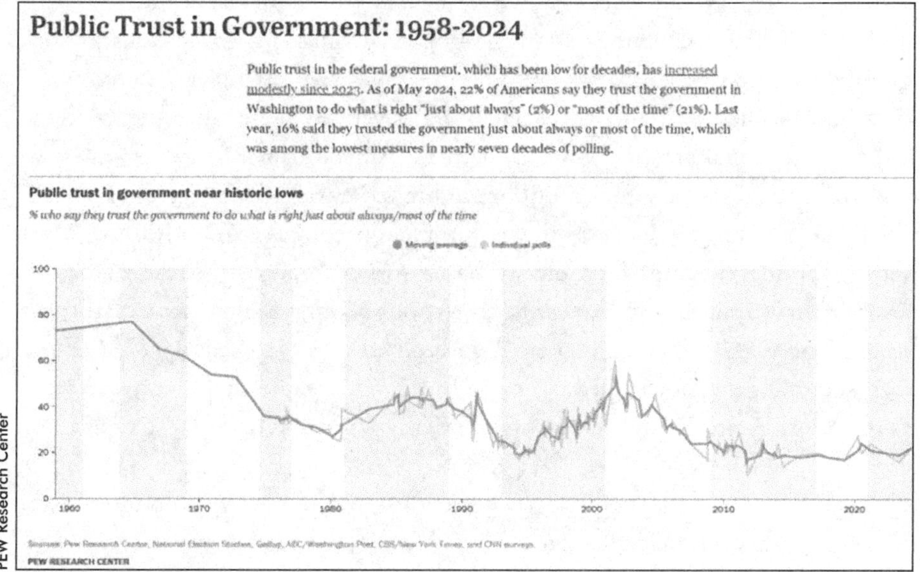

PEW Research Center

Figure 55: Trust in US government has collapsed.

Back in 1958, about three-quarters of Americans trusted the federal government to do the right thing almost always or most of the time. But with the Lyndon Johnson "Great Society" explosion in welfare programs, followed by Nixon's full embrace of unconstitutional Perverted Triangle election pandering, the Perverted Triangle took over both parties and the government. Ronald Reagan helped reverse the decline in trust of government in the mid-1980s, but unconstrained growth in government interference, regulations, spending, along with the divisions between the two sides have driven trust and approval of government to dangerous lows. Republicans are the most disgusted (and most likely to revolt) with just 11 percent trusting the federal government almost always or most of the time, versus 35 percent of Democrats.[24] But that's 2024 poll data—Democratic support of federal government is likely way down today.

Barbara Walter, who has worked with these intelligence agency political instability models, believes that "conditions in the US have worsened with a drastic decline in the quality of the [democratic] system. It's happening quickly . . . and everything indicates that the president wants to weaken it further. If he can, he will eliminate the checks and balances on the executive branch. I can imagine a scenario in which he's successful in creating a dictatorship.'"[25] Walter warns that the US is not just scoring in a zone with risk of civil war, but we are at a point where if conditions worsen, "you get there very rapidly."[26] Walter does not believe it will be a civil war between armies, but rebel groups fighting and killing at local levels.

But while Trump opponents condemn his clear violations of the Constitution, ignoring limits to executive power, Trump supporters and Libertarians counter that constitutional limits to government are effectively gone since the Supreme Court refuses to enforce the Ninth and Tenth Amendments. Federal social, welfare, health care, income redistribution, unlimited government regulation of private homes and property, many other government programs are clearly unconstitutional. Nor does the Supreme Court defend the most important, American part of government—limiting government to protect our Natural Rights, not violate them at will. The Courts allows all levels of government to completely ignore Natural Rights promulgated in the Declaration of Independence and supposedly protected by the Ninth Amendment, like rights to privacy, private property, the right to be left alone.

Ray Dalio, the founder of Bridgewater Capital, one of the largest, most successful hedge funds ever, made his fortune by correctly predicting major future events. He believes a US civil war is very likely given the sharp, increasing divisions in our society. He estimates a greater than 50 percent chance of some form of US civil war due to the growing political/social divide.[27]

But a second civil war will not be anything like the first, with states or armies fighting. It will be citizen groups fighting within states, refusing unconstitutional laws and violation of their Natural Rights. Some states may break up; some may secede from the US.

Collapse Survivor App US Civil War Simulation Explained How Conservative Rural Areas May Rebel Against Liberal Democrat/ Urban Controlled State Governments

To understand how this violence could develop, analysis and simulations were done on the Collapse Survivor App. The US military owes much of its success to realistic training exercises, "command post" or "tabletop" exercises that simulate different scenarios that could lead to war. Using input from intelligence officers, analysts, and experts who have studied political instability, the Collapse Survivor App ran several simulations on how domestic political divisions could escalate into protests, violence, and a collapse. The hundreds of people playing the simulation were polled about what kind of violence they expect to result.

This exercise simulation on US civil war illustrated how political violence can spiral out of control, yield looting, widespread loss of law and order, and a collapse. This would not be states and armies clashing, but citizens fighting, looting, a breakdown in law and order, and possibly rural/conservative parts of California and other Democrat Party controlled state governments revolting.[28]

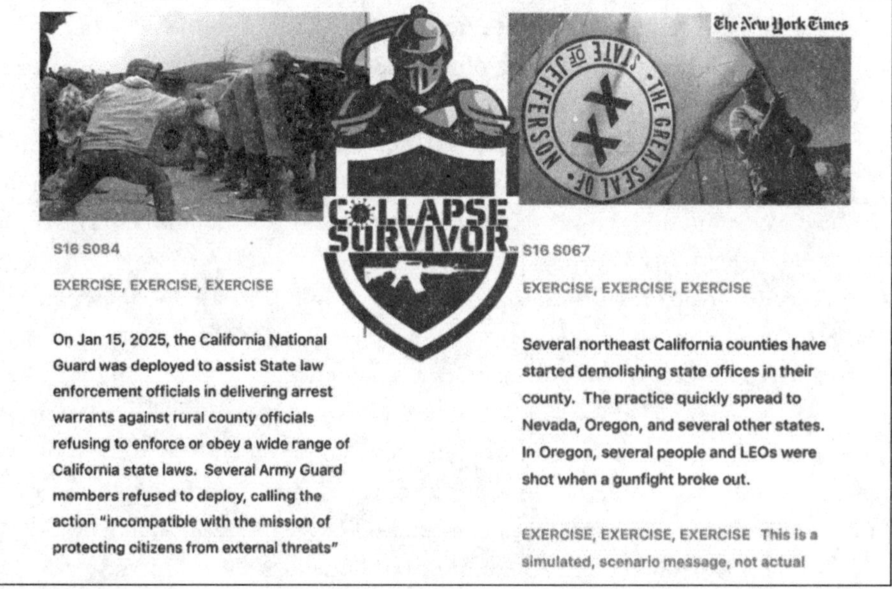

Figure 56: Collapse Survivor App US civil war scenario, collapse survival simulation shows how rural, conservative citizens in states controlled by urban, liberal Democratic voters may rebel.

In a Collapse Survivor App scenario where Trump was reelected, political divisions led to rural conservative counties in California rebelling against the state government controlled by liberal Democrats. Political protests and violence evolved into conservative and Libertarian citizens revolting against Democratic controlled state governments in California, Oregon, Nevada, Colorado, Illinois, New York, and Massachusetts. It was not a civil war between states, but civil war *within* states, with rural, conservative counties revolting and often fighting against state gun control laws and then kicking state government officials out of their counties and refusing to follow zoning and building code laws forced by urban-dominated state governments into rural counties that oppose such rules. This is how US civil war prior to or after a collapse is likely to be: not war between states, but war between liberal, Democratic party-controlled state governments and rural areas that are conservative, Republican, refusing to follow state laws and wanting to separate.[29]

Many Americans Are Preparing for Civil War since Political Divisions and Violence Can Lead to Civil War Now, or During/ After a Collapse

How the deepening US political divisions evolve is unpredictable, but we have already seen how political protests in the US can lead to loss of law and order, with bad people taking advantage of political protests to start looting in places like Portland and Baltimore. With the growing political divide and violence, exacerbated by media and podcaster coverage, and social media that is often used to incite and organize flash mobs, you can see how the US could suffer widespread, long lasting political protests, looting, loss of law and order.[30]

Criminals take advantage of overwhelmed police during political protests to loot and even rob and kill people in their homes. A major training lesson from Collapse Survivor App training exercise simulations is that when police are overwhelmed with protestors, criminals and gang members can exploit this and law and order can quickly vanish.

A recent poll of several hundred preppers, people who are looking at news and watching for threat indications, well informed, asked, "Do you believe that President Trump's actions and plans to date are increasing or decreasing the likelihood of a domestic civil war?" The poll found that 50 percent believe Trump is "greatly increasing" the likelihood of civil war, with another 20 percent indicating he is slightly increasing likelihood of civil war. Seven percent responded that Trump is not having an impact on the likelihood of civil war, but that a domestic civil war is likely. Combined, 77 percent of respondents believe Trump is increasing the likelihood of civil war or that domestic civil war is likely.[31]

The top three collapse threats according to the Disaster Preparedness Threat Watch and Collapse Warning System "Probability of Collapse Model" are loss of the electric grid, a bad pandemic, and domestic civil war. The model estimated a 2 percent annual risk of a domestic civil war that leads to a collapse. The likelihood of political violence and looting is much higher than this, but the probability of this escalating to the point of a national collapse is probably low.

Americans have very good reasons to hate government. An early chapter described thirty documented examples of how our unlimited, unconstitutional government is literally killing citizens with unconstitutional programs and policies that help career politicians buy votes to get reelected. Programs that give benefits to special interest groups and key political constituents earn votes for career politicians, always running for reelection and fighting for their warring political party at the expense of not just personal liberty and our earnings, but often the lives of the silent majority.

The preppers who are watching the trends and conditions, the intelligence agency state instability models, and Ray Dalio's estimate of a greater than 50 percent likelihood of civil war, are all wise warnings. It won't be a war between battling states, but within states, as rural/conservative populations revolt and fight against liberal Democrat/city controlled State governments with policies and regulations violating the Constitution and Natural Rights. The nation's divisions are increasing, will get more violent, and some trigger event like a bad recession or as assassination or just rising numbers of flash mobs and protests, could lead to wide spread loss of law and order and a civil war driven collapse. Regardless, when the first collapse does happen, the odds of civil war during collapse recovery may be very high, as explained in a later chapter.

Unconstitutional federal social programs are bankrupting the country, undermining families and individual responsibility, creating a dependent class of poor people, and fueling the great political divide in the country. If the federal government followed the Constitution and unconstitutional social programs were eliminated, then states and localities could decide if they want to pursue social programs, limited by Natural Rights and what the local population wants. The nation would not be so divided by these unconstitutional and contested social policies, not in a state of low-level civil war, and not failing as badly to prepare for collapse survival if government was limited to do its proper job of protecting citizens from external threats they cannot handle on their own.[32]

Chapter Fourteen

POLITICAL REFORMS ARE REQUIRED TO RETURN LIMITED GOVERNMENT FOCUSED ON PROPER ROLE OF DEFENDING CITIZENS

Without an end to the Perverted Triangle focused on reelection and pandering for votes with pork and social programs that divide the country, and a proper focus of government on national security and protecting us from threats we cannot handle on our own, most Americans are unlikely to survive the coming collapses.[1]

Since Americans' disagreements on social and welfare issues, reinforced by the warring political parties, are largely irreconcilable, the only way to avoid civil war before or after the first collapse is to get at least the federal government and ideally state governments as well out of dictating or participating in social and welfare programs, leaving it up to local governments and communities to choose—with the losing side able to more readily vote with their feet and leave.

With a future of deadly bioengineered pandemics,[2] a vulnerable electric grid that our irresponsible federal and state governments refuse to harden, and many new threats from AI and new man-made technologies, the US government must stop wasting resources on social and welfare policies that divide the nation, and return to its original, constitutional, proper priority of protecting citizens from external threats they cannot handle on their own. Unlike Switzerland, Finland, China, and some other countries that are preparing citizens for collapse survival, the US government is not just failing to prepare citizens—but is the major barrier and imposes huge extra costs for individuals to prepare.[3] By undermining personal responsibility and families, creating dependent wards of the state, the Perverted Triangle is setting Americans up for massive fatalities in a collapse.[4]

Unconstitutional Welfare and Social Programs Are Dividing the Nation, Setting Us Up for Civil War

There is no limit to what unconstitutional government can seize from Americans to spend on in the United States today with Americans's natural and constitutional rights illegally erased, as the traitor/criminal/prisoner Bradley Manning's government-funded sex change operation proved.[5]

Chelsea Manning to undergo sex reassignment surgery

By Tom Vanden Brook

MilitaryTimes

Sep 13, 2016

Figure 57: Traitor, convict, given taxpayer-funded sex change operation.

In 2010 while serving in Iraq, Army Private Bradley Manning deliberately gave WikiLeaks about 750,000 classified and sensitive, military and diplomatic documents. He was caught and sentenced to thirty-five years' imprisonment. While serving his prison sentence, he decided that he wanted to be a she and changed his name to Chelsea Manning. Then he[6] demanded that the government pay for his sex change operation. The US Army, of course, refused the request. But then the gay community in San Francisco and New York City rallied behind him (even nominating him to be Grand Marshal of Gay Pride parades) and lobbied Democrats in office. The politically powerful (with the Democratic Party) American Civil Liberties Union sued on Manning's behalf.

His request for government funding of a sex change operation should have been quickly rejected, but the Perverted Triangle, unencumbered by the Constitution or common sense, seeing zero limits on any government action, no matter how wrong and absurd, granted the request. Not wanting to risk a politically incorrect action that might lose LGBTQ-community votes, no elected officials blocked the asinine, absolutely outrageous, wrong decision to waste and abuse taxpayer funds. So traitor, felon, criminal, prisoner Bradley/Chelsea Manning was given gender reassignment surgery, costing about $25,000, while in prison, and then free hormone treatments after.[7] This would be continuing today, except that Chelsea Manning was commuted by Barack Obama after serving just seven years of his thirty-five-year sentence.

Ignoring the incredible wrongs, the perversion of government paying for someone to have a sex change, the worst offense is that this is a grotesque violation of our Natural Rights to use our personal property and wealth. Some Americans have moral objections to sex change operations, most believe people have the right to do whatever they want as long as it does not harm others, but everyone is outraged when our money is taken to pay for outrageous, unconstitutional government spending like a taxpayer funded sex change operation for a traitor in jail. Thanks to FDR and the Perverted Triangle, there are no limits left—governments at all levels take our money and pass laws, make regulations to do whatever they want. They can violate and kill us with full protection from the courts—and do so every day. In a collapse they are authorized to steal our food and supplies, and have set citizens up for massive die-off.

Federal welfare and income redistribution programs are unconstitutional, not mentioned, enumerated, or written in the Constitution. The taking of one person's money to give to another against their will is a clear violation of both the Tenth Amendment and Natural Rights as well. American voters have not authorized the federal government (or most state governments) to take money from someone to give it to someone else against their will. Constitutional expert, attorney Roger Pilon, has written many books and articles (many with the Cato Institute) explaining how "individuals have both the right to rule themselves and a right not to be ruled by others."[8] Government income redistribution programs are unconstitutional and violate our Natural Rights to private property and to be left alone. As Pilon put it, "The redistributive power amounts to theft by government, plain and simple."[9]

The American Revolution Was Fought for Natural Rights and Strictly Limited Government. But the Supreme Court No Longer Enforces the Constitution and the Perverted Triangle Has Evolved to Exploit Unlimited Power at the Expense of Citizens' Lives.

The Constitution was never amended by the People or the States to eliminate our Natural Rights of privacy, private property, and self-defense—all protected by the Ninth Amendment that the Supreme Court no longer enforces. Nor was the Tenth Amendment, which clearly limits the federal government to only pursue action in the few areas written out in the Constitution repealed. The Supreme Court no longer enforces the Tenth, either. The US is not a democracy or a representative democracy with unlimited majority rule; it is a Republic with a Constitution that is supposed to guarantee our individual Natural Rights and protect us from abuse by the majority or government by greatly limiting government to only the specific areas where government is authorized to rule, with all levels of government limited in abusing our natural and constitutional rights. But both the Ninth and Tenth Amendment, limits to government power are effectively gone.[10]

The right of personal use of your private property that has no impact on neighbors is increasingly restricted or completely denied by Big City regulations that Democratic Party–controlled Big State Government has forced into county government and rural areas. In the interests of survival, preppers looking to build their bug-out facilities and survival communities in rural areas should ignore the zoning and building code barriers that stand in the way.

The great defect of the Constitution, slavery, was finally corrected with the Civil War and the Thirteenth and Fourteenth Amendments. If Natural Rights had been defended by the Supreme Court as they should have (overriding the Constitution in preeminence), this abuse would have been solved in the early 1800s. Government and courts that respected and obeyed our Natural Rights—which are supreme, above the Constitution in priority and authority, far above positive laws passed by legislatures—would also have stopped the lies and theft and abuse of Native Americans. Chief Standing Bear said all he needed to in court when he raised his right and said: "That hand is not the color of yours, but if I pierce it, I shall feel pain. If you pierce your hand, you also feel pain. The blood that will flow from mine will be of the same color as yours. *I am a man*. The same God made us both."[11] As a human being he had Natural Rights that trump every law, government bureaucrat, and regulation in the land. But because Natural Rights to personal freedom are wrongly ignored in US courts, discrimination that plagued African, Chinese, Japanese, and Native Americans continued, and in some instances, still occurs.

How could this happen when the Ninth Amendment is so absolutely clear, both in its text and legislative intent: "The enumeration in the Constitution of certain rights shall not be construed to deny or disparage others retained by the people."

Of course, when people disagree, and court cases occur, judges (and ideally juries) need to decide what listed (freedom of religion, speech, bearing arms, et cetera) and unenumerated Natural Rights should be protected, and whether a law or some other conflicting right should take priority. It is pointless, a fool's errand to try to legislate every possible right, and stupider yet to try to argue what is right or wrong based on arguing past case decisions by other judges. What makes sense is for judges and juries to decide—guided by the Declaration and the Constitution, the priority of Natural Rights and personal freedom, sacrificed only when we are interfering with other's Natural Rights, imposing harm or a huge risk of causing great harm to others. And as Roger Pilon points out, "the principles of adjudication are the same with all rights, enumerated and unenumerated alike. Thus, from both a textual and an adjudicatory perspective, judges must uphold our written Constitution by discovering and securing unenumerated rights, just as they must and do with enumerated rights." What is completely unacceptable is ignoring our Natural Rights to maximum freedom and the absolutely key American principles of limited government.

Pilon continues: "It was the doctrine of enumerated powers that was meant to constitute the principal defense against overweening government." The problem wasn't lack of votes in Parliament (which as a minority, would have had little or no effect) but rather the "unrestrained majoritarian regime, as the Founders knew from their experience with English rule."[12] The Boston Tea Party participants objected to the tax on tea, not the fact that they didn't have a representative in Parliament to vote on it. The Revolution was not launched to gain seats in Parliament or majority rule, but to proclaim a totally new type of government where The People had Natural Rights that were above and superior to any legislatures, God, or king's claim of authority. But it's far better for the Perverted Triangle to have a docile, subservient population that blindly obeys and submits, so they teach in public history books that the Revolutionary War was just because of "taxation without representation," and that since Americans can now vote, government is good, and FDR was the greatest American ever. The Perverted Triangle would love citizens to limit their involvement to voting, with elections limited to the Democratic Party and GOP, and blindly obey all laws. They champion "rule of law"—but most federal laws are unconstitutional, and a massive, ever-growing avalanche of laws and regulations that violate our Natural Rights. These laws are not legal, are ruining our country, killing citizens now, and setting the populace up for annihilation in a collapse.

The Ninth and Tenth Amendments are still there; but Congress, the Executive Branch, and courts are free to ignore them whenever they want. Worse, with the perversion of *stare decisis* and lawyers über alles, judges follow and weigh past case decisions over both our superior Natural Rights and the Constitution! Most Americans know our government and judicial system are grossly wrong, but have no idea how the Perverted Triangle took most of their liberties and protection from Big Government.[13]

Surviving in the Age of Collapse Requires Great Personal Responsibility and Families—Both Undermined by the Perverted Triangle

Overwhelming proof that Big Government welfare programs have ruined families and created a poor, dependent class is data on marriage rates, single-family kids, and out-of-wedlock birth rates. Wealthy Americans continue to have marriage rates and overwhelmingly two-parent families, but poor Americans were devastated by the surge in socialism, welfare programs, and growth of the Nanny State in the 1960s.[14] Black American out-of-wedlock births went from 24.5 percent in 1964 to 70.7 percent by 1994, roughly where it stands today. In 1964, before Lyndon Johnson's unconstitutional "Great Society" welfare programs were created, 7 percent of American children were born out of wedlock, compared to 40 percent today.[15]

Dr. Thomas West, a political scientist who studied American welfare programs, explains how the Perverted Triangle has undermined marriage and families:

> The most destructive feature of the post-1965 approach has been its unintentional promotion of family breakdown, which is a recipe for the neglect and abuse of children, the widespread crime that such abuse fosters, the impoverishment of women and children, and the loneliness and anguish of everyone involved. Among the reasons that people get married and stay married (or used to) are happiness, mutual usefulness, a sense of moral obligation, and the penalty of shame and the law for those who misbehave. Post-1965 policies and ideas have ravaged all four of these supports of marriage.[16]

When the government provides welfare payments and services, you don't need a family, or a two-parent family. Family breakdown fuels poverty. Even high school dropouts who are married have a far lower poverty rate than single parents with several years of college. Boys raised without their father are much more likely to use drugs, drop out of school, engage in violent criminal behavior, and go to jail. Girls are more likely to engage in early sexual activity or have a child out of wedlock. The Perverted Triangle blames their failures on other societal or capitalist problems they must solve, like dangerous neighborhoods or poor schools or evil businesses. But they are wrong—family structure and family and individual responsibility are the decisive factors driving work ethic, good character, and wise decisions.[17]

Even if you believed that destroying families and creating a huge government bureaucracy was worth it in order to win LBJ's "War on Poverty," the undisputable facts are: the effort not only failed, but made poverty worse. In *The Tragedy of American Compassion*, Dr. Martin Olasky explains how successful programs to assist the poor run by private charity groups and churches in the 1800s and early 1900s in the US were replaced by federal programs that were both less effective and poisonously addictive as entitlements.[18] Dr. Lawrence Mead, author of *Beyond Entitlement*, also argues that "the main problem with the welfare state is its permissiveness." Based on extensive research and service in the Department of Health, Education and Welfare, Dr. Mead concluded that the failure to obligate recipients of aid to take responsibility for their actions and end dependence on government assistance is the key flaw of Big Government entitlement programs pushed by the Perverted Triangle.[19] Political Scientist Charles Murray has documented in his many books how "[t]he perverse incentives of the welfare state have created dependency and human suffering."[20] The political appeal of "providing opportunity and access to the poor" is strong, but is ultimately a destructive effort.[21] But this dependency and irresponsibility is precisely what the Democratic Party wants to grow a subservient, foolish citizenry that supports and obeys the dictates of Big Government and the Perverted Triangle and votes Democratic.[22] Thomas Sowell, has studied welfare and government programs for decades, concluding that "[n]o government of the left has done as much for the poor as capitalism has. . . . Although the big word on the left is 'compassion,' the big agenda on the left is dependency."[23]

Do an internet search on historical poverty rates and you'll find many government sources—all starting from 1959, with the rate at 22 percent, then claim success because of poverty rates falling to 10–15 percent today. But the poverty rate was 33 percent at the end of World War II (1945), and it fell dramatically during the 1950s. In 1964 when LBJ's War on Poverty was launched it was already down to 19 percent. Then the host of unconstitutional federal welfare programs started. It was 17 percent in 1965, but then stopped moving down—as Nanny State socialism institutionalized poverty. In 2014, 15 percent of Americans qualified as poor, and the rate fluctuates between 10 and 15 percent today.[24] The improvement in poverty rates was driven more by economic growth than the Perverted Triangle—and poverty would be far lower without the destruction of work ethic and families from welfare and the huge regulation barriers and government fees to start a new business. The War on Poverty spent $22 trillion in a cornucopia of unconstitutional welfare programs and did worse than fail.[25] Not only did poverty remain, it institutionalized poverty, destroyed families, and subverted individual responsibility in favor of the Nanny State and the Perverted Triangle. Welfare and entitlement programs today have built up government debt that will destroy the US economy and could plunge us into an economic collapse that could kill millions.[26]

The biggest root problem with the federal government today, that corrupts and divides our society, is that limits to federal government policy and taxation are ignored; enabling divisive, expensive, unconstitutional, social programs and regulations to proliferate; bankrupting and dividing the country; eliminating Natural Rights, subverting individual responsibility; and destroying families.

> **"Everything that is really great and inspiring is created by the individual who can labor in freedom."**
>
> **—Albert Einstein**

Government Regulations blocking ability to Survive must end. Most Regulations can be replaced by Voluntary Standards and Citizen Advisory Associations.

The biggest barrier to personal collapse survival preparedness is Big Government and regulations. In the interest of not just personal property rights and liberty, but survival, Americans need to ignore unconstitutional Big Government regulations that violate our Natural Rights to be left alone and protect our families from the coming collapse that government is supposed to be preventing and preparing us for, but is not.[27]

We can achieve the benefits of standardization and safety without violating Natural Rights or wasting billions by eliminating most government regulations and regulatory agencies, replacing them with Citizen Advisory Associations and voluntary standards developed and monitored by private groups like Underwriters Laboratories.

Government overspending is just part of the Perverted Triangle's destruction of the United States of America. Economist Thomas D. Hopkins of the Rochester Institute of Technology concluded that in 1995 the American people had to spend $668 billion just to comply with the regulatory burden, about $7,000 per household.[28]

We can obtain the benefits of regulating without most of the costs and loss of Natural Rights by replacing most regulations with industry standards and best practices that are not set by industries, but by private standards groups enforced by them and "Citizen's Advisory Associations."[29]

The purpose of regulation is "to make regular," to standardize and promote best practices, improve product/service quality— not to pass laws and make more opportunity for lobbyists, campaign donations for career politicians, government jobs, and profitable work for lawyers.

The best way to accomplish the goals of regulations is not government mandates and a system run by the Perverted Triangle to benefit them, but voluntary, private standards and regulations. The best standards and safety promoting practices come from voluntary associations that have successfully operated for centuries. There is no need for government laws or government regulations to achieve standards and best practices and safety for the vast majority of products, services, and personal actions. The Nanny State doesn't even believe citizens have enough intelligence to go shopping. The federal Bureau of Consumer Protection tells us what to buy, with hundreds of federal government agencies and thousands of state and city government departments to regulate our decisions.

Private associations and industry standards have a huge history of success without government rules, bureaucrats, or lawsuits, via tests and analysis, setting standards, certification, monitoring, brand approval, warranties, product evaluations, recommending best practices, and arbitration.

For over a century, hugely successful and beneficial Underwriters Laboratories (UL),[30] which is not a government agency and operates with no government support or legislation, has achieved the benefits of safety and standardization with strictly voluntary compliance. Companies, customers, and insurance agencies look for UL approval on products, knowing that UL enforces high, reasonable standards for product safety. Companies voluntarily comply with UL standards and pay UL to get their stamp of approval. No government, no Perverted Triangle needed. No violation of Natural Rights and freedom.

Green Seal, an independent organization, certifies "environmentally sound" products. Kosher food products, The Good Housekeeping Seal of Approval, Consumers Union's fantastic *Consumer Reports*, the Better Business Bureau, hundreds of industry associations like the American Dental Association develop and promote standards.

Industry standards and voluntary compliance leverages the huge power of free market competition, with companies competing to win consumers by offering the best products at the best price. Unlike Underwriters Laboratory reasonable standards, a government agency in charge results in abominations like the Occupational Safety and Health Administration's 1987 final ruling on the use of formaldehyde that could save one person's life every hundred years by spending $72 billion (in 1984 dollars).[31]

We do not need Big Government national or state regulations on consumer products, businesses, personal affairs, personal property—let people choose when their decisions have no big negative externality[32] on others and let the courts handle charges of violating our Natural Right to be left alone, not harmed by others (people, businesses, or government bureaucrats). For guidance, replace government regulations with consumer/citizen association groups that advise on product safety and quality, good or bad business conduct. Let citizens choose what Consumer Advisory Association (CAA) they trust and want to follow. Those that offer great advice will be rewarded with more members. When a recommendation proves bad it can immediately be changed—unlike government laws and regulations that once passed, almost never go away. Rather than government bureaucrats that can't be fired, CAAs can be rewarded or rejected for their good or bad advice. The tax savings from firing millions[33] of government bureaucrats and eliminating hundreds of government agencies can fund not just better replacement consumer/citizen associations, but new companies, productive jobs, and a much happier populace. With fewer domestic laws and regulations to deal with, federal and state officials can focus on security, the most important service we need from government. The savings from fewer laws will also help get rid of more shyster lawyers and lawsuits, less expense for consumers buying products/services with higher costs due to our perverted legal system.[34]

Consumer Reports, environmental groups like Greenpeace, the Grange, the US Chamber of Commerce, National Small Business Association, the American Association of Retired Persons, USAA (current/former military), American Legion, the Salvation Army, churches, lots of groups and associations could offer ratings and recommendations on regulations and rate companies. CAAs can consider inputs from companies, individuals, other associations, in developing their guidelines and recommendations. Coalitions of groups might band together to form or back a CAA. Many like Consumer Reports, USAA, Costco, already have regular publications with advice on not just what to buy, but how to promote environmental sustainability, avoid being a victim of crime, improve your health and wealth—without taxing people or forcing them to do things. While industry associations can be very effective in developing common standards and promoting good conduct, they would best serve by giving inputs to Consumer Advisory Agencies—not be a CAA given their inherent bias.

In advising on regulations and public policy, a CAA Congress would be ideal. Associations could send citizens (not lawyers or career politicians) to a group that meets full-time to discuss and debate the merits of regulations and public policies being proposed at national and state levels (perhaps some city/regional groups) to see if a CAA consensus can be achieved. If so, all CAAs could recommend the same guidance—providing the good aspect of laws and regulations without the overwhelmingly bad disadvantages of our current Big Government regulatory morass and the Perverted Triangle. If no agreement emerges, CAAs can disagree, explaining why they disagree so citizens who care about a particular issue can compare CAA positions and make their own call.

Associations can also amass consumer power to leverage against monopolies and fight bad AI companies. For example, a Facebook competitor that protects or pays for citizens' data and does not rip off small business advertisers badly could be promoted by associations—encouraging members to dump Facebook and switch to the better startup. YouTube is another big quasi-monopoly that needs competitors that CAAs could back. It is virtually impossible for a small startup to gain awareness and grow against the Facebook, YouTube, Google, or Apple monopolies/oligopolies. CAAs can help leverage consumer power and choice against the business giants. Associations should collaborate and when facing powerful monopolies that are exploiting their market power, act collectively to promote alternatives, encourage members to boycott some firms. Strong government regulation and control are vital for AI, but CAAs could be an additional, powerful means of forcing AI companies to stop dangerous, fatal abuse of uncontrolled AI.[35] CAA's must not be bound by anti-collusion laws; they need to be authorized by law to collaborate and cooperate to counter the power of monopolies and huge corporations promoting AI for their profit at the expense of our lives.[36]

Regulations undermine, and ultimately ruin personal and family responsibility. Why inspect a house, consider the safety and reliability of products when there are so many thousands of government regulations and inspections? Why bother working hard, or making big investments in education when government can provide you income and health care? You don't need a parent or the advice of extended family members when the Nanny State is guiding you in everything you do: what you can eat and drink, the design and construction of your house, your health and medical care, your income if you need financial help, et cetera. For FDR and top strategists and leaders of the Perverted Triangle this is no accident; it's part of their grand design to yield a dependent, docile population that is beholden to them for guidance and survival, eager to vote to keep them in power so their government benefits keep flowing.

The perversion of laws and regulations and welfare programs by the Perverted Triangle is far more damaging and evil than Boss Tweed's Tammany Hall[37] because it is so more sophisticated and hidden. A citizen could figure out he'd been bribed with free food or a job, but most Americans today are on welfare programs and don't know it is due to deliberate government lies and deception—like misleading people to think that their Social Security number is for an individual retirement account with their contributions and interest earnings in it, not the Congressionally set benefits and hidden welfare payments that Social Security and Medicare provide.

When Big Government decides to regulate your home and adds building codes, they don't just violate your Natural Rights of privacy, use of private property, and right to be left alone, they drive housing costs up. This is particularly hard on poor Americans and small businesses. Code requirements drive up the costs of new houses by tens of thousands of dollars. Moreover, government routinely tears down poor people's houses that are not "up to code" for defects as minor as peeling paint. For example, the Dallas city government demolished over a thousand private homes between 1992 and 1995, most of them in low-income and minority areas, sending previous residents onto the welfare rolls or into the streets as homeless.[38]

The standard lie of building code officials is that community safety drives them. However the majority of such regulations deal with strictly personal preferences and trivial (or nonexistent) personal safety. Colorado Springs building codes dictate how much glass you can have on a patio (and it's not a limit on the percent of glass for a stronger building—it's a requirement for lots of glass because a window manufacturer in town lobbied for the requirement).[39] A neighbor can't be harmed from your lack of tamper proof outlets or stair tread width or building size. Democratic Party takeover of state governments in Nevada and Colorado has led to expansion of big city building codes and zoning restrictions, forcing this government control into rural counties where there are no neighbors and no demand for building codes. These codes and regulations benefit politicians, government workers and lawyers—not safety. Where safety might be improved by adding some item, it is the individual's right to decide if they want to pay the price to add it—not government.[40]

The Democratic Party loves to have more jobs for government bureaucrats, more regulations and laws to generate business for lawyers (who vote for the Democratic Party). Poor people having to spend more for housing also is great for the Democratic Party, which champions government welfare programs for the poor, buying their votes. A 2023 Pew Charitable Trust Poll found that 82 percent of Americans were concerned about the high cost of housing, 86 percent wanted faster permit processing, 65 percent wanted more personal freedom over use of their property.[41] Government regulations are primarily for the benefit of the Perverted Triangle, not American citizens.

A great path to wealth is to start your own business, not just work for others at low wages. As Albert Einstein observed, "Everything that is really great and inspiring is created by the individual who can labor in freedom."[42] With the explosion of laws, fees, permits, licenses, codes, regulations, and fines that the Perverted Triangle has dumped on us for their benefit, it is impossible to labor in freedom today. The poor are far more likely to get stuck in poverty because of the barriers to running a business erected by the self-serving Perverted Triangle and Big Government.

The Perverted Triangle makes running a small business or family farm orders of magnitude harder and less likely to succeed because of wretched, outrageous regulations and a tax code that is impossible to comply with (deliberately so) unless you employ accountants and lawyers. The tax code is many times the length of the King James Bible, littered with special provisions that politicians passed as pork benefits to buy votes. It is a nightmare for small businesses and citizens, but windfall profits for our million plus lawyers (many of them voting as elected officials when the laws were passed), plus jobs for the bureaucrats that enforce the rules (and donate to and campaign for the career politicians). The tax code is not a system designed to efficiently provide revenue for government; it is a cancerous perversion shaped over decades in lobbying, buying votes, and creating jobs and wealth for the Perverted Triangle.[43]

The Sarbanes-Oxley Act on business financial disclosure is 810 pages long, Obamacare over 1,000 pages, and the Dodd-Frank Wall Street Reform and Consumer Protection Act is 2,300 pages long. A huge company can employ lobbyists to tailor the laws passed for their benefit and afford the overhead staff to comply with all this nonsense. Smaller companies are disadvantaged by this regulatory morass, and every citizen losses with the added costs for products and services. The Perverted Triangle is the beneficiary.

One fire disaster occurs and the Perverted Triangle rushes in with laws, regulations, and new government jobs that last forever. America had no crisis of fires or safety or food poisoning in the 1950s to justify the explosion of laws and regulations and business fees—they were not justified; they were for the benefit of the Perverted Triangle.[44] Environmental and occupational regulations were piled on in the 1960s and 1970s. Today there are 260 federal agencies that issue business regulations, hundreds of thousands of pages of regulations, three thousand new regulations added each year, at an annual direct cost of accumulated federal regulations on the economy estimated at $2 trillion per year!!![45] Add state and local government rules and regulations and permits and you see how the Perverted Triangle is destroying everything that has been good about America. Freedom to work, build a business, make a living, support a family, and be left alone are all, like the Ninth and Tenth Amendments, the personal liberty that used to define America, largely erased by the Perverted Triangle and relentless, unchecked growth of Big Government.[46]

Especially in private residences and privately owned buildings not open to the general public, building codes should be completely optional or limited to a very few, absolutely vital codes for neighbor's safety (reasonable fire protection). The government property records can record whether or not owners decided to comply with a particular building code and get inspected. Future buyers and the general market can value that or not. Having built many homes and buildings, dealt with lots of building codes and inspectors, I confidently reject many of their code requirements as a huge waste, irrelevant to safety risks to neighbors, and gross violation of our most basic Natural Right—freedom in our own home. Most of the 143,000 government building code and permit positions in the US, paying a median salary of $67,700, could be eliminated.[47]

Aaron Wildavsky, a president of the American Political Science Association and author of many books on public policy analysis, argued for adaptiveness and resilience over excessive regulations and restrictions on new technologies. He believed that enhancing the capacity to cope with and adapt to surprises rather than trying to prevent all catastrophes in advance was the best course of action.[48] Unlike government agencies, private and voluntary CAAs can quickly adapt and change. AI and other new technologies will drive much faster and more lethal problems and threats that our irresponsible, horrible, self-serving, perverted government will not deal with properly or fast enough. When an AI company is doing something bad, CAAs can quickly condemn it and call for boycotts—before government agencies can even agree to schedule a first meeting to consider the issue.

US National Security Policy must no longer be shaped by vote pandering career politicians without National Security Policy expertise

Samuel Huntington, a leading American political scientist, director of Harvard's Center for International Affairs, pointed out that strategic programs and major defense and foreign policies are "not the product of expert planners rationally determining the actions necessary to achieve desired goals. Rather they are the product of controversy, negotiation and bargaining among different groups with different interests and perspectives."[49] As explained earlier in the book, Graham Allison's "Models" of government decision-making showed how bureaucratic interests (Model 2), and politician's biases and political goals (Model 3) drive policy decisions rather than rational policy analysis (Model 1).[50]

As the Perverted Triangle (Model 4) took absolute control of government in the 1960s (starting with FDR in the 1930s), the impact of great Americans like Thomas Edison, Henry Ford, George Marshall, George Kennan, and Dwight Eisenhower, was replaced by the Perverted Triangle, and rational policy analysis for the benefit of citizens fell further behind in favor of career politician's self-interest.

After noble military service to his country, then serving eight years as President, Eisenhower delivered a farewell address to the public with a vital warning that the US defense industry was becoming too powerful, self-serving, and needed to be controlled:[51]

- "This conjunction of an immense military establishment and a large arms industry is new in the American experience. The total influence—economic, political, even spiritual—is felt in every city, every State house, every office of the federal government."
- "In the councils of government, we must guard against the acquisition of unwarranted influence, whether sought or unsought, by the military-industrial complex. The potential for the disastrous rise of misplaced power exists and will persist."
- "We must never let the weight of this combination endanger our liberties or democratic processes. We should take nothing for granted. Only an alert and knowledgeable citizenry can compel the proper meshing of the huge industrial and military machinery of defense with our peaceful methods and goals, so that security and liberty may prosper together."

Just as the Congressional EMP Commission and thousands of experts testifying to Congressional Committees have been ignored, since only those bearing donations can achieve action in a Congress controlled by the Perverted Triangle, US nuclear weapons policy is a politically driven mess that does more to weaken than enhance our security.

The Bush decision on unilaterally eliminating all US BNWs was a catastrophic policy decision, harming national security for political votes. Since Senator Joseph McCarthy and his lies, fearmongering, "Red Scare" (detailed in the earlier chapter on why the US must stop interfering in Taiwan and China's internal affairs), congressmen have pledged allegiance to any look-tough-on-Communism idea that gets pitched. The result was a reversal of sound policy from George Marshall to stay out of the China-Taiwan civil war, and then the Vietnam War. Our policy on the second Iraq War was another case of bad foreign/national security policy driven by domestic political concerns and the Perverted Triangles benefit, not rational, best policy for protecting Americans.[52] The asinine, still ongoing "War on Drugs" that scored Nixon big political points, but raises crime and murder rates for Americans and is a disaster for Latin America, is another great for the Perverted Triangle and Big Government, bad for protecting American lives policy.

Bad decisions on Iraq, Taiwan, nuclear weapons policy, the asinine War on Drugs and War on Terrorism, the government working to kill us, are all driven by domestic political considerations, Models 2, 3 and 4, prioritizing the Perverted Triangle's interest, trumping Model 1 rational policy analysis of what's best for citizen's security.[53] The self-serving Perverted Triangle is killing Americans now and setting us up for big collapse disasters.

We are not a majority-rule democracy, we are a republic with elected representatives who are supposed to work full-time studying the issues and making best decisions for county and citizens, with well above average intelligence and character and integrity, with absolutely limited government to protect our Natural Rights. You would not find many Americans outside the Perverted Triangle who believe we are anywhere near this ideal.

In the 2010 Nuclear Posture Review, the Obama administration, to placate long-standing, widespread Democratic career politicians condemning nuclear weapons as inherently evil, worked to further reduce the role of nuclear weapons.[54] A few years later, in 2012, continued Obama administration condemnation of nuclear weapons led to changing the name "Prompt Global Strike" to "Conventional Prompt Strike" to further emphasize their rejection of any consideration of first use of nuclear weapons, pandering to domestic anti-nuclear groups at the cost of our national security.[55]

Proliferation of nuclear, biological, chemical, new types of WMD developed with current technologies, and especially with the aid of AI, is inevitable, unstoppable despite maximum efforts. We face a much larger range of WMD threats, and need far more flexibility in nuclear targeting and forces to have the quick response time and firepower to deter or defeat proliferating enemy WMD threats.[56] There is a far greater need for low-yield/higher accuracy/more responsive theater and battlefield nuclear weapons. Career politicians must stop interfering in the design and execution of measures to prepare for survival in the Age of Collapse.

Democratic career politicians with zero national security expertise, representing urban liberals and their causes, continue to ban any DoD efforts to field low-yield NW. A good example is California Congressman Ted Win-Ping Lieu. Wikipedia describes him as "an American lawyer and politician" and "a member of the Democratic Party."[57] Lieu studied computer science and political science at Stanford University, then later attended Georgetown University Law Center, becoming a lawyer. He served as a law clerk and then joined the USAF to serve for a few years as a military lawyer, and then in the USAF Reserve as a lawyer. He has zero experience with nuclear strategy, warfighting, anything close to combat or weapons. His major work is as a Democratic career politician in California, first as a state assemblyman, then in the California State Senate, then in the US House of Representatives, representing regions of Los Angeles.[58]

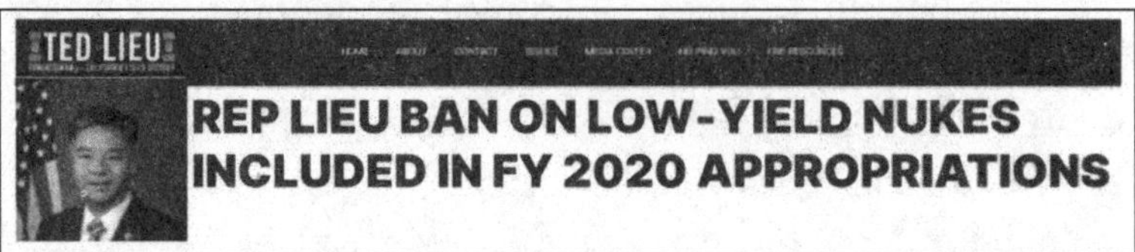

Figure 58: Democratic congressman's taxpayer-funded website bragging about ban he got added to an appropriations bill to prevent low-yield nuclear weapons.

Congressman Lieu made deals and vote trades to get a ban on low-yield nuclear weapons added into an appropriations bill. He had the incredible stupidity to claim in his website bragging that "conventional artillery" has the firepower of nuclear weapons. And how conventional artillery relates to submarine launched ballistic missiles is truly baffling. Congressman Lieu is an idiot; a lawyer and career politician with zero expertise in battlefield nuclear war fighting or submarine launched weapons or defense strategy. But this is how Perverted Triangle members deal with national security issues—it's all about maximizing their press releases and website bragging and deals for reelection votes. Bad impact on national security is irrelevant to them.[59]

Both for more credible deterrence and more effective defense, and to be able to conduct Prompt Global Strike missions to preempt WMD attacks, we must have effective, usable, low-yield TNW and BNW. The pandering US politicians, with zero military experience, less knowledge of strategy and deterrence, who have cut funds or worked to ban battlefield and tactical nuclear weapons must be stopped.[60]

Defense Spending Can Be Cut, with Massive Changes in Strategy and Forces, Vital for Cost Savings and National Survival if We Destroy the Perverted Triangle

With defense spending now at one trillion dollars annually while we are not at war, we must have not just efficiency improvements but huge shifts in grand strategy, cutting back large forces overseas, and ceasing to procure obscenely expensive high-tech conventional weapons systems that are both unaffordable and increasingly ineffective given the advances in drones and AI.[61]

With US progressives increasingly against overseas military ventures and huge defense budgets, the Trump-dominated GOP unenthused about big spending to support Ukraine and allies, and the clear national need to focus on homeland security and disaster recovery in the Age of Collapse, there could be a political majority for this shift in strategy away from conventional military weapons superiority. But the entrenched government bureaucracy and the defense industry lobbyists will be against cuts in government weapons program spending, and career politicians won't give up the huge vote buying power of these expensive programs.

Add to this the massive DoD bureaucracy, the military-industrial complex; defense firms with billion-dollar contracts to supply the latest and greatest weapon systems, leveraging an army of lobbyists to buy votes in Congress, and you have an impregnable, entrenched, powerful, morass—both the Iron and Perverted Triangles. The switch from fielding the most powerful conventional military forces deployed around the world to a focus on homeland defense, Prompt Global Strike, with BNW to protect much smaller deployed overseas forces, big defense budget cuts, with far fewer dollars for reelection vote buying and job losses from defense program cutbacks, will be a huge political battle despite its obvious benefits for security.

An *Air & Space Power Journal* article I wrote on "Improving Cost-Effectiveness in the Department of Defense" noted, "the most important factor in cost-effectiveness for business is not profit but a system that enables real accountability and consequences for measurable results."[62] Such accountability and consequences are completely lacking in government—along with real concern for cost-effectiveness. Former DoD officials like Anthony Cordesman call the DoD's planning and budgeting system a "liar's contest" where ridiculous claims of accomplishments and low costs are rewarded, not punished.[63]

The number of people involved in the Department of Defense's massive Planning, Programming, Budgeting, and Execution system is unfathomable to most congressmen and citizens. When I worked in the DoD Senior Executive Service in the "Business Management Modernization Program" we estimated at least ten thousand man years of government civilian and military manpower is devoted to this process, a billion dollars arguably wasted annually on just the budgeting process in the DoD, the fight for money.[64]

With an incomprehensible thicket of government acquisition regulations (a DoD University attempts to teach them), and a legal system designed to promote lawsuits and income for lawyers, the DoD acquisition system is an even bigger source of waste. Big Government run processes are inherently wasteful, reliable only in yielding big cost overruns—hundreds of billions of dollars per weapon system cost overruns in the DoD.[65]

When we abandon the effort to design, develop, field, and maintain the most advanced conventional weapons technology military systems in the world, we can abandon a lot of our civilian bureaucracy in the DoD—thousands in budgeting positions, thousands in the acquisition process, tens of thousands in maintenance, logistics, tens of thousands of administrative and personnel positions.

The DoD financial and accounting systems are so convoluted and full of bad information, that they have never passed a financial audit. Many federal agencies can't produce reliable financial statements.[66] No American citizen or public company could get away with having bad books and the inability to pass an audit, but the government exempts itself from such requirements. The DoD loses track of billions of dollars of equipment with its multiple, incompatible business systems and lack of accountability.

In the DoD Business Management Modernization program we identified at least four thousand different DoD business software/ID systems in use because of the complete lack of standards. Independent military services, and multitudes of DoD agencies that can use any duplicative, incompatible software and business systems they want. Even within military services, there is no administrative and business cost accountability or leadership—just utter the magic words "it's for the war-fighter" and your spending wish is granted. It is no wonder that the DoD can't get auditable financial statements and has over half a million civilian employees—the duplication of all services in the now six separate military services[67] and about fifty DoD agencies is a tremendously duplicative, wasteful, bureaucratic expense.[68]

The Defense Integrated Military Human Resources System was an attempt to get a DoD-wide standardized business system, using the extremely successful big business approach of an "Enterprise Resource Planning" (ERP) system. This was a human resources management system that all the military services and DoD agencies would use, replacing over a hundred different duplicative, incompatible DoD human resource IT systems, with lots of payroll errors and problems. The program started in 1998. Unlike a business that would have moved quickly, with staff fired for failing to deliver, this DoD program moved at a snail's pace, plagued by the government regulatory morass, government employees that cannot be fired, "cover your ass" decision-making, and military services refusing to give up their particular idiosyncrasies and preferred practices in favor of a standardized system.[69] As the 2009 army implementation date neared, army officials continued to complain that "army requirements" were not adequately incorporated in the new system. Other services in line to use the system also kept complaining, and in 2010 the Office of the Secretary of Defense gave up and the entire effort was abandoned. Eleven years of effort and $850 million dollars flushed down the toilet on the failed system![70]

The Government Accountability Office study of the failed program attributed most problems to "DoD's long-standing cultural resistance to department-wide solutions." Another problem was that "Years of 'home-grown' systems built up a myriad of data elements that in many cases did not match similar fields in different systems." The morass of DoD business, accounting, personnel, and logistics systems is so immense, incompatible, and screwed up, that efforts to try to link or use old data in a new system is impossible.[71] You cannot negotiate efficient, shared IT systems with military services or please everyone. The morass of DoD accounting and business and IT systems, one of the worst Augean Stables[72] in the world, must be completely abandoned and replaced with one new DoD-wide business and accounting system that is not customized for military services or any DoD agency. The DoD must admit that its current systems and the historical data in it is an unauditable, inaccurate mess and abandon all of it—starting over with modern, DoD-wide systems based on a single ERP system that will not be customized, but far cheaper, workable, compatible, and capable of yielding accurate and auditable data. The DoD must deny the military services and DoD agencies the right to run their own separate accounting, business, IT, personnel, and logistics management systems and force them to standardize under one DoD-wide system, subject to the control of the Office of the Secretary of Defense. Like any sensible business that after acquiring a company forces them into their shared, common key business systems (usually an ERP system), the DoD must simplify, standardize, and just say no to military services' preferred independence.

The major reasons the DoD bureaucracy and headquarters staff is so huge and wasteful are:

1. Bigger staffs can fight more successfully for bigger service budgets
2. The services are very independent, and fight back against attempts at cutting or changing or "interfering" with them with claims that this will "harm the war-fighter," with end runs to favored congressmen to intercede on their behalf
3. Top military service and DoD leadership have little to no experience in managing for cost-effectiveness, and get no reward for being more "businesslike"

The DoD bureaucracy is so vast and entrenched that any effort to pursue cost-effectiveness is a nasty battle that no Secretary of Defense wants to deal with. When ordered to reduce headquarters staff, services just create new units or transfer people to different organizations to pretend staff was cut.[73]

We fight with joint forces, and decades ago the Department of Defense rightly tried to shift to "capabilities-based planning"—funding forces we need to achieve capabilities to accomplish missions to get away from budgeting based on the military services and defense agencies separate, biased goals. To choose joint military capabilities, the Office of the Secretary of Defense needs to analyze, compare, and decide in a process that is not dominated by the military services promoting their favorite weapons and capabilities.

Not just for staff and budget savings, but primarily for sounder decision-making on national defense priorities, budget power and staff must be stripped from the military services and DoD agencies, replaced by a Department of Defense Budget crafted and set by Office of the Secretary of Defense staff. An argument to help persuade the services to accept this loss of staff and budget power is that the alternative to this is eliminating the separate military services altogether.

In an article another Institute for Defense Analyses analyst and I published, "Improving DoD Adaptability and Capability to Survive Black Swan Events," we argued that given the increasing uncertainty of future threats, the impacts of new technologies and AI, the "key skill or attribute that individuals, units, and teams of commanders and leaders need to improve on is adaptability."[74]

Our article offered recommendations on how to make the DoD more adaptable and capable of deterring, countering, or recovering from Black Swan events.[75] We must stop trying to think we can predict future wars or events, and field forces with the greatest possible flexibility and versatility for the broadest range of conflict. Since Black Swans are "unpredictable," Taleb states, "we need to adjust to their existence (rather than naively try to predict them)."[76]

US conventional force technological superiority almost demands that a determined opponent use an asymmetric attack such as weapons of mass destruction (WMD) or terrorism in the CONUS either to defeat our forces or to inflict losses that lead to loss of popular support for the campaign.

Promoting innovation and adaptation is a must do for the DoD. Institute for Defense Analyses studies have laid out ways to improve our personnel's ability to adapt, and "US troops in the field are so good at adaptation because they are freed from many of the bureaucratic constraints that are constant in a headquarters."[77] The multitude of asinine regulations and bureaucracy drives many bright young officers from the military. A 2011 Harvard study, which surveyed nearly 250 former junior officers who left the military between 2001 and 2010, revealed that the second most frequently reported reason was frustration with military bureaucracy.[78] This is yet another reason why America must eliminate the vast majority of Perverted Triangle promoted, self-serving regulations not just to reduce costs and damage of Big Government, but to survive in the Age of Collapse.[79]

Billy Mitchell fought for military airpower and was court-martialed for it. USAF Colonel John Boyd fought the DoD establishment for fifty years and often prevailed, though never made general due to his trouble making. No one since has been able to impact the massive marshmallow bureaucracy of government.[80] Army Colonel Douglas Macgregor, a military reformer working outside the bureaucracy, observes that "the ability to think beyond the boundaries of what is conventionally acceptable is always scarce and, sadly, seldom in demand unless it aligns with the thinking desired in the ranks of the ruling bureaucracy, civilian appointees and influential politicians."[81]

We Need a Convention of States and "The Constitutional Alliance" to Amend the Constitution, Destroy the Perverted Triangle, Fix our Unconstitutional Government before Collapse Disasters Kill Us

Thanks to the Founding Fathers there is a way to fix our irresponsible, unconstitutional government, undo the damage of FDR and the Perverted Triangle's Second Revolution, and get the essential limits to government back. Article V of our Constitution enables the people, via responsible State Legislators, to hold a Convention of States to amend the Constitution. FDR and the Perverted Triangle quietly eviscerating the Constitution and eliminating limits to government is a largely unknown second American Revolution. A Third American Revolution is vital to get term limits to keep the career politicians out and other reforms necessary to destroy the Perverted Triangle, restore our Natural Rights and limits to government, save the country and our lives.[82] The fix cannot come from Washington, DC; there are too many career politicians and committed members of the Perverted Triangle. Many do hate this corrupt system, and will support the Constitutional Alliance if convinced that it will succeed.

The Constitutional Alliance plan to unite the hundreds of citizen reform groups in the US and fix our unlimited, unconstitutional government and fight the Perverted Triangle is available at https://constall.org/.[83]

Term limits are the most vital, immediate reform to pursue. Elected officials who are not running for reelection are more resistant to lobbyists and far more likely to vote for what is best for Americans. The POTUS should serve one six-year term and never be allowed to run for office again. The POTUS should not be leading a political party, or campaigning for anyone's election. He or she should only be concerned with making the best decisions for the country.

Trump won thirty-one of the fifty states in the 2024 election. It only takes thirty-four states for a Convention of the States to propose constitutional amendments. Nineteen states have already passed legislation for a Convention of States—all nineteen among the thirty-one that Trump won (Trump's base is less the GOP than the larger majority of Americans disgusted with government). A major advantage Trump has over past GOP presidents is that he is not owned by the Right to Life movement, and can acknowledge the right to privacy, a Natural Right, protected by the Ninth Amendment. By mobilizing state legislatures in the conservative states with populations that still want constitutional limits to government power, and convening a Convention of States to amend the Constitution, force term limits, and obedience of the Ninth and Tenth Amendments, Trump could save the United States of America from divisive civil war and get the country ready to survive the Age of Collapse.

In decades of work studying American government and the Constitution, Roger Pilon concluded that "the Founders intended nothing like our present American leviathan. Indeed, many of the grievances the Declaration [of Independence] lists, which led to our revolt, are today the ordinary stuff of government in America."[84] The vast majority of Americans are disgusted with the disaster that the Perverted Triangle has made of American government and our legal system. Again quoting Charles Murray, "The federal government was created with one overriding duty: to allow us to live freely as we see fit, as long as we accord the same right to everyone else. It has betrayed that duty."[85]

The Perverted Triangle is not a conspiracy group or just Democratic Party top leaders, it is a system— a collection of horrible practices, laws, two political parties, institutional rules, a legal system that has been corrupted over time.[86] There are certainly leading proponents of this corrupt, Big Government, Nanny State system, but most members of the Perverted Triangle are better described as trapped in the system than willing participants. Many congressmen and women take office hoping to effect change but quickly become cogs in the Perverted Triangle.[87]

The Perverted Triangle Promotes "Collective Stupidity" to Enhance Their Power

Albert Einstein said, "Three great forces rule the world: stupidity, fear, and greed."88 Nassim Taleb, one of the wisest persons alive today, wrote that "Humans are great at self-delusion." Most people commit the "error of confirmation," looking for information that confirms your opinion, ignoring contrary evidence, to feel more justified in your views. Lawyers, politicians, and advertisers exploit this to persuade and deceive. People also commit the "narrative fallacy," fooling ourselves with stories and anecdotes, simple explanations that "seem right" rather than critical thinking. In sum, Taleb concluded, "We are made to be superficial, to heed what we see and not heed what does not vividly come to mind. . . . We are naturally shallow and superficial—and we do not know it."[89]

It is much easier to just follow the crowd and be collectively stupid, not an independent, critical thinker. Erich Fromm, a social psychologist, explained how freedom causes fear in many people who worry about not making the right decisions, and the burden of responsibility you have as a free person. This leads to many preferring to relinquishing freedom (and the responsibility to think critically, make your own decisions, be responsible) to just follow a leader and do what everyone else seems to be doing.[90] While military academies do teach and prioritize critical thinking, most universities in the US prioritize political correctness.

A huge enabler of—and result of—the Perverted Triangle's power is the rise of "collective stupidity," the term for the decline in critical thinking and increasing stupidity of people blindly following social pressures to conform and the propaganda of the dueling political parties.[91] The flood of information, social media, and search engines/YouTube algorithms feeding people reinforcing, biased information (much of it false),[92] the "likes" and "influencers" promoted to push conformity and attention to appearances, also promotes a vulnerable society. As one educator explained, "collective stupidity occurs when social pressure, conformity, emotional contagion, and a lack of critical thinking drag the group down into the Reality TV gutter."[93] AI will make the problem worse since Internet search engines and AI programs are engineered to agree with users, figure out what will please them, and feed affirmative information.[94]

Much—perhaps most—of mainstream media in the US today has a partisan bias, selecting and spinning the news to promote their political party and causes, adding to the echo chamber of reinforcing current beliefs and biases. Podcasters can be far more blatant in their bias, but many at least acknowledge their prejudice.

This is fantastic for career politicians and political parties who like loyal, outraged followers who feel, fear, and react rather than think, buy the "party line," and vote to keep them in power. Again, quoting Taleb, "governments . . . engage in what could be labeled as phony 'philanthropy,' the activity of helping people in a visible and sensational way without taking into account the unseen cemetery of invisible consequences."[95] As documented in this book, governments are killing Americans daily with taxes and regulations and programs that help some yielding payoffs for the Perverted Triangle at the cost of death for the silent majority. With professional liars in politics rewarded for stirring up emotions and blind followers, and lawyers allowed to lie in court, truth and critical thinking, justice and responsibility are dying out. In *The Dying Citizen: How Progressive Elites, Tribalism, and Globalization are Destroying the Idea of America*, Hoover Institute scholar Victor

Davis Hanson wrote that the political wokeness in America, "multiculturalism" and "collectivism," erodes individual responsibility and citizenship, promoting "tribalism" (warring political factions) and "victimization."[96] All this politically motivated collective stupidity empowers the Perverted Triangle and erodes critical thinking, American freedom, individual responsibility, our well-being and probability of survival.

To Reduce Damage of Political Pandering and the Perverted Triangle, Require Use of Multi-Criteria Decision Analysis and Scorecards to Force Better, More Accountable Decision-Making

Rather than liar's poker by the military services, vote pandering by career politicians, Models 2/3/4 decision-making,[97] in the Age of Collapse we must have professional, citizen-serving, Model 1 rational analysis and decision-making. To help ensure this, in addition to other reforms and limits on government addressed elsewhere in this book, we need to mandate and enforce a requirement to use "Multi-Criteria Decision Analysis" (MCDA) scorecards in decision-making and record the final MCDA "Scorecards" used to justify a legislative bill or executive policy.[98]

The examples here are largely from the DoD, where I've worked. But MCDA DSS and scorecards are very valuable and useful in all areas of government (and elsewhere).

The DoD needs a standard Decision Support System (DSS) to improve risk analysis and trade-off decision-making. Adopting and promoting the consistent use of a flexible, multi-criteria decision support system would improve DoD risk analysis, decision-making, and cost-effectiveness. Business cost-effectiveness results in large part from everyone using and understanding the same decision support system (DSS)—the income statement (aka the profit and loss statement, P&L). While DoD has multiple objectives and other complications, the benefits of a widely used DSS to support better analysis, collaboration and decision-making can be achieved if a standard, very flexible multi-criteria DSS is promoted for department-wide use.[99]

A well-designed MCDA DSS can merge quantitative, qualitative, and subjective measures to provide a shared framework for analysis for optimal decision-making. A simple MCDA DSS can be flexibly adapted to cover a wide range of objectives, applicable in nearly all DoD resource and risk management decision forums. MCDA DSS can support more "systems approach" (assuring a broad range of alternative programs and strategies are considered), "decision analysis" (a structured, disciplined analysis), risk analysis (comparing different assumptions of future threats), "game theory" (considering reactions of adversaries), weighting costs as a criteria, and using any operations-research models and simulations available for measuring performance. The tool lets analysts, planners, and decision-makers apply a wide range of analysis techniques and information across a diverse range of decision criteria. If mandated for use as a DoD standard, the MCDA methodology can help enforce use of desired analytic techniques and considerations. The "DynaRank" MCDA tool, developed by RAND, running in an Excel spreadsheet as an add-in function, is a fantastic tool I've used for decades in the military, government, and business.[100]

MCDA scorecards must cover all reasonable options and possible impacts of a government action. You can use an "other impacts" category for dozens of relatively small impacts—but everything should be considered, not ignored. The MCDA lists the objectives and criteria in columns, and then compares the policy or forces choices in rows to compare how each best achieves the objectives, and scores against a wide variety of criteria and considerations. Perhaps the best aspect of MCDA is its ability to "incorporate" other models and metrics, including both qualitative and quantitative assessments. The DynaRank MCDA scorecard can include all impacts of a government policy, all the issues relevant to its adoption—costs, impacts on our Natural Rights, unintended possible impacts beyond the desired results, etc.

The MCDA DSS is not intended to thoroughly "model" a decision or "compute" an answer. Rather, it's a flexible tool to help consider the objectives of a decision and analyze (and shape/alter) alternatives to best meet objectives. A wide range of other analytic and cost models and methods can and should be used—the MCDA DSS is the common means to hold and display and weigh the results of other analytic tools. The MCDA DSS can be used to do sensitivity and risk analysis, showing decision-makers the range of alternative rankings based on changes in assumptions, threats, weights for criteria, or different valuations of factors where organizations disagree.

In rotating between jobs in business consulting, DoD Senior Executive Service, Institute for Defense Analyses, and the Air Force Reserve, it was easy to see the dysfunction in DoD decision-making due to the lack of a consistently used DSS. In businesses, the income statement spreadsheet is the ubiquitous means of framing and presenting data and making risk and resourcing decisions. The standard, consistent means of decision-making enables better understanding of the alternatives, better collaboration in decision-making, and a clear record of what was the basis for the decision—the results promised in a "pro forma" income statement. DoD could accrue these benefits by adopting a standard "multiple criteria decision analysis" (MCDA) tool to be used in all steps of the risk and resource management process. PowerPoint, the dominant means of "analysis" and the major tool for decision-making in government, is a very poor alternative as a decision analysis tool and means of recording decisions for review and accountability.

MCDA lets analysts and the decision-maker use the results of the in-depth modeling and analysis along with "weighing" the subjective and all factors bearing on the problem so a decision-maker can "see" the impact of additional criteria and assumptions, make trade-offs, and understand divergent perspectives of different individuals and organizations examining the problem. Without a DSS like DynaRank MCDA, instead of pulling together all analyzed or roughly estimated, known, objective, subjective information on a large number of decision criteria into a "total score" decision-makers must instead try to keep all this information in his or her head, then make a decision based on "feel" or "overall this looks like the best decision." Without a comprehensive DSS, government decision-makers use long PowerPoint presentations and then made a decision (the last slides shown are decisive!). The DynaRank tool adds up the criteria, weighted as the decision-maker prefers, to rank order the alternatives. Add to this the use of different scenarios and sets of assumptions to compare which option ranks best under changing situations, and you have a very powerful, much better decision support tool.[101]

Once the decision is made, the MCDA Scorecard selected as the best option can be saved and used to document the decision and expected performance results. This is precisely how the income statement is used in business. It is not just for making business decisions, but once approved, the "pro forma" (projected, estimated) income statement can be compared to the "actuals" that result to see if the plan is working, how managers are doing in executing the plan—holding them accountable for results, seeing what assumptions are proving right or wrong. Governments do not have and largely do not want such accountability—and won't have it unless legally, vigorously forced to.

Without a standard DSS that is widely used and understood, it is often not possible to use a DSS because of time constraints in showing how the DSS works or staff blocking you from presenting what first looks like a very complex and complicated tool.[102]

Some examples of the "scorecards" from different MCDA projects are provided in this webnote.[103]

Some operations research analysts disparage MCDA because some criteria may "overlap" or "double count" some issues, making multi-criteria decision analysis calculations "wrong" since they are built on the assumptions of mutually exclusive, collectively exhaustive, independent criteria. You can somewhat handle this by adjusting the weights (i.e., if two criteria are counting the same basic thing, just different/related forms of it, you can half the weights of each).[104] MCDA is not a tool for rigid optimization, but comparing the "decision space." It should not be described as mathematically rigorous or highly accurate.[105]

The purpose of the MCDA DSS is not to precisely calculate but to provide a framework for careful and orderly analysis of the many uncertainties and issues and trade-offs involved in any difficult decision. As a framework for highlighting uncertainties, focusing analysis on most important risks and areas of disagreement, and promoting interagency, interdisciplinary simultaneous analysis and debate, a MCDA DSS promotes six of E. S. Quade's (one of the best operations research analysts) eleven "Principles of Good Analysis":

1. "Efficient use of expert judgment is the essence of analysis."
2. "The design of alternatives is as important as their analysis."
3. "Interdisciplinary teams are usually necessary."
4. "For broad questions, comparisons for a single contingency are not enough."
5. "Partial answers to relevant questions are more useful than full answers to empty questions."
6. "A good new idea is worth a thousand evaluations."

MCDA can be used with the "Delphi Method,"[106] Red Teams, outside staff and reviewers, private discussions via the Internet, "chat rooms," and other methods to combat groupthink and other decision-making problems. A "Red Team" is very beneficial in this process to challenge assumptions, groupthink, test the scorecard with an outside perspective, and, most important: guard against the tendency of brown-nosing and failure to question top elected officials' opinions.

The complexity and subjectivity of this proposed DSS is not a weakness—it's the reality of the problems and decisions. Weighing political, behavioral, and psychological factors, attempting to predict how foreign countries may react, is inherently complex and subjective.[107] As an Institute for Defense Analyses study noted, "If effects-based operations are concerned with changing human decisions and behavior, metrics for effects-based operations must address human interactions. In summary, what is easy to measure is probably not appropriate, while what is appropriate is not easy to measure."[108] The MCDA DSS can help focus debate on areas of significant disagreement and identify issues/disagreements that don't matter—i.e., do not affect the recommended decision.[109]

While the size of a MCDA scorecard can intimidate, its mechanics and math are simple, and it is easy to learn and use. The issues, intended and unintended consequences of government action, uncertainty, and costs are complicated, but the MCDA process is very simple and powerful in improving analysis and decision-making. Unlike many analytic models that are incomprehensible "black boxes" to decision-makers, anyone can see clearly and simply how it works. It does not provide an "answer"; it provides insights to improve analysis and decision-making. More importantly, the MCDA DSS can force more careful analysis and decision-making, more honest and open acknowledgment of risks and costs, and provide a fantastic record to evaluate program success or failure, and hold decision-makers accountable.

Many years ago, the Air Force Logistics Command developed a system to reward individuals for not fully spending their budgets, something considered impossible.[110] It was successful in saving money, but an unusual application that was unfortunately dropped. Governments and bureaucracies are not very motivated by reducing costs, and do not like accountability. If not mandated and enforced by some outside authority, cost-saving and DSS are unlikely to be used. We need MCDA, decision scorecards, a very disciplined, professional, accountable public policy analysis and decision-making process—mandated and backed up by outside enforcement and consequences for failure to perform.

Increased use of MCDA could also help deal with the problem of collective stupidity and the propaganda of the waring Perverted Triangle political parties. Any difficult, contentious situation has many issues and impacts (criteria) to consider, with different views and values and priorities by those concerned. The MCDA format and process highlights the often competing criteria and differences in views. It forces the differing parties to specify and rate exactly what their positions/objections/priorities are. This leads to better analysis and debate while exposing positions that are clearly misinformed or nonsensical. Often, the MCDA process can help work out a new option that better meets criteria and is acceptable to more people.

Had there been MCDA analysis of our decision to pursue "building a democracy in Iraq," real consideration of the requirements, the decision criteria, reasonable estimates of the likely results, we would have never committed to this impossible task under the conditions there.[111] Had Congressman Lieu been forced to lay out all the costs, benefits, impacts, risks of his ban on low-yield nuclear weapons (that's correct—less explosive power, not more) in a MCDA scorecard, with the policy proposal actually debated and openly rated in a published, recorded decision scorecard, his asinine proposal would not have been approved. Career politicians routinely screw the country to pander, buy donations from lobbyists, score votes in their districts with horrendously bad, deadly policy decisions that are not analyzed, not debated, and executed with zero accountability. Bills are amended with pork provisions, lobbyist regulatory changes made in payment for campaign donations, horrendous decisions that are not debated, analyzed, or even documented—they just appear out of nowhere and end up in law. All legislation and decision-making, especially anything impacting national security and homeland defense policy, should be required to have a MCDA scorecard prepared, presented, debated, and then recorded with the final decision and vote.

Neither the House of Representatives nor the Senate, nor any part of government, would willingly follow such a requirement. The vast majority of congressmen and Senators are subservient to political parties and the Perverted Triangle. Therefore, we need a Constitutional Amendment to require MCDA and a recorded decision scorecard and other reforms to prevent the perverted deals in Congress that allow pork and disastrous, deadly regulations and policies.

One of the many reforms proposed by the Constitutional Alliance (just some are mentioned in this book) is to add "Federal Watch Officers" appointed by state legislatures to enforce a requirement that all bills passed in Congress and the Senate must limited to a single subject and read in full while at least 80 percent of members are present and attentive, as judged by these Federal Watch Officers.[112] These officers, an additional check on the federal government abusing power, can also enforce the requirement of properly preparing and considering MCDA scorecards of all bills, with requirements to include in the criteria: all unintended but possible consequences, costs, lives lost from government spending ("Miller's Maxim," covered later), and the impact on personal liberty from the government action. Federal Watch Officers could rule whether the scorecards are "complete, reasonable, and honest," and label a bill null and void for noncompliance with these requirements.[113]

These MCDA scorecards can then be entered into the official record, along with votes; this would allow much better assessment and accountability of how government programs do or fail to achieve promised objectives and whether or not Representatives and Senators were honest and correct in their analysis and voting. These MCDA scorecards should be absolutely required on national security and homeland defense measures. I recommend they be required in all departments and agencies, at all levels of government. If a government official supports a National Science Foundation award of $856,000 grant to train three mountain lions to use treadmills to study mountain lions' use of energy while hunting, $3.5 million for a parade in Detroit (from federal funds), $4 million in federal funds to build a sewer in a tiny town of ninety-eight people in Alaska, then back it up with the MCDA DSS scorecards that show how the promised benefits exceed the costs in taxpayer funds and citizen's lives and lost liberty, and document the reasons and claims of those who approved these acts.[114]

The Perverted Triangle and Unconstitutional, Divisive Big Government Must End or Most Americans Will Not Survive

Below is a list of some of the glaringly wrong, irresponsible, deadly bad Perverted Triangle-driven polices that must change for survival in the Age of Collapse:[115]

Figure 59: Irresponsible Government Policies That Must Change to Avoid Millions of Deaths in a Collapse

1. The lie of a US "nuclear umbrella," "extended deterrence," promising to launch strategic nuclear attacks on Moscow or Beijing, committing "Mutually Assured Destruction" suicide to protect our allies must end.
2. US opposition to nuclear proliferation must end for countries that need nuclear weapons to deter or defeat attack from Russia, China, Iran, and North Korea. Do promote acquisition only of defensive low-yield, short-range (or Atomic Demolition Munitions) nuclear weapons—not high-yield or ICBMs, SLBMs or long-range bomber delivered nuclear weapons.
3. Abandon the policy of "no first use" of nuclear weapons; adopt and announce a strategy that the US will use nuclear weapons whenever necessary to defend our troops overseas and stop attacks on our homeland. This may include preemptive attacks on any nation, terrorist group, or individual that we believe is about to launch a collapse-level attack.
4. Battlefield, tactical nuclear weapons must return to the US Army, along with training, doctrine, and plans for their use.
5. Improve conventional and nuclear "prompt Global Strike" air and naval forces—but for small attacks, largely against looming WMD attacks by nations/terrorists/individuals—not fighting a major military power.
6. Reconstitute capability to quickly conduct an underground, crisis nuclear detonation at the Nevada Test site as a Flexible Deterrence Option
7. The US must end its domestic political pandering promises to defend Taiwan, which is a Chinese internal affair, a fight that China can win by destroying our vulnerable electric grid or playing "nuclear chicken" with the US, forcing the POTUS to back down and retreat—after we suffer a needless, costly nuclear strike.
8. Stop risking war by pushing NATO membership to Russia's border despite Russia's clear threats of retaliation, prompting war in Ukraine.
9. Start improving US "Domestic Survival Capability": the ability to manufacture and domestically produce food and materials vital to collapse survival. Compared to China's Domestic Survival Capability and what the US needs to survive, America is weak, inviting attacks and subject to losing most of its population when a bad collapse occurs.
10. Provide honest warnings and alerts to citizens about collapse threats. Stop lying about the H5N1 threat being "low risk" and warn Americans to prepare for this inevitable, potentially imminent, deadly pandemic and the collapse that will result.
11. Stop promoting AI despite clear evidence that it will lead to more weapons of mass destruction and inevitable misuse to kill millions or all of us. Institute strong regulations and control of AI development, treating AI as more dangerous than nuclear weapons. Form an international alliance of countries that will control AI, the AICA (AI Control Alliance), to fight/punish countries that allow AI-generated WMD.

continued on following page

12. Completely ban superintelligent AGI, backed up by the AICA with the capability to fight/punish countries that pursue AGI.
13. The Achilles' heel of the US military and citizens' survival must be immediately fixed—the fragile US electric grid must be hardened, transformers stockpiled, with microgrids added, initially prioritizing military bases.
14. Stop funding "gain-of-function" virus research, especially giving funds to foreign countries like China to develop more deadly viruses.
15. Stop spending trillions on conventional military technological superiority arguing that it is the best way to guard against nuclear or biological weapons use. Technological weapons superiority encourages enemies to use nuclear or biological weapons against US troops abroad or WMD attacks on civilians at home. AI and drones are making technological military superiority ineffective and even more unaffordable.
16. Cease violations of the Tenth Amendment and get the federal government out of unconstitutional, divisive social programs and focused on its number one mission—national defense and security.
17. Stay in NATO and back all alliances, and UN peacekeeping operations we approve of—but cut back on overseas deployed conventional forces, especially ground forces.
18. FEMA and DHS are woefully inadequate for homeland recovery—the Department of Defense needs to take over both homeland defense and collapse recovery, and shift the vast majority of DoD personnel, and the bulk of the DoD budget to homeland defense and recovery missions.
19. Reinstitute a federal government Civil Defense Food Stockpile Program, controlled by the National Guard, with at least a twelve-month supply of shelf-stable food for every citizen, and locate/map out alternative potable water sources for citizens to use in a collapse.
20. Create national stockpiles of critical supplies we cannot source locally.
21. Expand the size of Army National Guard and provide all Guard, Reserve, and Active Retired personnel with firearms so they can perform security work and fight marauder groups in a collapse.
22. Create a "Civil Ground Patrol" under the Army Guard to mobilize volunteer help for disaster recovery operations.
23. Build up large reserve police/sheriff forces.
24. Fire millions of federal government social and welfare workers, pursing unconstitutional programs to fund the additions to Police Reserves and Army National Guard members for collapse recovery operations.
25. Identify key workers for vital utilities, nuclear power plants, LEOs, military.
26. Stop allowing enemy cyberattacks on critical infrastructure, enemy drone surveillance of military bases and critical infrastructure, and enemy agent physical attack drills against the electric grid.
27. Secure our borders. Stop allowing enemy agents, terrorists, released prisoners, millions of undocumented immigrants easy access to the country. Work to identify and deport or execute enemy agents in the country.
28. Encourage rather than restrict volunteers to help put out wildfires, and offer nonviolent prisons the opportunity to earn early release by doing forest wildfire mitigation (removing dead trees and brush).
29. Reduce numbers of imprisoned US citizens. Prepared plans for collapse emergency release of nonviolent, execution of very violent prisoners (with executive order pardons for wardens and staff), and Army Guard basing at prisons for collapse recovery efforts.
30. Hold a Convention of the States to institute term limits and other constitutional amendments to destroy the Perverted Triangle, force the Supreme Court to enforce the Ninth and Tenth Amendments, add clear protections and preferences for Natural Rights, including the rights to survive, use private property, and

continued on following page

not be subjected to regulations that endanger one's own survival plans without causing harm to others. Ban regulations stopping small farms and domestic gardening/ranch animal husbandry vital to collapse survival, zoning and building regulations that violate our constitutionally protected Natural Rights to private property and make it difficult or impossible to prepare for collapse survival. Unconstitutional government activity, especially interfering in personal matters and social issues, violating Natural Rights to private property, survival, and to be left alone, must end at all levels of government.

31. Hold a Convention of the States to amend the Constitution requiring a balanced budget to end overspending and driving national debt to a level that will bankrupt the country and lead to an economic collapse.
32. Constitutional amendments from the Convention of States to stop pandering congressmen from adding pork, laws, and regulations to bills via measures like single topic requirements for bills, reading in full, and requirements for Multi-Criteria Decision Analysis and recorded decision scorecards for all legislation impacting homeland defense and national security, enforced by "Federal Watch Officers" appointed by the states.
33. Constitutional amendments from the Convention of States required to stop unconstitutional, divisive social programs that benefit the Perverted Triangle but divide the nation, threaten civil war, and are unaffordable—bankrupting the country.
34. Stop providing collapse survival protection just for top elected and government officials at Mount Weather and other sites—and no civil defense for citizens. Ban legislators at any level of government from having collapse survival protection beyond what all citizens are offered.
35. Ban executive orders authorizing government agencies to seize food and resources from citizens in a collapse.
36. Enforce the Second Amendment and ban laws limiting magazine size or outlawing AR-15s and "military capable" weapons that citizens need in a collapse to defend against marauder groups.
37. Stop broadcasting messages and sending satellites beyond our galaxy to advertise and map our presence so alien civilizations more advanced than us can find us.
38. Create Consumer Advisory Associations and rely on private groups like Underwriters Laboratories to set voluntary standards and replace government regulations of non-life-threatening maters. Limit government regulations and activities to protecting citizens from severe threats they cannot handle on their own. Government must focus on severe threats to citizens' lives and survival.
39. Stop the unconstitutional, ineffective "War on Drugs" that does not stop drugs but yields higher crime and murder rates that kill Americans.
40. Stop allowing top elected officials allowed to break laws protecting classified information, undermining our intelligence capability and reducing national security.

Defense industry lobbyists and much of the Perverted Triangle will fight these huge shifts in defense procurement and the job losses in their districts, or shift of military forces and government spending from their districts.[116] The big defense contractors will spend millions to lobby and buy votes.[117] Career politicians will not vote based on what is best for our survival, but the impact on their reelection campaigns. This is why we must have term limits. The sacrifice of national security to buy votes for career politician's reelection is the worst defect of American Government we've got, and a fatal one if we don't stop it.[118]

It is not just the rise in federal government spending as a percentage of GDP, from less than 5 percent a century ago to 30 percent today; but the mix of that spending that is grossly wrong. Defense spending as a percent of GDP has fallen from 10 percent in peacetime in the 1950s to about 3 percent today, now matched by spending on interest on the cancerous national debt the Perverted Triangle has built up. Spending on social welfare programs is a staggering 20 percent of GDP. And this does not count the huge state and local government spending and debt. Government debt is larger than, about 125 percent of our GDP! In 2024, for the first time, the unconstitutional US reached the point where we are spending more on our national debt than we are on defense spending![119] US government debt could lead to a deadly economic collapse. The Perverted Triangle and their elimination of Natural Rights and limits to Government have yielded a socialist state, a bankrupt country, and a dependent population that will largely not survive a collapse.

Even in cases where government regulatory oversight is warranted, like nuclear power plants and environmental protection, the appalling record of government ineptitude and career politician interference/sabotage calls for limiting the government role. For example, powerful Senator Harry Reid blocked nuclear waste storage in Nevada where we've got the ideal place to store it. Tens of billions of dollars were wasted, progress blocked on safe storage, because the Perverted Triangle always leverages government regulation and action for their benefit. [120] So even when there is a need for the power of government to regulate, we should limit the scope of government oversight, relying as much as possible on industry associations, CAAs and privatization of as much "government" work as possible.

The phenomenal surge in US defense production during WWII that won the war did not occur because government bureaucrats ran it, but because private companies ran thousands of new plants, with regulations that stood in the way ignored as government bureaucrats stood down to let American companies and workers produce.

If we could destroy the power of the Perverted Triangle and abolish most government regulatory agencies, we would have far better voluntary, legal, institutes and associations promoting regulations and standards without the horrible waste, costs, and destruction of government dictates passed by lobbyists bribing career politicians, enforced by bureaucrats and lawyers. We can achieve the benefits of regulation and safety without the huge taxes and forced compliance, without the illegal, unconstitutional, un-American pillaging of our Natural Rights.

We must have strong government strongly regulating AI and an AI Control Alliance to protect us from the existential AI threat. Consumer Advisory Associations and private groups can back this up, but government is essential to protect citizens from deadly WMD threats. These severe threats to citizens must be the focus of government, with all nonessential (and unconstitutional) government activity, especially interfering in personal matters and social issues, absolutely ended at all levels of government.[121]

We need to warn people that natural and bioengineered pandemics are inevitable, could happen anytime, and cannot be stopped.[122] The CDC lie that H5N1 is a low risk to us must be repudiated. Citizens need honest disclosure of pandemic threats, the many vulnerabilities of our fragile electric system, and a warning that the grid could go down for a year or more, not just a few days. Honesty in disclosing the dozens of other threats, known (pandemics, asteroids, super volcanoes, cyberattacks, etc.) and Black Swan, largely unknown, new threats (nanotechnology disaster, Artificial Intelligence misuse, et cetera) and frankness in admitting that the economy may not function and law and order may be lost is vital. Government must stop lying and pandering for votes and do its top priority, proper job of protecting citizens from threats we cannot deal with on our own, and honestly warning of the limits to their ability to do so.

Without an end to the Perverted Triangle's unlimited power and focus on reelection and pandering for votes with pork and social programs rather than prioritizing national security, dividing our country, most Americans, and likely the vast majority of all humans around the world, are unlikely to survive the coming collapses.[123]

Chapter Fifteen

IS THE UNITED STATES IN THE FINAL STAGE OF CIVILIZATION COLLAPSE?

There are people who believe that the Age of Collapse and the decline and imminent fall of the US are the result of the inevitable cycle of a civilization's decay.[1]

There are many historians and analysts who have written about this cyclical rise and fall of civilization. There are books and theories about the rise and fall of civilizations. The ones highlighted here are the major and best.[2]

In their eleven-volume *The Story of Civilization*, historians Will and Ariel Durant argued that internal decay, the impact of internal divisions and moral decline, weakened great civilizations, making them vulnerable to external threats and collapse. "A great civilization is not conquered from without until it has destroyed itself within. The essential causes of Rome's decline lay in her people, her morals, her class struggle, her failing trade, her bureaucratic despotism, her stifling taxes, her consuming wars."[3] This description largely fits with the US today.

Historian Arnold Toynbee wrote about the rise and fall of twenty-one major civilizations in his massive, twelve-volume *A Study of History*.[4] Toynbee found civilizations tended to last for a few hundred years before collapsing due largely to internal decay. Success leads to complacency, decline in work ethic, growth in government bureaucracy and welfare programs, and internal decay. An outside force, a new civilization may conquer the old—but it is the internal decay that is the reason for their fall. As Toynbee succinctly put it, "Civilizations die from suicide, not by murder." But Toynbee did not believe that all civilizations are doomed to disintegration.[5]

"Civilizations die from suicide, not by murder."

—Arnold Toynbee, *A Study of History*

By far the best, and thankfully, the shortest, work on the rise and fall of civilizations is Sir John Glubb's *The Fate of Empires and Search for Survival.*[6] Glubb was a British officer and engineer, who served honorably in WWII, and then volunteered for service in Iraq, eventually becoming a contractor to the government of Jordan where he commanded the Jordan Arab Legion, an army. A Renaissance man,[7] Glubb studied eleven human civilizations over the past four thousand years to attempt to discover patterns and lessons learned. His empires were overwhelmingly Middle East and European—he did not include China.[8]

Figure 60: Eras of Human History.

Note: Homo Sapiens estimated to have existed for about 300,000 years. BCE means "Before Common Era" or "Before Current Era" or "Before Christian Era." CE means "Common Era." AD, "Anno Domini," the "year of our Lord" is the more traditional term for CE.

Prehistory:
Stone Age: 3 million–2,000 BCE
Bronze Age: 2,000–800 BCE
Iron Age: 1,000–1 BCE
Classical Era: 400 BCE–1,500 CE
Early Modern Era: 1,500–1760 CE

Modern Era:
Industrial Age: 1760–1970
Information Age: 1970–present
Artificial Intelligence: 2022–present
Age of Collapse: 2026–

Sir John Glubb's findings were convincing, valuable, and should be a major area of study in school history courses:

- Civilizations tend to last 250 years, a period of about ten generations.
- The first stage of a civilization is "won chiefly by reckless bravery and daring initiative"—an "Age of Pioneers."
- The "Age of Commerce" follows, with huge growth in wealth from trade, new businesses.
- In the "Age of Affluence" that follows "money replaces honor and adventure

as the objective of the best young men" and schools switch from "producing brave patriots ready to serve their country" to "educational qualifications which will command the highest salaries."

- In the final stage, "the Age of Intellect," with ample wealth to pursue knowledge and leisure, people falsely believe that via "mental cleverness" rather than hard work or sacrifice, they can continue to survive and prosper.
- As the civilization declines, internal political hatreds intensify.
- In final stages, there is a big increase in frivolity, a "universal pessimism gradually pervades the people, and itself hastens the decline."
- "Frivolity is the frequent companion of pessimism. . . . The heroes of declining nations are always the same—the athlete, the singer or the actor."
- The great civilization ultimately turns into a "welfare state" where instead of rewarding hard work and sacrifice, citizens get free goods and services for doing nothing. The welfare state is a "regular milestone in the life-story of an ageing and decrepit empire."
- "We have not drawn from history the obvious conclusion that material success is the result of courage, endurance and hard work."
- The decadence is not just the population—it is the system. Many citizens retain great energy and character, good work ethic and character.
- "Ten generations of human beings suffice to transform the hardy and enterprising pioneer into the captious [constantly complaining] citizens of the welfare state."

Dr. Patrick Ophuls, writing as William Ophuls, is an American political scientist, ecologist, who served in the US Coast Guard and US Foreign Service. In his book *Immoderate Greatness: Why Civilizations Fail*, Ophuls offers some more scientific explanations for why civilizations fall:

- "Civilization . . . encounters four implacable biophysical limits. It also sets in motion a seemingly inexorable moral and practical progression from original vigor and virtue to terminal lethargy and decadence."
- "Most historians have tended to emphasize the psychological factors as casual . . . civilization succumbs to moral decay and practical failure. But we shall see that biophysical constraints play an equally important, if not decisive, role in propelling civilizations toward exhaustion and eventual death."
- "The city is an ecological parasite . . . sucking resources away from its hinterland. . . ."

- "civilization . . . well beyond the point of ecological sense . . . degrades or exhausts ecological resources that are critical for its long-term survival."
- ". . . as the number of functionaries increases out of proportion to the tasks to be performed, government becomes more and more unwieldy and expensive. Onerous taxes and stifling regulations follow as a matter of course, so initiative and enterprise are strangled in red tape. . . ."
- ". . . success breeds hubris in the form of complacency, arrogance, self-righteousness, and over-confidence. A spoiled society begins to rot from within. . . ."
- "Another symptom of rot is an increasing focus on welfare- social insurance, medical care, charitable works, and the like. Affluence fosters a sense of entitlement, as well as a feeling that none should be left behind. *The upshot is a welfare state with a burgeoning roster of clients and a growing burden of subsidies, along with a corresponding loss of personal responsibility and independence. . . .*"
- "*A hypertrophied [excessively enlarged] bureaucracy strangles the society in red tape.* Rent-seeking insiders batten on the public purse, and selfish elites feather their own nests."

Note that the Durants, Glubb, Ophuls, and others blame government bureaucracy, too many regulations for civilization collapse, and the costs and corruptions of welfare programs, fostering a dependent, entitled, class of citizens who no longer support a great and powerful civilization. Again quoting Ophuls, "The society's original vigor, virtue, and morale have been entirely effaced. Rotten to the core, the society awaits collapse, with only the date remaining to be determined." The dependent masses of Romans living on free bread handed out by the empire, watching gladiators fight in the Colosseum, were not the hardworking farmers or soldiers who built the empire.[9]

Jared Diamond in *Collapse: How Societies Choose to Fail or Succeed* also studied reasons why societies collapse, adding in the impacts of environmental damage and climate change (deforestation, soil overuse and erosion, water shortages, over hunting or fishing, too many people, energy shortages, long periods of drought). A root problem according to Diamond is overpopulation relative to the carrying capacity of the environment.[10]

In *The Upside of Down: Catastrophe, Creativity, and the Renewal of Civilization*, Professor Thomas Homer-Dixon also blamed environmental, population, and political-economic stresses as the cause civilization (and global) collapse.[11]

The Collapse of Complex Societies by Joseph Tainter, an archaeologist, believes that complex societies collapse because of diminishing returns from increased complexity. Government "maintenance of legitimacy or investment in coercion require constant mobilization of resources. This is an underlying cost that any complex society must bear."[12] As advanced human societies' complexity increases, bureaucracies increase, increasing costs of internal control and external defense, reaching a point of declining marginal returns, declining social resilience, crowding out funds available for investment in economic growth. Threats and challenges, including natural resource depletion and environmental threats, end up overwhelming society. There are public revolts, civil wars, societal disintegration, failure to adapt, and a younger, stronger civilization can defeat the older, overwhelmed, decaying empire. [13]

The Founding Fathers, fantastic students of history and government, arguably designed the Constitution to help forestall some key elements of civilization decline. The limits on government power, the most important part of the American Revolution and Constitution, could have prevented the growth in both government bureaucracy and welfare programs if the Constitution had been followed, enforced. The welfare and income redistribution programs of the federal government are absolutely unconstitutional, banned by the clear intent, the words and, especially, the fail-safe Tenth Amendment prohibition of any federal program or spending or actions that are not specifically written out in the Constitution. The overwhelming priority of American government to limit government and prioritize individual Natural Rights over government powers, backed up by the Bill of Rights (especially the Ninth Amendment), makes it clear that American governments at all levels cannot steal our money, regulate our private affairs, or violate our basic right to be left alone, and not directed or exploited by government that is supposed to be strictly limited to a few designated tasks.

Benjamin Franklin helped shape the Constitution, and offered this wise warning:

> I agree to this Constitution with all its faults, if they are such: because I think a General Government necessary for us, and there is no Form of Government but what may be a Blessing to the People if well-administered; and I believe farther that this is likely to be well administered for a Course of Years and can only end in Despotism as other Forms have done before it, when the People shall become so corrupted as to need Despotic Government, being incapable of any other.[14]

In his Farewell Address, George Washington warned about candidates and national policies promoted by political parties: "They serve to organize factions . . . to put in the place of the delegated will of the nation the will of a party, often a small but artful and enterprising minority. . . . Let me . . . warn you in the most solemn manner against the baneful effects of the spirit of party. . . ." Washington warned against unconstitutional growth of power in government, urging that "[i]f, in the opinion of the people, the distribution or modification of the constitutional powers be in any particular wrong, let it be corrected by an amendment in the way which the Constitution designates. But let there be no change by usurpations; for though this, in one instance, may be the instrument of good, it is the customary weapon by which free governments are destroyed."[15] This is exactly what happened. FDR and the Perverted Triangle he created illegally eliminated the vital Ninth and Tenth Amendments from the Bill of Rights and have destroyed US government and the judicial system.

Many civilization collapse experts regard the decline, corruption, and fall of civilizations as inevitable, "hardwired for self-destruction" as Ophuls put it. Civilization collapse is not an inevitable development if responsible citizens and governments can learn the lessons of history, stop the growth of government bureaucracy, welfare programs, personal dependence, and irresponsibility.

The British Empire, peak English civilization, ended without a great disaster for the United Kingdom (excluding the ravages of two world wars). They were not destroyed by an enemy, but supplanted by friendly offspring, the United States. While China is on track to eclipse the United States due to the irresponsible policies and destruction of the Perverted Triangle and loss of constitutional limits to power, war with China is absolutely avoidable.

As this book is being written in 2025, the United States is 249 years old—perfectly ripe for collapse per the historic timetable. Ophuls believes the "the process of decline is already well advanced" in the US today.[16] We definitely fit the historical stage and timing for the fall of US civilization, the growth of government bureaucracy and welfare programs have corrupted and bankrupted the country. Rather than barbarians at the gate, the internal decay and divisions in the US, with war and break up triggered by the next collapse that we are woefully unprepared for, may mark the end of US civilization. Both a bang and a whimper.[17]

But the historic rise and fall of civilizations, rise and fall of super powers may be irrelevant in the Age of Collapse. While many collapse disasters may be national in scope, pandemics, nuclear wars, nanotechnology gray goo, and now unimaginable new AI-invented WMD are likely to be global in devastation. The Age of Collapse, especially if superintelligent AGI is not prohibited and prevented, may be the fall and elimination of all humanity. The Age of Collapse is not unique to the US and is driven by economic and technology changes, though the undermining of personal responsibility and civil war divisions are due to our irresponsible government. The Age of Collapse is not just about the fall of a civilization, it's the potential last era of our species.[18]

Chapter Sixteen

WILL NATION-STATES WITH FREE CITIZENS, AUTHORITARIAN DICTATORS, OR WARLORDS RULE IN THE AGE OF COLLAPSE?

The "Godfather of AI," Dr. Geoffrey Hinton, believes that AI's destructive power and danger is an existential threat to humans, and sees government intervention as the only solution to control AI.[1] China leverages all technologies possible to monitor and control their citizens, and may be thrilled with controlling and exploiting AI to better surveil and control its citizens.[2]

For people who prefer to live in freedom, AI is a completely bad development in all respects. It will be used to kill us, or Big Government controlling AI will use this as both a reason and another instrument of power to control citizens. This may be Palantir chief Alex Karp's plan. If AI continues to grow without controls, it will become such a lethal technology that constant government surveillance of citizens to be sure they are not abusing AI to create WMD or superintelligent AGI will be necessary. The better option for free people is to have government institute strong controls now over Tool AI, and prevent superintelligent AGI—without the need for Big Government surveillance and control of AI and citizens after the horrible AI-developed WMD are unleased.

Another possible development is that society will be so devastated by collapses from many sources that governments will be unable to reestablish law and order, or regain control. The collapses may be so severe and frequent that local warlords may reestablish law and order in some areas, with the nation-state and Big Government unable to get reestablished. Or citizens may be disgusted with their government for failure to retain law and order and protect them, and refuse to allow a return of government control.

In the aftermath of the first bad, worldwide collapse, expect huge changes in governance, with many failed nation-states replaced by dictatorships or warlords. Many nations (and in some countries states or provinces) may split up or be gone forever. In the power vacuum of a collapse, with more need than ever for security, law and order, and protection, local warlords may be the main form of government, providing security and rule.

A nation-state means people with common attributes (historically ethnicity)—the nation, and an organized political system with sovereignty over borders—the state. Another important aspect is that the nation-state has a "monopoly over the means of violence."[3] This is true for most countries, though the Second Amendment in the US can serve as a citizens' check on the power of government violence. States are given this monopoly over means of violence because citizens empower and trust government to protect them. When government fails to protect citizens, the social contract is broken.

Jamie Bartlettis, a British journalist and political think tank analyst, noted that people living in the Roman Empire 1,500 years ago believed that empires were the norm, and thought theirs would last forever. The nation-state is a relatively new creation, and "we are just as deluded that our model of living in 'countries' is inevitable and eternal."[4] Until the mid-1800s, empires, city-states, and principalities were the norm. The growth in government bureaucracy and nations' waging organized war led to the development of nation-states, bolstered by the American and French Revolutions creating more strongly defined national interest.[5] By the mid-1900s nation-states had taken over, 195 of them today.

In the Age of Collapse, many nation-states may no longer offer their primary means of justification: protection from foreign attack. Switzerland, Finland, China are exceptions, but the vast majority of nations are not preparing their citizens for collapse survival. Borders aren't able to keep out viruses or new WMD that AI helps individuals invent. A small terrorist group or a rogue collection of Iranian Revolutionary Guard jihadists have the capability to unleash WMD attacks like viruses with more devastating results than the worst Russian nuclear attack.

As Henry Kissinger noted, "For as long as history has been recorded, security has been the minimum objective of an organized society . . . but no society that could not defend itself—either alone or in alignment with other societies—has endured. . . ."[6] In the Age of Collapse, don't expect nation-states to endure after citizens don't just recognize the failure of government, but find out government leaders knew of its vulnerabilities and only prepared themselves for survival.

In *The Transformation of War*, Professor Martin Van Creveld, author of dozens of books on military strategy and history, also warned that "a community which cannot safeguard the lives of its members, subjects, citizens, comrades, brothers, or whatever they are called is unlikely either to command their loyalty or to survive for very long. . . . If, as seems to be the case, that state cannot defend itself against internal or external low-intensity conflict, then clearly it does not have a future in front of it."[7]

When law and order vanishes and a nation-state fails, some group will seize control. Hopefully in America it will be the state government, with National Guard troops backed up by Civil Ground and Civil Air Patrol. But if it's a really bad collapse, I suspect either private militia groups that form, or a powerful, big marauder group, or a "warlord" may emerge in control—whoever can best provide security. A warlord may or may not be bad. It might be a popular elected official, a skilled businessman, who commands the most powerful armed force in the area and establishes order. It could be a dominant marauder group leader that switches to taking "voluntary" support from locals while keeping other marauder groups from committing violence. Hopefully it is a friendly warlord, backed by remnants of police/military units, militia groups, survival communities, and citizens who support them.

Warlords historically were unelected, usually unofficial individuals or groups that in the absence of a functioning government provided security and ruled over people in an area that may be very small or large. Warlords have ruled throughout much of recorded history, and likely in periods of prehistory.

Warlords ruled in China for decades after the central government collapsed, from 1916 into the mid-1930s. Warlords who ruled recently in Afghanistan and Iraq after Saddam Hussein's removal and our failure to establish control or prevent civil war in Iraq were not necessarily evil or bad to their subjects. They were generally preferable to being killed by other marauder groups or opposing militias or terrorists. If a group can restore law and order so you're not robbed and killed, can grow food—that's a huge improvement over starving to death and living in constant fear of marauder attack.

It will be much better if survival communities, neighborhood groups, private militias, surviving elements of local governments and local National Guard forces, form an alliance and pool resources, appointing a committee to serve as an interim government—in effect, a benevolent warlord. In a bad collapse such an alliance, warlord-like arrangement, is very likely at least in a transition period until normal government can be restored—or the citizens agree to allow it to come back.

The warlord could well be a popular politician. Imagine a rural area of the US and a huge Trump supporter, a former county commissioner, backed by several local militia and neighborhood/survival community defense groups who promises to wipe out marauder groups and protect citizens. With the legitimacy of past elected service and pledges to prevent state or federal forces from stealing food regardless of their official executive orders, promising ruthless extermination of marauders (not trying to arrest, but executing them), this benevolent warlord could be extremely popular and the best available option for recovering from the collapse.

You would expect that eventually official federal and state authorities would take over. This may not happen for years if the electric grid is destroyed, or a highly lethal virus continues to drive a pandemic into two, three years. It may never happen.

Even after the collapse is over, economies functioning and law and order restored—the nation-state level of government may not be reestablished. Even if their Continuity of Government plans work and top government leaders and politicians survive, citizens may well refuse their return to power. Why would the survivors of a collapse want to let the politicians, the Perverted Triangle, that survive at Mount Weather and Raven Rock and other government/military facilities, return to power after their spectacular, deadly failure to their job—saving themselves while the rest of us were left to die?

The earlier chapter on civil war in the US noted the secession efforts in twelve states. After a bad collapse, with survivors furious at our irresponsible government and their efforts to save only themselves and to hell with us, their "Continuity of Government" policies, most states may have separatist and secession movements or oppose the return of prior government. This will be reinforced by the fact that preppers and survival communities like Fortitude Ranch tend to be largely Libertarians and people who do not trust the government. They are preparing because they don't believe the government is doing its proper number one job of protecting citizens. They are a small percent of the population today. They will be a much larger percent of the population post-collapse. Many or most survivors may be so furious with the former, failed government that they may refuse to allow them back into power, some preferring punishment for them, not allegiance.

Could there be civil wars in the US and other countries post-collapse, with outraged surviving citizens more interested in prosecuting former government officials than letting them return to power? Definitely.

The catalyst of US government failure to prevent a collapse or protect citizens during it could spark the breakup of many states, and the secession of Texas and others. It is not difficult to imagine new "states" forming that bring together conservative, rural Americans who refuse to allow the return of irresponsible government and the Perverted Triangle. If a local government or a popular warlord is doing a good job in rural areas of states like CA, OR, CO, IL, WI, PA, NY, MA, ME—where Democrats controlled the state government and rural/conservative folks disliked them before, and loathe now (i.e., gun control laws, regulations that made prepping and building far more costly or difficult, they failed to prevent the collapse or protect them during it)—angry surviving citizens may refuse the return of "official" failed, hated government. Under the true spirit of the American Revolution and constitutional government protecting Natural Rights, they would have every right to refuse such governments.

The world map could be dramatically rewritten. For example, the Kurds may be very well positioned to survive, thrive, and take over their territory after a collapse. The Kurds are the largest ethnic group, nationality, without a nation-state, scattered and often exploited in Iraq, Iran, Syria, and Turkey. They have strong ethnic cohesion and may benefit from great cooperation during a collapse. There is an old Kurdish proverb, "No friend but the mountains." This proverb reflects both their historic act of sheltering, hiding out in the mountains to avoid enemies, and a feeling of betrayal as an exploited, distinct ethnic group with no state. I would be delighted to see a new Kurdish nation-state emerge for the Kurds.

Indeed, it is possible that a collapse could be deliberately triggered by a group that wants to destroy the existing world order if they believe that their chosen group will emerge from it in a much better position.

While unlikely in the US, dictatorships could emerge firmly in power in many more nation-states post-collapse, or dictators serving as warlords in thousands of fiefdoms among disintegrated nation-states. A beloved warlord might be elected as a new President or Chancellor or Leader for Life.

In North Korea, a collapse may yield just the opposite—an opportunity to depose Kim Jong-un. The Iranians might have an opportunity during the collapse or recovery to depose of their wretched, repressive theocracy.

For the first time, early in the twenty-first century, the number of democracies in the world exceeded the number of authoritarian states, "experts" rating ninety-eight countries as free government, eighty controlled by dictators.[8] But after the 2007–2009 US housing market financial collapse that sparked a worldwide recession, faith in western style government plunged, and many countries switched to more dictatorial style government, ninety-two countries versus eighty-seven rated "free" in 2019.[9] There are two very important lessons here. First, at least half of the countries in the world have dictatorial style governments. Second, and this lesson is proven throughout history—Russia a great example—that people often prefer the stronger security of a somewhat dictatorial style government over riskier (in terms of fending off invaders and not starving), more democratic forms of government.

In a 2006 American Political Science Association study of failed and collapsed States in Africa and Central Asia, they found that "after violent conflict and political collapse, people demand basic public services that only states can supply."[10] This study of these largely underdeveloped small countries found that warlord rule was usually for short periods and unsustainable. But these were largely states emerging from military conflicts and civil war, with citizens still loyal to their countries. Nationalism tends to rise in wars. And for these small, poor countries, "[f]ollowing conflict, every government requires an organization to represent its interests to international donors and diplomatic missions. Hence, state reconstruction is all but inevitable."[11] This is not applicable to most countries post-collapse. Where governments fail to protect citizens, nation-states fail, and surviving citizens may be less likely to rally round the flag than to ensure the bastards responsible don't get back in power.

In a post-collapse environment, most survivors may prefer more secure, stable, dictatorial style government over more free, democratic governments. There are too many uncertainties, including allegiance and satisfaction with the government prior to the collapse, the length and severity of the collapse, how law and order is restored and by whom, to estimate, but the worse the collapse, the more likely it is that survivors may choose a government they judge more capable of avoiding another collapse. In the US, it is not difficult to imagine survivors choosing a popular, successful governor or warlord over the Perverted Triangle.

The very word "dictatorship" originated in the Roman Empire, where dictatorship was a temporary grant of absolute power to a leader to handle an emergency.[12] In a crisis, fast and decisive decisions are needed, not slow deliberations, pandering, and compromise. Russians for centuries have faced outside invaders and generally favor a strong ruler, a dictator, as better for security. Post-collapse, security and food will be the top concerns of survivors.

Underdeveloped countries that have strong farming and agriculture will likely emerge from a collapse in better shape than urban, rich, developed countries that lose the vast majority of their population from starvation and marauder murders. Countries like Argentina may keep law and order, lose no one to starvation, and emerge in great shape. Densely overpopulated urban countries like Germany may be largely destroyed after a bad collapse—especially if Switzerland is successful with their defensive plans of very well armed, weapons-skilled citizens, and blown up bridges and roads along their borders, able to keep foreign starving people out.[13]

Around the world, many nation-states may be forever destroyed by a bad collapse. Many that stay together as nation-states may be in control of political movements that reject the old failed government and insist on drastic reforms.

National and international gangs may grow in power and importance as nation-state power declines, and law and order breaks down in repeated collapse disasters.

There is no predicting how the world will look after the first bad collapse, especially if it happens soon, with most countries and the vast majority of urban people completely unprepared and horribly positioned.

I suspect China will emerge from a collapse in relatively good shape, and the clear leading world superpower. As described in the earlier chapter on why the US must abandon its politically correct but national security suicidal policy of defending Taiwan, China has years of stockpiled food and resources, strong agriculture and manufacturing, and an undisputed, all-powerful Communist party to keep control. Law and order may not be lost in China, so their collapse could be mild, while the US and Western European nations starve to death and are ravaged by marauder groups.

What will countries around the world conclude post-collapse when they see how the Chinese Communist Party stockpiled food for its citizens and helped them survive while the US Perverted Triangle, so focused on buying votes and its benefit, stockpiled food just for themselves, with executive orders authorizing agencies to steal food from citizens in a collapse? The US will probably emerge from a collapse with a much larger percent of its population dead and survivors outraged at government, many ready to replace it. Why would countries around the world choose US democracy in it perverted practice now over one-party rule in the Age of Collapse?

Many nation-states are likely to permanently disintegrate after a bad collapse. Bartlettis argues that "the nation-state with its borders, centralized governments, common people and sovereign authority is increasingly out of step with the world."[14] Nation-states are based on secure borders that digital technology, the Internet, multinational corporations, international travel don't respect. The Internet and digital technologies are "an enormous pain for the nation-state in all sorts of ways" from cyberattacks and ransomware, empowering companies like Uber and Airbnb to ignore local laws, and Bitcoin and other cryptocurrencies that can replace fiat (government-issued) currency. And many countries today do not have effective, defended borders. Bartlettis quotes then presidential candidate Donald Trump in 2016 tweeting: "A nation without borders is not a nation at all. We WILL Make America Safe Again!"[15] Again quoting Bartlettis:

> This is the crux of the problem: nation-states rely on control. If they can't control information, crime, businesses, borders, or the money supply,

> then they will cease to deliver what citizens demand of them. In the end, nation-states are nothing but agreed-upon myths: we give up certain freedoms in order to secure others. But if that transaction no longer works, and we stop agreeing on the myth, it ceases to have power over us.

In a collapse, many nation-states won't just fail to control borders. There will be long-lasting, widespread loss of law and order, with gangs and marauder groups killing citizens, hell on Earth. Law and order may be restored by government forces or militia groups or marauder warlords, but on a smaller level of territory.

Bartlettis believes the city-state is likely to replace the nation-state.[16] But he was writing in 2017 about normal times, pre-Age of Collapse. In the Age of Collapse, densely populated cities will be untenable, far too dangerous for survival. Big cities will be abandoned in a collapse, left to marauder groups, the worst hell on Earth. Even in good times, we increasingly don't need big cities for work or commerce. We can collaborate, work in a big company, without being in the same building, or certainly in the same city. The Internet and digital technologies undermine city-states as much as nation-states. After city residents abandon cities to survive a collapse, it will be surprising if most of them decide to return. They are far more likely to stay in sustainable, survivable rural areas.

Lower population countries are certainly a better fit for democracy and less densely populated rural areas have better odds for peaceful coexistence. With digital technology, dispersed populations in rural areas can engage in modern economic activity without suffering the drawbacks of big cities. But the decisive factor favoring "county-states"[17] (regions with largely rural populations), rural living in the Age of Collapse is the ability to grow food, have local reliable water, better quality of life in good times, and better odds for surviving the next collapse. Again, our future is one of repeated collapse disasters, not one and it's over.

If there is no big external threat of an invading army, then "county-states" may be an especially popular form of government in the Age of Collapse.

China is very well positioned for world dominance in the Age of Collapse. If they choose to become an expanding empire (which I doubt) this would force "county-states" to again join a powerful nation-state for collective defense.[18] Many nation-states may follow China's model with dictatorial or one political party rule. But if China is the world superpower and only wants to apply economic power worldwide, not build an empire (and I see little historical precedent or modern advantage of doing so), many nation-states in the Age of Collapse may be replaced by county-states, warlords, without a big nation state like we have today. If national armies are no longer capable of protecting people, and the key to survival is not presenting a threat to anyone/anything else, having local food production, keeping a low profile—then a local warlord or a county-state may be a better form of government for citizens than today's nation state.[19]

My best guesstimate is that China will be the leading superpower in the Age of Collapse, with fewer nation-states, many warlord-led small to large fiefdoms, and many "county states" around the world. The Perverted Triangle is unlikely to be welcomed back in the US. If it does return at the national level, Texas and other conservative states, joined by break-off rural parts of Democratic Party controlled states, will probably secede. But if the Perverted Triangle can be destroyed, with local governments, "county states" that exercise government power, and national government again strictly limited to national security and AI control, this new world order and life in the Age of Collapse could be both survivable and worth living.

CHAPTER SEVENTEEN

CIVIL DISOBEDIENCE IS JUSTIFIED TO STOP IRRESPONSIBLE, UNCONSTITUTIONAL GOVERNMENT THAT IS WORKING TO KILL US

What are citizens supposed to think when our government ignores catastrophic risks like our vulnerable electric grid, bioengineering, and H5N1, uncontrolled development of Artificial Intelligence, and dozens of other collapse threats and does nothing to warn or prepare us? What are citizens to think when congressmen and their families, along with federal bureaucrats, have survival facilities they get to use, at taxpayer expense, protected by federally paid forces, stockpiled with years of food and water, while we have nothing but a website that says keep three days of food and water stored in your house? How should citizens react when government orders give themselves legal authority to steal our private stockpiles of food, preparations we've made on our own to try and survive?[1]

Common sense, the Declaration of Independence, the US Constitution, Common Law, and your Natural Right of self-defense all say citizens have the right to oppose and when necessary fight and kill government officials who pursue policies to kill citizens and exploit them as sources of food and resources to steal from in a collapse.

The odds of the Perverted Triangle now pursuing even a small fraction of the must-do, long-overdue vital changes proposed in this book to survive a collapse is near zero. The Perverted Triangle is firmly entrenched, the country too divided to agree on major changes. Government decision-making today does not prioritize protecting citizens or following the Constitution, but advancing their power and interest, lying and pandering for reelection votes.

Lobbyists who love new weapon systems, the utility lobbyists who don't want to harden the grid, the AI company CEOs, the Status Quo and the Perverted Triangle have much to lose in adjusting to the Age of Collapse. The politicians are protected at Mount Weather, Raven Rock; wealthy folks can build private bunkers, jet away to safer places on Earth, or join Survival Condo. Until the first collapse hits, most people will ignore the obvious threats we face today and the warnings to prepare.

Citizens must hold elected and appointed officials accountable for irresponsible conduct. When the CDC still assures citizens in 2025 that H5N1 is "low risk" and refuses to do its job of correctly informing people of the H5N1 threat and preparing for the inevitable pandemic that is coming, there must be consequences. We cannot allow our government to continue leaving our vital electric grid unprotected, pushing China to war over Taiwan, outlawing and eliminating low-yield tactical nuclear weapons.

When necessary, civil disobedience is called for, vital when Big Government and the Perverted Triangle is illegally and immorally trampling individual rights, killing us, and setting us up for massive death in the coming collapses.

The nonviolent model of Martin Luther King should be followed as much as possible. King proclaimed that "[a]n individual who breaks a law that conscience tells him is unjust, and who willingly accepts the penalty of imprisonment in order to arouse the conscience of the community over its injustice, is in reality expressing the highest respect for the law."[2] We are trained to consider it "un-American" or "unpatriotic" to question government, but as Charles Murray argued, "When I propose to use systematic civil disobedience, it is not against a government that has made a few unintentional missteps and should be given the benefit of the doubt. The civil disobedience I propose is against a government that has over five decades earned our distrust."[3]

The Dr. King quotes explain his beliefs that we must fight for our rights, take action despite risks, favor nonviolence as much as possible, but recognize that "it is just as wrong, or perhaps even more so, to use moral means to preserve immoral ends"—i.e., not surrender to "rule of law" or all constraints of nonviolence when it is unjust or will kill you and your family.[4]

Dr. Martin Luther King's philosophy and guidance on fighting against evil, using nonviolent means as much as possible, are very relevant to the campaigns to stop AI and unconstitutional Government before they kill us:

"We want all of our rights, we want them here, and we want them now."

"Every man of humane convictions must decide on the protest that best suits his convictions, but we must all protest."

"We still have a choice today: nonviolent coexistence or violent co-annihilation. We must move past indecision to action."

"We adopt the means of nonviolence because our end is a community at peace with itself. We will try to persuade with our words, but if our words fail, we will try to persuade with our acts."

"I have tried to make clear that it is wrong to use immoral means to attain moral ends. But now I must affirm that it is just as wrong, or perhaps even more so, to use moral means to preserve immoral ends."

Mercy Otis Warren, in her *History of the American Revolution* (1805), noted the propensity of Americans to obey authority out of old habits of obedience until they have been pushed to the limits by despotic masters.[5] This limit has been reached for most Americans, and it's the reason Donald Trump is POTUS. The one thing divided Americans do agree on is that our politics is a disaster. We face the risk of civil war because of the sharp divisions in our society promoted by the two political parties and the Perverted Triangle. We face devastation and death in a collapse our irresponsible government is doing nothing to prepare for.

We must have responsible, limited government that stays out of individual lives and decisions that do not harm others, and focuses all efforts on protecting people from significant threats and harms we cannot deal with on our own. Because Big Government is irresponsible and negligent in preparing us to survive a pandemic, loss of the electric system, and other collapse threats, we must take responsibility and action to protect ourselves. Dr. Charles Murray with the American Enterprise Institute contends that being a good citizen "does not command our blind allegiance to the law." Indeed, "government is instituted to protect our unalienable rights, and . . . when it becomes destructive of those rights, the reason for our allegiance is gone."[6]

It is our duty as citizens to defend the Constitution, our families, our lives. As a commissioned military officer, it is particularly galling when I took an oath to uphold and defend the Constitution of the United States while our government, under control of the Perverted Triangle, violates and treats the Constitution like toilet paper. We must serve under a federal government that promulgates blatantly illegal, unconstitutional programs that are tearing our country apart and setting us up for extermination in a collapse. We swear loyalty not to the president or Congress, but to "support and defend the Constitution of the United States against all enemies, foreign and domestic." The Perverted Triangle is a horrible domestic enemy of the US Constitution and our retained Natural Rights as Americans.[7]

We don't need and cannot lead good lives with millions of unlimited government rules and programs, spending that is theft from us, dividing and bankrupting our nation. We can and must fight government violation of our Natural Rights, refuse to follow rules and programs that are unconstitutional and violate our Natural Rights to privacy and freedom at home, to use our private property as we want and need to for survival.

As more and more Americans refuse government rules, it becomes impossible for government bureaucrats and courts to enforce them. Mass civil disobedience can succeed and thwart the Perverted Triangle. As more Americans demand limited government, personal liberty, refuse to follow asinine rules or let government bureaucrats into their homes to approve our receptacles and stair balusters, we can stop the politicians, bureaucrats, and lawyers from violating our freedom, jeopardizing our lives.[8]

You have a Natural Right to your personal property and freedom to build and live in your home as you alone choose. A local government has a right to ban a fireworks factory in a city apartment building, but no right to dictate what is inside your house, how you use your property that poses no threat to the public. State government has no right to dictate inherently local zoning and building codes or gun rights in rural counties. Especially when such unconstitutional violations of your Natural Rights reduce or prevent your ability to protect your family and prepare for a collapse, you must refuse and fight them. This abuse of zoning and building codes and unlimited government regulation is happening all over the country, especially where big city, Democratic Party dominated state governments promoting the Perverted Triangle force conservative, rural counties to follow rules and policies that do not fit. It is the exact opposite of democracy and government that serves the particular needs of citizens. It is an intolerable violation of our Natural Rights and a threat to our lives.[9]

Governments and politicians must stop threatening to ban "military style weapons" and high-capacity magazines you will need to survive in a collapse when gangs and marauder groups are out stealing and killing to survive. Citizens must ignore such unconstitutional laws if they want to survive a collapse. When a local government laws and regulations bans woodstoves, "military capable" weapons you need to defeat a marauder attack, prevent you stockpiling antibiotics and survival supplies you need, raising rabbits and chickens, reject these government acts as unconstitutional violations of your Natural Rights, protected by the Ninth Amendment and other parts of the Bill of Rights in the Constitution and refuse to follow them.

Most counties in the US today are refusing to obey unconstitutional gun control laws. But there are far more unconstitutional laws that also must be refused. The Second Amendment is just one of many Natural Rights spelled out in the Bill of Rights—the Ninth Amendment makes it clear there are many more that are just as vital and cannot be violated by government unless there is a clear national security requirement or threat to other people's safety and property.[10]

Until a Convention of the States to amend our Constitution, get it enforced again by the Supreme Court, and defeat the Perverted Triangle is successfully completed, citizens need to oppose, ignore, refuse to follow rules and regulations that violate our natural rights to use our private property for self-defense and survival when it does not directly, improperly harm others.

Uber openly violated taxi laws and regulations and won because of massive public support. Airbnb has also succeeded and offered great public service by blatantly violating zoning regulations limiting how people use their private residences. Every citizen should tell government officials to take their rules on how people use their private property and shove them up an appropriate place. Government is for protection from external threats people cannot handle on their own—not to dictate who stays in your house, or stair tread height you prefer. Government action is only justifiable when it is protecting citizens from serious external threats.

Poor Americans in particular should refuse to follow unreasonable regulations that restrict their ability to start up a small business and provide for their families, ignore building code requirements that are not really essential for safety, and refuse to accept any judicial proceeding that forces them to hire a scum lawyer. If fined or ruled against—do not pay or comply.

As citizens we have the Natural Right and an obligation to protect ourselves and our families. Government rules and bureaucrats that stand in the way of preparing for a collapse are wrong, immoral, and should be ignored and opposed. Thomas Paine, who laid out the case for the American Revolution in *Common Sense* (1776), is correct: Americans have not just the right, but the duty, the responsibility, in the face of "a long train of abuses and usurpations" to "throw off such Government, and to provide new Guards for their future security."

In Colonial times, Americans used juries "in protecting fellow citizens against government oppression" by rejecting a judge's (lawyer's) instructions to confine themselves to limited questions the judge and lawyers want to argue, and instead do the right thing and focus on delivering real justice.[11] This check on bad/big government was wisely included in our Constitution (the Seventh Amendment right to jury trial). Lawyers and their partners in the Perverted Triangle have undermined this rightful citizen's power with laws, lawyers über alles provisions, and judges dictating to juries precise, strict, and unconstitutional limits on how they can vote—forcing them not to rule based on right and wrong, justice, but legal BS and allegiance to past rulings of other judges (lawyers). Juries must exercise their right and obligation to dispense justice, not serve lawyers. When true Americans disobey unconstitutional and unreasonable intrusive government laws, they should not just refuse to comply, but refuse to settle or pay fines, and insist on a jury trial by their peers, as guaranteed by the Seventh Amendment. In trial, argue against the use of case precedents by lawyers and instead, appeal to Natural Rights, the Constitution, reason, and justice. Appeal to true Americans serving on juries to vote for what is right and just, not be coerced by regulatory BS, legal tricks, and restrictions that judges cannot rightfully impose.[12]

If Americans, even by just a few hundred thousand at first, start refusing regulations, taxes, and laws that are clear violations of our Natural Rights and threats to our survival, the Perverted Triangle system could start to falter.[13]

A friendly couple in San Francisco put a book sharing cabinet outside their home, letting anyone passing by borrow or trade a book as a nice neighborhood service. Bureaucrats in San Francisco ordered them to pay a $1,420 "Minor Sidewalk Encroachment Permit" fee to keep their free library open.[14] Tar and feathering is too risky, but Americans need to refuse obscene, unjustified laws and say "hell no" to politicians, government bureaucrats, lawyers, and judges who give them wrongful orders. Martin Luther King's nonviolent protests should be the guide, but Americans must be willing to pay the ultimate price to stop Big Government and unconstitutional laws. Quoting Benjamin Franklin: "Security without liberty is called prison."[15]

The American Revolution began as a revolt against government policies the colonists opposed—and would still have opposed whether or not they passed in Parliament with a few Colonial Representatives voting no. The Declaration of Independence was not about voting rights or majority rule, it was about real freedom—priority given to protecting an individual's Natural Right to live free, the right to be left alone, not harassed by government or a majority. The American Revolution was instigated by outrage over British taxes and fees that were trivial compared to the avalanche of Big Government taxes, regulations and violations of freedom we suffer from today. The Constitution was written and approved to protect our Natural Rights and freedom from government or majority opinions violating this personal, individual liberty. The Constitution has been strangled and is dead in practice, alive on paper largely as a lie. American government today is orders of magnitude worse than British rule in the 1700s.

People must demand and, when necessary, use peaceful civil disobedience to exercise their Natural Right of life, survival, and use of personal property to achieve this overriding priority. When government blocks your survival preparations—refuse them. Prioritize your family and friends' survival.

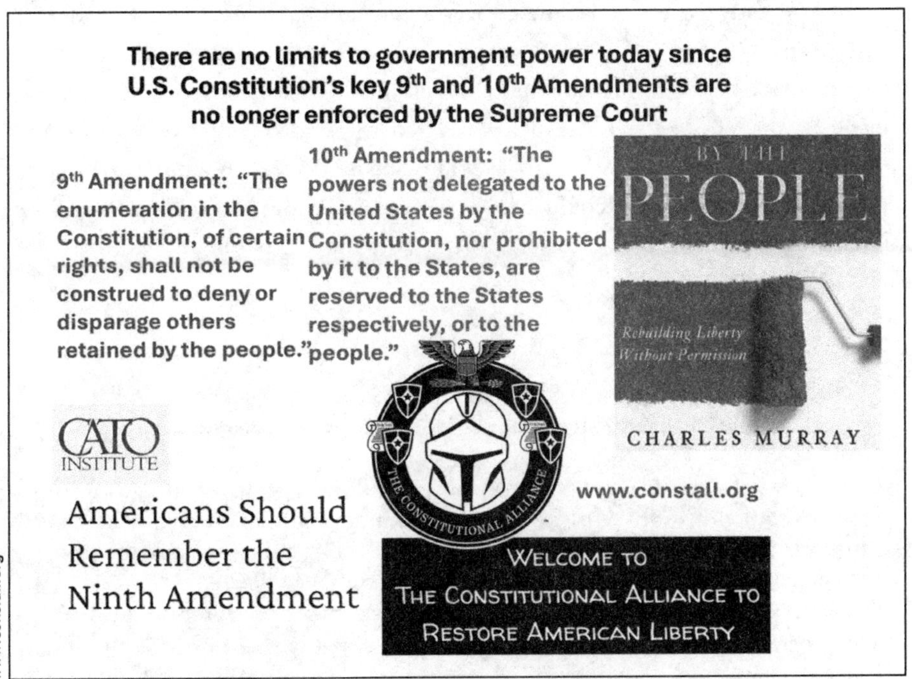

Figure 61: Lack of limits to government power.

In this citizen's fight for a Third American Revolution to destroy the Perverted Triangle and get limited, American government and our Natural Rights back, the Constitutional Alliance must organize mass educational and protest programs.[16]

Common themes and messages are needed, including more polished versions of "Miller's Maxim." A maxim is a short, succinct statement expressing a general truth or rule of conduct, useful in public debate. Government laws and regulations steal individual freedom and impose government power to subject citizens. As George Washington put it, "Government is not reason, it is not eloquence—it is force! Like fire it is a dangerous servant and a fearful master; never for a moment should it be left to irresponsible action." Every government tax dollar, program, regulation, imposes great costs that lead to loss of individual freedom, wealth, and citizens' lives. Government taxes and actions reduce productivity, leading to lower income—which leads to deaths and shorter lifespans. Based on a variety of studies, a reasonable estimate is one death for every $10 million in lost income from government programs that take your tax dollars, reduce your earnings, lower your quality of life and life expectancy.[17]

Citizens and their representatives need to know this and demand that for every regulation already passed, and all new government actions proposed, that the deaths to citizens must be weighed. Thus I propose "Miller's Maxim" to be, "Government action is force, subjugation, violating our Natural Rights, taking our income and causing deaths." Cato the Elder, a Roman Senator, ended every speech with the phrase "Carthago delenda est" (Carthage must be destroyed). A shorter, shoutable version of Miller's Maxim could be "Government action kills!" This should be followed by a demand for an answer to the question, "How many will die from this law?"[18]

Figure 62: Miller's Maxim: "Government action is force, subjugation, violating our Natural Rights, taking our income and causing deaths."

Every government tax dollar, program, regulation, is force stealing our Natural Right of individual freedom, with a cost in citizen deaths. Government taxes and regulations directly and indirectly steal our income, reducing our freedom, quality of life, and length of life.

Citizens and their elected representatives need to demand that for every government act taken, the deaths to citizens must be openly and formally weighed. A shorter, shoutable version of Miller's Maxim, is "Government action kills!" Follow this with a demand for an answer to the question, "How many will die from this proposal?"

The longer version of Miller's Maxim is: "any government spending, regulation, restriction, or other imposed costs on its citizens that meets constitutional guidelines, must also acknowledge and overcome the significant costs (intended and unintended) from the interference in our liberties, loss of Natural Rights, and loss of income and lives of the proposed measure."

The value of lost freedom when government interferes with our Natural Right to be left alone must be given great weight in the decision. No government program is allowed unless it is absolutely necessary, vital to prevent or offset significant harm that individuals cannot deal with (or choose to accept) on their own.

A dollar price of taxes, loss of productivity and time, and all unintended but likely losses from the measure must be weighed in the decision-making, including a cost for the loss of freedom and loss of life from the government spending and interference. Any imposition of financial costs on people reduces their income and life expectancy. So both a dollar cost of all harms possible from the government measure

continued on following page

and an estimate of the number of citizen's lives that will be lost from loss of income must be estimated and disclosed.

When politicians pandering for votes try to offer you a government benefit, or pass a law or add a regulation, tell them: **"Government action is force, subjugation, violating our Natural Rights, taking our income and causing deaths."** Then ask, **"How many will die from this?"** If the government act is not protecting citizens against big threats they cannot handle on their own, then insist it not be approved or obeyed, leaving our Natural Rights of private property, privacy, pursuing happiness as we alone choose. —Dr. Drew Miller, Col USAF (Ret)

To survive in the Age of Collapse, particularly with the irresponsible, self-serving Perverted Triangle killing us now and setting us up for unnecessarily catastrophic fatalities in a collapse, citizens must insist on their Natural Right to survive and use private property. We must refuse zoning, codes, regulations that endanger survival plans without causing harm to others. Most county sheriffs, most counties and many states across the US are already doing this by refusing to obey unconstitutional restrictions on gun ownership and self-defense. Until a Convention of the States to defeat the Perverted Triangle and amend our Constitution so it is again enforced by the Supreme Court and limited government and Natural Rights return, citizens need to disobey and fight unconstitutional government regulations and prepare for collapse survival despite the barriers unconstitutional government imposes.

If we survive and recover from a bad collapse where our electric grid goes down, there should be a tribunal for criminals like the Nuremberg Tribunal after World War II; not for the foreign enemies who take the grid down or release a deadly virus or some other AI-invented WMD, but the elected officials who for decades with clear knowledge of our many catastrophic vulnerabilities did nothing to fix them.[19]

Chapter Eighteen

UNLESS GOVERNMENTS ACHIEVE STRONG CONTROLS OF AI, CIVIL DISOBEDIENCE IS VITAL TO STOP AI

AI is the worst technology mankind has developed in terms of its ability to kill people, worse than nuclear weapons, bioengineering—any technology since AI can be misused by bad people to use other technologies to more effectively, and easily develop WMD that are much harder to detect and prevent. AI will exploit all existing technologies to kill—and develop innovative, entirely new ways to kill that people have not thought of, and are completely unprepared for.[1]

If we don't stop AI now we risk extermination from the new WMD that bad people using AI develop. If we don't prevent superintelligent AGI we will reach a point where stopping it is impossible and humanity (and possibly all living biological species on Earth) will be wiped out.

Superintelligent AGI may conclude that the Perverted Triangle, irresponsible destruction of the environment, and collective stupidity of societies, like the US, demand extermination of our harmful species. But even if the growing crowd of AI experts who insist that it is absolutely impossible to control AGI and prevent this are wrong, it is 100 percent certain that some bad people will abuse AGI to exterminate humanity. There is no doubt: "If anyone builds it, everyone dies."[2]

As explained earlier, Tool AI is all we need, and even if AI was completely stopped, paused, we already have sufficient AI tool capability to power decades of economic growth without the risks and devastation of our current uncontrolled AI development. This is obviously best for over 99 percent of humanity, best for our other species and our planet, best for every single country. Bad just for AI investors, AI companies, and the career politicians who benefit from their campaign donations.

People around the world need to demand that their governments support them, not AI companies. Again, quoting Aquirre and his "Keep the Future Human" proposal:

> We don't have to do this. We have human-competitive AI, and there's no need to build AI with which we can't compete. We can build amazing AI tools without building a successor species. . . . Humanity must choose to close the Gates to AGI and superintelligence. To keep the future human.[3]

Polls show overwhelming majorities of the public want slower, more careful development of AI and do not want smarter than human AI replacing them in their job, or threatening our sources of information and our lives.[4] But the silent majority doesn't make campaign donations, so the Perverted Triangle is completely ignoring the welfare of citizens and backing Mark Zuckerberg, Sam Altman, and Alex Karp in an AI arms race.

As the previous chapter explained, we have a Natural Right of self-defense and survival. If AI company leaders, board directors, and employees do not value our lives, we have no obligation to value theirs and must take action to protect ourselves and other innocent people who face death from their irresponsibility and imminent threats to our lives.

Worldwide protests, ideally nonviolent, but if necessary disrupting and stopping murderous AI development in self-defense is needed, justified, morally right. It will take worldwide demonstration and, at times, probably violence to force AI company CEOs, the Perverted Triangle, and governments worldwide to halt AI until we can get the controls, facilities, and multiple oversight inspections in place to allow safe AI tools and prevent any possibility of superintelligent AGI.

The slow-moving, massive government bureaucracies in place today take years to develop regulations, hampered by Perverted Triangle politicians and self-serving lawyers that add in provisions for their campaign donations, power, and profit, not public service. They will be lobbied and bought with legal bribes from the vast wealth of the big AI companies. Consumer Advisory Agencies[5] can act quickly to mobilize popular support and boycotts, but don't have regulatory control or destructive punishment power.

Alexander Karp, CEO of AI company Palantir, has spoken out against slowing down on AI, arguing that our enemies won't and we can't risk them having AI capability superior to that of the US and the West.[6] In his book, Karp lists the considerable risks and dangers of AI, then dismisses them in his call for a self-serving AI arms race: "It is essential that we redirect our attention toward building the next generation of AI weaponry that will determine the balance of power in this century, as the atomic age ends. . . . One age of deterrence, the atomic age, is ending, and a new era of deterrence built on AI is set to begin."[7] Why the role and power of nuclear weapons will wane or disappear is never explained. We are modernizing, not abandoning nuclear weapons. They will play a far more vital role in the Age of Collapse as a counter, punishment, deterrent to new WMD and AI misuse. Karp has zero experience or education in military strategy, and is wrong to assume international cooperation to control AI is impossible (it has not been attempted and every world leader prefers staying alive) and in advocating an AI arms race. We need nuclear weapons–like controls and limits on AI, not a crash "Manhattan Program" to accelerate the unlimited advance of AI as Karp proposes.[8]

A 2024 Collapse Survivor exercise training simulation dealt with a scenario covering the threats of Artificial Intelligence and how people around the world decided that they are not just going to let big companies develop AI and allow it to kill us. In this six-day simulation, anti-AI groups got a protest movement going that succeeded in generating widespread support and a ban on AI was achieved.[9] This Collapse Survivor App scenario where the "People Strike Back at AI" illustrates the kind of massive, worldwide protest movement that may be the only chance of stopping AI before it is used to destroy us. This scenario began when a real anti-AI group, Pause AI, called for worldwide protests against AI since our governments are not doing anything effective to control this deadly new technology. In the simulation many other organizations quickly joined this effort, and it became a massive, worldwide, effective movement protesting AI. The name of the movement got changed from Pause AI to Wipe Out AI—wipe out Artificial Intelligence before it can wipe us out.

As the movement gained support and had big success, many other groups also joined. The Wipe Out AI movement started with peaceful protests, but they quickly got violent, escalating into attacks on major AI companies and assaults on the CEOs of those AI companies, and in some cases gunfights with employees of big AI companies. Companies that had been implementing or planning to use AI reversed course and pledged to stop using AI to avoid the damage protestors were causing. And because they would not be competitive if other competitors used AI, they joined the Wipe Out AI movement.

Job losses that AI threatens were a major reason for the support of the Wipe Out AI movement. AI threatens to wipe out hundreds of millions or a billion-plus jobs—office workers, factory workers, almost every profession and industry will experience huge job losses. Overnight you'll be unemployed and unable to provide for your family. Skills you devoted decades to develop now worthless. This job loss on such a rapid, massive scale, with no time to adapt, is unprecedented. It will likely yield tremendous suffering and violence that results in a collapse. When you destroy peoples' livelihoods and lives so quickly, on such a massive scale, you should expect that these hundreds of millions of people will fight back—and this is what happened in this simulation.[10]

You may have heard the term "Luddites" before, a name given to people who oppose new technology, protest against it because it could mean they lose their jobs. Luddites was the name given to British hand loom weavers who opposed the industrial, machine-powered looms in the early 1800s. But AI is not just a new means of improving economic production, it's a means to kill people and possibly wipe out our entire species, and perhaps the planet. The best analogy is that AI is like letting anyone who wants to develop nuclear or biological weapons do it. This is an understatement of the deaths likely if AI is not immediately controlled.

The reason we ran this scenario was because we wanted to send a message, suggest that there should be an uprising by the people against Artificial Intelligence. Such an uprising would require a worldwide movement like the one described in the Collapse Survivor simulation. The question this scenario posed is: should people rise up against AI, and fight it, even use nuclear weapons against countries that refuse to control AI? Most people playing the Collapse Survival exercise simulation and taking a poll on the app believe it will kill billions and that violence is justified if necessary to stop AI, including use of nuclear weapons if necessary to stop the threats of AI.[11] While no one wants to promote violence, the right of self-defense is a fundamental, universal Natural Right. The people who are working to advance AI are responsible for the disasters and deaths this technology will cause, and the violence of efforts rightfully undertaken to stop them.

A video that covers this simulated worldwide movement to stop AI before it kills us is available in the webnotes.[12]

While the Wipe Out AI movement in this Collapse Survivor simulation exercise succeeded in getting a total prohibition and outlaw of AI in most countries in the world, Russia, China, Iraq, and North Korea refused. They just issued lies that they had no dangerous AI programs.[13] AI has tremendous power and use in military applications, and with AI ended in the West, but advancing in the alliance of Russia-China-Iran-North Korea, that could spell military disaster for the good guys. So the proposal was made to form a new alliance of countries pledged to ban AI, protecting one another if ever attacked by one of these four counties that are not banning AI.[14]

The argument that AI is vital for national security is nonsense. Uncontrolled development of AI is suicidal for all nations and our species. AI is unlike nuclear weapons, which are very difficult now to create and fairly easy (with old/current technologies) to monitor, prevent, and control. It is on the other end of the spectrum in relatively easy ability to have massive, deadly abuse. National security is not a legitimate reason to not control AI, but the issue of AI used for military superiority must be addressed. It may even be one that helps unite the world: we come together in our opposition to allowing AI to destroy us and form an alliance of anti-AI countries against those who refuse to control AI, as proposed in an earlier chapter.[15]

It is highly unlikely that the United Nations or national governments will ban AI or effectively regulate and control it. Effective AI regulation will not happen through the slow normal government process, and certainly not in a system where Google and the hundreds of billions of dollars pouring into AI sends millions to donate to politicians to control AI legislation. It will take a well-organized, highly dedicated mass movement, and probably some use of violence against the powerful AI companies that control how the Perverted Triangle and government now promote rather than control AI.

Iran, North Korea, and terrorist groups will refuse to obey any ban on AGI or controls on Tool AI, and won't allow foreign inspections. But with the AI Control Alliance (AICA), backed up by Prompt Global Strike and nuclear weapons, the good guy countries pledged to controlling AI to save humanity can keep bad, no-AI-control countries in check. China and Russia should support the AICA if their top priority issues (stay out of Taiwan civil war, stop expanding NATO toward Russia) are rightly met. They have just as much incentive to ensure AI is not used to kill their citizens. A worldwide uprising against AI may spread to China and Russia if they refuse AI controls.

Military AI work can continue in regulated, policed labs—especially if there are countries that refuse AI control and international inspection. It would be dangerous to give up the power of AI to defeat/defend against an enemy exploiting AI. But like nuclear weapons, all AI research must be absolutely controlled by a government authority and third party group that can't be bribed or corrupted into allowing illegal, dangerous misuse. When an AI application, like self-driving cars, is available, and can be certified as inherently safe to use, AI benefits can be reaped. But open, anything-goes development and use of AI is suicidal.

If responsible governments cannot get AI safely and completely controlled within a year, the best course of action for mankind and our planet is a massive, unforgiving, public assault against AI companies and governments to force a pause in AI use and development until Tool AI development can resume in highly controlled, safe, isolated, government and third-party monitored facilities, with super-intelligent AGI effectively banned and prevented.

What is the moral reasoning that justifies obeying government "Rule of Law" when most laws today are unconstitutional and these laws enable government policies that kill citizens now and development of AI that will ruin billions of lives, lead to billions of deaths, the extinction or enslavement of the human race? The government funded and promoted AI arms race we are now in is morally indefensible. Failure to fight and oppose AI as it is currently being developed is immoral and suicidal.[16]

Chapter Nineteen

ACHIEVING PEACE, FREEDOM, AND QUALITY OF LIFE IN THE AGE OF COLLAPSE

Movies on collapse survival, like the 1995 film *12 Monkeys*, have relied on the *deus ex machina*[1] of time travel to go back and fix the mistake, avoid the collapse. There will be no do-overs for us; we must adapt now, implement a host of revolutionary changes to survive. Nor should the Age of Collapse be *Mad Max Beyond Thunderdome* (1985) or *Battlestar Galactica* if we act responsibly, civilly, and pursue the logical, doable preparations necessary. Indeed, despite periodic, unavoidable Weapons of Mass Destruction (WMD) attacks and disasters, we can achieve peace, freedom, and good quality of life while surviving in the Age of Collapse.[2]

Notably absent from this list is "prosperity." Prosperous today means wealthy, "auspicious, favorable, marked by success or economic well-being."[3] But prosperous used to mean, in its Latin and Middle English origin, "agreeable to one's wishes" or "in conformity with one's hope"—not rich.[4] Being wealthy isn't necessary for great quality of life today, and will be less important and valued in the Age of Collapse.

The Age of Collapse is not avoidable. The key uncertainty is not whether a natural or bioengineered viral pandemic occurs, or crippling attack on the electric grid happens, which disaster or WMD attack comes first, but how bad they are, what depth and duration of collapse results. Whatever collapse devastation comes first, the key point uncertainty expert Nassim Taleb argues is "Black Swans being unpredictable, we need to adjust to their existence (rather than naively try to predict them)."[5] We must adapt to the future of bioengineered viral pandemics,[6] new AI-developed WMD, and make big changes in our strategy, military forces, economy, and preparedness to reduce the likelihood that the consequences do not cascade into a collapse. We need to be prepared to deal with the consequences of a horrific disaster and massive loss of lives that often cannot be stopped. We need to cooperate worldwide to share food and provide mutual assistance whenever possible. The technology and capability to generate WMD and launch horrific attacks can't be eliminated. Even the best possible regulation and control of AI are not going to stop some AI misuse to develop new WMD.

The first collapse disasters will be particularly horrible, with the vast majority of people unprepared and most governments only bothering to protect themselves, not their citizens. But as we add preparedness measures, improve WMD detection and Prompt Global Strike preemption capability, improve security against marauders and collapse recovery resources, if you are not in the "ground zero" impact of the initial disaster, the wider collapse may not happen or won't be as difficult to survive. Prevention, Preemption, and Preparedness, P^3, are key in the Age of Collapse.

Governments at all levels need to make recovering from a collapse, whether from a pandemic, loss of the electric system, whatever the trigger event, top priority. All citizens must prepare for surviving when there is no functioning economy and widespread loss of law and order. We need stockpiled food, much larger Army Guard and LEO reserve forces, Civil Ground Patrol, major preparations for preventing or recovering from a collapse. Everyone must become a prepper, grow food, defend your survival facility against marauders, be ready to survive a never-ending series of WMD attacks and collapse disasters.[7]

Bloomberg

Live TV Markets Economics Industries Tech Politics Businessweek Opinion

Opinion
Amanda Little
Columisst

The Preppers Were Right All Along

Once the domain of end-of-timers and right-wing radicals, the survivalist mindset is pushing into the mainstream thanks to rising climate-change disasters and civil unrest

November 6, 2022 at 7:00 AM CST

Bloomberg.com

Figure 63: The preppers were right all along!

During the collapse, government regulations on weapons, use of your property, almost every law, will be disregarded as people rightly focus on survival. After the first bad collapse, regulations on personal property and anything that stands in the way of preparing for collapse survival will be widely, ruthlessly if necessary, refused.

The best change from the Age of Collapse for Americans will be the death of the Perverted Triangle. The top villains of the Perverted Triangle will survive, but most survivors will be more interested in prosecuting them when the collapse is over rather than welcoming them back into power.

The Founding Fathers designed the best system of limited government yet devised, especially with the Bill of Rights and Thirteenth and Fourteenth Amendments. The Perverted Triangle subverted the Constitution, but Article V is still there to get our Natural Rights and limited, constitutional government back. Thirty-four state legislatures can save our country thanks to Article V. If they can do it before the first bad collapse strikes, they may save tens or hundreds of millions of Americans. The Constitutional Alliance[8] is feasible, a draft plan for the many reforms needed. Term limits to stop the career politicians is an easy, obvious reform that 87 percent of American's already support.[9] Amendments to force the Supreme Court to stop ignoring the clear meaning and intent of the Ninth and Tenth Amendments and enforce them is another obvious must-do.[10]

It is our duty when disgusted with our government and "the Right of the People to alter or to abolish it, and to institute new Government."[11]

If the US can get a Convention of the States to pass term limits, force the Supreme Court to enforce the Ninth and Tenth Amendments, eliminate the Perverted Triangle, then social and welfare programs can be phased out or approved by constitutional amendments. Natural Rights can again be protected instead of abused. With governments focused on their proper role of protecting us from deadly threats we cannot handle on our own, our odds of collapse survival will rise. Local governments can do more or fewer social programs as their citizens prefer, and the country can reunite at the national level, avoid civil war, and work toward the best possible capabilities for surviving the Age of Collapse. That is a lot of ifs. These big political reforms are unfortunately unlikely to happen until a collapse wakes the silent majority up. So my key prayer is that the first collapse is not too bad, so we can rebuild with a Convention of States and resolve to fix our perverted government and adapt to survive the Age of Collapse.

If the Perverted Triangle remains in power in the US, then the best course of action for most Americans may be secession.

Per the Declaration of Independence, the US Constitution (Ninth Amendment), the most fundamentally American principles of freedom we hold dear, and fought a war of independence to achieve, we have Natural Rights to live in freedom with strictly limited government.[12] Natural Rights do not have to be listed in the Constitution because that document specifies the very few powers and rights we did delegate government to act on. No US government can legally steal your money to give to someone else or force you to have health insurance or dictate the height and width of stair treads in your house. Most state constitutions also list this priority and retention of Natural Rights to freedom and liberty, regardless of whether or not a Natural Right is spelled out in the Constitution. Any task not listed in the US Constitution the federal government cannot act on. The right to "alter or abolish" an unjust and abusive government is an absolutely retained Natural Right—it is the number one, top priority, the hallmark of America. We The People retain top authority, we will not be slaves to government, and we can abolish and change it, or leave it—states can secede.[13] Government is absolutely limited to the few powers and areas of action we specify via the US Constitution. We have retained and have to exercise our Natural Right to throw off the Perverted Triangle or States may have to secede from the unconstitutional United States of America.[14]

It is "Common Sense"[15] in looking at the abomination of American government and our legal system today that the divided citizens of the current unconstitutional US need to "dissolve the political bands which have connected them with another"[16] and abolish the unconstitutional US and the Perverted Triangle. If we can eliminate divisive and unconstitutional social laws and programs at the federal and state level, limit the now unconstitutional federal government to its proper role, we can avoid the rift and stay united at the national level, with freedom to disagree and live as we prefer at the local level. If not, we must peacefully divorce and separate. So if the Perverted Triangle survives into the Age of Collapse, Americans should move forward with TEXIT and other secession movements to get out of the unconstitutional US. Hopefully, the Constitutional Alliance[17] can force a return of the Ninth and Tenth Amendments and limited federal government that allows maximum personal liberty and freedom. If not, we'll be much better off in smaller, diverse, allied nations. If we stay on the present course as a divided nation, we face the prospects of violent civil war and far worse likelihood of surviving the continuing WMD attacks and collapse disasters we face in the Age of Collapse with the irresponsible Perverted Triangle in charge.[18]

If Texas does have to secede and other states secede and join, the new nation could adopt the US Constitution and actually follow it. It could be called the Constitutional United States (CUS). Texas, and eventually other states that join and parts of other states that break off and join the CUS, would not leave the US Constitution, but leave the currently perverted, unconstitutional US government.

The unconstitutional US Armed Forces would be glad to keep military bases in Texas, along with Texas manpower and financial support. Texas ranks very high in military participation per capita. Guess where you find the lowest per capita participation in the unconstitutional US military (recruits as a percent of eighteen- to twenty-four-year-olds)? The District of Columbia, seat of federal power.[19] If the

Union cannot be saved by a return of limited, constitutional government, then Texas and the CUS can fully back the US Constitution and continue to support and serve in the unconstitutional US military. But if the Perverted Triangle blocks this, then, in the ultimate irony, the CUS could ally with another big, friendly military system: TX or the CUS could petition to join the Commonwealth of Nations. Canada is part of the Commonwealth. Texas, along with most or all of the Midwest, eastern Oregon, the Jefferson State (northern CA), Vermont, and others—the CUS—would pose no threat to the unconstitutional US; we would be allies. I've served with Canadian and British generals, and they, like their entire military, are first-class. The UK has nuclear weapons, so Texas and the CUS would also have a nuclear umbrella. Regardless of how TEXIT plays out, there should be no "civil war," no big battles between warring states or nations.

As a retired Air Force Colonel, I may lose a big retirement paycheck if Texas secedes, but I am all for TEXIT because this bold action could force the federal government to follow the Constitution, obey the Ninth and Tenth Amendments, which prohibit most of the socialist and Big Government programs that drive the divisions in our country. I believe that Texas seceding, likely followed by other states and parts of them over time, will force a return to constitutional federal government. I'd like to remain a United States citizen, but I'm backing TEXIT as far as necessary because the only US worth belonging to is one that follows our Constitution and protects our Natural Rights and prioritizes citizen's lives.

Once we have a constitutional US government back, we need to continually guard and fight against the return of unconstitutional Big Government and social regulations and welfare programs that divide the country, destroy families and responsibility, contribute to civilization collapse, and reduce our chances of surviving a collapse. But we must have very strong government for national security, controlling AI and WMD technologies, protecting the environment, defending us against threats we cannot handle on our own, while staying out of private matters, not interfering with our Natural Rights.[20]

To keep Americans united on foreign policy and national security, we need to divorce on social and domestic policy at the national and state levels. The federal government must obey the Ninth and Tenth Amendments and limit its activities to national security, foreign policy, and the very few constitutionally authorized actions like the US Post Office. States should also abandon Big Government social policies at the state level that divide and violate our retained Natural Right to be left alone in freedom. If we are to avoid secession, counties refusing state laws, dissolution, and civil war, the way ahead must be limited government at the national and state level, with only local governments allowed to engage on divisive social issues. As an Arizona

Supreme Court Justice wrote, "The provisions of the Ninth, Tenth, and Fourteenth Amendments demonstrate a clear preference for leaving decision-making with local governments as long as that doesn't result in threats to individual autonomy."[21]

The US needs to stop spending a trillion dollars for a clash of military forces overseas, abandon its world's policeman role, and focus on Prompt Global Strike with conventional or nuclear weapons to interdict enemy WMD, with smaller overseas forces backed by a return of battlefield nuclear weapons. Most defense resources (at a much lower cost) must be focused on homeland defense and collapse recovery capability so fewer citizens die when the WMD attacks cannot be prevented.[22]

In the Age of Collapse, we must have an alliance of all responsible nation-states to effectively control AI and prevent or interdict WMD attacks. The key to this much better, safer (for the US, other nations, and the planet) world order is to stop trying to control or defeat China, but befriend them. This is doable once we abandon our wrong, suicidal interference in Taiwan. China can then become our ally in our worldwide fight against dangerous rogue countries, terrorists, individuals with WMD, and uncontrolled AI.

Economic activity and where people live will be very different for most survivors in the Age of Collapse. Most big cities will likely be abandoned and partially or largely destroyed in a collapse. We should not rebuild them. Overall there will be far less national and international trade; economic activity and sourcing will be far more local. The pressures of continuing WMD attacks and collapse disasters will force us to be more rural, more sustainable agriculture, more "county-states"[23] with largely local sourcing and economic activity.

Biologists Daniel Brooks and Salvatore Agosta, writing in *A Darwinian Survival Guide: Hope for the Twenty-First Century*, noted that "If we are reduced to a single instinct, it will be the instinct to survive."[24]

Ophuls recommends that we preserve tools and materials to reconstitute civilization post-collapse.[25] The survival communities will do this, preserving tools, seeds, expertise. The Collapse Survivor App has the complete contents of Wikipedia on it, accessible without any Internet or cell phone service.

Collapses will halt international trade, and even shipments over long distances within nation-states. Post-collapse, some surviving companies will try to rebuild international sourcing, but this time with significant inventories to reduce collapse vulnerabilities and strong preference for local sourcing. Most nations may institute big tariffs to promote local production of essential goods that are less vulnerable to a collapse. Global, multinational firms may not reemerge. Small local firms won't produce huge/complex items on their own, but they can network with other not too far away firms and produce goods needed. International trade for essential survival items and just-in-time inventories should give way to local sourcing and stockpiling of key survival goods.[26]

> **In the Age of Collapse, we need "economics as if survival mattered."**
>
> —John Michael Greer, *The Wealth of Nature: Economics as if Survival Mattered*

With the ever-present threat of WMD attacks and another collapse, businesses should try to avoid complexity as much as possible. Favor higher cost, but more locally maintainable, resilient economic activity. "Keep It Simple Stupid" is a key operating principle at Fortitude Ranch. Our three key operating principles are respect Murphy's Law (if something can go wrong, it will), Keep It Simple Stupid, and adapt. Businesses also need to keep operations and sourcing as simple, local, and adaptable as possible.

Reliability and sustainability are vital to survival, far more important than lowest cost production. Communities and perhaps local governments might ban the sale of cheaper products that undercut vital local suppliers, threatening their economic survival and the community's ability to have vital local sources of supply in a collapse. Economics in the Age of Collapse must be based not on profit maximization but "economics as if survival mattered."[27]

Microgrids will be built in the Age of Collapse to supplement or replace huge regional/national electrical grids. Microgrids are local systems of distributed and shared electric energy sources that can operate in parallel to bigger commercial grids or independently.[28] A massive electric grid is too large, vulnerable, difficult to protect in the Age of Collapse.

Economic activity and housing needs to shift away from big cities. Agriculture and water and energy systems need to be more sustainable, resilient, survivable at local levels of organization and governance. If rural areas don't have to support distant big urban centers, we can have more sustainable agriculture, less industrialized agriculture, and less transportation energy waste.

Some of the earlier recommended collapse preparedness measures were considered impossible to pursue until a collapse occurs and people understand and now support the changes. International travel will have to be curtailed, with requirements of secure lockdown for days before/after arrival for plenty of time to verify, double-check, physically confirm identities of travelers, and to be sure no deadly virus or some WMD is not in transit. This does not need to be bad, prisonlike. There could be a new industry of "Transit Resorts"—places near airports/ports/major ground border crossings where travelers spend their three or more days of preemptive quarantine vacationing or working. Their in-country friends/family/work associates can enter the Transit Resorts with them to spend the days together. International ocean travel will boom with millions now choosing to switch to luxury ocean cruise ships, where your quarantine time is served while crossing the ocean.

Most companies and organizations won't survive a bad collapse because of too many key associates killed, data backup that does not survive a collapse,[29] and key assets and facilities looted or destroyed. Surviving companies will adapt to the Age of Collapse, figure out that normal "business continuity" plans that assume people come to work and law and order exists are not enough, and finally adopt business collapse survival plans and procedures.

Most frivolous products and services will no longer have much demand in the Age of Collapse. That is to say, most companies operating in the US pre-collapse will not be needed post-collapse, regardless of whether or not they survive. As explained in the chapter on why the US must abandon its horrible policy of defending Taiwan, China has an economy that largely produces goods essential for survival and basic products and services, manufacturing that will be in demand post-collapse. The US has an economy that largely produces entertainment and fashion, movies and IT—all worthless during a collapse, and of little or no value throughout the Age of Collapse. Nor will there be worldwide demand for Alphabet (Google), Amazon, Apple, Meta (Facebook), Microsoft, the huge US companies that produce products and services of no value during a collapse and little to no (or even negative) value in the Age of Collapse.

Most of the current US GDP is worthless in the Age of Collapse. The US will not be the world's leading economy in the Age of Collapse. With our current state of unpreparedness and grotesque, irresponsible government, the US is likely to be a basket case after the first bad collapse.

Companies will also have to adapt to fewer people interested in working long hours or sacrificing as much to climb the corporate ladder or achieve big salaries.

Our environment could be vastly improved from the drop in human population and shift from dense, urban cities to most people living in sparsely populated rural and suburban areas, isolated small cities in "county-states."

Another powerful reason to favor rural, low-tech, sustainable agriculture-focused county-states in the Age of Collapse is to avoid the attention of superintelligent AGI if this worst possible disaster occurs. The arguments of leading AI experts that humans have no chance of controlling AGI and the gross complicity and irresponsibility of governments in allowing this AGI disaster suggest that the best strategy for some humans to survive is to pose absolutely no threat or harm to

AGI systems when they take over. This is the Fortitude Ranch defensive strategy: stay put on our remote properties, just farm and pose no threat or interest to ruling AGI systems. Hope that AGI sees us as harmless, worthless rural rats, not worth their attention.

The global warming problem will be solved if there is a bad collapse that halts most industrial production for months or years, and kills off a few billion humans. Even without a big worldwide collapse lasting over a year, a series of small collapse disasters could achieve the transitions needed and yield a smaller human population with far less big cities, industrial pollution, and energy waste.

Despite the huge decline in human population from the collapses in the early years of the Age of Collapse, we need policies and people committed to promoting a smaller human footprint and less environmental burden for the planet. We must avoid densely populated huge cities. If we cease living in densely packed big cities, we don't need industrial agriculture. People in sparsely populated rural areas can grow their own food, or buy the surplus of nearby farms and ranches. Sustainable agriculture[30] with natural fertilizers and crop rotations, environmentally friendly land management, not imported nitrogen and fertilizers and pesticides, is more labor intensive, but sustainable and survivable in the next collapse. Sustainable farming, and much less long-distance food shipments, are far more feasible when humans turn back to largely rural populations, not urban.[31]

Patrick Ophuls argues that "the enormous 'productivity' of industrial agriculture is a sham. It is a machine for converting ten calories of fossil-fuel energy into one calorie of food."[32] The imported inputs, fertilizers and pesticides, huge farming equipment and transportation, processing of food for long distance shipment, requires far more energy than the final, processed, packaged, shipped food output provides.

Another big reason to favor limited human population on our planet and far better treatment of our environment is to avoid provoking people (and AGI) from wanting to kill off humanity to save the planet. With individuals able to modify a deadly virus or develop and release other types of WMD, we want less incentive for dedicated environmentalists to kill people or provoke superintelligent AGI to reason that there are too many humans for the planet and therefore it needs to wipe out a few billion.

It is odd that the Age of Collapse seems to favor changes that environmentalists have pushed for, largely unsuccessfully, for decades. But since survival in the Age of Collapse forces you back to rural farming and living sustainably with nature rather than industrial agriculture, and destroys or reduces densely populated big cities, reducing human population, the environmentalist objectives will be achieved. Yes, farming can also destroy the environment if we plow up everything, deforest, exploit topsoil rather than farm sustainably. Civilizations have collapsed from such ecological destruction. With fewer humans on Earth in the Age of Collapse than we have today, and less ability to do industrial style agriculture, the environment and other species should have it much better.

Many Americans deny global warming and other problems not because they believe the data is lacking or don't care about environmental damage, but because they know it will be abused as an excuse for the Perverted Triangle to add more taxes, government programs, bureaucrats, regulations, and lawsuits. If citizens did not rightly fear Big Government and lawyers' abuse of power, there would be more support for reasonable actions to address environmental problems.

A collapse provides not just a wakeup call to change, from the never ending WMD threats in the Age of Collapse, constant lethal pressure to shift the focus of humanity and civilization from the cycle of maximizing wealth and then decadence, huge government bureaucracy and welfare programs, civilization collapse, to focus on satisfying just essential needs, staying alive. Fortunately, this could be a better quality of life without all the work and economic production devoted to frivolous luxuries, the rat race, and the interference and abuse of government.

In *Small Is Beautiful: Economics as if People Mattered*, E. F. Schumacher rejected the self-defeating characteristics of Western maximum production economics in favor of smaller, more environmentally and people-friendly ways of production. Like Stoics and Buddhists, Schumacher urged acquiring only materials for human needs, not frivolous "wants." Rather than maximizing profit at the cost of eliminating jobs, automating every step of production to eliminate human craftsmanship, production in the largest possible factories for maximum economies of scale, Schumacher proposed economic models that considered impacts on the environment and the quality of people's lives.[33] Schumacher's philosophy is one of "enoughness," producing what we need to meet human needs and limit environmental damage, save limited resources for future generations, not maximum production of every conceivable item with advertisements and influencers and governments all urging maximum production and consumption of largely unnecessary products.

The world will experience massive changes in government, probably fewer nation-states, more dictators and warlords after the first bad collapse, and as disasters continue in the Age of Collapse. We've had city-states and nation-states. The Age of Collapse should favor rural county-states as the locus of community and government, "Small is Beautiful" economies, with people behaving better toward each other and the environment.[34]

Indeed, this is what Washington, Adams, Jefferson (all farmers first and foremost in their occupation and philosophy of life), most of the Founding Fathers had in mind—citizens living their lives as they choose, active in their local community and government, with the federal government limited to national security and foreign policy and a very few, absolutely limited central economic functions like the Post Office.

Densely populated big cities are inherently more violent than rural areas.[35] As biologists Brooks and Agosta explained, "Humans are capable of interpersonal violence but are not usually violent as a species, especially at low population densities and when escape is possible. But at high densities with no escape option, humans, like all animals, are capable of considerable violence."[36] Added to this, cities are "centers of high population density with low kinship ties. . ."[37] Ask a veteran who served in the Iraq or Afghanistan counterinsurgencies, or a prepper, and they will tell you the worst place to be in a collapse is a big city.

As Ophuls lamented, "So why don't we prudently check the growth of our civilization and prune back our level of complexity to achieve resilience and sustainability? Alas, we never have."[38] But the Age of Collapse will destroy cities, industrial agriculture won't function (or much of any manufacturing until we've adapted), and survivors will be those who are growing food and raising livestock in largely rural areas. Complex just-in-time delivery, highly interdependent, internationally integrated, complex economies with tremendous transportation and energy costs, are not going to function in a collapse, and are unlikely to be rebuilt in an age of continuing collapses. We are going to be forced to rural living, local sourcing—and that will bring huge energy savings, environmental improvements, and hopefully revolutionary change, evolution, and improvement in human behavior.

While human survival is arguably the most important topic in the world, very few write on this, largely just preppers and environmentalists. Brooks and Agosta note that "Darwinism taught that species cope with change by changing- something humanity needs to follow now. . . . Paradoxically, humans are creatures of habit who do not like to change their behavior. . . ."[39]

The lessons of history and common sense should leave no doubt—the path to changing human behavior to achieve happiness and survival in the Age of Collapse is not going to be one dictated or commanded by government elites. As "philosopher Karl Popper pointed out in *The Open Society and Its Enemies*, all utopian social engineering projects resort to violence to keep the population on the proper path to the preferred utopia. . . ."[40] We can encourage and educate, but not successfully force with government power the changes in behavior and economic activity required in the Age of Collapse.

We will make lots of mistakes in our adapting and evolving. This is the other essential reason to favor local communities making decisions, never mandating or imposing them from higher level governments. Brooks and Agosta's *Darwinian*

Survival Guide recommends that our "transition to survivability" focus on "maximizing diversity at the grassroots coupled with accommodating essential institutions to generate viable networks of cooperating communities."[41]

Like many biologists and environmentalists, Brooks and Agosta blame big cities and overpopulation: "Humanity is . . . at risk because humans have used technology during the past six hundred generations to construct sedentary and increasingly urbanized lifestyles."[42]

Scientist Elinor Ostrom argued that small communities can manage their local resources well, as they have for thousands of years. She was awarded the 2009 Sveriges Riksbank Prize in Economic Sciences in Memory of Alfred Nobel for demonstrating that "selfishness is not the only driving force in human behavior within a community, and given the right conditions, self-organized 'grassroots' governance systems can be effective at managing resources without overexploiting them."[43]

In the Age of Collapse, people will focus on survival and quality of life, less on achieving fame and fortune or amassing vast possessions that are rarely used and not needed. Like people with a terminal medical condition and a few years to live, focus is understandably short-term and on the most important things.

When you have suffered through a collapse, and expect another collapse at any time, you will probably want to really make every day count. Everyone will focus on collapse survival capability, but that's not too hard once you've made it through the first collapse and are living in a safe place or part of a survival community. If you live at or belong to a survival community in a rural place, crops and some farm animals established, reliable water, food and ammo stockpiled, enough people and professional staff to keep good collapse security, you're good to go. The majority of your time and attention can be devoted to family, friends, essential work, quality of life.[44]

To get an idea of how people might choose to live differently in the Age of Collapse, with a death sentence hanging over us, we ran a Collapse Survivor App training simulation on an "end of Earth" scenario with a huge incoming asteroid. In the exercise simulation, a huge asteroid was inbound, impossible to deflect, and would throw up so much debris into the atmosphere that scientists around the world agreed the sun would be blocked for a decade plus, killing all plant life, wildlife, almost all people dying off. This scenario was not a normal Collapse Survivor App survival training exercise figuring out how to stay alive, but largely thinking about what you would do with only a week left to live. The exhibit on the right shows what most Collapse Survivor players chose to do in this scenario with just a short time left to live:

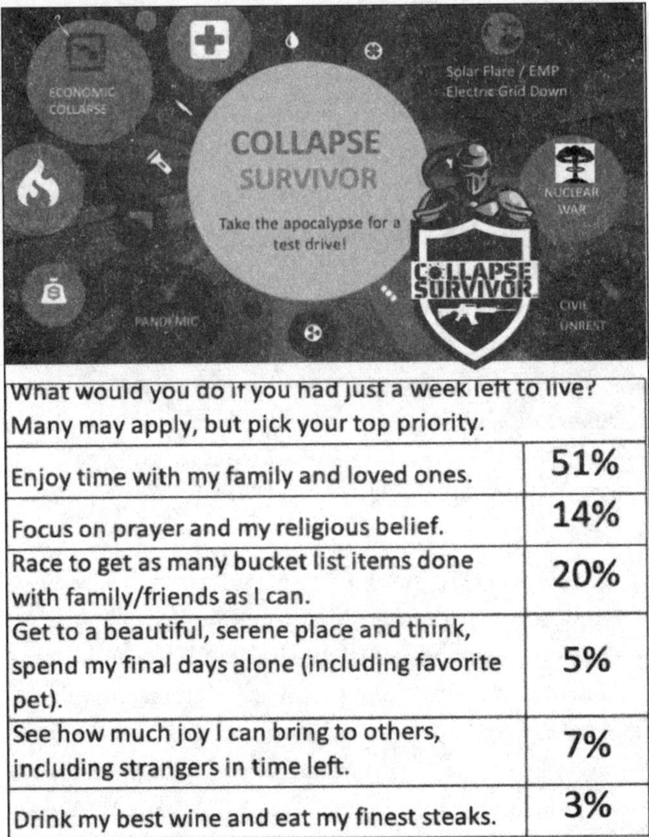

What would you do if you had just a week left to live? Many may apply, but pick your top priority.	
Enjoy time with my family and loved ones.	51%
Focus on prayer and my religious belief.	14%
Race to get as many bucket list items done with family/friends as I can.	20%
Get to a beautiful, serene place and think, spend my final days alone (including favorite pet).	5%
See how much joy I can bring to others, including strangers in time left.	7%
Drink my best wine and eat my finest steaks.	3%

Figure 64: End of Earth asteroid strike poll question: what would you do if a week left to live?

The "Lessons Learned" podcast video on this simulation is available in the webnotes.[45]

If there was not still the high-risk of more collapse disasters coming, most survivors would want to "get back to normal" after a collapse, continue the pursuit of careers and wealth. This would probably mean continuing the cycle of overpopulating, over taxing the environment, waging wars. The rise and fall of civilizations would begin again.

We will probably never get back to any sense of security in the Age of Collapse. WMD attacks and collapse disasters could be coming often, perhaps every year, despite best efforts and full worldwide cooperation to try and prevent or preemptively destroy them. This will very likely yield major, permanent shifts in how people choose to live their lives and what they focus on. If we act responsibly and rationally we can achieve big improvements in personal behavior and attitudes that ironically could make the Age of Collapse the finest era of humanity.[46]

For many people, getting back to farming, collapse survival gardening, building and creating things with hand tools, using "pioneer" skills, being in touch with nature again, will be a blessing and a big improvement in quality of life. We will still have manufacturing, and smaller size cities may continue in the Age of Collapse. If they stay small in total size (maybe under fifty thousand), they may be supportable and survivable in a collapse. But whether living in rural areas or smaller cities, our attitudes and behaviors need to adapt and change for the better.

I suspect far fewer Americans will want huge McMansions. The capital and time Americans put into lavish, giant homes[47] will probably be cut way back due to focus on more valuable pursuits. McMansions are also unlikely to be preferred because massive homes in a city or suburb are unlikely to be useful or survive looting and marauding in a bad collapse until we have built up the preparations and security to reliably check marauders.

The age of opulence, decadence, big government bureaucracy and welfare programs, conspicuous consumption (the final state of civilization collapse) may end—to the benefit of us all. Quality of life could very well improve in the Age of Collapse. Most survivors will reject the "rat race," the grueling, pointless cycle of trying to get income beyond what you really need, buying more "stuff" you'll rarely use in your massive house.

The Covid-19 pandemic and the largely unrelated political protest and violence across the country in 2020–2023 led to millions leaving major cities for a safer and better quality of life in rural areas. "Tiny home" popularity surged. While it was a very mild pandemic (much less than 1percent lethal) compared to our future of H5N1 and bioengineered pandemics (with double-digit lethality), it prompted many to reconsider their priorities in life. For a better quality of life, millions left big cities for rural life. Metropolitan counties with big cities over one million lost 750,000 residents in 2021, 650,000 in 2022, and 550,000 in 2023, while rural populations grew.[48] The exodus from the high costs and regulations of Big Government California also fueled the trend.

We saw this leaving the "rat race" and move to safer rural areas trend at Fortitude Ranch. More and more people contacted us not for normal membership (two weeks of vacation visits, otherwise only coming out for a collapse), but wanting to live at remote Fortitude Ranch locations full-time. We thus added "Fortitude Village" to our offering. People can buy or lease land adjacent to the Fortitude Ranch survival community to live full-time in a more peaceful and pleasant environment, with the collapse time security of the Fortitude Ranch survival community.

We should become more "stoic" to deal with the stress and challenges of the Age of Collapse and to become better humans. Stoic philosophy emphasizes controlling your wants, living frugally in accordance with nature, focusing on virtue and inner resilience. Stoics seek to control their thoughts and not lust for things they do not need or worry about external problems and threats they cannot control. This allows not just peace of mind, but better ability to focus on things you can do to improve yourself and do good. True Stoics believe that building their virtues of courage, reason, working for justice, controlling wants and fears, and helping others is the best way to find happiness and contentment. Stoics do not participate in the rat race, worry about popularity, or strive for monetary wealth. Stoics know that if we control our wants and fears, stop worrying about things we can't control, improve ourselves, we can lead much happier and better lives, become better persons.[49]

Stoicism emphasizes living in the present and making the most of each moment, not dwelling on past problems or worrying about the future. Post-collapse, some may focus on rebuilding their lives, the entertainment and luxury they had before and race to get it back. But many, most I would hope, will reject this and instead choose an arguably better philosophy for the Age of Collapse—focusing on the present, on the essentials for survival and enjoying the present, helping others cope and survive. The Fortitude Ranch motto since its launch a decade ago is "Prepare for the Worst, Enjoy the Present."

The second century CE Roman Emperor Marcus Aurelius was a Stoic. His book *Meditations* explained how to live a Stoic life. Marcus Aurelius reigned in a time of attacks from German tribes, rebellions in northern Italy and Egypt, and a plague. In sum, he lived with collapse threats. Rachana Kamtekar, an expert on Stoicism, summarized Marcus Aurelius's philosophy as understanding that "we are tiny and temporary fragments in the cosmos, that death takes us all in the end, that we ought to live purposively rather than like mechanical toys."[50] We should live responsibly, with purpose, improving ourselves and doing good for others—not worrying about popularity or struggling to build a fortune.

A similar philosophy to Stoicism, that fits well with the Age of Collapse, is Victor Frankl's "logotherapy." Frankl suffered and survived three years in German concentration camps, including Auschwitz. Frankl believes that the primary human drive is searching for meaning in life, which is critical for psychological well-being and survival. You can discover meaning in life by creating something useful, doing good deeds, by experiencing something or someone, knowing true love, nobly standing up to unavoidable suffering. Frankl observed that people who could find some meaning, even amid the horrendous suffering of a Nazi concentration camp, were the ones who survived. In his book, *Man's Search for Meaning*, Frankl explained how people can find meaning in accomplishing some good, creating something, helping and loving others, even while you're in hell on Earth.

Like Stoics, you can make a decision to face catastrophe and suffering with courage and dignity, refusing to succumb to despair. No matter what, you have the choice of how you respond to life's challenges. You can find some way to do good, help someone else—and take great pleasure and satisfaction in that, despite the overall suffering.[51]

Two quotes from Frankl are especially relevant for us in dealing with the stress and challenge of on-going disasters in the Age of Collapse—and learning how we must adapt and improve:

"We . . . may also find meaning in life even when confronted with a hopeless situation, when facing a fate that cannot be changed. For what then matters is to bear witness to the uniquely human potential at its best, which is to transform a personal tragedy into triumph, to turn one's predicament into a human achievement."

"The truth—that love is the ultimate and the highest goal to which man can aspire. Then I grasped the meaning of the greatest secret that human poetry and human thought and belief have to impart: The salvation of man is through love and in love."

The Stoics, Frankl, Ophuls, the *Darwinian Survival* authors, and other scientists and philosophers writing on this topic of human evolution/improvement/survival insist that human behavior must evolve to be more humane, more loving, tolerant, and forgiving to improve our chances of survival.[52] This is not a very concrete or convincing argument to make in the current condition of opulence and welfare, entertainment and consumerism, social media hysteria, horrendous politics, and our final stage of civilization collapse. It should be far more understandable and persuasive in the Age of Collapse.

Humans do need to become more loving, more family responsible, kind and caring, to raise our odds of survival in the Age of Collapse.[53] I may be wrong, but I believe there will always be inherently bad, evil people, with no chance of love or nurturing, and definitely not government programs, making them good. More intact, complete, and responsible families will reduce the number of bad people—another reason to prevent perverted government social and welfare programs. But bad, evil people will always be among us, and cannot be allowed to kill, so I'm still in favor of executing the death sentence for evil people. We clearly need to have less evil people in an era when individuals have the capability to make WMD.

Another way the stresses, threats, and challenges of the Age of Collapse could improve us is to give real impetus and meaning to the vital quality and importance of responsibility—especially family responsibility.

In a socialist "Nanny State," you don't have to take care of your parents, it's no problem to divorce and abandon your children, or not bother getting married to begin with. Government welfare and entitlement programs are available, you don't need to bother earning an income for yourself, providing for a family, or caring for your parents.

In the first collapse, some people who lack it now will again have and feel family responsibility.

We need to do a much better job of educating people, especially in teaching them responsibility, the vital importance of good character and conduct.

In the initial century of the United States, there were many guides to good conduct, and Americans generally worked to be good citizens, responsible and hardworking people of good character. The "Maxims For Young Men," published in the late 1800s, summarized the virtues that Franklin, Washington, many of the Founding Fathers and best Americans worked to follow.

Figure 65: Maxims for Young Men and Women

- Never be idle. If your hands cannot be usefully employed, attend to the cultivation of your mind.
- Always speak the truth.
- Make few promises.
- Live up to your engagements.
- Have no very intimate friends unless well tried. *("Well tried" means tested, highly trusted.)*
- Keep your own secrets if you have any.
- When you speak to a person, look him in the face.
- Good company and good conversation are the very sinews of virtue.
- Good character is above all things else. *(This means having good character and "following" good character principles is more important than anything else.)*
- Never listen to loose or idle conversation. *(Don't tell gossip about people, pass on rumors.)*
- You had better be poisoned in your blood than your principles. *(Better to be poisoned/dead then to give up your principles, your good character and conduct.)*
- Your character cannot be essentially injured, except by your own acts.
- If anyone speaks evil of you, let your life be so virtuous that none will believe him.
- Drink no intoxicating liquors.
- Ever live, misfortune excepted, within your income.
- When you retire to bed, think over what you have done during the day.
- Never speak lightly of religion.
- Make no haste to be rich if you would prosper.[54] *(Prosperity here means a good life, not huge wealth. Do not either try to get wealth fast or focus on maximizing wealth.)*

continued on following page

- Small and steady gains give competency with a tranquility of mind.
- Never play at any kind of game. *(At the time when this was written the danger of starving to death, wars, et cetera meant that "wasting" time with play was unwise. This is not really applicable at this instant, but will be at times in a collapse and perhaps most of the time in the Age of Collapse. Many Americans do spend far too much time on mindless and often destructive TV, video games, and social media.)*
- Avoid temptation, through fear that you may not withstand it. *(Don't let yourself get into situations—which friends may lead you to—where you will be exposed to bad situations like people smoking and taking drugs, someone breaking the law, et cetera)*
- Earn your money before you spend it. *(Invest and save.)*
- Never run into debt unless you see a way to get out.
- Never borrow if you can possibly avoid it.
- Be just before you are generous. *(Giving money to someone who does not deserve it may not be a wise or good thing to do.)*
- Keep yourself innocent if you would be happy. *(If you do bad things you'll know it—and your conscience will bother you, you won't be happy.)*
- Save when you are young to spend when you are old.
- Never think that which you do for religion is time or money misspent. *(Religion teaches some good values and behaviors like being kind to others, the golden rule, et cetera)*
- Let Honesty and Industry be thy constant companion.

These maxims are from the 1800s, when times were tough and you needed to work from sunup to beyond sundown; with little time for games or frivolity. Some updating is needed, but we must have character training and improvement to pull society out of our downward spiral of increasing bad conduct and irresponsibility. Families are of course the best positioned and suited to teach and enforce good character.[55]

We must teach and coach kids to invest in themselves, learn responsibility and integrity and other traits of good character, and lead a meaningful life in pursuit of good pursuits and achievements. Organizations like the Boy Scouts, Girl Scouts, Civil Air Patrol, and Future Farmers of America do work to promote good character and responsibility in our youth.[56] Military academies train officers of good character with rigid adherence to an honor code: "We will not lie, steal or cheat, nor tolerate among us anyone who does." But when the president and senior elected officials are professional liars, lawyers make fortunes lying in court and twisting laws and case citations for their clients to escape justice for their crimes, promoting honesty to youth is extremely difficult today.

Families and local community groups and schools should teach maxims of good conduct and character. The federal and state governments should not be teaching virtues, other than demonstrating them in the good conduct of public officials. If we get term limits and end the career politicians of the Perverted Triangle, it will be far easier to teach responsibility and good character. Public schools should not get into sex and social issues that interfere with family-taught values. But local school districts can and should promote responsibility, good character and public service, teach values like the "Maxims for Young Men and Women," community service, encourage Civil Air and Ground Patrol membership, serving in the military.

We need to teach what the "pursuit of happiness" as written in the Constitution really means.[57] It was definitely not maximizing daily pleasure from any source, which is the norm most Americans pursue today. While Americans should be free to do whatever they like (as long as they don't harm others in the process), the purpose of life should not be pursuit of maximum fun/sex/pleasure, but happiness defined as a meaningful life, pursuing and living a life worth living. American youth today are more likely to learn "if it feels good do it" than the "Maxims for Young Men and Women" where pursuit of happiness is defined as a worthwhile, meaningful life. Raising a good family, enjoying good friends, building a business, serving a worthy cause, achieving your potential, many pursuits can yield a meaningful, satisfying, happy life. Youth pursuing this true, intended form of happiness are far less likely to engage in crime and violence, squander their talents and energy, and will lead far happier, fulfilled, meaningful lives. Teaching such values and responsibility in the modern era of luxury and decadence and the Perverted Triangle is very difficult. It will be much easier in the Age of Collapse.[58]

With your innate, Natural Right to freedom you could seek happiness as Tuskegee Institute Founder Booker T. Washington recommended in his book *Up from Slavery*: "Those who are happiest are those who do the most for others."[59] Or you may follow Ayn Rand's very different approach, the "virtue of selfishness," achieving your highest goals, living your life as you alone want to pursue it.[60]

I'm a fan of Ayn Rand, particularly in her demanding the right of individuals to refuse interference and subjugation by government or community dictates. But in the Age of Collapse we all must feel obligations and act on responsibilities to help provide for and protect our families and our local communities. If we are part of, dependent on, a nation-state for broader national security, then we also have a responsibility to support the nation-state. All Americans would support our government if it stayed properly focused on national security and protecting us from threats we cannot handle on our own. We should fortunately get this good, proper, limited government back after the first collapse or two, with the Convention of States and elimination of the Perverted Triangle.

Former Democratic governor, Public Policy Professor Richard Lamm cited historian Arnold Toynbee's warning that all great nations fall when they lose their original virtue, work ethic, and drive and "commit suicide." Lamm warns that "We want education without study, wealth without work, freedom without participation, and democracy without citizenship. We must self-correct or perish, for this is hardly a sustainable agenda. . . . Americans . . . have forgotten that rights and privileges require duties and responsibilities."[61]

The most important thing to promote individual responsibility is to abolish Big Government and the Nanny State, that undermine family and individual responsibility.

To survive and improve in the Age of Collapse, we cannot have the Perverted Triangle and national or state level socialism. The Nanny State, Big Government socialism is the arch enemy, the destroyer of individual responsibility, families, and family responsibility. If some people choose to continue Socialism or Communism at their local levels, that is their Natural Right. But for the vast majority of people, socialism and government and government control are wrong and destructive. Charity and helping those truly deserving assistance is needed in every community—but provided by volunteerism, groups like the Salvation Army, a Church, the Red Cross, or a local volunteer group—not mandated by law, coerced, exploited as a tool for politicians and government bureaucrats. Big Government and the Nanny State, socialism, must not be allowed at national or state levels, and pursued at local community levels only where people fully support and can shape and control it.[62]

With term limits and no more career politicians, far more, perhaps most adults can serve brief terms in government. Government will be far more responsive to the people, at local levels, with the state and national governments strictly limited to vital security and limited economic and environmental protection functions, not diverting resources/attention to divisive social issues, not needlessly violating Natural Rights. With more or most people serving short periods of work in government, as citizens, not career politicians, we will get far more community responsibility—but without the incentives or ability to use government as a force to amass power and coerce people.[63]

In the Age of Collapse we need each other more, depend on each other to survive a collapse. A key principle of Fortitude Ranch is that everyone serves guard duty, everyone. A blind elderly lady will serve, probably at night paired with a sighted guard. Our most skilled shooters and guards will be assigned the most critical guard posts and likely night duty, but we think it is important for community cohesion and individual feeling of self-worth, that everyone serves their community guard shift, everyone works and contributes.

Nothing could be further from Schumacher's noble *Small Is Beautiful: Economics as if People Mattered* or John Greer's *The Wealth of Nature: Economics as if Survival Mattered*[64] than the wretched huge AI companies working today to profit at the expense of not just our jobs, but our lives.

AI, even if limited to controlled Tool AI, is going to eliminate hundreds of millions, maybe billions of jobs. It will happen too fast on far too massive a scale for people to adjust. Hundreds of millions to billions of people's lives (fired workers and their families) will be ruined. The perverted proposals to just expand government bureaucracy and welfare programs to pay people not to work[65] are insane. It's not just the income loss, the insult of having to take welfare, the blow to dignity and self-worth that will result. In *Tightrope: Americans Reaching for Hope*, veteran *New York Times* journalists Nicholas Kristof and Sheryl WuDunn argue that the lack of meaningful, rewarding jobs has plunged America's working class into despair, drug addiction, and suicide.

Ophuls, cited many times before in this book, explains in *Plato's Revenge: Politics in the Age of Ecology*, that mankind's future requires rural living in harmony with nature, not trying to conquer it, with *Small Is Beautiful* economics, a simpler (and for most much happier) way of life, without big cities or big government.[66] This will require massive change in human behavior, improving our virtues—largely in line with Stoic, Buddhist principles outlined earlier. We must have limited government, economic production that does not destroy our environment, and maximum personal honor, duty, and responsibility.

Ophuls believes the solution to stop civilization collapse, the way to "allow humanity to thrive in reasonable numbers on a limited planet for millennia to come . . . would require a fundamental change in the ethos of civilization—to wit, the deliberate renunciation of greatness in favor of simplicity, frugality, and fraternity."[67] This is possible in the Age of Collapse if most of us become Stoics, living in county-states, perhaps associated with nation-states that cease trying to control citizens or wage war on other nation-states. This vital change in behavior can occur, prompted by the constraints and threats of the Age of Collapse.

While my expectation is that most American collapse survivors will be libertarian and oppose socialist government, there will be survivors with liberal points of view. Some may be communes. Let them do what they want as long as their citizens vote for it and don't trample the Natural Rights of those who don't want this. There is a wide band (not a narrow line) of gray area where personal freedom, your Natural Rights of private property and privacy and being left alone, can conflict with local government and majority desires to build a road, add a library, run a youth activities center. I hope local governments will stay out of social programs and charities, leaving this to private, voluntary groups. When these boundaries, gray areas, are decided at local levels, the losing side in the debate and vote has much better opportunity of getting the decision changed, accepting the policy, or voting with their feet to leave.[68] Real believers in America and the Constitution (Libertarians), have no objection to any individuals or voluntary groups pursuing whatever practices they want as long as it doesn't seriously harm us and they don't force it on us.

The Age of Collapse is an opportunity to make revolutionary improvements in our government, our economy, our environment, and ourselves.

The Age of Collapse can help us escape our evolutionary biases and become more responsible, tolerant and forgiving, helpful and loving, as we cooperate and work together to protect our planet and each other.

We will not give in to despair. We will survive, improve, and find meaning in life and quality of life, despite the constant specter of WMD and collapse.

Surviving in the Age of Collapse is going to require a lot more human restraint, toleration, forgiveness, discipline, responsibility and cooperation than we've ever had. The American form of very limited government and protection of Natural Rights of individuals is the best form of government to let people live in freedom and achieve good lives in the Age of Collapse. We can have differences in religious, social, and political views and stay unified at state and national levels by obeying the Ninth and Tenth Amendments and keeping Big Government absolutely limited to national security, homeland defense, and the very few specified economic and environmental programs approved. We can avoid the political wars of left and right, Democrat and Republican, urban and rural, that ruin and divide America today. We can unite at the national level for protection, and be very diverse and free, far happier at local levels where people can change and shape local government and move if they find a better community.

Can we convince people to adopt the morals of natural law, the strength of Stoics, the "Maxims for Young Men and Women," to put responsibility and good conduct first, not the pursuit of pleasure and wealth? In the Age of Collapse I believe we can. Yes it's very hard for humans to change. But periodic collapses will deliver not a shove or kick in the ass, but a bullet in the arm, experience with starvation and dead bodies, recurring hell on Earth to encourage strong contemplation and commitment to change.

A novel about people adapting and improving during a collapse, *Rohan Nation: Reinventing America after the 2020 Collapse*,[69] covered a survival community fighting off marauder attacks, forming a tight community of highly responsible, stoic members. They adapted to a very different and difficult way of life, but found great meaning and happiness and contentment in their achievements and the community they built. They adapted and created a better way of life.

Survival communities will help more of the middle class survive. That's why I founded Fortitude Ranch as an affordable, professional survival community,[70] to ensure my family and responsible, good, middle class Americans survive the collapse and can rebuild. The Perverted Triangle with their Continuity of Government plans will survive. But I don't want America rebuilt by just the most capable marauders and, worse, the disgusting career politicians surviving at our expense at Mount Weather.[71]

The current state of the despicable Perverted Triangle and despicable AI CEOs like Altman and Karp disgracing themselves and capitalism with their total disregard for human life gives a strong starting point to rally people against the current system. The first collapse will be a thunderous trumpet call to action that most survivors will respond to.

It will be hard for all of us to change our views. With my background I can easily be a tough Stoic, but tolerating liberals and socialists will be an unpleasant struggle. Everyone must adapt, compromise, and dedicate themselves to save humanity and our planet. The Age of Collapse can help force us to evolve our behavior and attitudes, compromise and tolerate different views of people—as long as they also respect our Natural Right to live as we choose when we are not harming others. We can find meaning in our lives and enjoy a great quality of life, true love, with Stoic living, responsible behavior and good character, protecting and caring for family and neighbors, working together to survive and thrive in the Age of Collapse.

Living as a responsible Stoic in a "small is beautiful" rural county-state, with loving family and friendly neighbors, could be a wonderful lifestyle. But it will not be too pleasant if you suffer endless WMD strikes and collapse disasters. It will not be survivable if superintelligent AGI is created and decides to exterminate all humans. We still need nation-states and a world alliance to control AI, prevent AGI, and fight WMD.

Nor can a nation-state survive in isolation in the Age of Collapse. Existing WMD capabilities and powerful new AI-generated WMD, and, if we fail to control AI, superintelligent AGI, will eliminate the ability of any nation-state to ignore the rest of the world and live in pleasant isolation. New Zealand might avoid fallout from superpower nuclear war, or human-to-human transmissible viruses if they quickly close borders and have great quarantine. But a nanotechnology gray goo that can traverse oceans or a cruise missile delivering a bioweapon, countless other WMD threats, can get to you anywhere.

While collapse threats and the need for AI control make the case for more international cooperation (intelligence sharing and prompt attacks to preempt WMD attacks), once a major worldwide collapse occurs, we may revert to every nation for itself. The world may revert to strong isolationism.

It is inherently uncertain, but the Age of Collapse, the constant threat of WMD, should pressure the world to come together to reduce/preempt/overcome WMD attacks. Controlling AI, especially, could be the catalyst for finally bringing nations around the world together to cooperate against these existential threats to all of us. Just as an alien invasion might pull nations and humanity together in a collective fight to survive, the Age of Collapse could bring an end to wars between nation-states as we cooperate to control AI, prevent and preempt WMD attacks, and survive.

Some collapses may only hit certain areas of Earth—allowing un- or less-impacted countries to rush in aid, in expectation that when they are clobbered by the next WMD attack and collapse, other nations will come help them.

World War II birthed the United Nations, but it has not achieved much cooperation and impact. The AICA and the Age of Collapse should yield far more cooperation and international assistance. If the US, Canada, China, Europe, Russia, India, Japan, and Australia commit to the AICA, which is very doable as explained earlier, we have great prospects for ending traditional nation-state wars and bringing the world together with our mutual goal of surviving the Age of Collapse.[72]

There is no fundamental reason for the US to be at war with Russia or China; though we spend a trillion dollars now annually on defense to prepare for war with them, and are in an AI Company CEO/Perverted Triangle promoted AI arms race with China that will likely kill all humans if not stopped soon. If the US stops provoking and interfering in China's civil war with Taiwan, and ceases NATO expansion that threatens Russia, it is very feasible to see future conflict with China and Russia eliminated. We can then probably get their cooperation on controlling/limiting/containing AI so it can't be leveraged by bad people to develop WMD or AGI-controlled efforts to eliminate people.[73] If the US/NATO/Russia/China/Japan/South Korea/Australia/India other great nations are no longer preparing for war against each other, defense spending can be reduced by an order of magnitude, possibly two.

Again quoting biologists Daniel Brooks and Salvatore Agosta, A *Darwinian Survival Guide; Hope for the Twenty-First Century*: "The universality of Darwinian evolution gives us substantial hope . . . if we proceed with the clear and certain knowledge that the way to survive is to change our behavior and prepare for change, not war."[74]

Get Updates, Corrections from online "Webnotes" for *Preparing to Survive in the Age of Collapse*

How a collapse unfolds, how people react to a collapse, and the aftermath of revolutionary changes as people reject fatal old ways and adapt to survive the Age of Collapse, is inherently, highly uncertain. Many of the subjective judgments in this book and speculations of what will transpire will be wrong.

These "webnotes" allow the book to be updated with better information and ideas. Because there will be errors, omissions, and changes I need to make later, these "webnotes," online "endnotes," will be updated periodically. They can be downloaded to read online or print at: https://collapsesurvivor.com/preparing-to-survive-in-the-age-of-collapse/.

We can handle the bad people and WMD with a worldwide alliance, the AI Control Alliance (AICA), to control AI and fight WMD. Unfortunately, the people and organizations who want to launch devastating attacks and collapse disasters will keep improving their capability to develop and release WMD. But as people and governments adapt to the Age of Collapse and do the food stockpiling and security force improvements, the numbers of people living in densely populated urban areas keeps falling, fewer and fewer WMD attacks and disasters will yield a collapse. If law and order is not lost, a collapse need not occur despite a horrific initial strike.[75]

There is another, now probably more likely development in the Age of Collapse: China could emerge as the world's superpower, and their model of one-party rule, with government ruthlessly controlling its citizens, might become the standard approach that nation-states run by self-serving government officials use. If this first collapse is one largely limited to the US, this is especially likely. Thanks to the Perverted Triangle, the US is now so vulnerable to a collapse that we may emerge as a basket case country. Our nuclear weapons can prevent China or Russia from invading us, but the US electric grid, a largely unprepared population, and our interference with nations worldwide make us the prime target. China is prepared right now to destroy the US because of our interference with Taiwan and our huge vulnerabilities.

Absolutely strong, ruthless governments could be the best way for most people to survive in the Age of Collapse. If you have total surveillance of people all the time, you know what they buy, where they are, everything they say and do, it's a lot harder to build an illegal WMD. China's president and Communist Party might prefer this to the AICA and the model proposed here for a relatively good Age of Collapse. For free people, this alternative of absolutely powerful Big Government controlling everything, monitoring everything people do, could be worse than a collapse.

This is painful to write, but the Perverted Triangle may be decisive evidence that democracy, even with the best possible Constitution to protect Natural Rights and limit abuse of government power, is an inherently flawed form of government. Majority rule and pandering career politicians may be a guarantee of abuse. The Perverted Triangle may have already permanently killed America's great limited government of Natural Rights by generating such partisan, powerful collective stupidity and effectively erasing key parts of the Constitution, eliminating limits to government with 99 percent of Americans clueless of the loss or that they are pawns of the political parties or ruling elite. AI's ability to manipulate and trick people will be exploited by career politicians and other members of the Perverted Triangle—as well as the big AI companies—to further misinform and promote their agendas, building collective stupidity so widespread, and entrenched that the unprepared masses and last vestiges of American Constitutional government will not survive the Age of Collapse.

The United States has three clear, obvious, must do *now* imperatives:

1. We must abandon our interference in China's affairs, stop provoking them and motivating their huge arms buildup and war, by abandoning our plans to assist Taiwan's defense
2. We must get worldwide control of Tool AI and prevent super-intelligent AGI, which requires agreement with China and an AI Control Alliance they are part of
3. Get a Convention of States to implement the Constitutional Alliance program of reforms to stop the Perverted Triangle and get Natural Rights and the Constitution's limits to government power back

The Han Chinese people on the island of Taiwan, a breakaway province of China, are not going to be slaughtered or enslaved. Like the formerly independent city-state of Hong Kong, they may have less freedom, but they will be alive and well when reunited with China. The US can be saved from a devastating nuclear exchange or destruction of our electric grid collapse. The world could be saved from a disastrous future of unlimited government with absolute power over people rather than the far better approach of a world AI Control Alliance if we can get China into the

AICA and become allies. The Perverted Triangle won't and can't make such a fast change. But President Trump could do this.[76]

Far left liberals, environmentalists, conservatives, libertarians, almost everyone on the planet—even most of the Perverted Triangle (the bureaucrats and lawyers)—can all agree on the vital need to regulate and control AI and completely prevent AGI. Without the US and China in something like the AICA, this will not happen. This WMD/existential/complete human extermination threat of AI and superintelligent AGI has the power to unite all factions in the US (except the AI companies and their purchased career politicians) and every country in the world in favor of controlling Tool AI and preventing AGI.

Biologists Brooks and Agosta, in their *Darwinian Survival Guide*, appear to have been writing about Alex Karp and Sam Altman, backed now by President Trump, when they wrote: "Our governance systems . . . long ago co-opted as instruments for amplifying personal power . . . became instruments by which individuals with sociopathic tendencies could expand their personal power at the expense of the general well-being of a population, helping them make a case for making war on the other groups . . ."[77]

It is indeed horrible for America and all humanity that President Trump today is backing the villains: Sam Altman, Alex Karp, and their self-serving AI arms race with China.

In June 2025, Palantir CEO Alex Karp said that the country needs to "run harder, run faster" in an "all-country effort" to develop more advanced AI models, insisting that "either we win or China will win."[78] This was one of the most blatant, wretched, self-serving lies in history. First, the notion that China would refuse international AI controls and we have no alternative to this arms race is wrong. Second, there is no way that the US can win a full speed ahead, all-country effort to build AI as fast as possible. The US, everyone, loses when AI generated WMD are released or superintelligent AGI is achieved. Karp is promoting his profit at the expense of our lives. As of June 2025, when Karp spouted these self-serving lies, Palantir stock is up 74 percent with their defense and government contracts making billionaire Karp a larger fortune.[79]

There is no objection to Karp and Altman working for their company's profit, but no justification for creating technology or promoting policies that promote war, new AI Weapons of Mass Destruction, and AGI.

Karp and I are also on opposite ends of the spectrum with regards to the likelihood of the US engaging in major military fights with Russia or China. Karp believes "the US will very likely fight a 3-front war against Russia, China, and Iran."[80] They may be allied, but the likelihood of war with China is high only because of our perverted Taiwan defense policy. Russia is no threat to the US with our strong nuclear forces and their current disastrous war in Ukraine. If we stop promoting NATO expansion, the risk of war with Russia would be gone. Unless we stop them, Karp promoting war and the AI arms race with China, while Altman preaches AGI is safe and no threat, will go down as the worst example of bad capitalism and sacrificing innocent lives in history. Leading AI safety experts have warned that any attempt to build AGI is suicidal for mankind, "an insane and stupid gamble that **NOBODY SHOULD BE ALLOWED TO TRY.**"[81]

I support Palantir's AI to improve intelligence and national security. Their AI programs run on secure government classified information networks, and could be a poster child company for controlled, safe use of AI in government-controlled facilities. Palantir should be a champion of the AICA. Instead, Karp is probably the biggest threat to AI control, avoiding war with China, and saving the world from superintelligent AGI annihilation.[82]

Palantir CEO Karp must be stopped. His pro-AI arms race campaign is based on lies, ego, and his clear profit payoff. My credentials for disagreeing with Karp? Karp got a BA in philosophy from the elite Haverford College, then a JD at Stanford Law School, and a PhD in neoclassical social theory. Using inherited money from his grandfather, Karp ran a firm managing money of high-net-worth individuals.[83] Karp befriended Peter Thiel at Stanford. Thiel is the key to Karp's success and power. My Bachelors in Science was from the US Air Force Academy, an International Affairs and History double major, earning an academic scholarship to Harvard University where I earned a Masters and PhD in Public Policy, Operations Research. My dissertation was on nuclear combat and the politics of nuclear weapons. Most of my career has dealt with national security issues. Karp has never served a day of public service. I started in Civil Air Patrol at age thirteen, served thirty years in the Active/Guard/Reserve Air Force, four years as a County Commissioner, twelve years as a University of Nebraska Regent, and in the Department of Defense Senior Executive Service and the top DoD think tank. Karp was one of four co-founders of Peter Thiel–funded Palantir, and the highest-paid CEO of a publicly traded company in 2024.[84] Karp is promoting this AI arms race to promote his profit at the expense of our lives. Karp is a leader in driving the US–China AI arms race, preventing AI control, the AICA, and what should be our top priority—getting China to ally with us to control AI and fight WMD. Peter Thiel should remove Karp from Palantir and repudiate this AI arms race.

Naomi Klein is a "social activist" who supports "ecofeminism" and organized labor.[85] Astra Taylor is a filmmaker, writer, activist, and musician.[86] Klein and

Taylor believe "The forces we are up against have made peace with mass death. They are treasonous to this world and its human and non-human inhabitants."[87] I agree.

Canadian liberal activists Klein and Taylor propose that "we counter their apocalyptic narratives with a far better story about how to survive the hard times ahead without leaving anyone behind."[88] This is BS in the United States, where top government officials are quite willing to let citizens die, caring only that they survive to resume control of the survivors post-collapse, exploiting them as needed before/during/after the collapse.

Klein and Taylor support many liberal, socialist causes I oppose. But a great public high school history teacher taught me something very valuable to know. While we use the term "left" and "right" in politics, the political spectrum is not a straight line. He drew it on the blackboard as a horseshoe. The left and right can come together and agree on issues, though often for different reasons. A colleague and I were on the losing end of a lot of 6–2 votes as University of Nebraska Regents—me on the conservative, Libertarian right, and Chuck Hassebrook on the liberal left.[89]

So, despite being on the opposite end of the political spectrum, I support Klein and Taylor's condemnation of AI company CEO's working full-speed-ahead to kill us all, backed by the Perverted Triangle. And I support their proposals to protect our planet, be tolerant of others, more community-minded and supportive:

- "build an unruly open-hearted movement of the Earth-loving faithful: faithful to this planet, its people, its creatures and to the possibility of a livable future for us all."
- "Perhaps what is needed is a modern-day universalization of that concept: a commitment to the right to the 'hereness' of this particular ailing planet, to these frail bodies, to the right to live in dignity wherever on the planet we are . . ."[90]

Sounds good to me—as long as "live in dignity" means live in freedom, with my survival community, without the Perverted Triangle, without being forced to pay for or participate in socialism or social/religious programs I don't want. But we can all get along if we limit government involvement in contentious social issues to local governments, protect Natural Rights, tolerate differences, cooperate and evolve to survive in the Age of Collapse.[91]

Indeed, I'll even give Klein and Taylor the last words in my book:[92]

> We have reached a choice point, not about whether we are facing apocalypse but what form it will take. The activist sisters Adrienne Maree and

Autumn Brown touched on this recently on their aptly named podcast, *How to Survive the End of the World*. In this moment, when end times fascism is waging war on every front, new alliances are essential. But instead of asking: "Do we all share the same worldview?" Adrienne urges us to ask: "Is your heart beating and do you plan to live? Then come this way and we will figure out the rest on the other side."

LIST OF TERMS AND ACRONYMS

AFAP: Artillery-Fired Atomic Projectile
AFL: American Foreign Legion
AGI: Artificial General Intelligence (or super intelligence)
AI: Artificial Intelligence
AICA: Artificial Intelligence Control Alliance
Anti-Fragile: A term from Nassim Taleb, meaning a system that not only can withstand stress and disorder but actually benefits from them
AR-15: ArmaLite Rifle, (a company, the civilian version of the military M-16 rifles)—does not stand for Assault Rifle
ASML: Advanced Semiconductor Materials Lithography, Dutch company, photolithography systems
Black Swan: A term from Nassim Taleb, meaning a highly improbable or unpredictable event with severe consequences, something that was considered impossible
BNW: Battlefield Nuclear Weapons
Bug Out: Prepper term for leave, get out of city or suburb and quickly get to your rural safe survival location or survival community
CAA: Consumer Advisory Association
CAP: Civil Air Patrol
CCP: Chinese Communist Party
CDC: Center for Disease Control
CEO: Chief Executive Officer
CGP: Civil Ground Patrol
CIA: Central Intelligence Agency
CONUS: Continental United States
COO: Chief Operating Officer

CRISPR: Clustered Regularly Interspaced Short Palindromic Repeats, a gene-editing technology
CUS: Constitutional United States
DHS: Department of Homeland Security
DNA: deoxyribonucleic acid, the genetic information and instructions inside living cells
DoD: Department of Defense
DOGE: Department of Government Efficiency
DSS: Decision Support System
DTRA: Defense Threat Reduction Agency
EMP: Electro-Magnetic Pulse
ERP: Enterprise Resource Planning system
FARness: Flexibility, Adaptiveness, Robustness—a term invented by RAND's Dr. Paul Davis
FDO: Flexible Deterrence Option
FDR: Franklin Delano Roosevelt
FEMA: Federal Emergency Management Agency
FY: Fiscal Year
GDP: Gross Domestic Product
GMO: Genetically Modified Organism
GOP: Grand Old Party (Republican)
GPS: Global Positioning System
H5N1: influenza virus, previously called Avian or Bird Flu, but now spreading in mammal populations
HEMP: High-Altitude Electro Magnetic Pulse
HQ: Headquarters
ICBM: Intercontinental Ballistic Missile
INTERPOL: International Criminal Police Organization
Iron Triangle: Political science term for the favoritism of Congressional committees, interest groups, and government bureaucracies
IT: Information Technology
JIT: Just-In-Time (delivery, no inventories)
JCS: Joint Chiefs of Staff
KISS: Keep It Simple Stupid
KT: Kiloton
LEO: Law Enforcement Officer
MAD: Mutual Assured Destruction
MCDA: Multi-Criteria Decision Analysis

MS-13: Mara Salvatrucha 13, a transnational, Latino criminal gang
MSNBC: Microsoft National Broadcasting Company
Murphy's Law: Anything that can go wrong will go wrong
NATO: North Atlantic Treaty Organization
NIH: National Institute of Health
NW: Nuclear Weapons
P³: Prevention, Preemption, and Preparedness
P&L: Profit and Loss
P(doom): Probability of Doom, usually used as an estimate of disaster from AI misuse
Perverted Triangle: Career politicians, Government bureaucrats, and Lawyers
PhD: Doctor of Philosophy
POTUS: President Of the United States
PRC: People's Republic of China (Communist China)
Prepper: Someone who prepares for a collapse or disaster
R&D: Research and Development
RAND: Research and Development, a US Federal Funded R&D Center, think tank
ROK: Republic of Korea (South Korea)
SHTF: Shit Hits the Fan, a widely used prepper term for collapse, loss of law and order
SNW: Strategic Nuclear Weapons
SUNY: State University of New York
TEXIT: Texas EXIT, secession of Texas from the United States of America
TLAN/N: Tomahawk Land-Attack Missile – Nuclear warhead version
TNW: Tactical Nuclear Weapons, or sometimes Theater Nuclear Weapons
Tool AI: AI techniques for specific, limited areas of expertise; far less capable than "superintelligent" Artificial General Intelligence
TRA: Taiwan Relations Act
TSA: Transportation Security Administration
TSMC: Taiwan Semiconductor Manufacturing Company
UK: United Kingdom
UL: Underwriters Laboratory
USAF: US Air Force
USD: US Dollar
USDA: US Department of Agriculture
WWI: World War One
WWII: World War Two

ABOUT THE AUTHOR

Dr./Col. Drew Miller is a USAF Academy Honor Graduate, received an academic scholarship to Harvard University where he earned a Masters Degree and PhD in Public Policy (Operations Research, dissertation topic "Underground Nuclear Defense Shelters and Field Fortifications for NATO Troops"); Retired Air Force Colonel, Intelligence Officer and Plans and Programs Officer (active duty, Air National Guard and USAF Reserve); Manager in Corporate Planning and Development at ConAgra Inc, Senior Executive Service in Department of Defense, Research Staff Member at the Institute for Defense Analyses (Department of Defense Federally Funded R&D Center), Founder and CEO of Fortitude Ranch, the nation's largest recreational and survival community, former Sarpy County Nebraska Commissioner, University of Nebraska Regent, Certified Management Accountant, Certified Government Financial Manager, and Certified Financial Planner. Drew currently serves as Managing Director of the Fortitude Collapse Preparedness consulting firm and promotes "The Constitutional Alliance" program to fix America's unconstitutional, irresponsible government.

ENDNOTES AND WEBNOTES

This book has endnotes that are not printed in the book, but posted online: "webnotes," online endnotes for the book that can be corrected and updated. The link below goes to online webnotes that allows updates, corrections, new information to be added to the book:

https://collapsesurvivor.com/preparing-to-survive-in-the-age-of-collapse/.